SCALE MODEL WARSHIPS

SCALE MODEL WARSHIPS

Edited by
John Bowen

MAYFLOWER BOOKS
MAYFLOWER BOOKS, INC.,
575 LEXINGTON AVENUE,
NEW YORK CITY 10022.

Frontispiece. A European Championship winning model at 1/100 scale of the Italian destroyer *Impavido* by Giancarlo Barbieri, a contributor to this book. (Photo: Giancarlo Barbieri)

Published in the United States by Mayflower Books Inc, New York, New York 10022. Originally published in England by Conway Maritime Press Ltd, London SE10 9JB

First American Edition

ISBN 0 8317 7702 8

Manufactured in Great Britain.

Foreword

The warship, particularly the powered fighting ship, has long been a popular subject for modelmakers all over the world. Whether it is due to the removal of some of the official restrictions on the availability of plans and other data of the vessels, or to the ability of the mass communication media to publicise many details of a country's latest warship even as it is being built, there is no doubt that recently there has been an upsurge in the construction of both static and working scale models of naval vessels.

It is an inescapable fact that as this interest has grown so has the desire to learn how to get started on this branch of ship modelling. The newcomer, looking at the development of the world's fighting fleets during the last hundred years, is confronted by an array of craft of all shapes and sizes, whose armament and equipment has become progressively more complex.

To help the beginner — and the more experienced modelmaker whose interest has lain hitherto with other ship types — we have called upon the experience and expertise of a number of builders of warship models of international repute to provide a series of introductory guidelines.

With such a vast subject it is clear that the content of any book can cover only certain aspects of the whole. So the aim throughout has been to set the modelmaker on the right path, first by introducing him to the value and necessity of research and to the requirement for accurate plans and coupling this with information on where to find such material. The subsequent chapters on techniques concentrate on basic elements which provide a sound basis for the modelmaker to develop his ability in his own way. Throughout, full use has been made of line diagrams and of a judicious mixture of photographs of models and of actual vessels. The latter have been selected to emphasis some particular details and to illustrate in general the value which can be gained from their use. Backing up the information thus imparted is a comprehensive bibliography showing those books and journals — technical, reference, pictorial and historical — which contain material that will be of value and interest to the modelmaker.

The plastic kit, despite the hostility once directed towards it, has been the means whereby many were first introduced to ship modelling. The marked improvements in recent years both in authenticity and accuracy, and in the manufacturing processes, have assigned today's kit its own particular place in the sphere of model warship construction. This has been recognised by the inclusion of a chapter devoted to these specialist techniques.

Many fine models of warships, built by professionals and by amateurs, can be seen in museums in many countries, where they form a permanent record of the development of the fighting ship, and are in themselves a delight to study. But for sheer pleasure the sight of a true-to-scale well built and detailed model of a destroyer or corvette, battleship or submarine, early ram or a circular ironclad, afloat in its natural element is hard to beat.

We hope that what has been written in the following pages will encourage still more modelmakers to experience these feelings.

JOHN BOWEN

Acknowledgements
The publishers gratefully acknowledge the help and courtesy of the staff in the Draught Room of the National Maritime Museum. Many other people assisted, but we would particularly like to thank all the warship modellers whose models are pictured in the following pages. The photographs came from many sources and are usually credited after the captions: any uncredited are from the camera of the editor, John Bowen. However, in this context we are indebted to Mr A S E Browning, CEng, MRINA, MIES, Keeper of the Glasgow Museum of Transport, for the supply of otherwise unobtainable photographs. Finally we must thank the family of the late Lt Col H T N Batchelor for the use of his notes, drawings and photographs, and for access to his fine model of HMS *Pheasant*.

Contents

Sources of information 1

by ALAN RAVEN

The scale modeller, whether only partly serious or a fanatic, has to depend as much upon sources of information which relate to the full size vessel as on his modelling skill. A look back over the years shows that many, many models, although built to high standards, were spoilt because they were not to scale, contained poor detail work, and did not represent the prototype at any one time in her life. In some instances these faults can be put down to lack of intelligence, a highly casual approach to accuracy, or a preoccupation with the working part or other aspects of the model. However the most important factor in the construction of a scale model is the quality and availability of source material. In most cases a modeller will respond to working with full and accurate source material and produce a model to match. Once having worked with such material he will be extremely reluctant in future work to fall back on those which are suspect. We can see therefore that the standard of scale warship models depends largely upon that of the basic data. In fact, 99% of the subjects for modelling are chosen by exposure to types of source material. In the past this has usually meant photographs, but gradually the easier availability of plans of various types has had an influence until today many modellers select their ships by plan availability rather than anything else.

For far too long the modeller has used sources (in most cases commercial ones) which, possibly through his lack of knowledge of the subject, he has assumed to be correct only to find out later during the course of building his model that the plans are badly inaccurate and/or incomplete. Worse still, after the model has been finished he may be told publicly that it does not represent the real thing; this can be shattering. With the foregoing in mind, my comments on the sources publicly available will be based, in the case of official material (such as builders' plans), on ease of interpretation and in the case of commercial plans on ease of interpretation, quality of draughtsmanship, accuracy to prototype and so on. These opinions are mainly subjective, and so those I make about commercial sources, especially the plans, *will be mine alone and stated without any influence or pressure from other sources.*

SOURCES

Source data falls into three major types: Plans, commercial and official. Photographs, from commercial and official organisations. Books, magazines, and similar publications.

There is also a fourth source — the publicly available official documents (other than plans) describing in various ways the ships and equipment carried. These can be useful to the modeller on an occasional basis but not as a general rule. The trick in using this fourth source is knowing when it is going to produce something useful. Perusing official documents and knowing how to interpret them is sometimes a bit confusing, often very time consuming, and requires a degree of intelligence to extract full value from such research.

PLANS

Over the last 20 years the number of warships modelled can be related directly to the drawings available, and it is only with the large number of plans which have come on to the market in the last five years that many new models have appeared. The set of plans to which the modeller works is *the* key piece of data; it will determine the standard and accuracy of his model, and may even decide if the model gets completed.

A modeller should make every effort to obtain plans which are accurate. With official builders' plans a degree of authenticity is built in, but this is not always so with commercial ones, and enquiries should be made before purchase as to the source of the plan. A good set of commercial plans is usually of greater value to the modeller than the parallel official set, because they will have been cleaned up and made clearer, include template outlines of equipment (hopefully) drawn out accurately and fully, and have had the alterations and additions existing on the official set taken into account, so that the plan will represent the vessel at a particular date in her life. Regardless of type of ship, an ideal set of commercial plans will satisfy the following criteria:

a Be of a named ship, ie HMS *Bluebell* 1942, and not '*Flower* class corvette circa WW II.'
b A pure profile and plan view.
c A simplified profile showing the outline form of the various deckhouses and so on.
d A set of plan views of the weather decks, with the above deck superimposed in dotted outline.
e Where necessary the reverse profile, as ships sometimes are radically different in layout port to starboard, eg aircraft carriers.
f A set of superstructure sections to indicate back and front of bridge and fore and after views of deckhouses.
g Where necessary, equipment such as DCTs, ship's boats etc, drawn out separately and possibly to a larger scale to make clear the complexity of these items.
h A set of hull lines.
j Where appropriate full colour and/or camouflage details.
j The scale(s) to which they are drawn clearly shown.
k Have been based on official sources (ie builder's plans), photographs, etc.

The list may seem formidable but there is no reason why most items should not be covered. Any set of commercial plans which includes the majority of the above can be adjudged by the modeller to be worth buying. This is not to say however that a plan lacking a fair percentage of the requirements is of little value, just that the more complete plan will indicate the extent of the draughtsman's knowledge of the full size subject, and of the material from which he has worked.

Commercial plans mainly cover ships of the twentieth century, with the bulk of these being plans of vessels which saw service during World War II.

COMMERCIAL WARSHIP PLAN RANGES

Plans Drawn by Norman Ough. (Available from David MacGregor Plans, 99 Lonsdale Road, London SW13 9DA who also distributes smaller numbers of warship plans by E N Wilson and warship and gun drawings by John Lambert.) Until a few years ago these plans, drawn between 1950 and 1964, were the only available high quality drawings of British warships, and they still remain some of the best obtainable. The greater part of each plan was compiled by using photographs as the main source, with (in some cases) some unofficial help from the Admiralty and other sources that included the chance to use official plans of the 'As Fitted' type (see the section on official plans) and design General Arrangement drawings. Norman Ough, during the interwar years and during World War II, built several highly detailed models of Royal Navy warships,all being based on a combination of 'As Fitted' plans, good photographs, and in some cases visits to the actual ship. Although he later destroyed the 'As Fitted' tracings he made, he retained enough information to produce with the help of the previously mentioned sources, this range of plans, a range which includes battleships, submarines, and drawings of ships' boats, guns, etc. Most of the plans are very complete and display a high degree of skill in draughtsmanship and layout. He was many years ahead of his time and his range of plans was no mean achievement. As one would expect, by using photographs as the primary source, the degree of accuracy is not as high in matters of proportion and of shape of superstructure as in plans prepared from official sources. This is the major fault of Norman Ough plans. However this need not deter the modeller as they include a remarkable range of detailed drawings of equipment, and the plans are worth having for this alone.

Plans Drawn by Alan B Chesley. (Available from Floating Drydock — address below.) These plans depict US ships as they appeared during and just after World War II and include battleships, aircraft carriers, cruisers, destroyers and destroyer escorts. Drawn over the last decade using official material, I believe these to be among the best plans of US warships, and the scale of $\frac{1}{8}$in = 1ft (1/96) allows for plenty of detail to be included. Some are drawn with more detail than others and some ships unfortunately are shown in pure profile and plan only without breakup or detail, but even so give the modeller an invaluable source of reference. Among the range is a set for the aircraft carrier *Belleau Wood;* these particular plans are beautifully drawn, as are those for the destroyer escort *Otter*. With most of the plans a reasonable number of fittings are drawn out separately in full detail and are highly recommended for anybody building US ships of the World War II period or just after.

A & A Plans. (Distribution arrangements uncertain at time of going to press.) Drawn by Alan Raven and John Roberts, the plans cover, with only a few exceptions, various Royal Navy vessels as they appeared during World War I and II, and is the only collection of any size to do this. Types depicted range

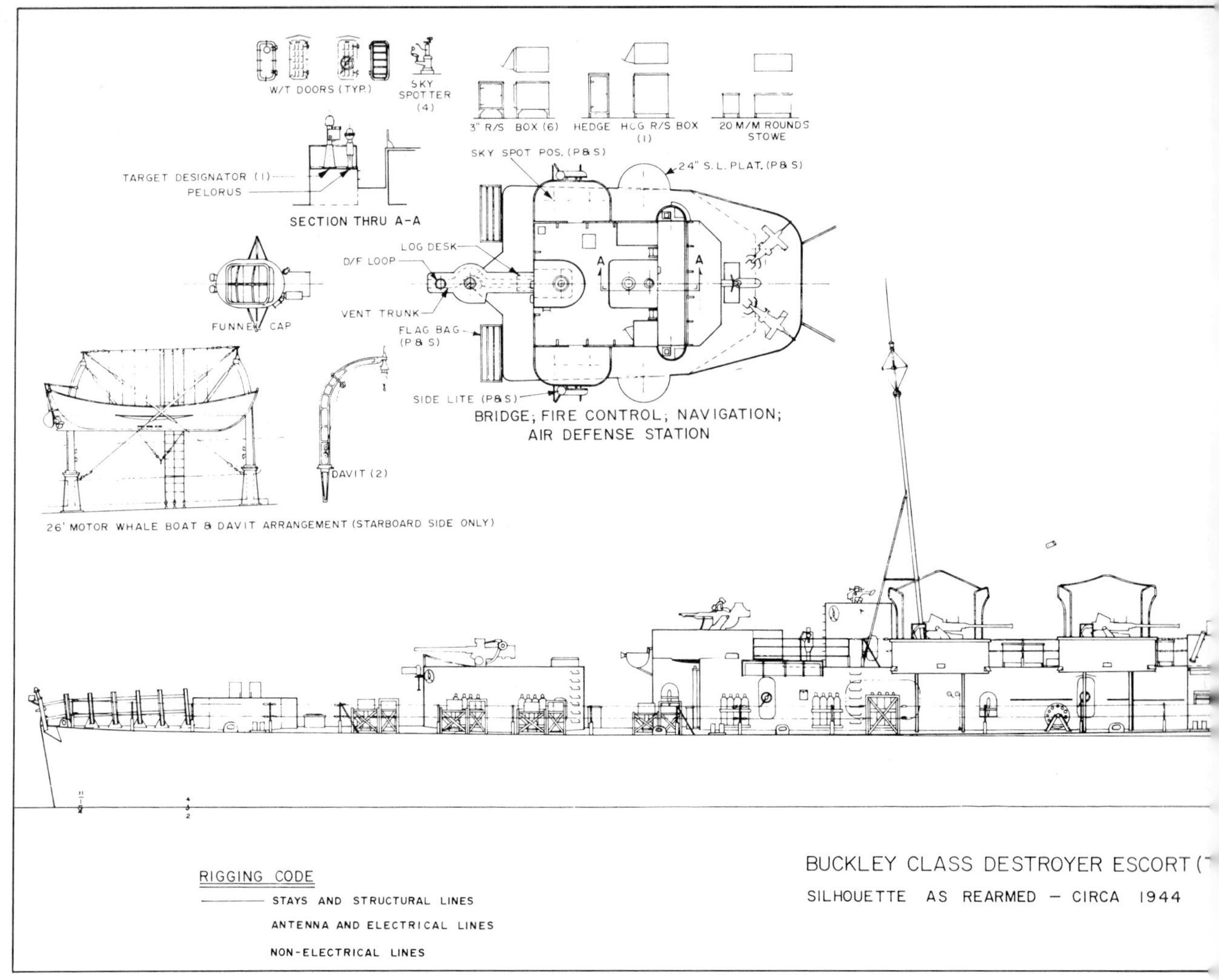

The Chesley 1/96 scale plans for the *Buckley* class destroyer escort USS *Otter*. Superimposed on this clear and well drawn profile are some of the excellent detailed drawings of the major fittings included on the second sheet of the set. Another useful feature is the inclusion of port side views to illustrate differences between the two sides of a structure.

from battleships and battlecruisers down to coastal craft, but no aircraft carriers. Drawn to a scale of 1/16in = 1ft (1/192) the plans usually consist of two sheets, the first giving a pure view plan and profile, the second containing lines, sections, superstructure break-up etc. They lack separately drawn out detail drawings of ship's boats, guns and so on. Many of the plans, all of which have been prepared using official builders' plans and photographs, show ships at periods for which there is no directly dated official plan and in this respect are unique. This series is among the better of the commercial ones and as far as accuracy is concerned, although not perfect, are certainly of very high standard, and any of the range can be recommended as forming a reliable basis for an accurate model.

Plans Issued by Jecobin Ltd. (31 Romans Way, Pyrford, Woking, Surrey GU22 8TR, UK.) A new range of plans which has appeared during the last

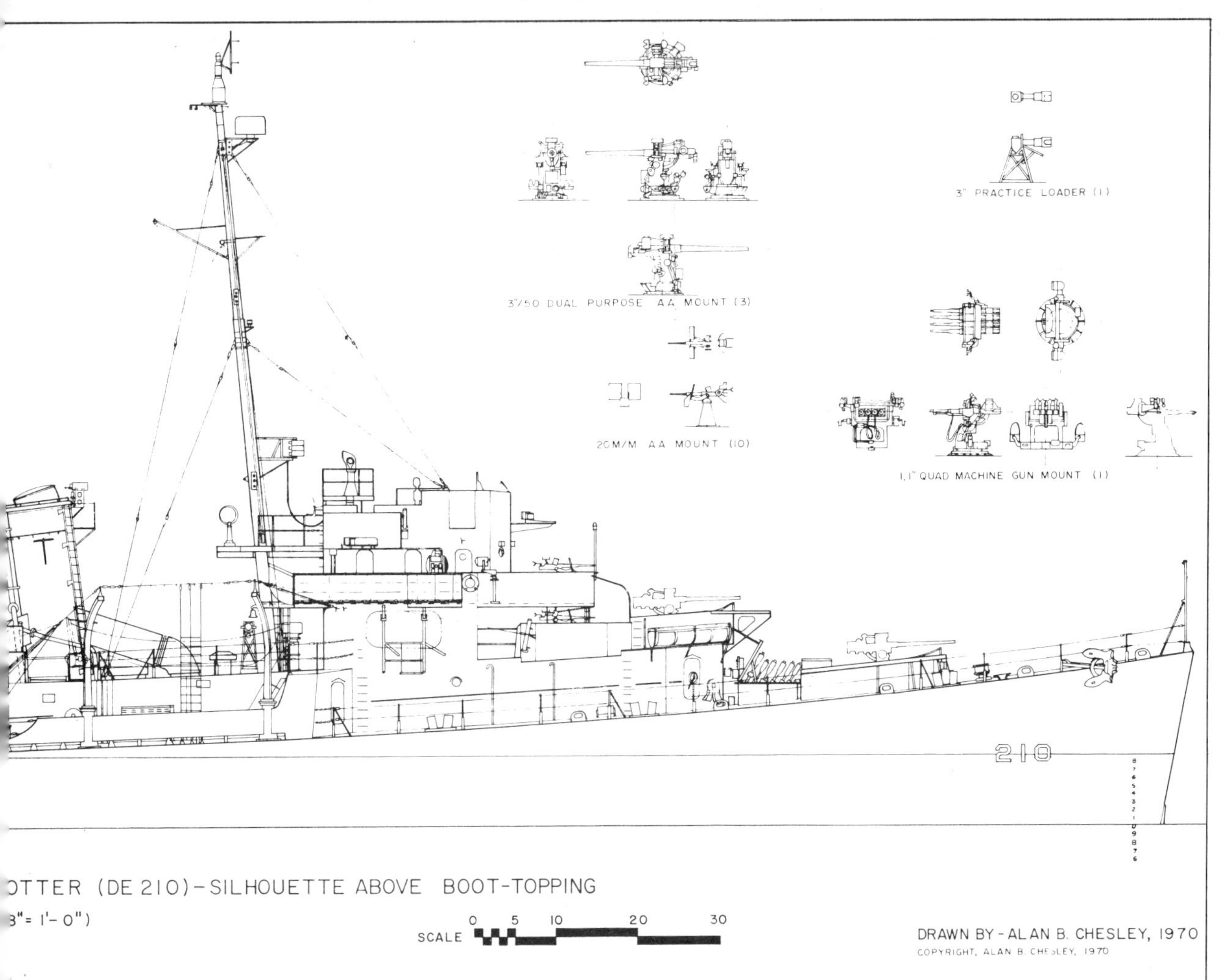

three years, they are the only ones dealing with modern Royal Navy ships. Drawn to a scale of 1/16in = 1ft (1/192) each plan consists of one sheet with the exception of the three sheet set of the aircraft carrier *Hermes*. (This set is the *only* commercial one available for a commissioned British aircraft carrier.) Security reasons have meant that all the drawings have been prepared using photographs and without the help of official plans, so not surprisingly they contain similar types of errors to those in the Norman Ough plans. They are competently drawn, and show a great amount of detail, but unfortunately for the modeller there is no separate break-up in plan view of the various weather deck levels, and showing the underneath deck shape in dotted form with the higher deck overlaid in pure form, and at 1/16in = 1ft scale, is not good enough to enable the modeller to get his basic deck shape correct, and I feel this is a major fault of the plans. However at the moment they are the only modern Royal Navy ship plans and with some care and research they can form the basis for a model. Underwater shape details have to be conjectural, since lines are omitted (except for the *Hermes* set) and details are restricted to those shown on the superstructure sections.

Plans Issued by Floating Drydock. (PO Box 16066, Philadelphia, Pennsylvania 19114. USA. This company also distributes smaller commercial plans ranges covering warships, armament and fittings.) All the plans are based on official sets and are really cleaned up tracings of them. They cover US ships mainly of the World War II period, and are usually available in two scales, 1/8in = 1ft (1/96) and 1/16in = 1ft (1/192). Being tracings each set varies in the amount of detail it shows, but some of the plans containing very full detail have been listed separately. As they are traced from the official general arrangement plans the accuracy is not open to doubt,

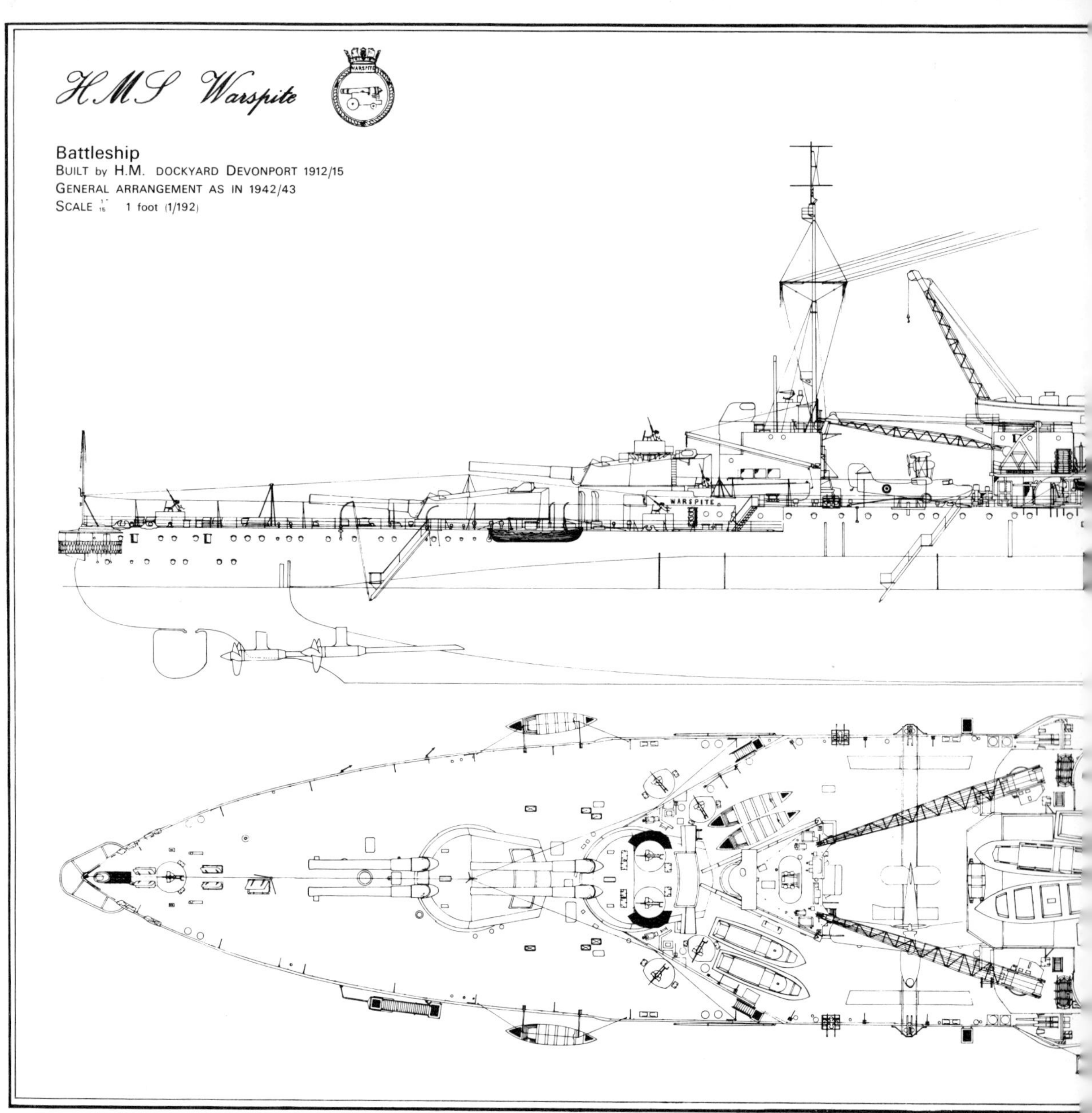

HMS *Warspite.* A & A Plans drawing of the ship as in 1942/3. One of the features of these plans is the amount of very fine detail included on the profile and deck arrangement drawings.

but official sets often use a simple outline and templates to indicate different pieces of equipment and any modeller using traced official sets should bear this in mind. The range covers battleships and aircraft carriers, down to escort craft. Any modeller thinking of a World War II USN ship could do far worse than consider these plans.

Plans Issued by Musée De La Marine. (Palais de Chaillot, 75116, Paris, France.) These cover French ships mostly as they appeared during the immediate

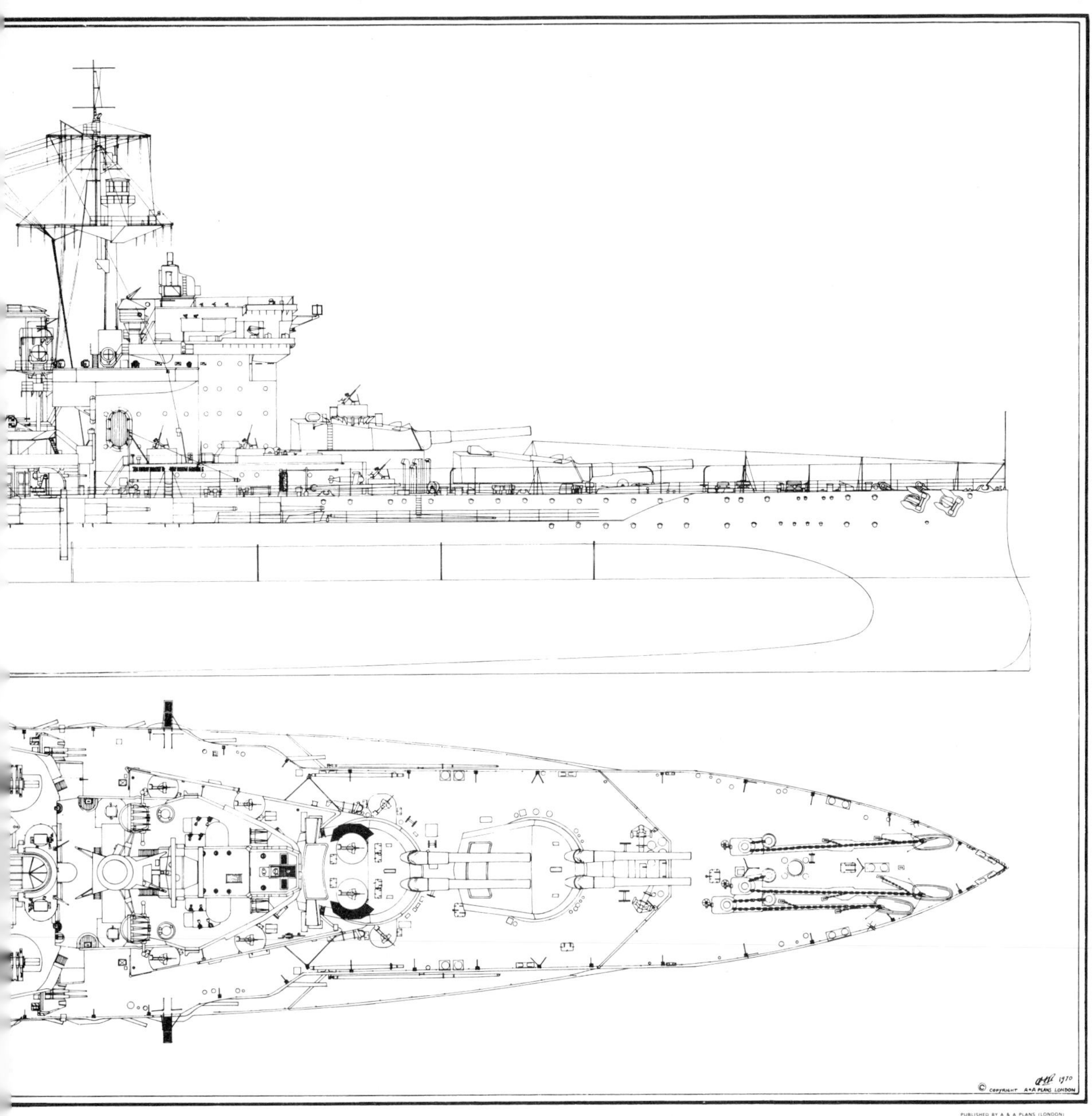

post World War II period based on models in the Museum, and range from battleships to submarines, including a set for a former British light fleet carrier HMS *Colossus* in French Service as the *Arromanches,* and a set of the submarine *Surcouf.*

A number of the plans are available in two scales, 1/100 or 1/50. All are based on official material and are competently drawn, and give in some instances a high degree of detail. Each is a printed production, not a dyeline as are most commercial plans, and comes complete with a folder containing a potted history of the ship and a list of the other available plans. They are the only worthwhile commercial plans of French warships, and although the amount of detail varies a little they are well worth considering.

Plans Drawn by P A Webb. (PO Box 60, Williamstown, Victoria 3016, Australia. Also available from Floating Drydock.) A large range of plans drawn over a number of years depicting

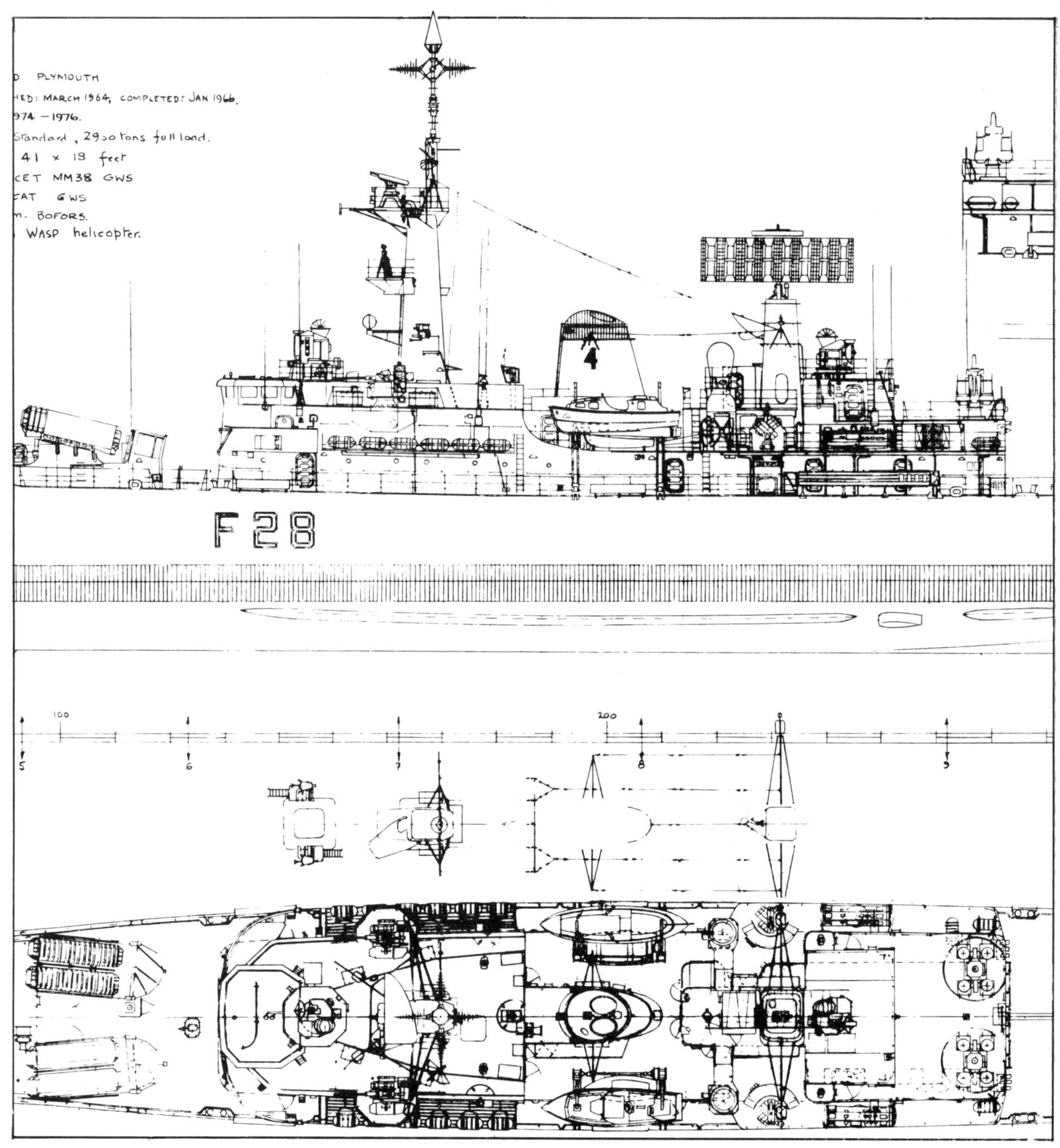

Above. The midship area of HMS *Cleopatra,* by Jecobin Ltd. Much reliance is placed on numerous cross sections to convey details of fittings, rather than the inclusion of separate drawings on the plans.

Opposite. Part of the plan of the French aircraft carrier *Arromanches* (ex HMS *Colossus)* from the Museé de la Marine, Paris. The numbers refer to the separate detail drawings on the plans of the item concerned. Note the useful cross sections in way of the shipside platforms and openings.

Australian, Canadian, British and American warships mostly of World War II vintage, along with a few postwar vessels. The major part of the range consists of properly printed profile and plan views on one sheet, all ships being printed to an approximate common size, resulting in a variety of scales from 1/16in = 1ft (1/192) down to 1in = 60ft (1/720) for large vessels. Some are detailed, some not so detailed, and none show either break-up details, lines etc. They have a very limited appeal for the modeller, and are

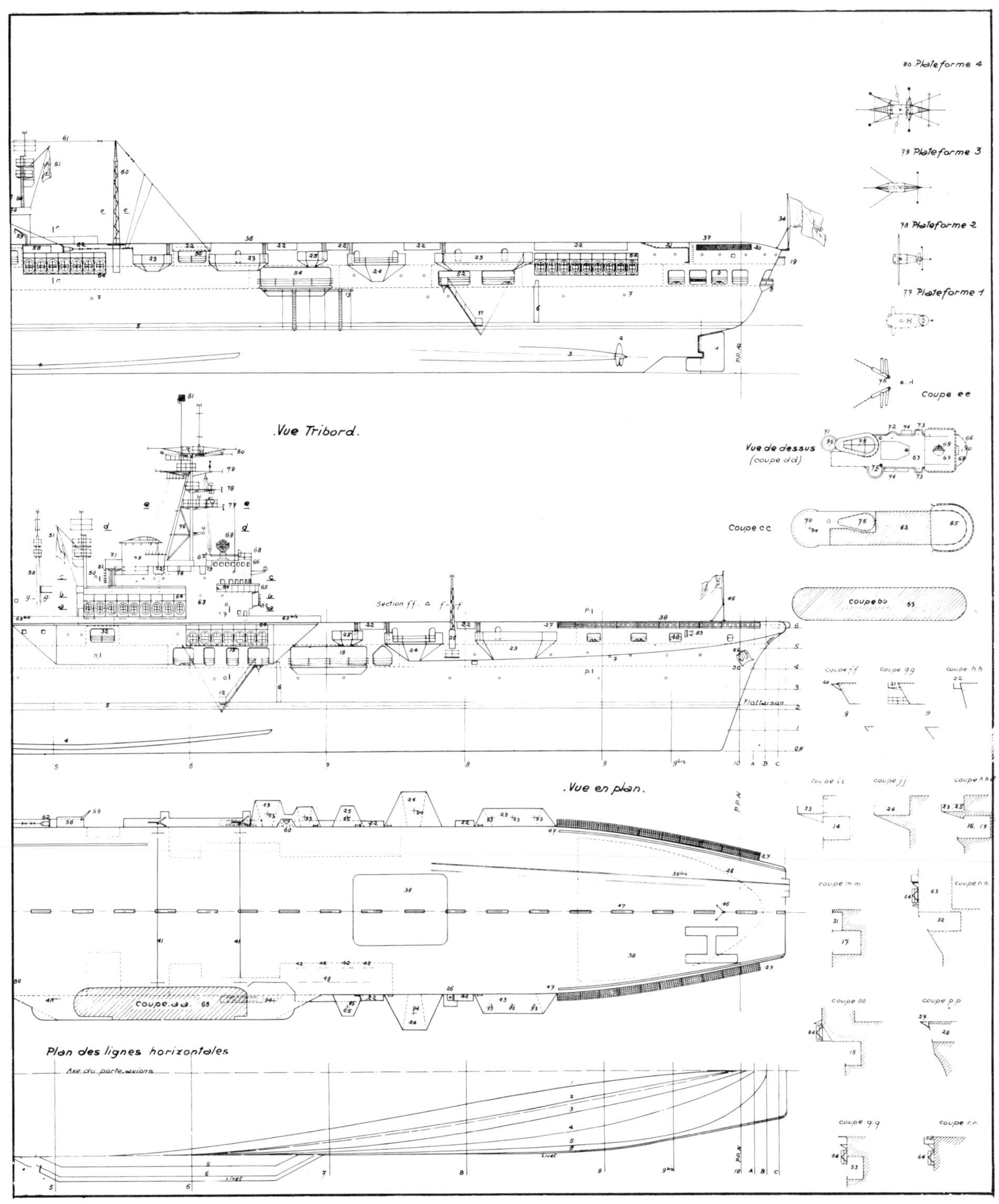

really prints suitable only for framing. However, there is available another range much more suitable for modellers. This contains mainly Australian and American vessels drawn to a scale of $\frac{1}{8}$in = 1ft (1/96), amd each set consists of at least two sheets, sometimes three. Except for the *Yamato* set, all are drawn using official plans as a basis. Official plans vary considerably in the detail they contain and this is unfortunately perpetuated in these plans. Some are superbly detailed and are a joy to look at and to use, and the three sheet set for USS *Fletcher* as in 1942 is a prime example; it shows very full detail of most fittings along with full camouflage details, completed by a printed folder giving a short history of the ship.

Plans such as the latter are of a sufficiently high quality that many modellers will find them perfectly adequate in themselves without having to search for further data, such as photographs. Others, especially those of Australian vessels, are not quite as detailed, and considering the scale are slightly lacking in supplementary detail; any modeller prepared to seek out other sources for additional data will find them extremely valuable.

Plans Issued by MAP Ltd. (PO Box 35, Hemel Hempstead, Herts HP1 1EE, UK.) A range of plans covering a period from the turn of the century up to the near present day. Most, if not all, appear to have been prepared by a modeller to go with the model that he has constructed, thus resulting in some odd scales and a varied level of detail, draughtsmanship, and accuracy. Unfortunately, many are lacking in all but the barest detail, some are blatantly inaccurate, bearing little resemblance to the real ship. Because of the variety of scales, styles, amount of detail and so on, it is a little difficult to discuss the range generally and to give an opinion as to the average standard. The last ten years has seen the availability through national archives in various countries of official builders' plans, and this has resulted in the appearance of many new and worthwhile plan collections which contain an accuracy previously lacking. With one or two exceptions, notably the set of the old armoured cruiser HMS *Kent* the MAP range does not appear to have moved with the times.

Plans Drawn by G Trenk. Although few in number these plans rank among the best of the commercial ones available. Covering German Capital ships of World War I vintage they are superbly drawn to a scale of 1/100 and contain very full detail. All have been prepared with a high degree of skill from official plans, and to a degree of accuracy difficult to match. The plans are remarkably complete and would require little follow-up research by a modeller to produce the finest model.

Plans Drawn by F Prasky. (Feuchterslebengasse 69-71/5, A-1100 Vienna, Austria.) Unfortunately this excellent series depicts only a handful of ships. It covers vessels of the Austro-Hungarian Navy of around the World War I period, and includes a beautiful set for the battleship *Viribus Unitis.* Like the plans by Trenk they are drawn to the highest standard and contain the fullest detail that the scale will allow. The *Viribus Unitis* is drawn to 1/200, the others 1/100. All are properly printed and come in a folder along with colour details. For the modelmaker interested in this particular navy, I recommend these plans wholeheartedly, and hope that the range will expand in the future.

Right. HMAS *Vendetta,* taken from the 1/96 scale range of plans by P A Webb. Whilst a lot of detail has been included, breakdown drawings are needed in many instances to augment that shown.

Plans Issued by TV Verlag. (2106 Berdestorf, Postfach 11129, Hamburg, West Germany.) A small range of properly printed plans of German ships drawn to a high standard. It includes a beautiful two sheet set for the cruiser *Prinz Eugen* as in 1945, which has just about everything for the modelmaker, including colour details. This set, drawn to a 1/200 scale, is recommended as is the E-boat set drawn to a scale of 1/50. It is to be hoped that the range will be expanded in the near future as there is a need for good plans of ships of the German Navy of the World War II era.

Plans Drawn by R F Sumrall. (Available from Floating Drydock.) These plans have been around for many years and cover ships of the American and German navies of the World War II era. The drawings, to a scale of 1/32in = 1ft (1/384) except for the U-boat plans which are to 1/16in = 1ft (1/192), are generally to a competent standard and are stated to be based on official sources. However, I am not completely convinced as to the accuracy of some of them and the amount of detail shown varies. For the builder of miniature models these plans might be adequate, but for those building the larger scale models incorporating a high standard of detail and accuracy, my advice is to consider alternative sources first and use these plans as a back-up source where necessary.

Plans Drawn by E H Wiswesser. (Available from David MacGregor Plans.) A very large range covering US, UK, German, French, Italian and Japanese vessels, mainly of World War II types, mostly to 1/32in = 1ft (1/384) scale. Many of those examples which I have seen are very sparse in detail, and inaccurate, a prime example being the plan for the American cruiser *Atlanta* (CL-51), shown with 1945 period configuration and equipment, even though the vessel was sunk in 1942.

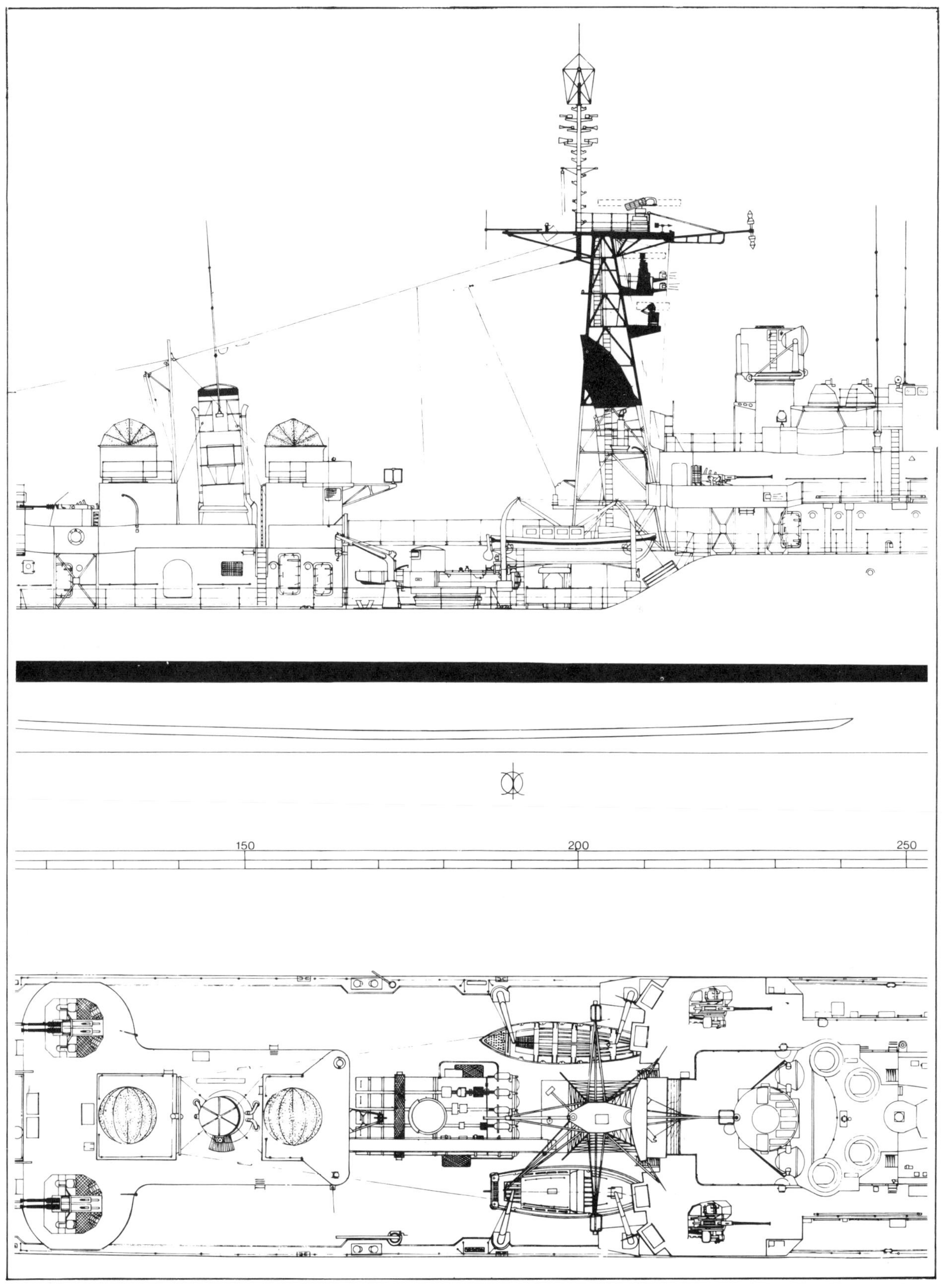
150
200
250

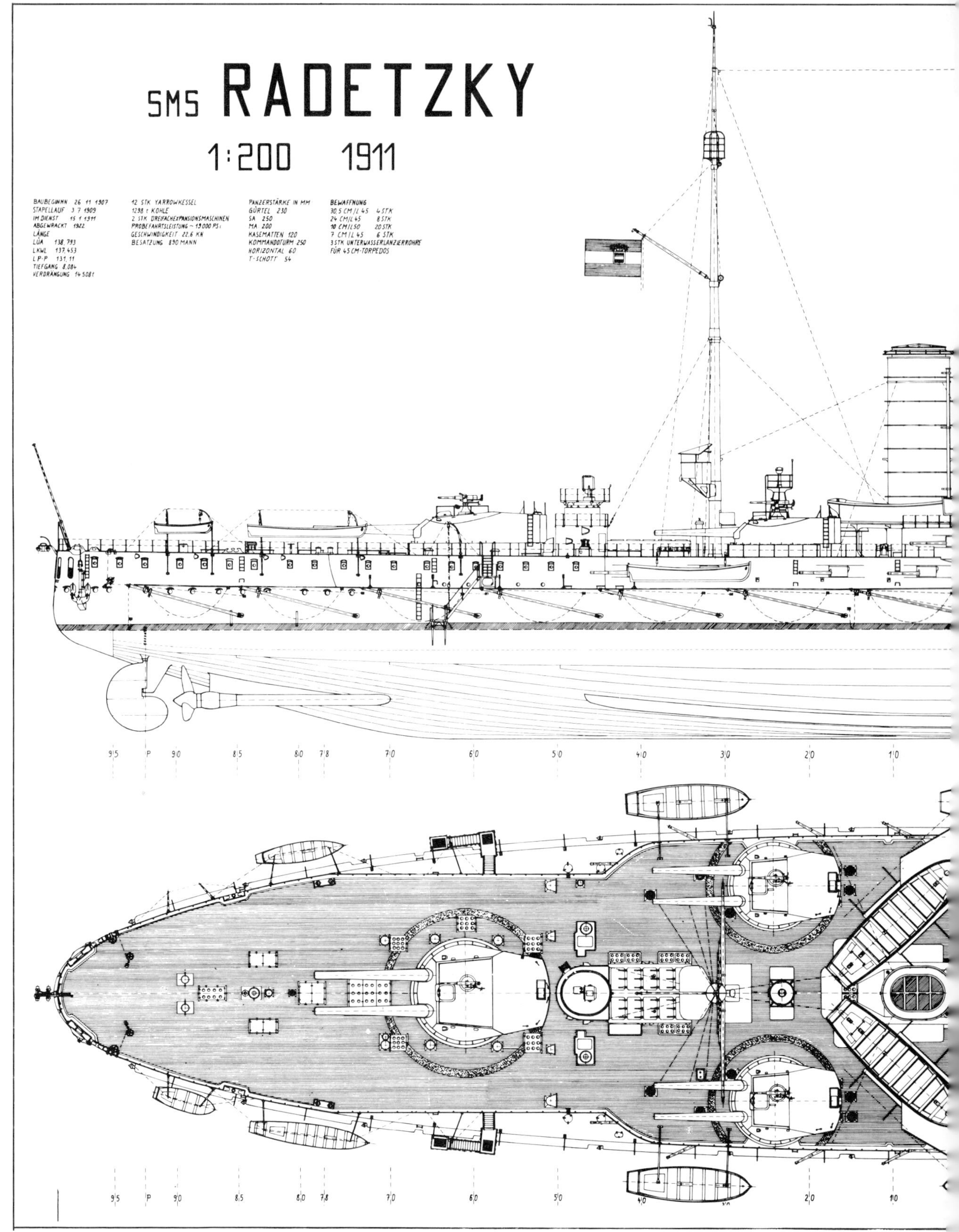
SMS RADETZKY
1:200 1911
BAUBEGINNN 26 11 1907
STAPELLAUF 3 7 1909
IM DIENST 15 1 1911
ABGEWRACKT 1922
LÄNGE
LÜA 138,793
LKWL 137,453
LP-P 131,11
TIEFGANG 8,084
VERDRÄNGUNG 14 508t
12 STK YARROWKESSEL
1298 t KOHLE
2 STK DREIFACHEXPANSIONSMASCHINEN
PROBEFAHRTSLEISTUNG ~ 19 000 PSi
GESCHWINDIGKEIT 22,6 KN
BESATZUNG 890 MANN
PANZERSTÄRKE IN MM
GÜRTEL 230
SA 250
MA 200
KASEMATTEN 120
KOMMANDOTURM 250
HORIZONTAL 60
T-SCHOTT 54
BEWAFFNUNG
30,5 CM/L 45 4 STK
24 CM/L 45 8 STK
10 CM/L50 20 STK
7 CM/L 45 6 STK
3 STK UNTERWASSERLANZIERROHRE
FÜR 45 CM-TORPEDOS
95 P 90 85 80 78 70 60 50 40 30 20 10

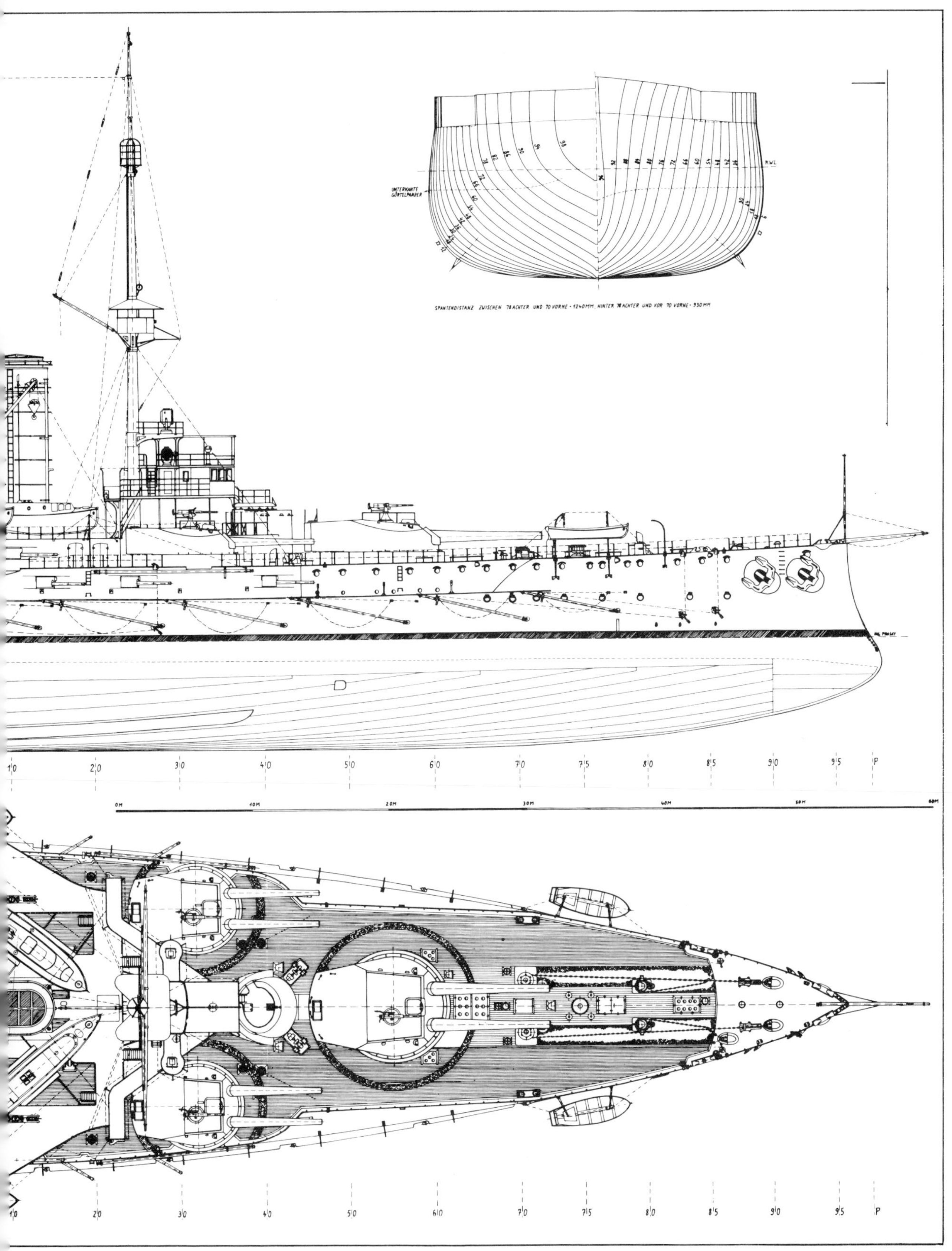
UNTERKANTE GÜRTELPANZER
KWL
SPANTENDISTANZ ZWISCHEN 78 ACHTER UND 70 VORNE - 1240MM, HINTER 78 ACHTER UND VOR 70 VORNE - 930MM
10
20
30
40
50
60
70
75
80
85
90
95
P
0M
10M
20M
30M
40M
50M
60M

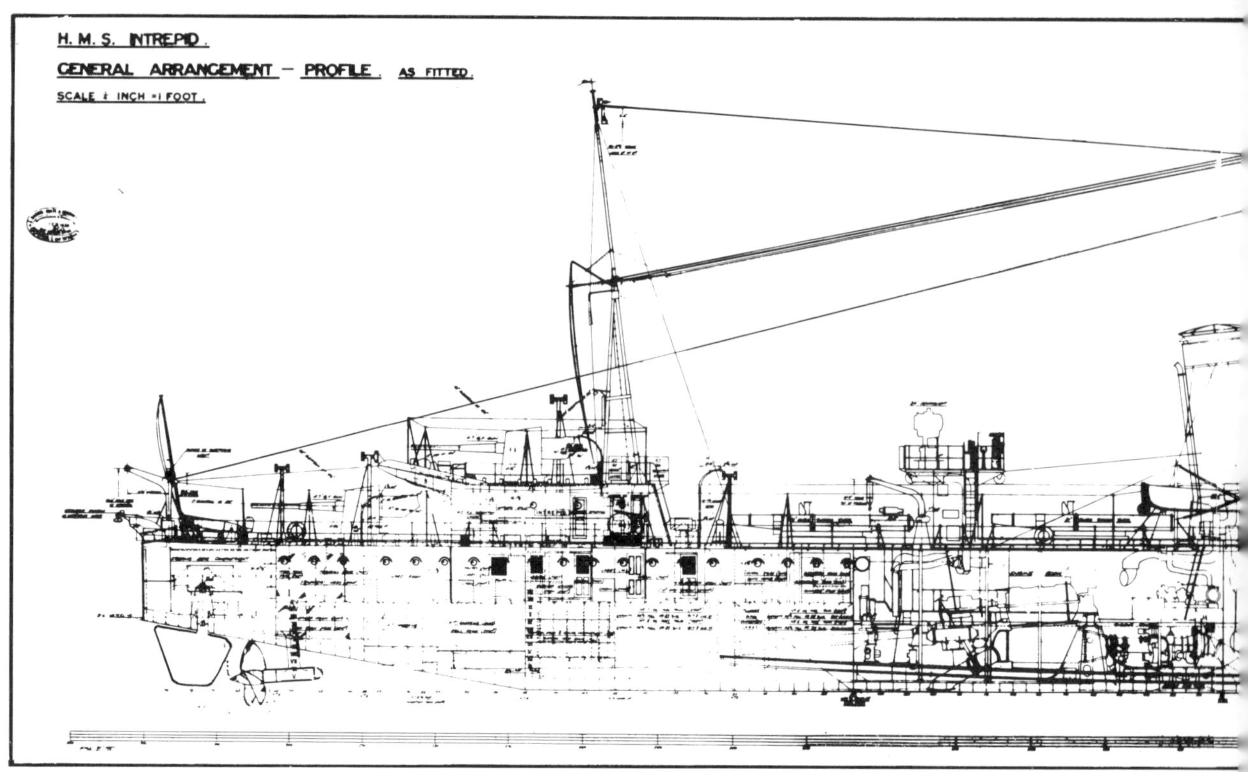

Plans Drawn bv G Barbieri. (Via Ortolani 55, 40139 Bologna, Italy.) A high quality list of Italian ships of World War II types with a few modern post war vessels; most are drawn to a scale of 1/100, with the smaller ships to 1/50 scale. The draughtsmanship is first class, and many of the plans contain very full detail, frequently set out on a separate back-up sheet. Ships covered range from a battleship down to a torpedo boat, but there are no submarines. The modeller of Italian warships would do well to consider these plans; if coupled with additional data, he will be able to produce models that are accurate and detailed. All plans are based on official material, with a corresponding degree of built-in accuracy.

Above. A typical original 'as fitted' profile which contains both inboard and ouboard detail, but with some of the latter indicated only by outline.

Previous page. F Prasky's fine plan of the Austro-Hungarian battleship SMS *Radetzky*.

Plans Drawn by A C Stephens. (Available from David MacGregor Plans.) Numbering about a dozen plans depicting British destroyers of World War I and pre-World War I vintage, all to 1/16in = 1ft (1/192) scale; a fair amount of detail is drawn out separately at $\frac{1}{8}$in = 1ft (1/96). They are based on the official 'As Fitted' plans and require little additional research by the modeller to produce accurate first class models.

Plans Drawn by Franco Gay. These plans, which cover Italian ships of World War II period, are among the better of the warship plan ranges; they are very well drawn, contain much detail and being based on official plans ensure an acceptable degree of accuracy.

OFFICIAL PLANS

Most of the official plans of twentieth century warships have become available to the public only during the last ten years. Surprisingly, there are still two major navies where this is not so; the French and the Russian. The lack of plans from the Russians one can perhaps understand as being one of the products of a closed society, but that of the French remains a puzzle and one can only hope that in the near future their archival material will be made public. For the other major navies the amount of material, including plans, is very large and in most cases fairly comprehensive.

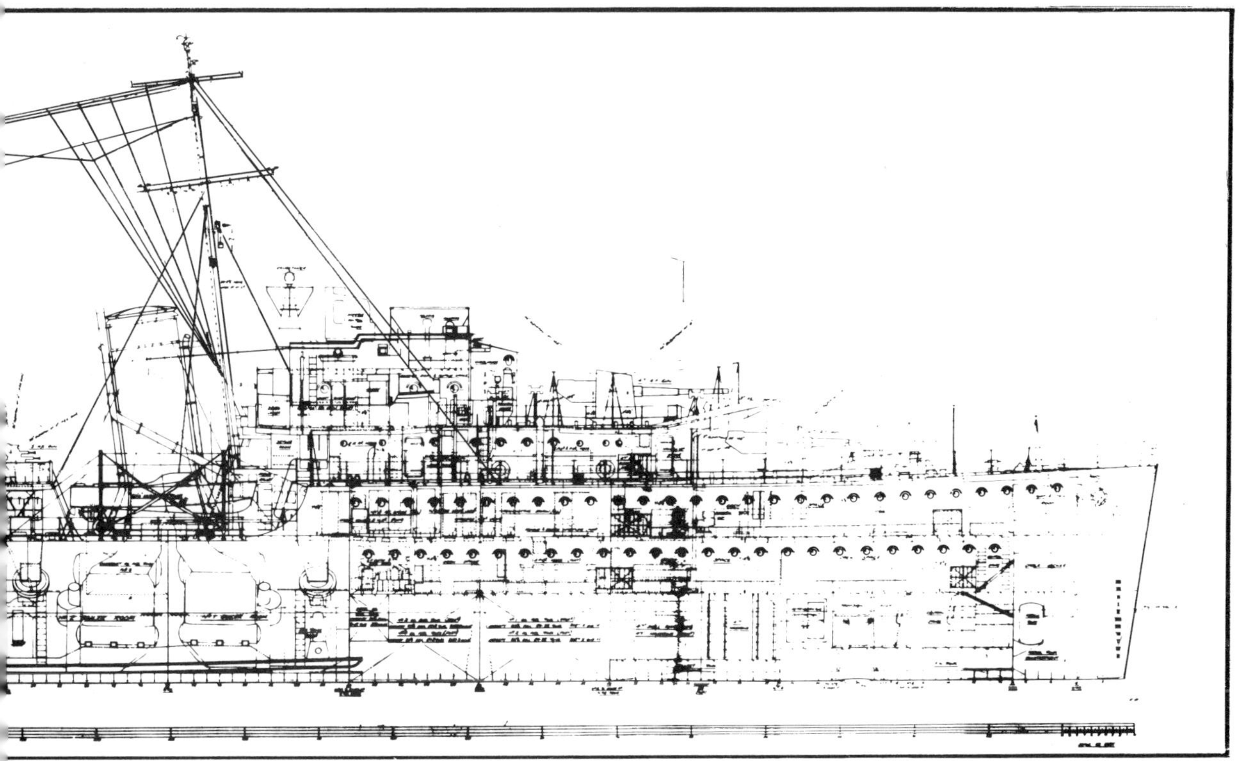

The official plans which the modeller will find most value will be those of the general arrangement type listed by ship's name rather than class heading, thus the modeller will be assured of a set of plans of a particular vessel. General arrangement plans can, and do, vary considerably from navy to navy and also within each navy according to a combination of factors prevailing at any one time, and official plans may often require a degree of interpretation not needed of commercial ones. Apart from the general arrangement set, which shows the profile and weather decks the modeller may require (depending on the standard to which he wishes to make his model) a rig plan showing full details of rigging, aerials etc, a shell plating expansion giving the plating arrangements on the outside of the hull, a set of lines and a sheer drawing, and a set of sections, the latter being particularly useful in giving additional superstructure details. Plans headed 'contract plans' or 'design plans' should be avoided if possible as they are plans for a class of ship rather than a named vessel and the amount of detail is usually on the sparse side. Other drawings of value are the working drawings; these are produced by the builders and are detailed plans of all the many parts of the ship's structure. They are not always available, and do require some research and interpretation.

One of the major sources, when available, for appearance details of various equipment are the manuals that describe the working of items such as gun mountings, directors, torpedo tubes and so on. These manuals contain drawings and photographs of the piece of equipment which will be of great assistance to the modeller. Another source for details of fittings are shipbuilding and naval architecture text books and manuals of seamanship, which include drawings of such items as capstans, boat davits, anchors, chain gear and so on, but the modeller must take care to match the period of the ship to the date of issue of the manual. Luckily some of the better commercial plans already include details of ship's boats, gun mountings, radar aerials and so on. In the case of gun manuals care should be taken not to confuse the mark of gun with that of the mounting, as in most cases the two are quite separate, the most important being the mark of mounting, and this must be ascertained from documents or ship's plans beforehand.

In official plans, one item usually lacking in detail is the ship's boats, of which there is a considerable number of types. Official sources for these are extremely scarce, and usually refer to boats of the pulling type, so it may be necessary to rely on photographs for information. Among the most prominent features of modern warships are the many aerial arrays which dominate the rig. On the postwar official plans available the arrays are usually shown only in outline, with many of the very small aerials not drawn at all, and as with the boats the modeller will have to resort to photographs for details, with the same procedure possibly having to be followed for some of the open gun mountings. Some rig plans, especially those of the late nineteenth century, also contain considerable superstructure detail, which can be useful in helping to understand the general layout of the vessel when used in conjunction with the general arrangement set.

Some of the most detailed plans from the 1880s to the present day are those of German vessels; an adequate number of draughtsmen plus a short life per ship has meant most plans being kept up-to-date and not covered in alterations as is the case with British plans. It is possible to obtain plans of almost every major German warship from the German Archives, and modellers will find the plans a delight to use.

British warship plans of all types, beginning from the introduction of steam up to the end of World War II, are available as part of British Public Records from the National Museum at Greenwich in London. Whilst there are plans for most individual ships, due to varying circumstances prevailing at any one time in the above period the quality, clarity and style of drawings varies widely. Many are beautifully detailed and clean, while others show only the barest detail, with fittings not drawn in but only indicated by a cross in the appropriate position. In some plans the rig is not shown at all, and this is where a rig plan is an absolute necessity. Wartime alterations where shown are usually incomplete and often indicated in only the barest outline. This is in marked contrast to plans of American warships, where it was was the policy to dispose of the out-of-date drawing as soon as a new set was drawn up showing the new configuration in complete form; these plans are thus completely devoid of alterations. This of course makes it easier for the modeller to understand the plan, but makes his task of tracing alterations more difficult. Luckily not all previously drawn sets of the same vessel were destroyed, but the retention of these over the years has been haphazard to say the least, and

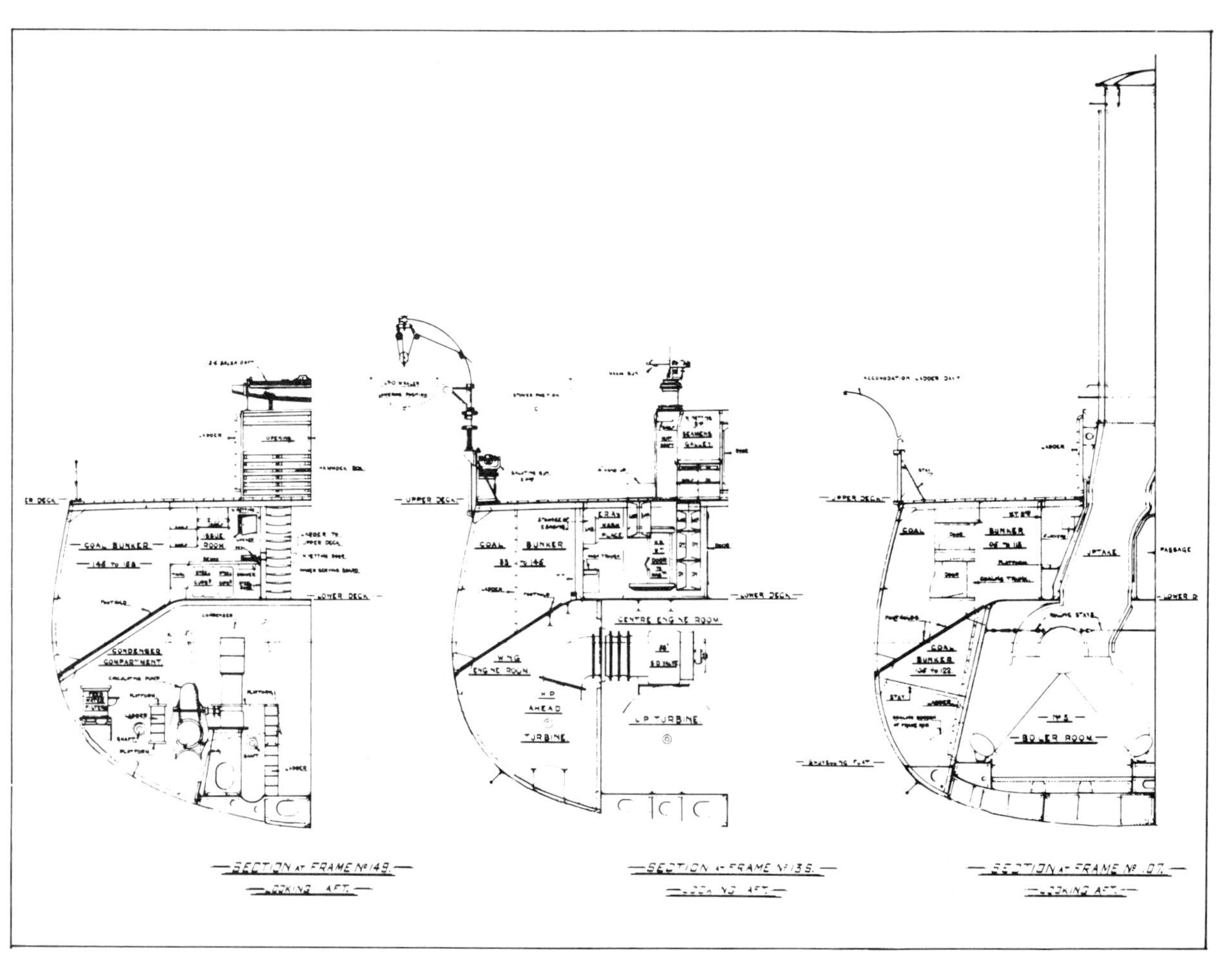

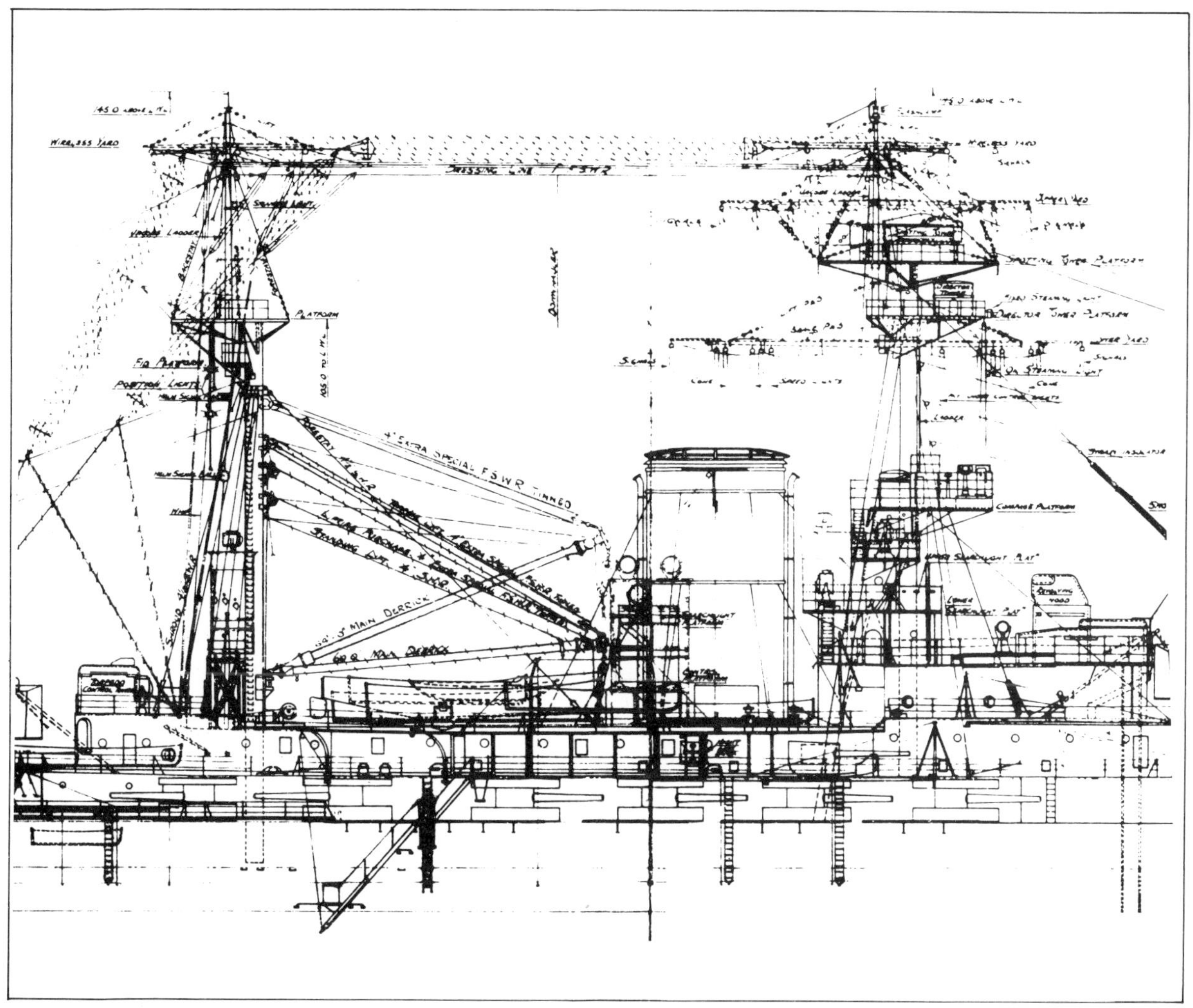

Left. Typical details from an Admiralty 'as fitted' Sections plan.
Right. Part of the 'as fitted' Rigging Plan of HMS *Resolution.* Close inspection will show that certain parts have been deleted by crossing out. This was done on the original tracing in coloured ink, and at the same time any additional equipment is drawn in with the same coloured ink. A different colour of ink is used for modifications, or 'alterations and additions' (A's & A's), made at each refit. As these reproduce in monochrome on a print, the only way to sort them out is by studying the character of the draughtsmanship, by the use of correctly dated photographs, and having some knowledge of the history of the ship. (By courtesy of the National Maritime Museum)

to make things more difficult the American Archives are by no means as fully documented as are the British. Both Archives are still receiving material in substantial amounts from their navies on an ongoing basis, and in America the material being made available under the US Freedom Of Information Act has meant an increased flow of documents to archival status. However the availability of general arrangement plans is usually restricted under the official USN policy of keeping under cover plans of ships still in existence until the last ship in that class has been disposed of, or is above a certain age. This is the reason why plans of *Essex* class carriers have been unobtainable until very recently.

The modeller of British ships is hampered to a certain extent by the working of the 30 year rule, which means his chances of obtaining ship plans that are less than 30 years old is small.

Of all the major navies of the twentieth century the one having least archival material in plan form is the

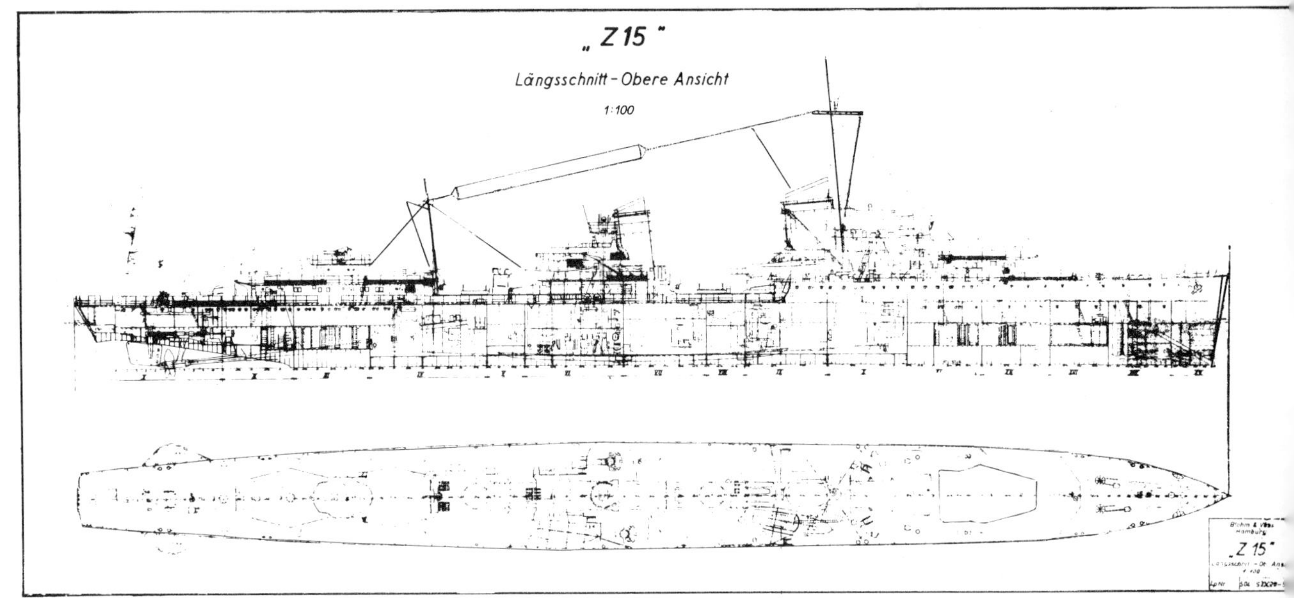

Japanese. At the end of WW II the Japanese destroyed vast quantities of documentation including ship plans. It was said for many years by uninformed persons that *all* plans had been destroyed. This is not true for, although they had destroyed much, respectable quantities remained in various locations in the homeland. The bulk of this was seized by the Americans and shipped back to the United States, with some finding its way to Britain. In 1964 these documents, which included general arrangement plans, were passed back to the Japanese and recently these have become at least partially available in reproduced form as folders of plans, each folder containing four sets. Unfortunately some important ship plans were lost, including the general arrangement sets for *Yamato* and *Musashi.* Happily the set for *Shinano* has survived but only the design set is available to the public, with the detailed general arrangement set still being witheld.

Most Japanese plans are detailed and clear, but some of the war-built ships are a little skimpy in detail. Like the Americans they redrew plans completely to depict a later configuration, a good example being two complete sets for the command cruiser *Oyodo,* one dated 1943, the second dated 1944 after refit.

PHOTOGRAPHS

Photographs are one of the prime sources of information for a modeller. Regardless of the completeness of the plans, manuals and working drawings, he should in every case obtain, or try to obtain, photographs of the ship in question. Apart from those of ships of the Japanese Navy which are only seen in books and magazines, photographs of ships of all the major navies are available from several sources. Like commercial plans some photographs are comprehensive and reliable, some are not and care should be taken when using the poor ones to make a check on them, especially as to the given date, for often this is incorrect. By far the best kind are those sometimes labelled 'fitting out', usually taken as a matter of official record or for the builder's private file. These are the ones to be located since the amount of information they contain is overwhelming. Unfortunately over the last one hundred years not all navies and builders adopted this policy, although the situation has been improving gradually over the years until today most vessels coming into service are comprehensively covered in their 'as built' state.

Without doubt the largest and best collection of photographs in the world is held by the National Archives in Washington DC. Unfortunately a large part of the collection is unlisted and it will be many years before the whole lot is sorted out. When the collection is made available in its entirety undoubtedly it will contain some surprises. Among those available are the 'fitting out' sets taken at various yards and consisting of a number of close-up views showing the vessel in full detail. Copies of many of these sets, as well as all round views of individual types of gun mountings, can be obtained from the 'Floating Drydock' Company, and although not of the same quality of reproduction as those from the National Archives, they are adequate for modelling purposes.

The modeller of British ships is not as well served as those making American vessels, although on occasion the photo coverage can be remarkably complete. The largest collection of British warship photographs is held by the Ministry of Defence and consists almost entirely of general views. There are some close-up shots but these are very few in number and other sources should be tried for this type. If you are making a WWI ship or one built between the wars then some of the finest close-up alongside photos can be obtained from the Perkins Collection held at the National Maritime Museum, London. The Imperial

Opposite: A shipbuilder's plan of the German destroyer *Z 15*. This one is well detailed, whereas some show many of the fittings in outline only.

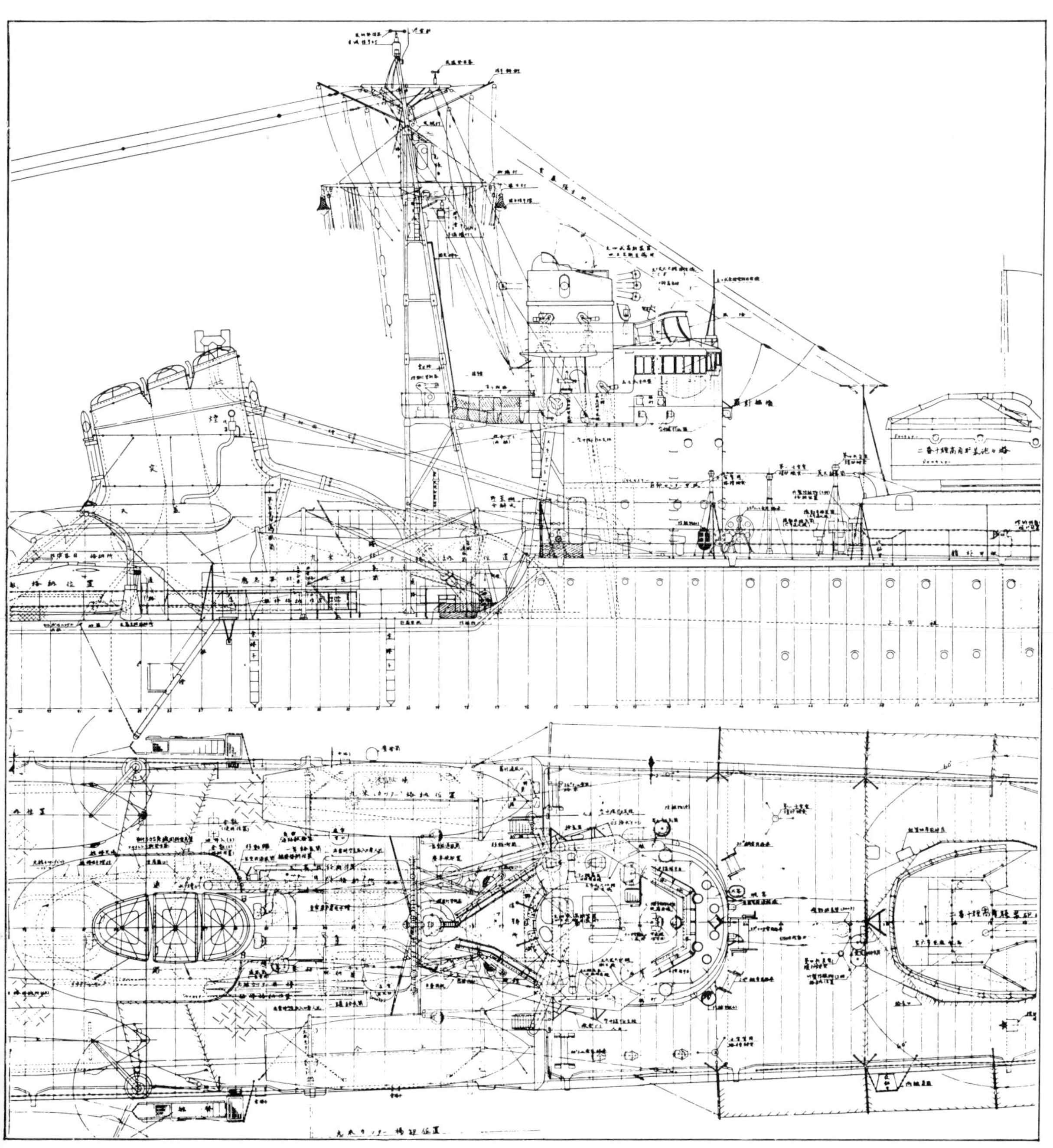

Below. Although this section of the drawing of the Japanese destroyer *Akitsuki* contains a great deal of information, the mass of superimposed detail on the plan view does make for some difficulty in its interpretation.

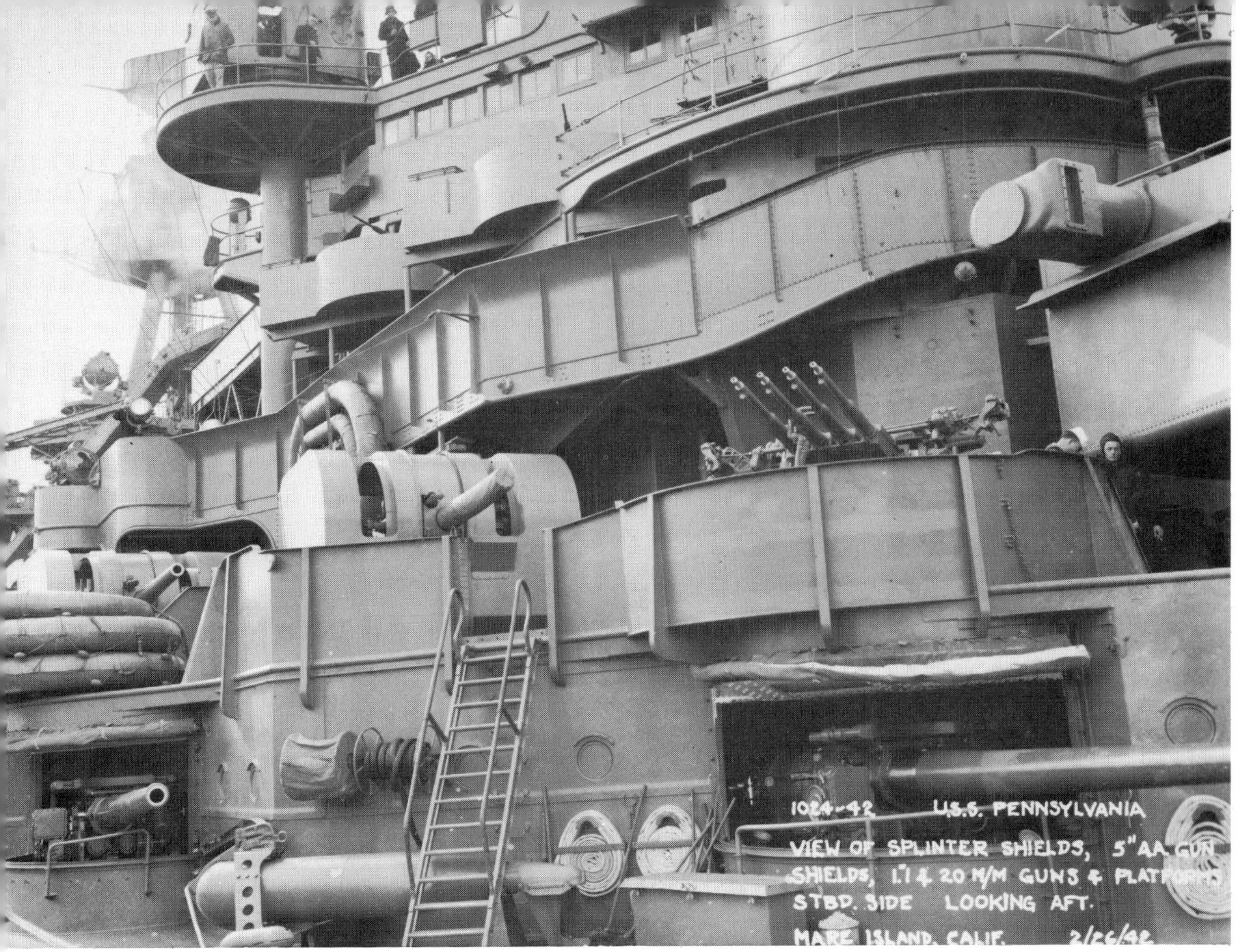

1024-42 U.S.S. PENNSYLVANIA
VIEW OF SPLINTER SHIELDS, 5" AA. GUN
SHIELDS, 1.1 & 20 M/M GUNS & PLATFORMS
STBD. SIDE LOOKING AFT.
MARE ISLAND, CALIF. 2/26/42

Opposite top: Typical of the material available from the US National Archives is this close-up of the USS *Pennsylvania* refitting at the Mare Island Navy Yard.

Opposite bottom: HMS *Royal Sovereign.* A good example of the standard of the close-up shots to be found in the Perkins Collection in the Photographic Section of the National Maritime Museum, Greenwich, London.

Below: HMS *Cleopatra,* a *Leander* class frigate built 1964. Described as a ship portrait, photographs such as this (by C & S Taylor) show a wealth of detail. Similar shots of naval vessels can be obtained from the Ministry of Defence (Navy Department).

War Museum, London also holds hundreds of close-up and on board views, but the system of listing is such that a modeller may well be disappointed with the result; the best method is to make a personal visit, state his case fully and conduct his own search. This also applies to the National Archives collection which contains a reasonable number of general views and as these are listed, in most cases correctly, they form a source of wartime photographs worthy of consideration. With the National Archives they hold photographs of ships other than those of their respective navies. The National Archives for example have views of British ships of WWII, while the Imperial War Museum have some American vessels along with a few French and a handful of Japanese.

Another good source of British warships are those from Wright and Logan of Southsea, Hants. Most are general views but are usually of the highest quality, as to are those of Beken of Cowes, Isle of Wight; Sky-fotos, of Ashford Airport, Hythe, Kent have many aerial photographs of vessels of several nationalities taken in the Channel in the past fifteen years. Sources are rather sparse for the French ships, but one that is first class is Marius Bar of Toulon, along with those from the Musée De La Marine in Paris, with German vessels being obtained from Verlag Foto-Drüppel in Wilhelmshaven, West Germany.

Hopefully this chapter will begin to make the modeller aware of the richness and variety of subjects

Three museum models. In fact these are all shipbuilders' original models, but several points have to be kept in mind when using such models as data sources. To begin with it is essential to establish the accuracy of the model in relation to the period of the vessel's career being modelled. Sometimes these models may have been built to the original design for the ship, as would appear to be the case for the Japanese destroyer *Sazanami* (top), whilst others like HMS *Finisterre* (centre), show the ship as completed. Then certain curious conventions were used in the construction of these models in past years. Much use was made of natural coloured woods, and there were some odd painting and finishing schemes. The plating of fittings was much in evidence, as can be seen on HMS *Hexham* (bottom), and on some of the other photographs in this book. Where, for instance, a vessel or class of vessel only survived for a few years, and did not receive much publicity, then models can be very useful. *Sazanami,* built 1899 by Yarrow & Co Ltd, London, for the Imperial Japanese Navy. Scale 1/48. HMS *Finisterre,* completed in 1945 by the Fairfield Shipbuilding & Engineering Co Ltd, Glasgow, for the Royal Navy; one of the first group of 'Battle' class destroyers. Scale 1/48. HMS *Hexham,* paddle minesweeper, completed in 1917 by the Clyde Shipbuilding Co Ltd for the Royal Navy. Scale 1/48. (Photos by courtesy of the Museum of Transport, Glasgow)

waiting to be worked. There are many more books and plan sets and small individual nuggets of information, but space is limited. If the modeller follows the golden rule of obtaining where possible official, or commercial material prepared using official sources, coupled with photographs, he will not go far wrong.

COMMERCIAL SOURCES FOR PHOTOGRAPHS

UK

Navpic, J W Goss, 64 Gains Road, Southsea, Hants
Real Photos Ltd, 69 Stanley Road, Broadstairs, Kent CT10 1BL
C & S Taylor, 3 North Avenue, Eastbourne, East Sussex BN20 8RB
Wright & Logan, Albert Road, Southsea, Hants PO5 2SE
Skyfotos, Ashford Airport, Hythe, Kent

USA

Floating Drydock (for address see above)

Germany

Foto-Drüppel, 2940 Wilhelmshaven, Rheinstrasse 50

France

Marius Bar, Toulon

Malta

A & J Pavia, Tessy House, Fleur-de-Lys Junction, Birkirkaar

OFFICIAL ARCHIVES

UK

The National Maritime Museum, Greenwich, London SE10 (for photos, plans, and documents)
The Imperial War Museum, Lambeth, London SE1 (for photos and documents)
The Public Records Office, Ruskin Avenue, Kew, Surrey (for photos and documents)
Ministry of Defence (Navy), Section 423B, Foxhill, Bath, Avon (for photos)
The Naval Historical Branch, MoD, Empress State Building, London SW6 (for information)

USA

National Archives, Plans Division (Warships), Washington DC 20408 (plans of ships up to WWII)
National Archives, Audio Visual Branch, General Services Administration, Washington DC 20408 (photos down to 1957)
Naval Photographic Center, Department of the Navy, Anacostia, District of Columbia (photos from 1958)
US Navy Printing and Publications, (Official Plans), Washington Navy Yard, Washington DC 20390 (official plans not yet in National Archives)
Naval History Division, Navy Historical Center, Washington Navy Yard, Washington DC, 20390 (for information)

Germany

Bundes-Archiv-Militarchiv, 78 Freiburg-im-Breisgau, Weisentralstrasse 10 (Hochhaus) (for photos, plans and information)
Institut für Zeitgeschichte, Leonrodstrasse 46B, 8000 München 19 (for photos and information)

France

Musée de la Marine, Palais de Chaillot, 75116 Paris (for information)
Etablissement Cinematographique Photographique Armée (ECPA), Fort D'Ivry, Ivry-sur-Seine 94203 (for photos)

Netherlands

Director of Naval History, Ministry of Defence (Navy), Bagarstraat 19, 2518 AE The Hague

Japan

Museum of Maritime Sciences, Senpaku Shinko Building, 35 Shiba-Kotohira, Minato-Ku, Tokyo
War History Office, Defence Agency Japan, 1 Honmura-cho, Ichigoya, Shimjuka-ku, Tokyo

Note that a list of naval history sections in the world's navies is printed in *Warship International* 1977 No 2, pages 172-173.

Hull construction 2

by DAVE SAMBROOK

There are several methods of hull construction which may be used in the building of model ships. My personal preference is for a planked hull as this is strong, light and has the maximum internal space for the installation of motors, batteries and radio control equipment.

PLANKED HULLS

The method which seems to offer the strongest structure is to form a profile backbone into which are slotted solid frames at stations plotted from the drawings. These are then braced accurately at right angles to the backbone by use of triangular section balsa and this will produce a rigid structure upon which to attach the planks. Before planking commences it is required to build up bow and stern with solid block, rough shaped and rebated to accept the plank ends; these areas are best formed in this way as it avoids having to pull planks into a sharp radius thus giving rise to the possibility of structural failures.

An advantage to constructing a planked hull with block bow and stern is that the making of a ram or bulbous bow is reduced to a simple wood carving job. When these operations have been carried out planking up may commence. This is best carried out from the deck edge (thus establishing a clear sheer line) towards the keel working from side to side alternately. When the hull has been completely planked the blocks at bow and stern should be carved to shape and the whole hull may be sanded smooth.

In the case of a capital ship with external bulges, such as HMS *Queen Elizabeth,* the frames for these should now be fitted, the extreme ends being made of block and the remainder planked as with the hull. The next operation is to plot the position of the bilge keels and attach them. These are made from plywood or thin brass sheet glued into a shallow slot cut in the hull along the appropriate line.

Where an opening occurs, such as at the cable

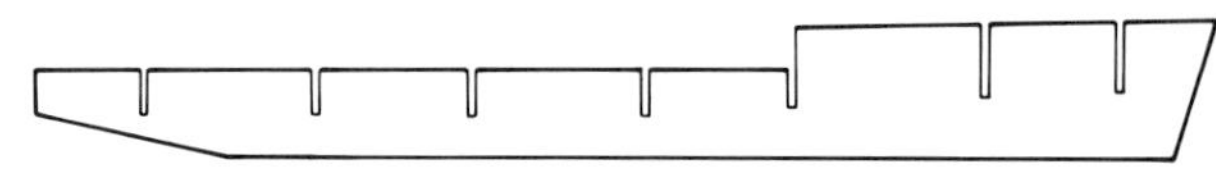

PLANKED HULL CONSTRUCTION 1: PROFILE

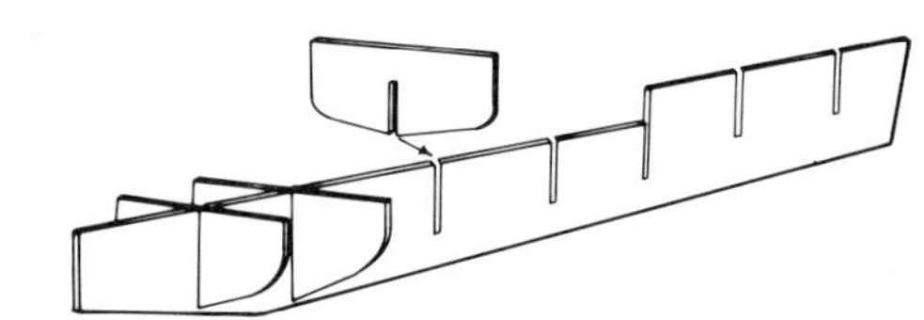

2: SOLID FRAMES

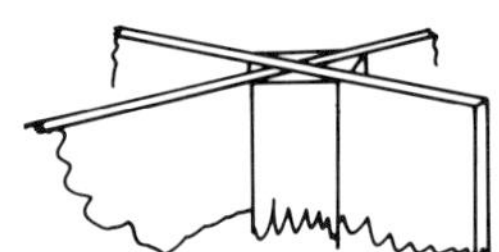

3: BRACES OF TRIANGULAR BALSA

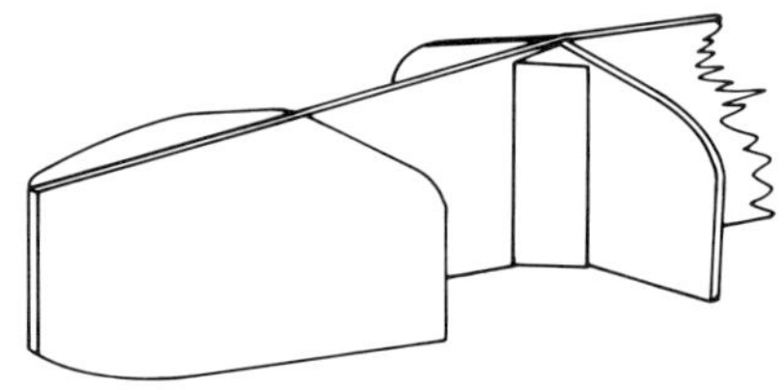

4: SOLID BLOCK BOW AND STERN

Opposite top: HMS *Repulse* by W S Bolton, 3/32in = 1ft, as in 1940. Note the bilge keel, the prominent armour belt and the heavy superstructure.
(Photo: W S Bolton)

Bottom: The famous British aircraft carrier HMS *Ark Royal* in 1940. This photo shows clearly the large openings in the sides of such vessels. Note the armour belt, visible between the lighters, and the supports to the gun sponsons.
(Photo: Conway Picture Library)

handling decks of aircraft carriers, these may easily be constructed by the following methods. Mark out on the hull surface the overall dimensions of the opening from deck to deckhead and bulkhead to bulkhead, then cut away. When this is done build a box on the inside of the hull matching the shape of bulkheading on the ship's drawings, and fit with all the various hatches, watertight doors and other deck fittings in this space, as these will prove almost impossible to fit after this stage. With all these operations complete it is now possible to plate up around the opening to the correct shape, including any plating which forms a bulwark. Any stiffeners in way of such openings will need to be fitted before the plates are fitted.

Where a steel bulwark extends above deck level as part of a vessel's side plating, such as in a *Flower* class corvette, this will need to be constructed so that it blends in with the shell plating. The first step is to make a paper pattern of the shape of the bulwark in question. In the case of the *Flower* class, for example, this extended aft right round the upper deck from the break of the forecastle. The pattern should allow a small overlap at the bottom to facilitate fixing to the hull. This lower edge can either be rebated into the hull or blended into the hull plating. When this fits satisfactorily it should be transferred to a piece of thin sheet metal and cut out; any openings such as freeing ports should be cut at this stage. The bulwark should then be curved to shape and glued in place but it will, of course, be necessary to represent the ship's plating on the inner face at this stage before any internal stiffening, in the form of stays or angle bar connections between deck plate and bulwark, is fitted. Finally the capping rail of steel bar or timber should be fixed in place.

The propeller shafts and their supporting brackets (if any) should be made and fitted at this stage. For working models I make the propeller shaft tubes from brass tube with turned brass bearings soldered into each end. At a point about half-way along the tube I drill a hole for a greasing tube, and solder this in position when the shaft tube is in place. The 'A' brackets are made in a similar manner to the tubes, but with the addition of their supporting arms. It is better to leave these off until the plating has been fitted in this area. Where the shaft tubes pass through the hull the position of these openings should be marked out and the required holes cut in the hull. A jig will have to be made to support the outboard ends of the propeller shafts in the correct position; when aligned fix the shaft tubes and 'A' brackets (if the plating has been fitted) with a 5-minute epoxy and fair the shaft tubes into the hull. The rudder, or rudders, can now be made and a tube for each post fitted into and secured to the hull. The rudder post is then passed through, and an arm soldered to the top

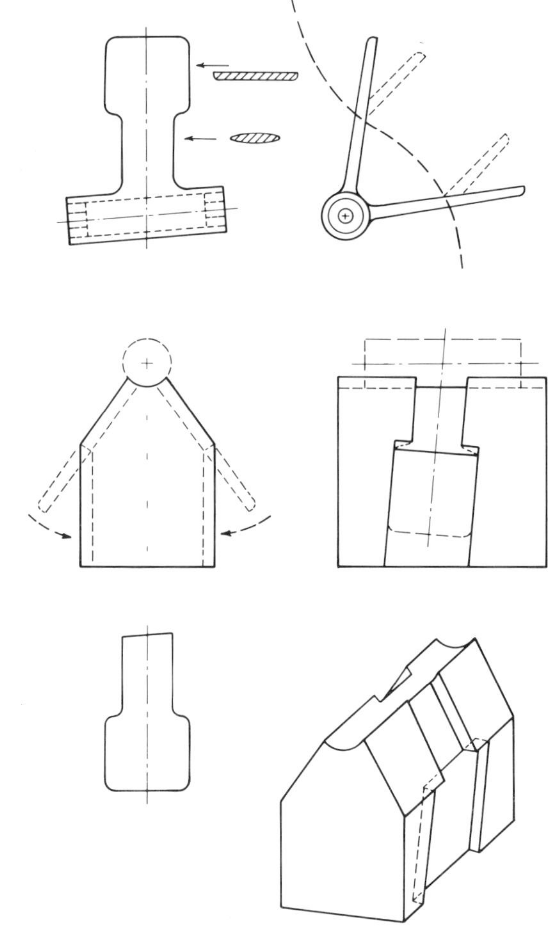

PROPELLER SHAFT BRACKETS

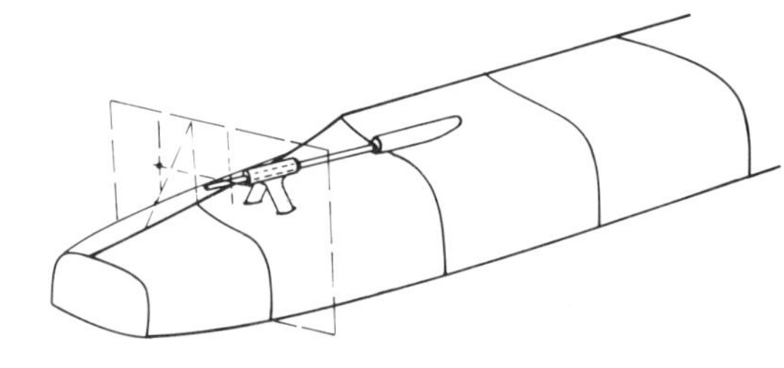

PROPELLER SHAFT ALIGNMENT

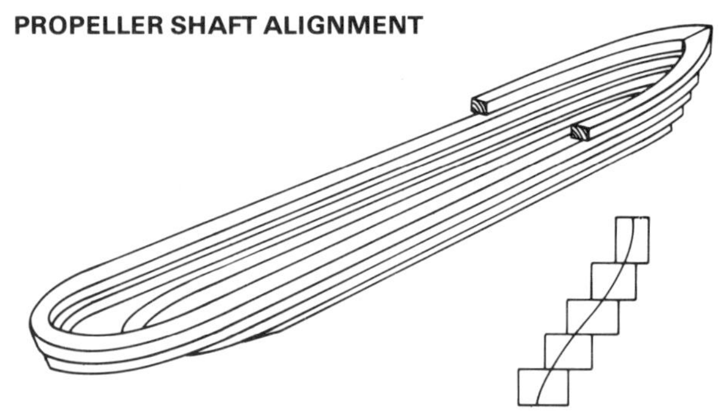

BREAD AND BUTTER HULL CONSTRUCTION

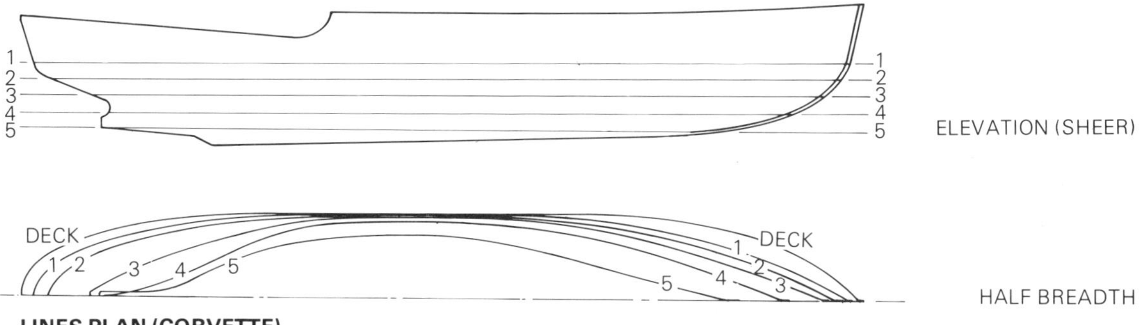

LINES PLAN (CORVETTE)

of the rudder post to take a push-rod for operating the rudder.

BREAD AND BUTTER HULLS

An alternative system of making a hull is the 'bread and butter' method, whereby several planks of wood are laminated together. A lot of hard work may be avoided by glueing together with a waterproof glue a few planks to make up the required thickness in the following way. Referring to the draught you will see on the elevation a number of horizontal lines and on the half breadth plan a series of curved lines similarly marked which show the shape of the hull at these levels. If planks are cut to these shapes a considerable amount of carving will be saved. The number and thickness of the timber will vary from ship to ship, according to size and type, but planks between $\frac{1}{2}$in to 1in (12mm to 25mm) are generally best.

Below: A planked model in frame of the Italian minesweeper *RD7* of the First World War period. Built by Giancarlo Barbieri, it is to 1/50 scale.

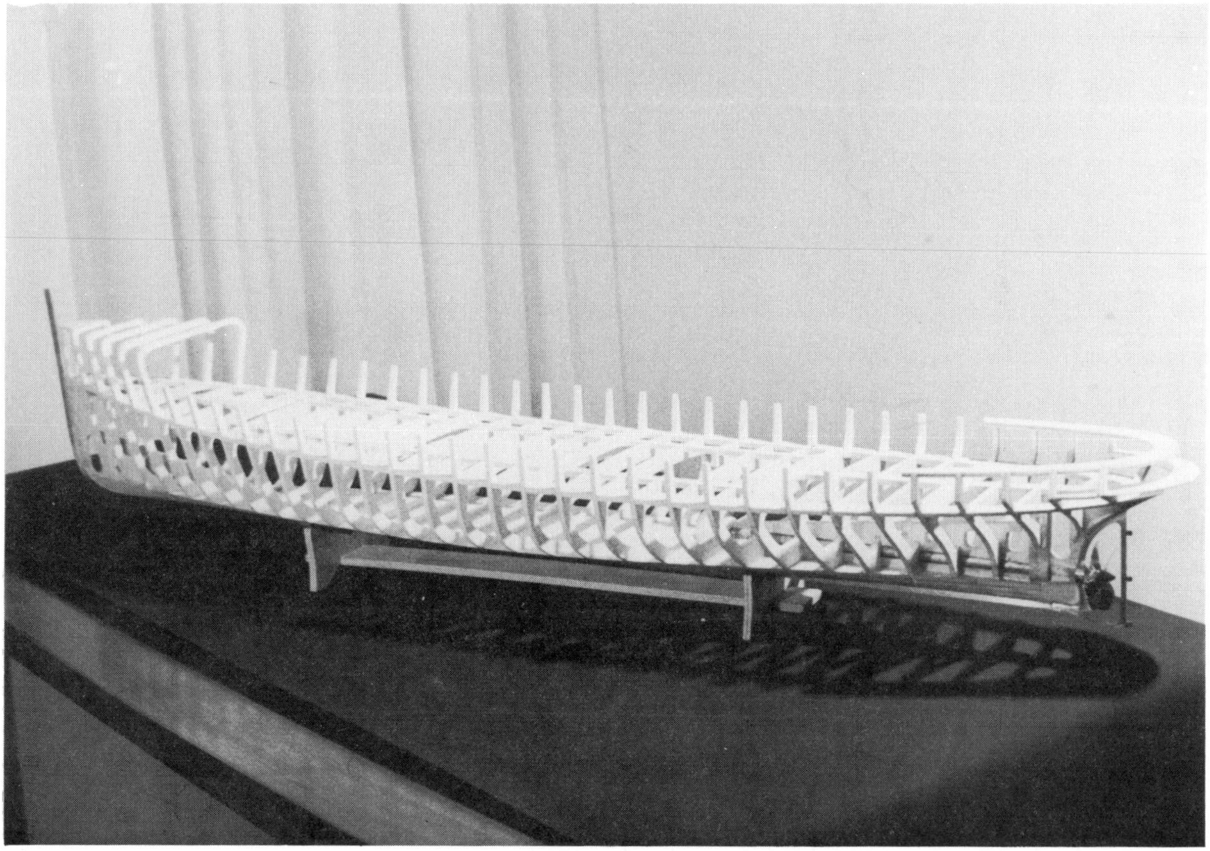

Some care should be taken when assembling the planks and the best way is to mark the centre line and one or more station lines all round. Never glue more than two planks together at one time and fix them securely with clamps or screws whilst the glue dries. When all are assembled the hull may be carved to final shape with the aid of templates to check the shape. In order to ease the difficulty of hollowing out the hull a large part of the centre of the upper planks may be cut away before assembly — these pieces can provide enough wood for the lower planks. Be careful though that you do not undercut the next lower plank as the inner cutting line must use the lower plank as a guide. When the outer surface of the hull has been smoothed to a suitable surface the interior may be smoothed off until the thickness of the hull is approximately $\frac{1}{4}$in (6mm). As the hull has been made from flat planks the top edge will be a straight line, which means it is necessary to mark out the true shape of the deck edge or sheer line and carve to shape.

As an alternative to the above-mentioned method of 'bread and butter' construction the following system offers a simpler and more economic way of doing things, and is suitable for the vast majority of warship hulls. Problem shapes are discussed later. The accompanying drawing is based on a typical cruiser hull. Thirteen stations are used in the example for simplicity, but ideally there should be more, for the more there are the greater will be the accuracy of the hull.

Trace out the full model size of the hull profile and body plan on to a piece of paper. If a sheer draught or lines plan is not available the above can be obtained

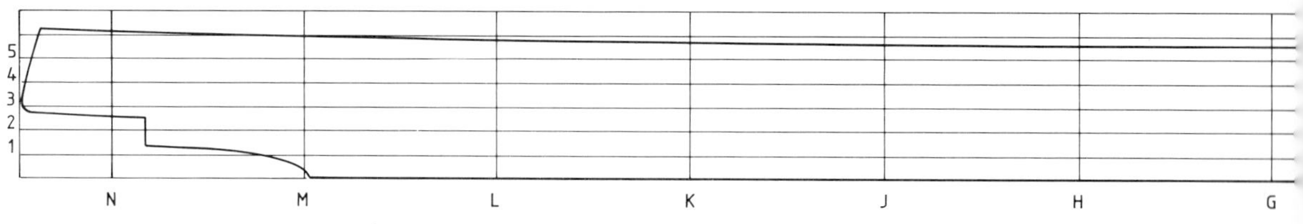

STAGE II
OUTLINE OF LAMINATIONS 1 & 2 AND DATUM LINE 2

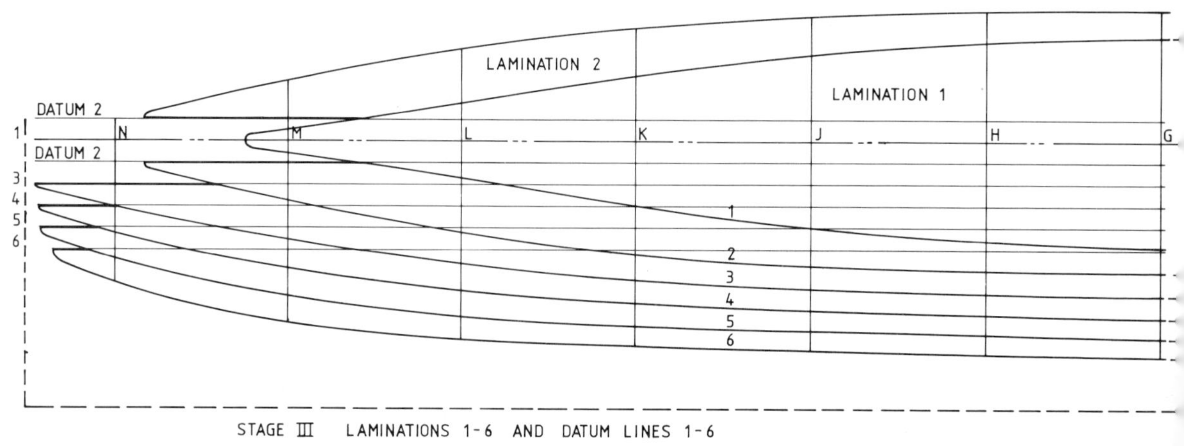

STAGE III LAMINATIONS 1-6 AND DATUM LINES 1-6

TYPICAL CRUISER HULL

from the inboard or outboard profile and sections. Do not draw in any horizontal lines except a base line.

Select the thickness of wood to be used and mark out the horizontal lines upwards from the base line, numbering the lines as you go; the line spacing must equal the thickness of the wood. If you are using balsa or obechi from a model shop it will be an imperial size such as $\frac{1}{4}$in or $\frac{1}{2}$in (6mm or 12mm), but if you purchase from a timber merchant it will probably be a metric size.

Decide how much you would like each lamination to overlap the next for a good glue joint. As a guide I usually make it $\frac{1}{2}$in (12mm) for large hulls and $\frac{3}{8}$in (10mm) for small ones. Now calculate the minimum width of wood from which to make the hull. The length will be at least that of the hull.

Width of plank=2 [(Number of laminations — 1) x overlap] + beam.

In our example the number of laminations is 8; overlap is $\frac{1}{2}$in (12mm); beam is 5in (127mm).

Applying the formula:

$$\text{Width}=2\left[(8-1)\times\tfrac{1}{2}\right]+5$$
$$=2\left(7\times\tfrac{1}{2}\right)+5$$
$$=7+5$$
$$=12\text{in}$$

To obtain wood of this width or more, several planks will have to be glued edge to edge. In this case, three sheets of 4in(102mm) wood should suffice if you are using balsa. If you intend using wood from a timber merchant check the flatness of the planks as they often curl after planing. Pine is best avoided as it is unstable. Mark straight onto the wood the centre line

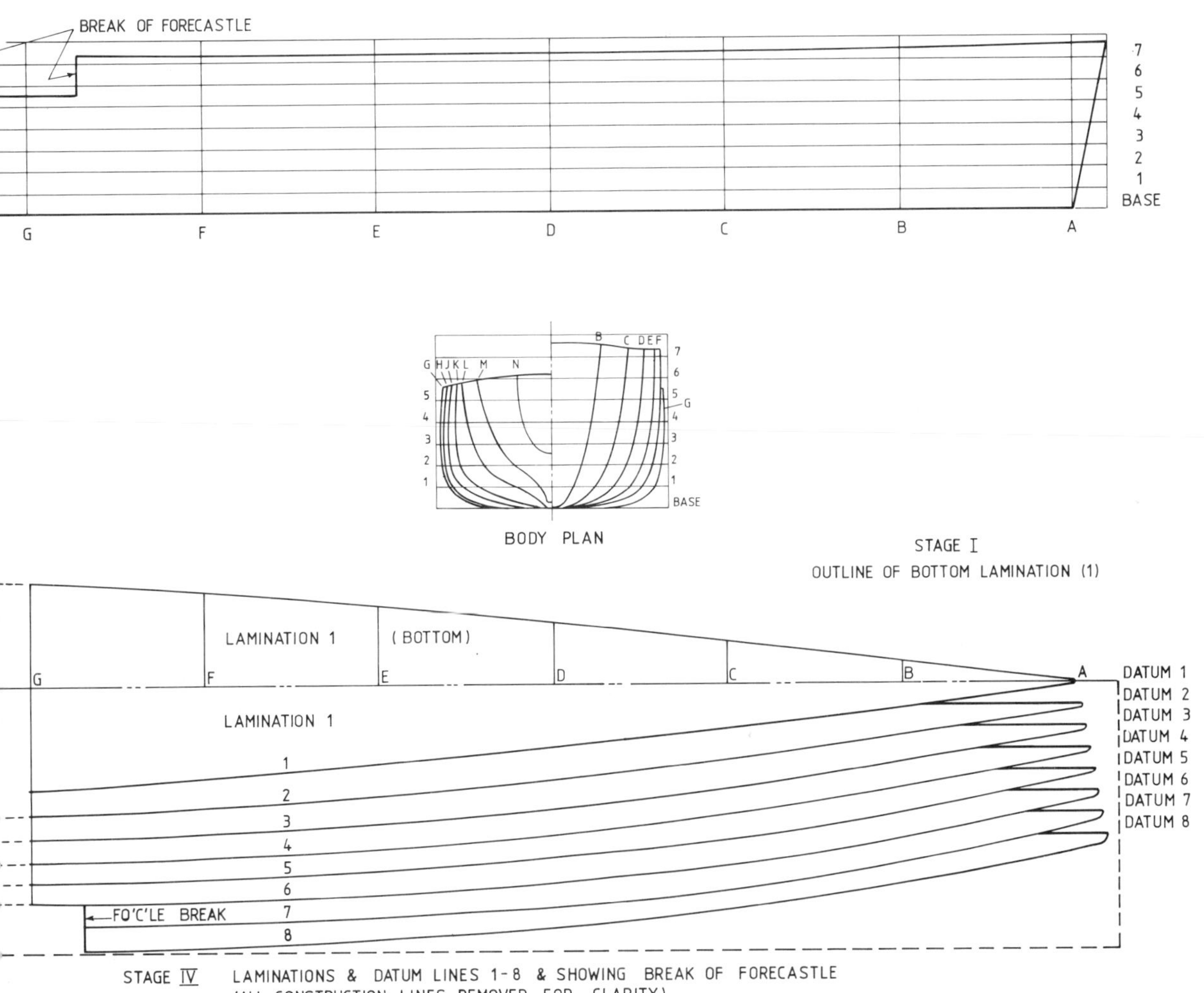

STAGE IV LAMINATIONS & DATUM LINES 1-8 & SHOWING BREAK OF FORECASTLE (ALL CONSTRUCTION LINES REMOVED FOR CLARITY)

Below: The flexibility of the bread-and-butter method of hull construction. At the top are hulls for a *Daring* class destroyer and for the cruiser HMS *Sheffield.* In the middle is the hull for a flat-bottomed shallow draught vessel; the sides are bread-and-butter construction, with a flat board for the bottom. In the bottom picture are the two parts of a hull built up using the economical cutting method described in the text. One part shows the boards glued up while the other shows the other half after being carved to shape.
(Photos: Author's collection)

Opposite: Problem shapes. HMS *Caledonia* an ironclad of 1862 (originally a wooden ship of the line, lengthened and altered to an ironclad on the stocks). Note the sharp tumblehome, the armour belt at the waterline with the additional wood sheathing immediately below, the stern walk, the decorative work, and other prominent hull details.
(Photo: Conway Picture Library)

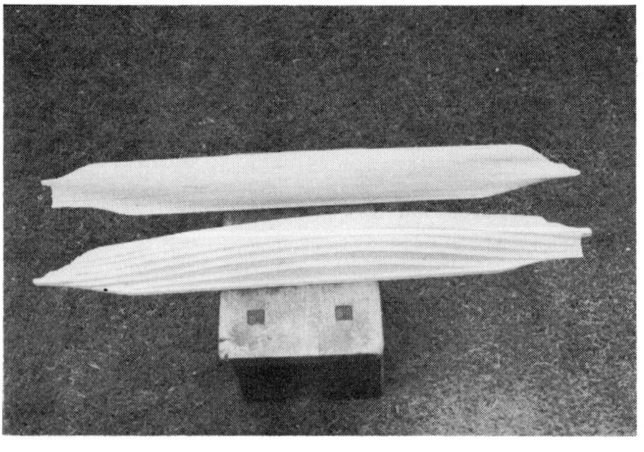

with the stations at 90°. You should have at least as many stations as on the drawing, certainly no less.

Plot the bottom lamination (No 1) on the wood. Using dividers, measure the width of each station on line 1 and mark off the widths as you do so on both sides of the centre line at each station. Join up the dots with a smooth curve to obtain the shape of this piece. Note that this curve starts just forward of station A due to the rake of the bow and that it finishes abaft station M. See stages I and II on the drawing. Stage I area is left clear of other workings so as not to confuse those who have not done any marking out of this nature before.

Mark off a new datum line each side of the original centre line at a distance equal to the overlap selected. In this case it is ½in (12mm). Mark out lamination 2, using line 2 on the body plan and datum lines 2 on the wood. This is shown in stage II on the drawing. Note that in this instance lamination 2 can be seen to finish between M and N on the profile. Plot this point by measuring its distance from N.

Mark out datum lines 3 and, using line 3 on the body plan, plot the shape of lamination 3.

For laminations 4 to 6 — observe that stations G, H, J and K incorporate some tumblehome. This shows clearly on the body plan. Be careful here! If the tumblehome shows up on G, H, J and K we must assume that its total extent is from F to L. Under these circumstances the width of the actual lamination is greater on the lower surface so, when taking measurements for laminations 4, 5 and 6 you must use the line under the lamination, that is line 3 for lamination 4 etc — but only where the tumblehome occurs. All other stations are measured in the usual way.

Stage III shows all the laminations up to quarter deck level. Observe the false datum lines 1 to 6. Finish off the marking out of the rest of the laminations. On hulls with a lot of sheer you may have fairly short pieces at bow and stern. Take particular care when marking these out.

Stage IV shows the final product with all construction lines removed for clarity. The dotted line around stages III and IV shows the plank of wood and how little is wasted compared with the old-fashioned way. The result shown in stages II and IV will, of course also appear in mirror image on the other side of the centre line!

Cut round the outside of the top lamination. When you cut the inside line on this piece you will be making the first cut on the next one down, and so on. When all the cutting out is done the whole lot can be glued together, the one-piece bottom being a great help in the building up. If there is the slightest difference in thickness from one side of the sheet to the other the hull will become lop-sided, due to the accumulated error, so lay out the laminations as they are shown on the sheet and swop over every alternate piece from one side to the other. This will cancel out any error due to thickness or density. Cascamite glue can be used for all types of wood during assembly. It has the advantage that you can make it thick or thin. Make it thin and watery for balsa wood, as a lot of water will be absorbed. Wipe off with a damp cloth any that squeezes out otherwise it will set very hard and make rubbing down difficult.

Shaping the hull is a long job so do not rush at it. It is a good idea to cut out your deck(s) using the plan view on the drawing and pin it in place temporarily, lest you cut too much off during the shaping of the top edge of the hull. A balsa hull can easily be shaped by using a razor plane and sandpaper. With hard wood hulls a disc sander on an electric drill saves an awful lot of hard work, but do wear industrial or leather gloves.

PROBLEM SHAPES

As mentioned earlier, there are some problem shapes. For bluff bows and round sterns use a block of wood as this system cannot cope with these shapes. Rebate the block to accept the ends of the laminations for strength and alignment. In the case of transom sterns the shape will usually be shown in the body plan or sections. Make this up before assembly and use it to align the ends of the laminations when glueing up.

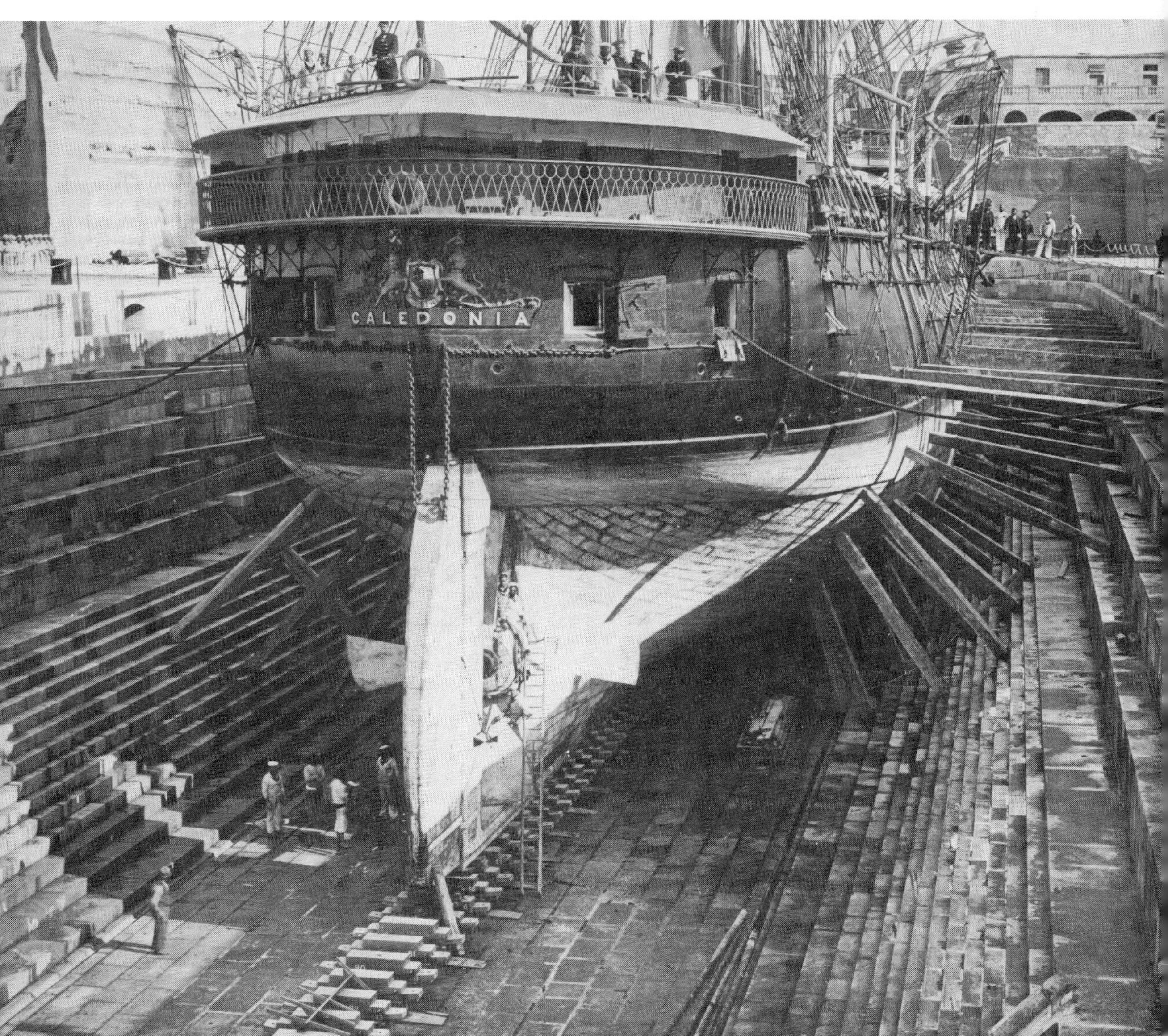

A certain amount of tumblehome can be accommodated such as is found in many British vessels, but not to the extent of some French types around the turn of the century. Bulges are best added after the rest of the hull has been shaped as it is extremely difficult to carve these in one piece.

HULL OPENINGS

Having built the hull, the next job is to add the deck, and this is done in more or less the same manner, regardless of the method of hull construction. Decks are cambered to allow the water to run off. As the curve of the camber is an arc or a circle (on most warships it is about 1 in 50), make a template to check for accuracy. When the deck beams have been cut and slotted to accept the longitudinal girders they can be fixed in place. It may be necessary to make openings in the deck, in which case cut away the beams just inboard of the longitudinals and fit a doubler onto the removed section. When the necessary frames for the removable sections of the deck have been made, the decks can be cut from thin plywood ($\frac{1}{32}$in or $\frac{1}{16}$in, 0.8mm or 1.6mm) and fixed in place.

In order to ensure that the ship is watertight in all respects it is necessary to build coamings round openings in the deck structure. These can be planned so as to be hidden within the various superstructure blocks. Despite this, I have found that given sufficient freeboard water will not normally enter a joint at the deck edge of a ship if it is carefully fitted.

Other methods of dividing the hull to gain access to the interior are possible. One of these is to split the hull along the waterline, and fit a false deck to the lower half of the hull for the upper portion to sit upon. To ensure a watertight structure a tall coaming is built upon this deck to the top of which is fitted a waterproof cover. A further variant of this method, which is suitable for submarines and any other vessel with exceptionally low freeboard, is to fit a sealed pressure plate to an opening in the deck.

In order to prevent water creeping in through various openings, such as stern/shaft tubes, hydroplane pivots, etc, it is a good idea to fit a bicycle tyre valve to the pressure plate so that when the whole hull is assembled it is possible to use a bicycle pump to raise the air pressure inside the hull, for it is vastly preferable to have an outward leak of air than an inward one of water.

One other type of hull division which I have found useful on a very shallow draught river gunboat hull was to build the hull, which is flat-bottomed, out of $\frac{1}{16}$in (1.6mm) plywood. The hull in effect is a pair of boxes, the central one being rectangular in shape containing all the motors, batteries and radio-control equipment and having an access hatch in the top with a raised coaming which protrudes into the engine

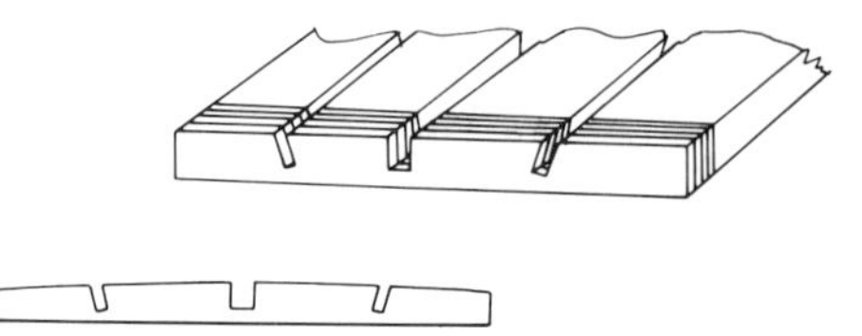

TEMPLATE FOR CAMBER OF DECK BEAMS

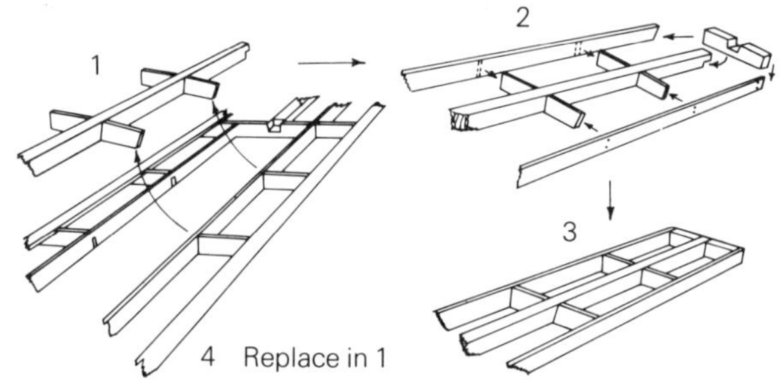

CUTTING AN OPENING IN THE DECK

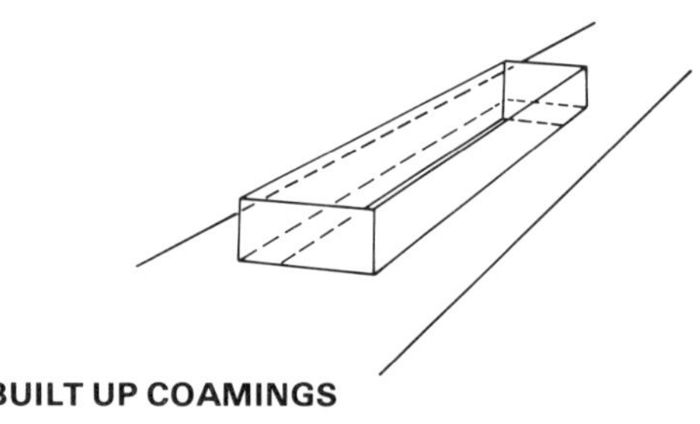

BUILT UP COAMINGS

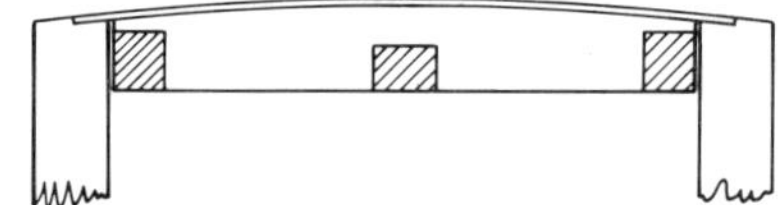

FLUSH HATCH FITTING AT DECK EDGE

HULL DIVIDED AT WATERLINE

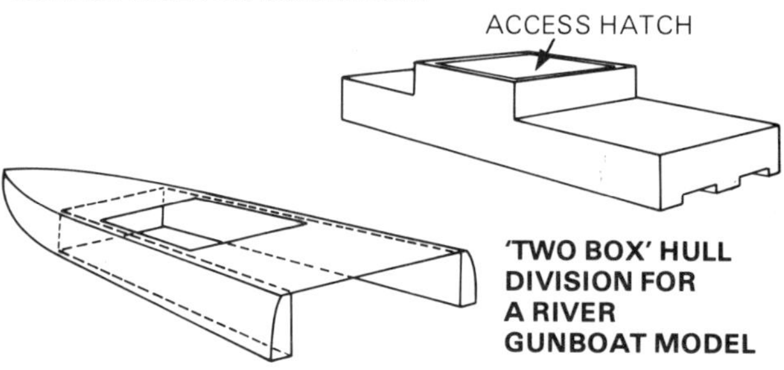

'TWO BOX' HULL DIVISION FOR A RIVER GUNBOAT MODEL

Above: Another problem shape. Note the very prominent armour belt with its square cut top edge and extending well forward. The casemates in the hull for the two aftermost guns have been plated over.
(Photo: USN)

Below: HMS *Wild Swan.* This 1/48 scale model of the composite sloop of 1876 is interesting for the way the builder, R Dawes, has divided the hull horizontally in order to gain access to the interior without having to disturb all the rigging; it will be a working model.
(Photo: John Bowen)

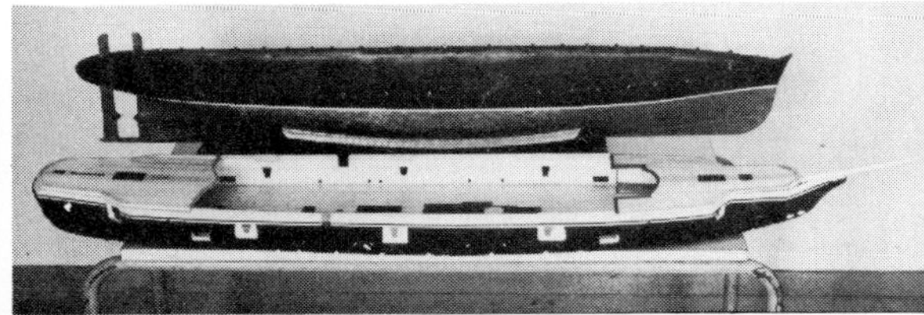

room casing through the deck of the other box. The latter consists of the remainder of the ship's hull, complete with upper deck. The advantage of all these schemes, which split the hull at places on or below the waterline, is that there is no longer any need to make any allowance for unrigging the ship to gain access to the interior. This means you can rig a vessel completely, even including deck awnings, as there is no need to disturb them once built. Also, as the power plant and controls are totally separated from the rest of the model, work may be carried out on them without fear of damage to the more delicate parts of the structure.

PLATING

If you intend to plate the ship's hull, it is important to have a shell plating expansion for the ship in question, since this shows the positions of the plates. Having marked out the portlight openings you must not forget that all ships have a considerable number of openings in the shell plating below the waterline for such things as intakes, Asdic domes, outlets, and so on. Where these occur the hull should be treated to prevent water soakage when the shell plating is cut through to represent these. On most ships having an Asdic dome these were retractable either partly or completely into the hull and a properly constructed opening must be made through the shell plating. Before plating commences though it is important to complete the work on all the ports in the ship's side. These should be drilled out and painted a suitable colour, then a short piece of perspex rod should be inserted. Plates should be applied with careful regard to the plating expansion, note being taken of the direction of lapping of plates and which strakes are 'in' and which are 'out'.

Where early destroyers' 'turtleback' forecastles are concerned the plating is usually laid as deck plating except, of course, there is greater curvature to the plates across their widths.

Several materials may be used to simulate plating effect such as gummed paper, thin card or litho plate, which is a thin aluminium alloy used to make printers' plates (it is usually possible to obtain used plates from printers as they have little value once used). This material is easily cut using a scalpel and steel rule. If it is necessary to put a curve into the plate it may be softened by annealing and fixed in place with a glue such as Uhu. It also has the advantage that it requires no sealing before painting. Scuttles (portholes) should, of course, be cut in the plates corresponding to those in the hull. After these are fixed in place rigols should be added — these are the small curved gutters fixed above them.

DECKS

Decks and deck coverings vary widely in their construction and appearance. In destroyers the wide plate at the deck edges, called 'stringer' plates, are usually 'flush butted'. That is, the ends of each plate are brought together and joined underneath by a 'butt strap' or wide strip of steel treble-rivetted to each plate end, thus giving a flush surface. The decks are then laid with a centre line strake with three others, 'clinker' fashion, across to lap the edges of the stringer plates. Sometimes, instead of this, the strakes of plates are laid in and out as is the shell plating of the hull. The plate ends are usually 'joggled', that is shaped at the aft end to lap over the end of the next plate, to which it is then riveted. Where the seam edge of the next adjacent strake of plating crosses the joggled end lap of two plates the section of joggled plate — so far as modelling is concerned — can be cut away under the seam to give a straight seam to the plating. In full size practice a different method of plate preparation is adopted to ensure watertightness at this point, and the modeller will have to take steps inside the hull to do the same.

Where the weather decks are bare steel, they are covered with footstrips laid in a fore and aft direction in the waist of the ship, and in a 'herring-bone' pattern or straight across the forecastle and part of the quarter deck. Sometimes they are arranged radially about the cable holder. They are short lengths of steel usually about $1\frac{1}{2}$in (38mm) wide and of varying lengths rivetted or welded to the decks to improve footholding on a wet deck. These can be represented by cutting thin strips of litho plate, plasticard or card and glueing them to the decks with rapid epoxy or impact glue.

All round the edges of the decks is a continuous wooden rail bolted to the deck. Normally this is inside the guard rails, and is approximately 4in (102mm) high and $2\frac{1}{2}$in (63mm) wide. It is called the 'spurnwater', and is there to prevent wash water from the decks streaking the overside paint. It is often of bare wood scrubbed clean, but on most of the modern warships that I have seen it has been painted buff colour.

When decks are not planked, large areas are covered with a composition called 'Semtex' which is trowelled onto the plates and contained at the edges with small steel beadings. When it is dry it has a matt surface with a similar appearance to dry asphalt. It is usually painted dark green. Steel decks are sometimes painted black or dark grey and often the forecastle ahead of the breakwater is painted with red lead. Of course, these colours will vary if the ship is carrying a camouflage scheme. In British destroyers prior to the

'CLINKER' DECK PLATING FOR A DESTROYER

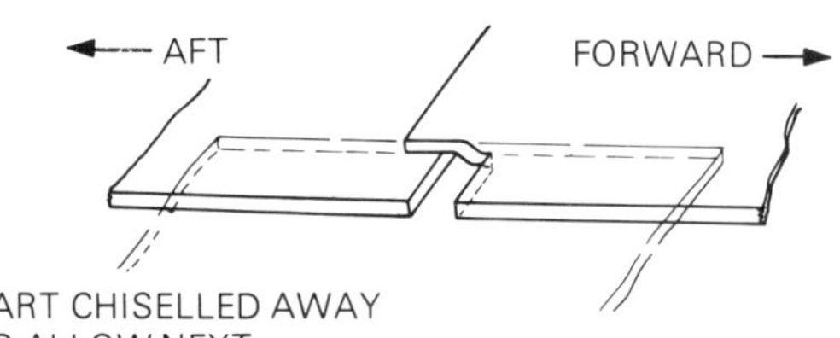

PART CHISELLED AWAY
TO ALLOW NEXT
STRAKE TO PASS

JOGGLING OF DECK PLATES

Opposite top: HMS *Devonshire.* Another problem with modern warships is the ripple effect on the shell plating caused by welding, well demonstrated here in this photograph taken after she had been commissioned in 1962 at the builders' yard. Note the recess for the anchor.
(Photo: Conway Picture Library)

Bottom: The corvette *Kromantse* by J Bidgood. This working model, whilst showing the clean lines of a modern warship, also shows some of the problems of these vessels — the pronounced knuckle and sharp flare forward, the stabilisers, and the tuck in aft in way of the shafts.
(Photo: John Bowen)

CAMPAIGNER
F 17

Below: HMS *Tallyho*. Perhaps the most complex hull shape of all, and certainly one to provide a modelmaker with some interesting constructional problems to overcome. Another case for horizontal division — main hull with separate upper casing and conning tower?
(Photo: Conway Picture Library)

Opposite: The German armoured cruiser *Blücher*. There is a wealth of hull detail in this photograph — the plated-in casemates for the anti-TB guns right aft alongside the stowed anchor, the prominent sidelights with their rigols, the torpedo nets, the heavy fairlead aft at the top of the stern contour plate, and the armour belt carried well aft.
(Photo: Drüppel)

Tribal class the material 'Corticene' was used in place of 'Semtex', which was a form of linoleum about the same colour as milk chocolate, and this was laid in squares and confined at the joins and along the edges by brass strips screwed to the decks. In the most recent destroyers and frigates a new non-slip material in pieces 12in x 6in (305mm x 152mm), with a surface like coarse emery cloth, is fixed to the decks in place of metal footstrips.

In large warships, such as cruisers and battleships, planking was the usual form of deck covering, normally of teak or Borneo whitewood, for British ships the planks being 5in (127mm) wide in sloops and *Algerine* class minesweepers; 7in (178mm) in cruisers; and 9in (229mm) in battleships. The edges of the planks are bevelled to form a V groove which is filled with oakum and is sealed with pitch. The deck planks are laid from the centre line outwards. The

butts are shifted so that the ends of the planks only occur in the same line every fourth plank. At the edge of the deck and around gun barbettes a finishing plank, called a 'cutting' board, is fixed to the deck. Where the deck planks meet this they have their ends cut to a bevel at one-third of their widths and notched into the 'cutting' board.

It is not difficult to represent a planked deck in model form. If the deck is made of plywood first rub matt white paint into the grain as a filler so that none remains on the surface of the wood. When dry, draw on this with indian ink and ruling pen or a very hard pencil to lay out the planking. The whole surface can then be painted over with clear dope which sinks into the deck giving a matt waterproof surface.

Another method with which I have had some success is to lay individual deck planks. This is a good method if, as with a *Flower* class corvette, there is a mixture of deck coverings. It is possible to work to quite small scales with this system.. Cut strips of thin obechi to the correct scale width (the full size plank is 5in (127mm) wide on this size of ship), and having carefully plotted out the plank positions and buttshifts, make up and position the cutting boards at the edges of the areas to be planked and at any hatches and ventilators passing through the decks in this area. Having done this, carefully lay the deck planks to fit the pattern drawn on the deck(s), finishing with a coat of clear dope to seal. In larger scale models the pitch seaming between planks may be represented by glueing strips of black paper between the planks, carefully trimming smooth, and sanding after laying.

Hatchways in decks have their coamings fixed to the decks with an angle bar. Those in the way of blast from heavy guns have 'blast plates' fitted, which are sloping strips of steel going from the deck to part way

up the coaming to deflect the blast. They are fitted not only to the hatches in line with the gun muzzles, but to those near the turrets as well, as blast acts in both directions.

GLASS REINFORCED PLASTIC

A type of hull which has much to commend it is the GRP moulded hull. This can be made fairly readily, but involves considerable work. It is necessary first to construct a wooden pattern of the hull required. This may be done in a manner very similar to the method described in the section on 'bread and butter' hulls except, of course, it is not necessary for the pattern to be hollow. Finishing off the surface should, however, be to the highest possible standard as every mark and blemish will transfer itself to the female mould which is made from this pattern. Before use it is probably wise to screw a block to the top enabling it to be gripped in a vice for ease of working.

Having achieved an accurate shape with the help of templates, apply a good primer, such as car type cellulose primer filler, rubbing down with wet-and-dry paper until a really smooth grain-free surface is achieved.

If the hull has any tumblehome it is vital that the mould be a two-part arrangement otherwise it will prove impossible to remove from the pattern. In order that the mould may be made in two parts it will be necessary to attach a flange with plasticine along the keel line as this provides a means of bolting the two halves of the mould together. It is also a good idea to provide a flange at the deck edge as well as this stiffens the mould and provides strength.

Before making a start on the mould make sure that the pattern has the required wax releasing agent applied and polished to a smooth finish with no blemishes. After this, apply the polyvinyl alcohol until continuously coated and allow to dry thoroughly.

When the releasing agent has set, building up of the female mould may start commencing with the gel coat, which is usually jelly-like and sticks well, not running off vertical surfaces. Make sure that the corners are well filled with resin and that there are no missed patches, then leave to harden. Next, using 1oz chopped strand mat cut into strips and lay-up resin, which is more fluid than gel coat, lay strips around the flanges first, stippling in the resin with a stiffish brush; then lay up the remainder of the mould with wider strips, say 4in to 6in (100 to 127mm) wide laid across the hull. Where sharp changes of shape occur care should be taken to try to avoid air bubbles. To obtain a strong mould three layers should be built up, working in alternate directions. When this first half of the mould has hardened, remove the keel flange piece and prepare the second side with release agents, including the keel flange face and lay up the second side as for the first. Leave for a week to cure thoroughly and before removing from the pattern drill a series of holes at 2in to 3in (50-76mm) centres around the keel flanges to enable the two halves to be bolted together.

Once curing is completed separate the halves, carefully wash off the polyvinyl release agent and check that there are no faults in the surfaces of the mould halves — any faults should be filled with glass fibre paste and the surface refinished with wet-and-dry paper.

With the female mould completed and reassembled, prepare the interior with the two release agents, as described previously. Apply the gel coat and lay up as before using three layers of mat. Again, allow a week, if possible, before removing from the mould. When free from the mould clean the release agent off and check for and fill any faults in the hull surface. Having cleaned the moulding, rub down with fine wet-and-dry paper to give a good key for the paint finish to adhere to.

WOODEN HULLED CRAFT

In the case of wooden hulled craft, such as HDMLs and MTBs the best method I have discovered of obtaining a smooth finish is to use household wood primer as a surface filler as this gives a good hard finish which takes paint well.

When building a hard chine hull, as with most MTBs, the hull should be framed up in much the same way as previously described, with the exception

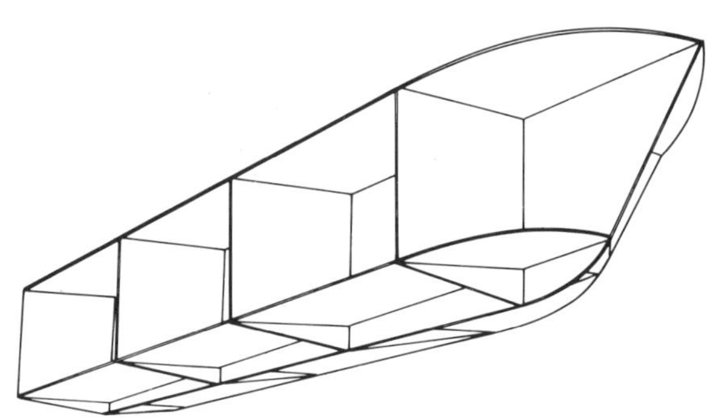

FRAMING FOR A HARD CHINE HULL

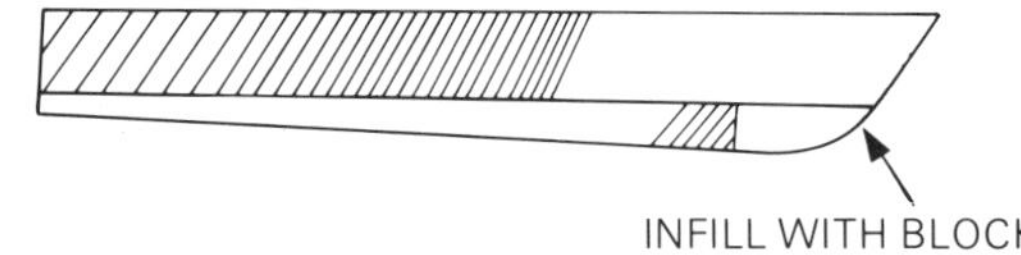

DIAGONAL PLANKING

that a lower 'chine' deck should be inserted to give a chine break to the hull. With the framing completed, planking up of the hull may begin. I use a method cribbed from a very old kit no longer available, which is to lay the bottom and side planking diagonally as in full size practice, except that as you plank forward from the stern the width of the planks should narrow allowing a natural flare to occur towards the bow. At the extreme bow, below the chine break, it is probably best to use block as a filling to avoid weakness. Where ports occur in the hulls of these wooden hulled craft they can be made by taking a piece of brass tubing of the correct diameter and cut to a suitable length slightly longer than hull plank thickness. Having cut the required number, plug one end with wood or glass fibre paste and paint the interior black or dark grey then, using a clear casting type resin or 'Devcon' 5-minute epoxy, fill to the brim. When set, this will give a realistic looking port which, when bonded into the hull, will be totally waterproof. The necessary hole to take these may be cut accurately using the same size brass tube as for the porthole, and sharpening the face of one end, pressing gently against the hull side, rotate slowly until it cuts its way through the hull.

GUMMED PAPER HULLS

Gummed paper strip may be used in the construction of hulls and to do this one must first build a mould over which the gummed strip is laid. To enable the removal of the mould it must be made in several pieces in such a manner as to allow it to be screwed together, and to prevent the first layer of gummed paper adhering to the mould a layer of tissue or toilet paper should be placed in position first. The layers of gummed strip should then be placed diagonally across the mould, in alternate layers. To ensure strength at the bow, a small wooden block should be set into the forefoot. When the hull has hardened and is free from the mould, the internal structure may be built in.

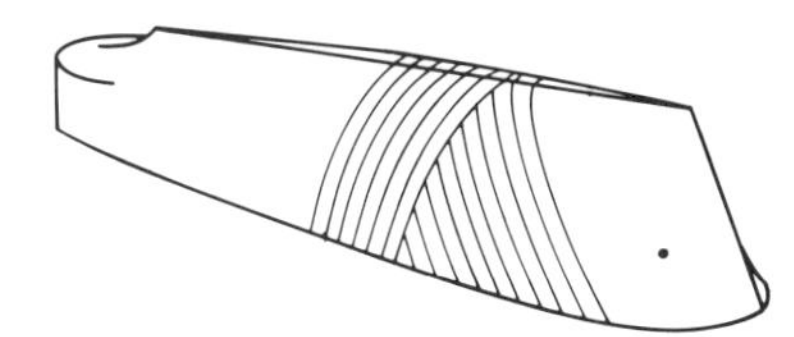

GUMMED PAPER HULL

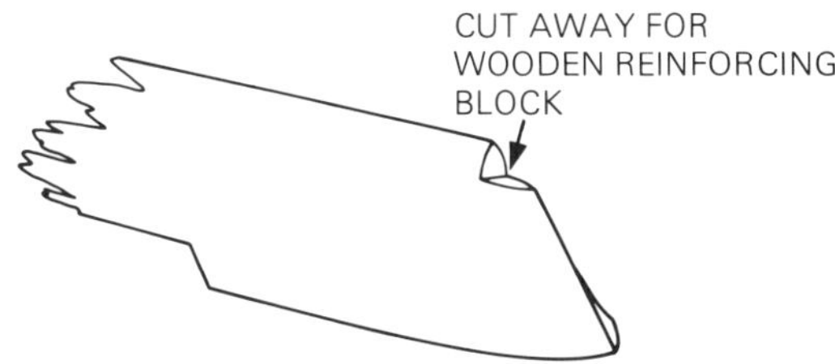

FORE FOOT IN A GUMMED PAPER HULL

Below: The wooden hull of an Italian minesweeper of the *Legni* class, at 1/32 scale by Giancarlo Barbieri. (Photo: Giancarlo Barbieri)

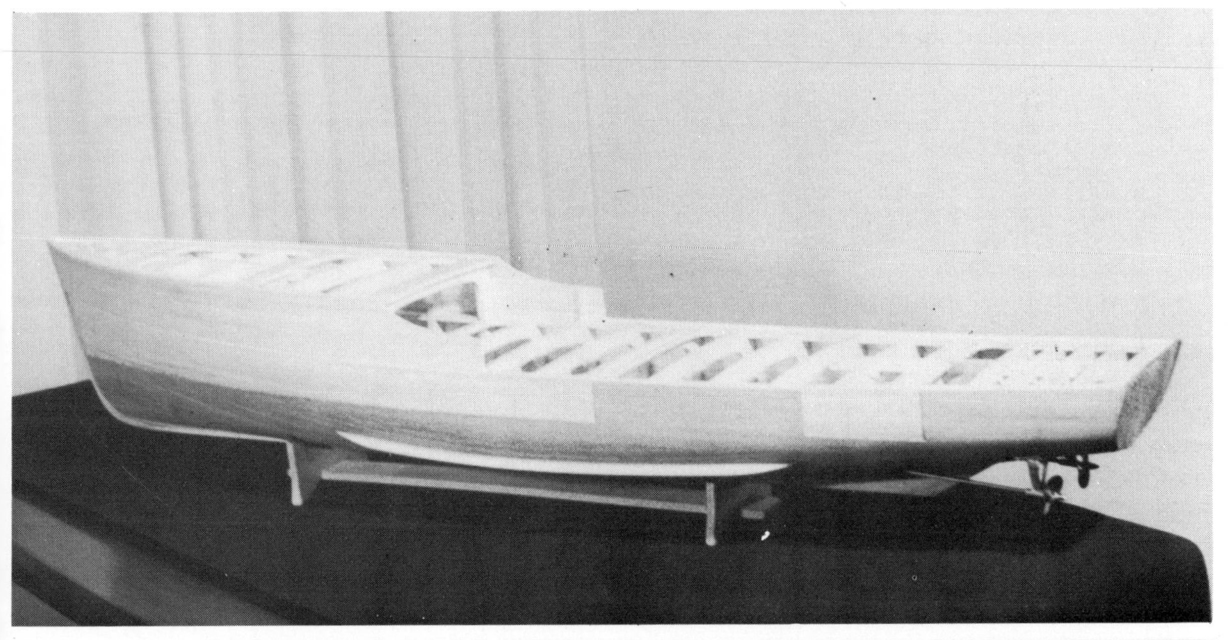

Tinplate construction 3

by H T N BATCHELOR

One of the best warship models to have been built in recent years using metal or tinplate construction is undoubtedly that of HMS Pheasant, *the work of the late Lt Col H T N ('Nick') Batchelor. Some time after he had completed the model he decided to write a very detailed step-by-step account of the building of this model. Regrettably he died before he had been able to do more than make some notes about the way he produced different parts for the model, and do a preliminary draft of the first couple of chapters. His relatives have made this material available to us in the hope that it might be of use, and we are very grateful for this generous gesture.*

This chapter has been put together from these notes, with the addition of some further material where necessary. No attempt has been made to present a cursive description of the building of a tinplate model; rather it is a series of detailed jottings on various aspects of the work of building the hull for such a model. For once the work on the hull has been mastered, the construction of the upperworks should be quite straightforward. It is apparent that Colonel Batchelor intended to write the book as though he was chatting to a group of interested modellers, so we have not altered this approach where it occurs in his notes.

The use of 'tinplate' is no new and novel form of ship model construction. The late Norman Ough was perhaps the one man who, in the immediate post-war years, really focussed attention on the true potential of this medium for the construction of accurate scale working models. He built several such model warships to prove his ideas, and whilst he did not publish very much about his methods, he did carry on a lengthy and detailed correspondence with Colonel Batchelor and with other modelmakers. **Editor.**

INTRODUCTION

If an accurate scale model hull is to be produced using tinplate there are two plans, apart from the customary lines plan, which are necessary — a plate line body plan and a shell plating expansion plan. Later the plans showing the plating of the weather decks will be required.

The plate line body plan looks, at first glance, very like the body plan found on the lines drawing, but whereas this latter may consist of half sections at displacement or other arbitrary stations, in the plate line body plan the half sections are at the frame positions. Superimposed on this plan are lines depicting the run of the decks and the run of the plate seams, showing whether they are in or out strakes, or in and out strakes. The extent, fore and aft, of each strake is also shown, as are the limits of any stealers. The shell plating expansion plan shows the position and extent of every plate on one side of the hull, indicates the nature of each strake (in or out, or in and out) and the type of riveting in the seams and butts — such as single, double or treble riveted, and so on. (**NB** These notes refer to vessels of riveted construction. Different techniques were adopted where all-welded construction is concerned, but so far as the modelmaker is concerned the all-welded hull virtually has a flush surface. It is only at close quarters that the welds joining the plates are apparent.)

Here it must be emphasised that a shell expansion plan is a diagrammatic plan — it does not give the actual size and true shape of each plate. The following description of how such a plan is prepared will explain this more fully. On a base line which represents the centre line of the ship along the underside of the keel are drawn to scale and the correct distance apart the true profile of the stem and the stern of the vessel. The position of each frame is then marked off along the base line and a

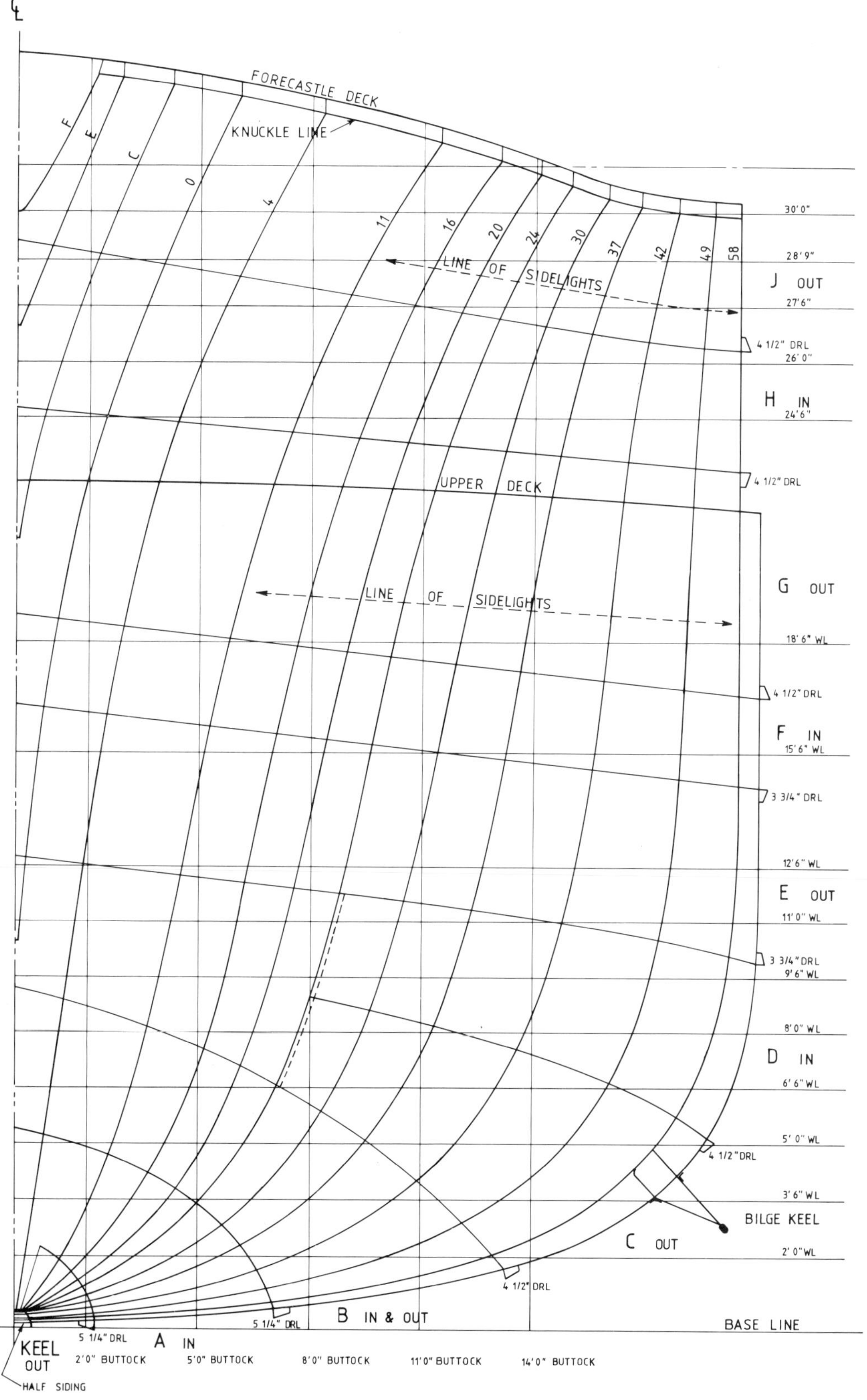

℄
FORECASTLE DECK
KNUCKLE LINE
F
E
C
0
4
11
16
20
24
30
37
42
49
58
30'0"
28'9"
J OUT
27'6"
LINE OF SIDELIGHTS
4 1/2" DRL
26'0"
H IN
24'6"
4 1/2" DRL
UPPER DECK
G OUT
LINE OF SIDELIGHTS
18'6" WL
4 1/2" DRL
F IN
15'6" WL
3 3/4" DRL
12'6" WL
E OUT
11'0" WL
3 3/4" DRL
9'6" WL
8'0" WL
D IN
6'6" WL
5'0" WL
4 1/2" DRL
3'6" WL
BILGE KEEL
C OUT
2'0" WL
4 1/2" DRL
5 1/4" DRL
B IN & OUT
BASE LINE
5 1/4" DRL
A IN
KEEL
OUT
HALF SIDING
2'0" BUTTOCK
5'0" BUTTOCK
8'0" BUTTOCK
11'0" BUTTOCK
14'0" BUTTOCK

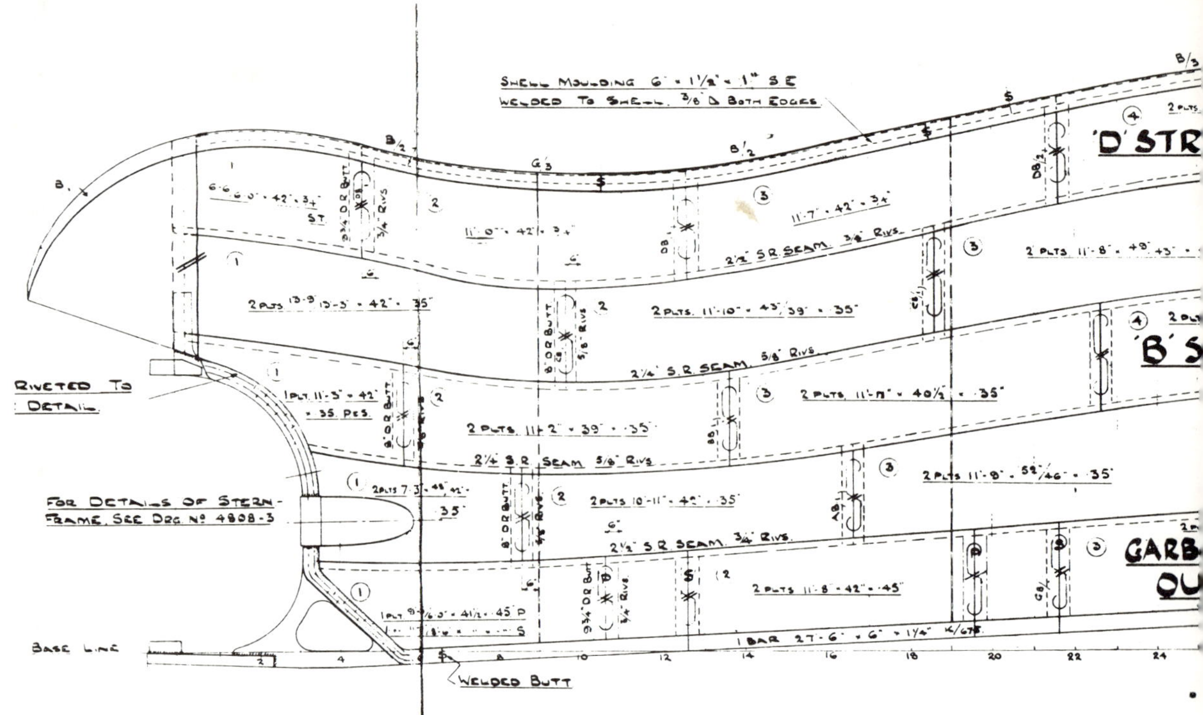

perpendicular line erected at each of these points. The girth of each frame from the centre line of the keel to the edge of the upper or weather deck is measured from the plate line body plan, and this distance marked out to scale, from the keel up, on the perpendicular at the corresponding frame line on the shell expansion drawing. When all these heights, or girths, have been taken and marked in, a fair curve is drawn through these points from stem to stern to represent the line of the deck at side. It is because the hull has been expanded transversely only, and not longitudinally, that the very peculiar shape is imparted to the deck line. By using the same method of measuring or girthing from the plate line body plan the run of each plate seam can be transferred to the shell plan. It is at this point that the draughtsman's knowledge of steel construction, and of the requirements of any statutory rules and regulations, comes in as he works out the various plate lengths and hence the position of the butts. How he does this does not really concern the modelmaker; the end product of his expertise is there on the shell plan ready for use. Plate line body plans and shell expansion plans also contain a lot of other information, such as the position of the internal stringers, longitudinals, flats or decks, etc, the majority of which are of no practical value to the modelmaker, as he will be installing the internal bulkheads, stiffening and so on to suit his particular requirements.

Above: A typical shell expansion (of a small vessel for clarity); riveted construction, with buttstraps at the ends of the plates, lapped seams. This particular drawing shows the ordered size and thickness of each plate.

Right: The author's 1/48 scale model of HMS *Pheasant,* here seen afloat in his test tank.

THE MASTER MOULDS

I build my tinplate ship on wooden masters, and several are required for my method of construction. In the case of *Pheasant* three were needed for the basic building of the hull and those parts of the decks which were integral with the upperworks. The first was for the hull itself, the second to take the major part of the upperdeck and its superstructures, and the third to provide the backing for the building of the waist, quarterdeck, dorsal and the after part of the superstructure.

The hull master must be built exactly to the

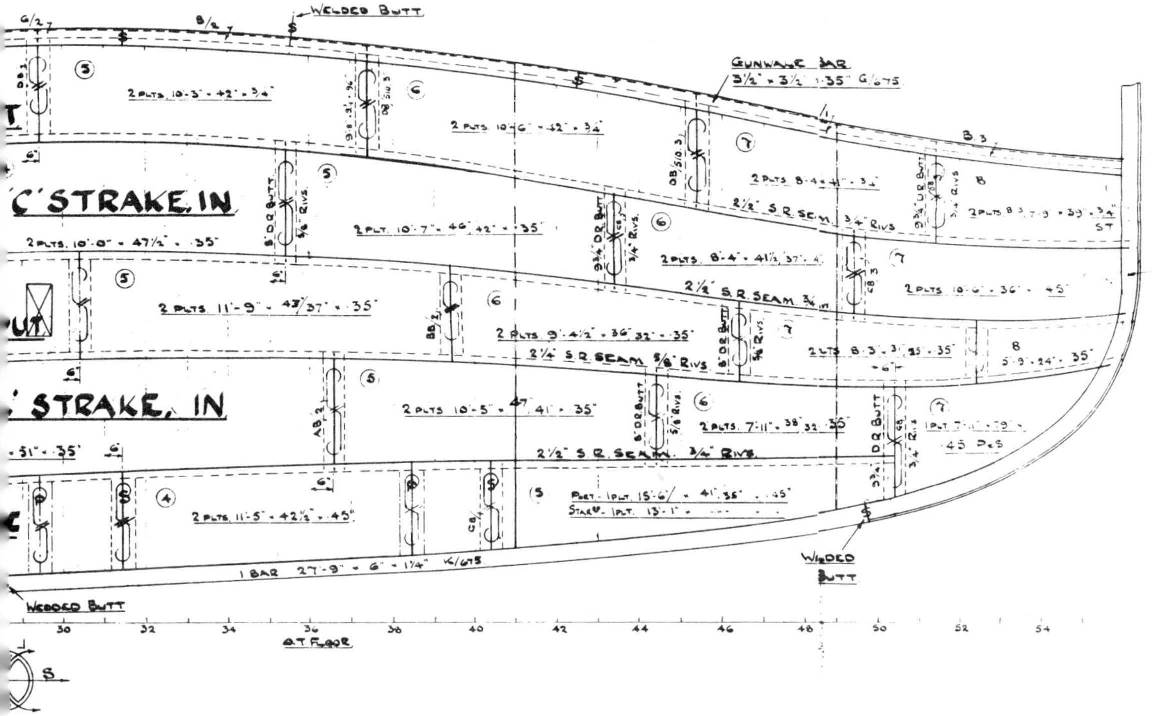

WELDED BUTT
GUNWALE BAR
'C' STRAKE. IN
' STRAKE. IN
2½" S.R. SEAM ¾" RIVS.
2¼" S.R. SEAM ⅝" RIVS.
1 BAR 27'-9" × 6" × 1¼" K/675
WELDED BUTT
30
32
34
36
38
40
42
44
46
48
50
52
54
A.T. FLOOR

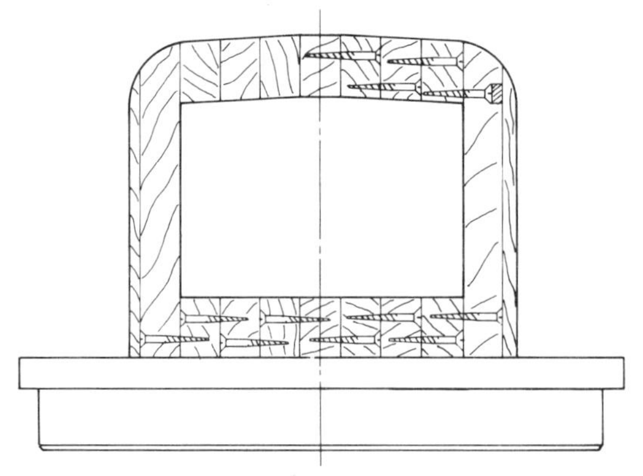

A SECTION OF THE HULL MASTER

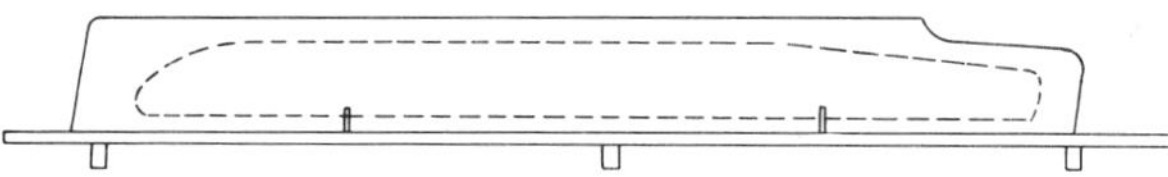

HOLLOWING OUT THE HULL MASTER

TEMPORARY PROTECTION FOR THE STEM

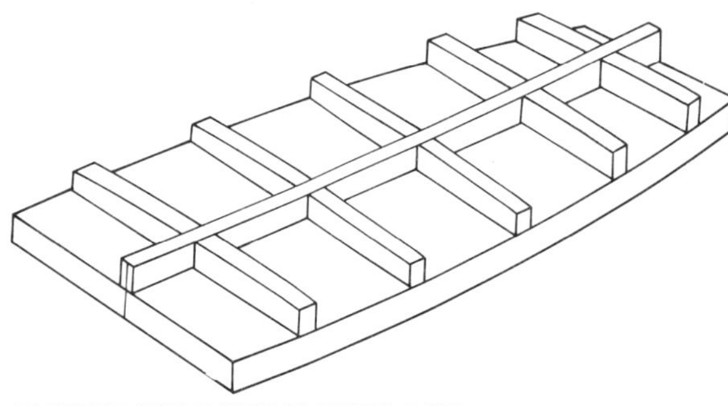

MASTER FOR DECK PLATING AND SUPERSTRUCTURE UNIT

drawings, with the extra or overdepth required for a true datum above or below, depending upon how you look at it, the actual sheerline of the decks. An allowance must be made for the thickness of the plating which will be used. It can be built of any softwood, the bread-and-butter method being the best. With a hull of the type of *Pheasant's* since the stem rakes inwards the requirement of having to dismantle the master to lift off the finished plating can be disregarded, though with many hulls this is imperative. Because of this, the planks can be in either the horizontal or vertical plane, and I strongly recommend the latter. It is far easier to plane the edges of ten one inch planks really true, and with the aid of a flat base to lay them up to match exactly before shaping starts. Once the master has been assembled, take it to pieces again and remove as much of the centre part as the final shape will allow; this is not essential, but it will reduce considerably the weight of a large block. Then reassemble the block and carve to shape, using all the recognised dodges, templates, etc. The quality of the finished hull will depend on the excellence of the work carried out on this master. There is only one thing to watch while shaping the master block; the stern is quite robust, and should not suffer any damage, but at the stem things are very different, and some form of temporary protection, such as a piece of heavy quality foam sponge, should be tacked in place.

When all is to your satisfaction, any imperfections such as gaps between planks, knots, and so on, can be made good with a suitable filler and sanded fair. Follow this with one coat of thin white hard matt undercoat paint, and when dry rub absolutely smooth with flour paper; the master is then ready for marking out.

Transfer on to the master all station lines, water lines, and the deck sheer line from the drawings. These are best done with a sharp chisel-pointed HB pencil, so that they can be erased and altered if needed. A strip of thin acrylic sheet about a half to one inch wide makes an excellent flexible batten for this job.

The other two masters which I needed were made next. These were replicas of the decks in question, and provided the outline of the scuppers, thus giving the plan shape of the respective decks which then fitted the hull accurately when complete; they had the required camber and the correct sheer. The accuracy of the sheer is very important since upon these masters the whole of the ship's upperworks will be built.

LAYOUT OF PLATING

This is best done by direct application of guide lines on the master, using a pencil of a different colour to

METHOD OF MARKING OUT ON A HALF MODEL

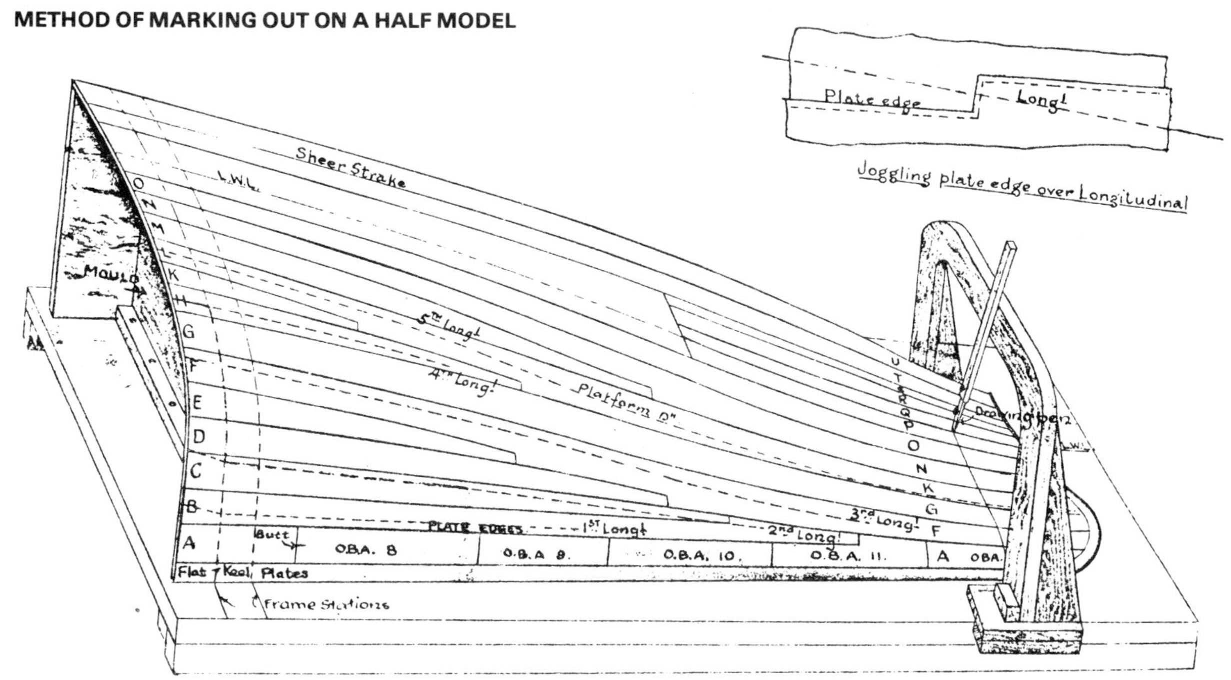

that used for other markings. Start from the key plates from which the whole system (so far as the model is concerned) springs — the stem piece, the stern plate, and the plates carrying the stern tubes. These and some of the other early ones are the most difficult you will have to make.

In marking out the plating remember that it is built into the hull from aft forward, so that all joints lap away from the forward movement of the ship through the water. Usually one line of plates, or strakes of plating as they are customarily called, will be an 'inside run' and those on either side will probably be an'outside run', thus producing the in and out system. The run on the sheer or deckline is an outside run. The vertical divisions, or joints at the ends of the plates are lapped, and follow the same principles roughly as brickwork, that is to say the ends of the plates in any one run must not coincide with the run above or below. Both the longitudinal and vertical joints between plates must start and finish clear of all major openings into the hull, such as ports and escape hatches.

Once the masters have been completed preparations can be made for building the hull. Before all else provision must be made for the stern tube assemblies and the rudder post. Important points to remember are the longitudinal run of the stern tubes in relation to the centre line of the hull, the angle or rake of the propeller shaft, and clearance between the tips of the propeller blades and the hull plating. Start by making the stern tubes. I recommend that the gland is placed on the outboard end, where it will be easier to adjust and maintain. On a 1/48 scale model the propeller shafts will be about 5/32 in or 4mm diameter, and they should be made from ground rustless steel, or silver steel. The construction of the tubes themselves is quite straightforward, and the details are all given in the sketch.

So to the propellers. It is not out of the question to build these yourself, particularly if you have some knowledge of the characteristics of warship propellers; you will probably produce a more authentic example than those available commercially. However, if you are buying them fully finished, be sure that they are bored and tapped the correct size for your shafts. Should the matter of the propellers look like holding up the work, the answer is to make a simple pair of blanks of the right diameter, so that you can get all the stern gear lined up correctly.

I do not recommend making the 'A' brackets at this stage, but the rudder post must be decided upon, although it will not be fitted till later. There is no need for the whole rudder at this stage but the post, or stock, and its bearing tube, must be prepared, though not finished off. This is important as there is a rather tricky plate through which it passes into the hull. At 1/48 scale the stock will be not less than 3/16in or 5mm diameter, and this will determine the size of the brass or copper tube carrying the bearing bushes at either end. Plain bushes rather than a gland will

Left: The after end of *Pheasant* showing the rudder, 'A' bracket, propeller shaft and bossing. The rudder has been enlarged in this instance as it is a working model.

suffice here since the top of the tube will be well above the waterline.

With all the bits and pieces ready the hull master must be prepared to accept them in exactly the right position. First the tube carrying the rudder stock. Mark the position of the centre of the tube on the centre line and drill a hole at least ½in deep, and without burring the end drive into the hole a length of 3/16in diameter rod, leaving just sufficient for the bottom bearing of the rudder tube to be put on upside down. Thus when you come to assemble the pierced plate, this proceedure will ensure that the rudder tube protrudes through the bottom of the hull in the correct place when you come to solder it in position.

Now for the stern tubes. Ascertain the point of entry into the hull plating; for example, on my model this was 6½in (165mm) from the point of major diameter of the propeller. So I prepared a piece of straight rod 5/32in (4mm), threaded one end, screwed it home into the blank (or the actual propeller) and cut off at this dimension. I then unscrewed it and formed a true point on the opposite end, returned it and checked the measurement.

In exactly the same way as for the rudder post tube, the position for each stern tube must be defined clearly, so that when the necessary plates are prepared each stern tube can be fixed so as to remain in its correct position. With the position of the major diameter of the propeller fixed in relation to the rudder post, place this trial assembly in such a position relative to the outside surface of the hull master so as to satisfy all the requirements outlined previously. The point on the temporary shaft will then indicate the exact point of entry through the plating. I find the best way of setting up such a trial assembly is with the aid of a good lump of plasticine. When the alignment and clearance requirements are correct the point should be in light contact with the surface of the master. Mark the spot directly under the point. Draw a line fore and aft through this point to represent the centre line of the stern tube, and draw a second line through the point at right angles to the master centre line as far as the load waterline. Mark up the opposite side of the hull master identically.

The next step is to cut channels or grooves into the hull master to accept the stern tubes with fair clearance. If you have hollowed out the master then drill straight down the grooves into the hull interior; this will provide clearance for the whole propeller shaft later on. The object of all this is so that later when finishing and fitting the plates carrying the stern tubes they will be in the correct position, and the tubes themselves will enter the hull at the correct angle in all planes.

The point has now been reached where a start can be made on the actual plating, but before doing so some hints and tips on working and soldering tinplate will not come amiss.

WORKING TINPLATE

So far I have made no mention as to the source of the material. Of course you can buy tinplate in flat sheets, but the handiest and most readily available source of supply is the common tin can — soup tin, fruit tin, etc. Just remove the ends and their rim, open out and flatten on a hardwood block. So far as plate sizes go, if you cannot adhere strickly to the original shell plating plan, then plates should be about 8in (200mm) long on average — long lengths are unwieldy and awkward to handle — and of a width to suit the particular hull shape, probably 1-1½in (25-38mm).

To obtain good results with tinplate always treat it kindly — gently but firmly; only in exceptional circumstances hit it, and then never with a conventional steel hammer. Homemade tapping heads can be turned up from Nylon 6 or Nylon 66 rod to your own desired shape. Before any plate or other part for the model can be shaped it has to be cut to

PROPELLER SHAFT BEARINGS

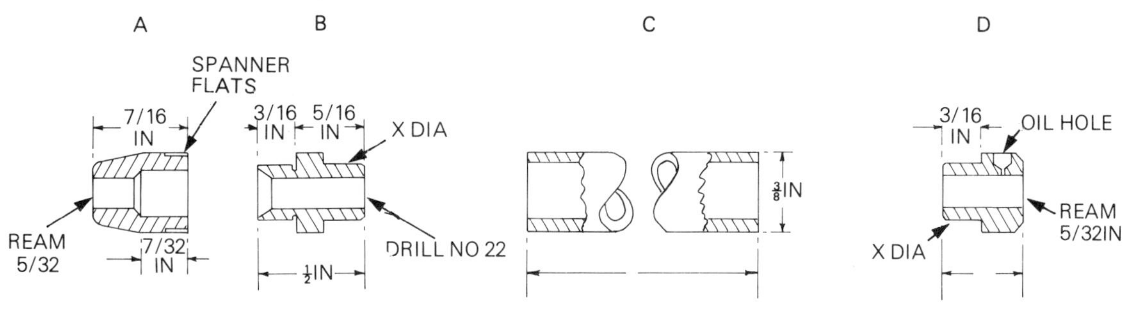

THREAD ¼IN x 40tpi

DIA AT X: FIRM FIT FOR SOFT SOLDERING INTO TUBE C

MATERIALS:
A BEARING CAP, BRONZE
B AND D GLAND AND INNER BEARING, GUNMETAL OR HARD BRASS
C STERN TUBE, ⅜IN O. D. COPPER TUBE

ASSEMBLY:
SWEAT B AND D INTO TUBE C, AFTER LOCATING STERN TUBE IN PREPARED HULL PLATE, WITH SHAFT TEMPORARILY IN POSITION FOR ALIGNMENT

PROPELLER SHAFT FITTING

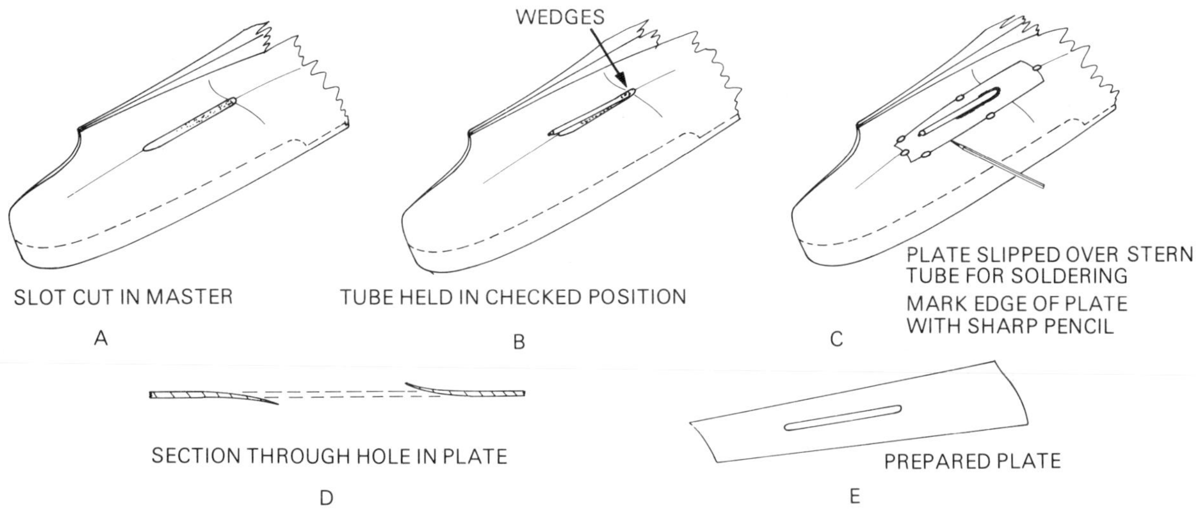

size. If you use snips or shears there will always be a tendency to curl up, often with a kinked or frilly edge. To avoid this, always rough cut every piece about 1/16in (2mm) oversize in all directions, and only then take it down to working size. This may not be the finished size but even so should always be as close as you can get to it, leaving only the minimum to be cut or filed off when finishing.

Final finishing and trueing up of tinplate parts follows exactly the same system throughout building the whole model, it is not confined to the hull plates alone and therefore what you do now for the hull plates will, in principle, serve throughout all your work. There are only two file types suitable for tinplate; for rough work use *smooth grade* files and for finishing work *dead smooth,* never coarser than a No 4 cut. The smooth file is only suitable for cutting along the run of the work piece while it is well supported for its whole length. By clamping a suitable backing to the workpiece against an adjustable work table the part to be trimmed can be so held with the marked finish line uppermost; the file can then be worked against the edge with the cutting face held vertically. Final finishing off should be done by 'draw-filing' with the work piece turned vertically, and again well supported for its full length.

The method which I have evolved for making up the plates is simple in practice. The shape of a plate is achieved by stroking or rubbing it — not by hitting it! This is done by using a series of home made tools and

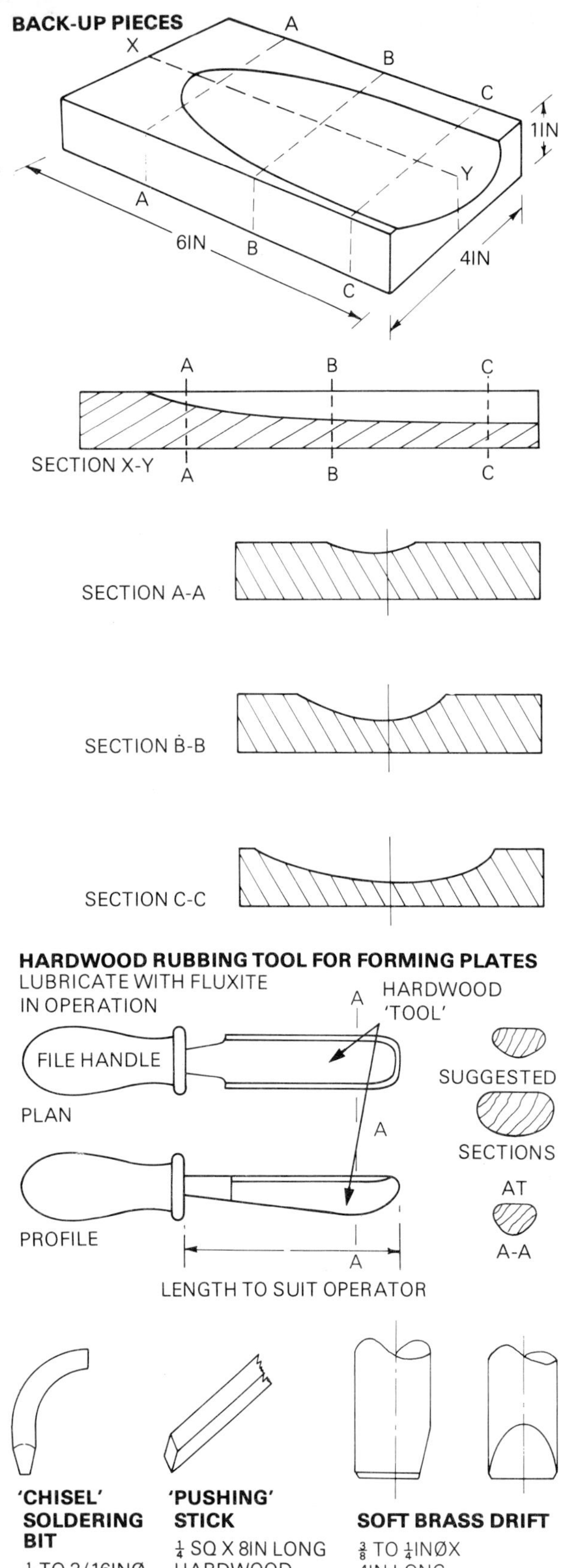

a variety of backing-up pieces the most useful of which are a piece of lead sheet about 6in (150mm) square by 1/8-3/16in (3-5mm) thick — the thicker the better — and a piece of hard rubber sheet, rather larger and thicker, and in any event hefty enough not to 'walk about' on the bench while you are working. Lastly a series of back-up pieces made out of good quality close grained hardwood such as walnut (from old furniture), obeche, or Honduras mahogany. These should be at least 1in (25mm) thick and 4-6in (100-150mm) wide; length will depend on their particular shape. The number required will depend on the individual, but it is worth while trying to work a varied number of curves into the declivity so that one or two pieces will provide most of what you want. They should be well finished with fine sandpaper, so that there are no defects on the surface which will repeat on the plates. These tools are used with a variety of hardwood pushers and rubbers. To form a plate, lay the prepared flat material as closely as possible to its correct position on the master, and this will show you exactly what must be done to make it fit snugly in place. During the shaping up process keep checking the plate on the master — it is not so easy to take out curves once you have set them into the plate.

SOLDERING TINPLATE

Here are a few simple tips which I have found useful when undertaking soldering work with tinplate components. First of all there is the old saw about cleanliness. I cannot emphasise enough how important this is, and in this connection there are one or two peculiarities to watch. I have mentioned elsewhere the use of Fluxite as a lubricant; this is important as any other contaminant or lubricant must be rigorously removed from all components if sound soldered joints are to result. If any component or part of the structure should become contaminated it can only be cleaned satisfactorily with organic solvents such as Trichlorethylene. Generally caustic solvents, readily available commercially as liquids, are worse than useless as they have two unpleasant effects. They seldom remove the contamination completely, only thinning it out to a fine film which you are unable to detect and only discover because the soldered joint is superficial, and does not run through completely. Then, being of a chemical nature, unless the whole assembly is very thoroughly cleaned of their presence afterwards, rust and corrosion will result remarkably quickly.

The next ones to watch are the soluble oils or suds used as a machine lubricant. Parts from the lathe may become contaminated quite easily, and this will pass on when contact is made with tinplate or other adjacent parts. Most of these substances are water soluble and cannot be removed by the use of organic solvents; the only defence here is thorough washing in hot water with a good detergent powder or liquid. After all the above operations, precautions must be taken to protect the work against corrosion during construction time, before final sealing and painting is possible. Later on you will find that quite large sub-assemblies will be completed and fitted to the model before it is possible to protect or paint any part of them. Here again Fluxite comes into its own. It should be applied immediately after degreasing or washing operations in readiness for soldering. As soon as a particular soldering job has been completed only clean off the obvious excess of flux before cleaning up and finishing the joint tidily. Then give the joint a wipe with a soft rag well steeped in Fluxite to spread a protective film over it.

When building tinplate models under no circumstances should acid fluxes be used, and similary I do not recommend the use of resin-cored or other supposedly corrosion-free cored solders. The former will forever give trouble with corrosion in the joints, and the latter is extremely difficult to clean off effectively.

The actual process of soft soldering tinplate is relatively easy, and the most important requirement for model shipbuilding is a soldering iron with a fine-pointed chisel-shaped bit. The ideal is an electric one with an on/off switch in the handle, and it should be of a type which provides considerably more heat output than the type designed for electrical or radio work.

When working with tinplate use only wood or some other inert material to back up the work; the same applies for any jigs or fixtures. Never use metal, for this will only conduct heat away from the job. Suitable hardwood, well steeped in Fluxite used in conjunction with small wooden holding sticks makes for simple and quick work. The sticks may tend to burn, but boxwood, again well steeped in Fluxite, will last almost indefinitely. Finally keep a stout metal plate handy to the work area, brass or copper is of course best, and use this for the quick cooling of components and other small assemblies after soldering. Quenching in water is not recommended for tinplate; however there are times when this may be your only salvation.

To make a first class job of soldering the plates to each other on the master, the procedure which I have adopted is as follows. First form the plate for the area to be covered, check it thoroughly, and trim and finish it on all sides. The question of the amount of overlap will depend on the scale to which you are working, the size of the model, and to a certain extent on the thickness of the plate being used. For a model at 1/48 scale it should be not less than 1/8in (3mm). In certain cases, for stealers and other difficult plates or those taking particular loads — for example round the stem and rudder post and in way of the 'A' brackets — a slightly different technique is required.

To begin with, the small heavily shaped plates — that is those which will lose their edges under adjoining plates — should be made to pass under their neighbours by more than the standard 1/8in (3mm). Where the final seam between plates will rest in a position of extreme curvature allow something like ½in (12mm); if necessary the plate edges can be notched or nicked to within 1/8in (3mm) of the seam line to improve the snugness of the fit and to facilitate the shaping. To make this system effective such plates will need to be soldered again on the inside when the hull is removed from the master. Secondly, some stealer plates, either at their ends or along their length, may need to exceed the overlap in order to obtain a fair run to the plating; these too should be double soldered.

The standard 1/8in lap should not require to be double soldered; if your technique is as it should be then the solder will run right through the joint in one operation. This is how it is achieved. Smear the edges which mate with adjoining plates well with Fluxite, place the plate in its correct position and hold it there with drawing pins. If you think it necessary you can tack it to its neighbours with spots of solder, but these should be kept to a minimum. Using a fairly stout pushing or holding stick hold the plates in close contact where you wish to place the solder tack and apply it with a very hot tool within as small an area as possible. Make sure that the plates do not spring, either during this or any other soldering operation. If one does it should be removed and discarded and a new plate made.

To complete the soldering job first finish the joint at the after end of the plate to the one behind, working across the master with holding stick,

SOLDERING PLATES

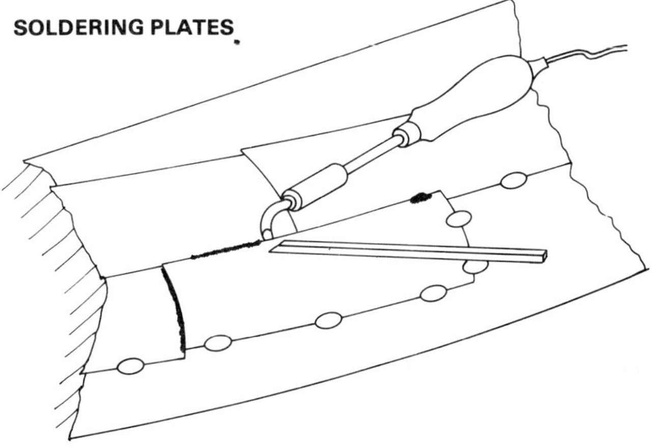

DIAGRAMMATIC PREPARATION OF A PLATING JOINT

A: AS SOLDERED, SHOWING HOW EXCESS SHOULD BUILD UP (IF JOINT IS REALLY SOUND FILLET WILL FORM BELOW)

B: AFTER APPLICATION OF GRAVER, NEAT SMOOTH AND VERY SMALL FILLET FORMED AT JOINT. UNDER PLATE FINISHED SMOOTH

C: APPLICATION OF SHARP CHISEL WILL CLEAN EXCESS FROM OVER PLATE. LEAVE USEFUL FILLET INSIDE HULL

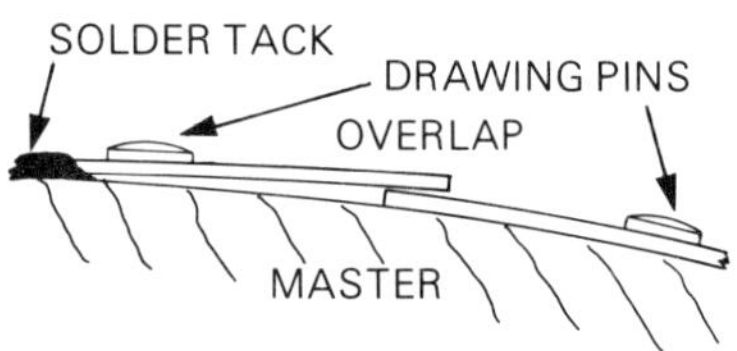

D: NEW PLATE SECURED IN POSITION

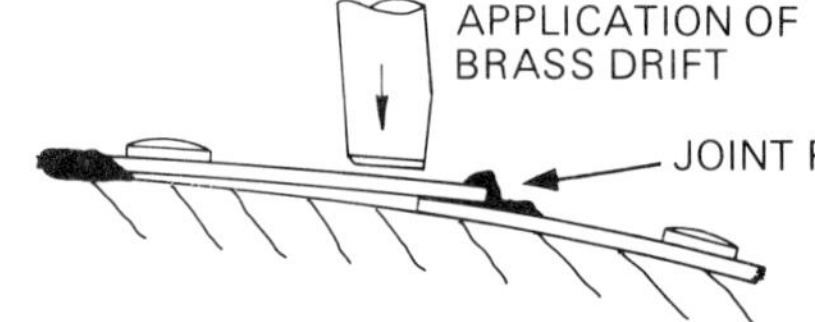

E: PLATES SOLDERED ON VERTICAL JOINT WITH POSITION OF DRIFT TO CLINCH HOME OVER PLATE

F: SECTION OF COMPLETED JOINT CLEANED UP

DIAGRAMMATIC COMPLETION OF PLATING OVERLAP ON ALL VERTICAL HULL PLATE JOINTS

OUTER BOTTOM PLATING METHOD OF ARRANGING STEALERS

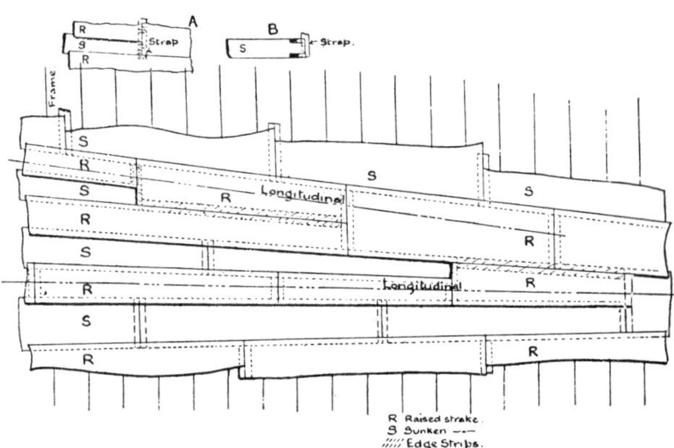

drawing pins and soldering iron — but do not go round the corner at all. Then from a point about $\frac{1}{2}$in (12mm) forward of the corner complete about 1in (25mm) of the longitudinal seam. The plate will now be really firm, so with the help of a soft brass drift close the gap on the overlap of the plate. Having done this solder the rest of the seam. That is all there is to it. You can now work steadily on and complete the whole of the plating — but do not forget to attend to those plates which require to have openings cut in them for such fittings as portholes, escape hatches, which must be done before the plates are soldered into place.

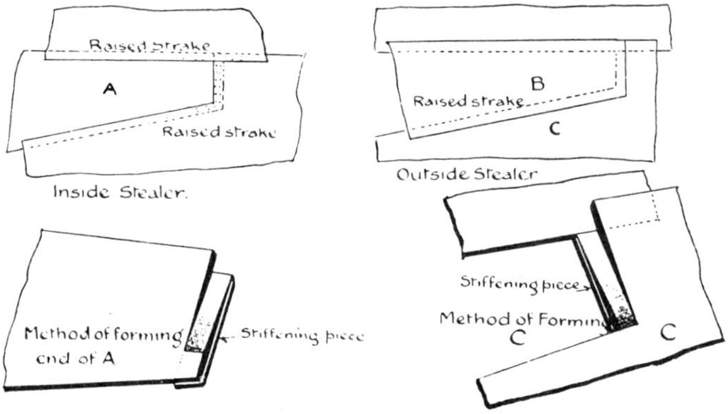

Raised strake
A
Raised strake
Inside Stealer.

Raised strake
B
C
Outside Stealer

Method of forming end of A
Stiffening piece

Stiffening piece
Method of Forming C
C

METHOD OF FORMING STEALERS

CLEANING UP SOLDERED WORK

Later on attention will have to be given to the cleaning up of the seams after soldering — another of those imperative tasks to be performed throughout he construction of the model. Every time a soldered joint is completed it must be cleaned up for excess solder, squareness, neatness and so on. If this is not carried out throughly a very messy model will result. Cleaning up the seams on the hull is the simplest and most straightforward of all these tasks. Almost any well honed and polished hand tool that suits your taste will do this job. I prefer to use a sort of graver and a pair of small flat hardwood chisels with specially prepared oblique cutting edges. Always leave a minute fillet of solder at the turn of the joint, and it is much better to leave a skin of solder on the exposed edge of the plate or component, however small, as an anti-corrosion protection. Tinplate, once cut and prepared will have no 'tin' or protective agent on these cut edges so it is up to you to put something there.

PLATING THE HULL

Start the plating by completing the two plates which hold the stern tubes, then fit the stem and stern plates. Thereafter, working from the stern forward, complete the run down the centre line of the bottom of the ship; this will take in the plate that holds the rudder post, the stern post and the sharp curve at its top. This part of the ship requires careful attention, as at this stage the plating will have little to hold it in position other than the drawing pins which secure each piece as it is added, so be sure all is well and nothing moves as you proceed. Up forward, towards the forefoot position you may find advantage in leaving out some of the smaller highly curved plates and their attendant stealers until later on.

From this point on it is just a case of working away methodically strake by strake until the hull is complete, and ready to be removed from the master. Once free of the master the hull needs careful handling for without internal stiffening it will be quite 'live', and the first job will be to complete any 'double soldering' to those plates and positions inside the hull which require it. Once this has been completed, check the hull closely to make sure that it is not distorted in any way, then proceed to the internal stiffening.

STRENGTHENING THE HULL

It is obvious that before starting on the model you will have decided on the type of power plant to be fitted, and also on any other major internal items such as radio control equipment. The internal strengthening of the hull will therefore have to be arranged in conjunction with and to suit the various components of this equipment. First of all longitudinal members must be fitted along the length of the hull; these must be a good close fit to the inside of the plating. Start with a central girder working from under the position of the engine bed plate, and preferably making this in one piece. Remember it must be of the exact dimension within the hull to support the underside of engine bed plate at the correct height. This member should run the full length of the hull plating along the centre line of the ship's bottom. Next proceed with one or more members either side of the central one, the number depending on the size of the model and the strength required; the spacing should be the same on both port and starboard sides. They should run parallel to and be the same height as the centre girder, and therefore 'run out' as the hull plating curves towards the bow and stern. A series of transverse floors should be fitted

Below: *Pheasant* under construction, showing the run of the bow plating: note the knuckle just below the deck edge. (All photos by the author)

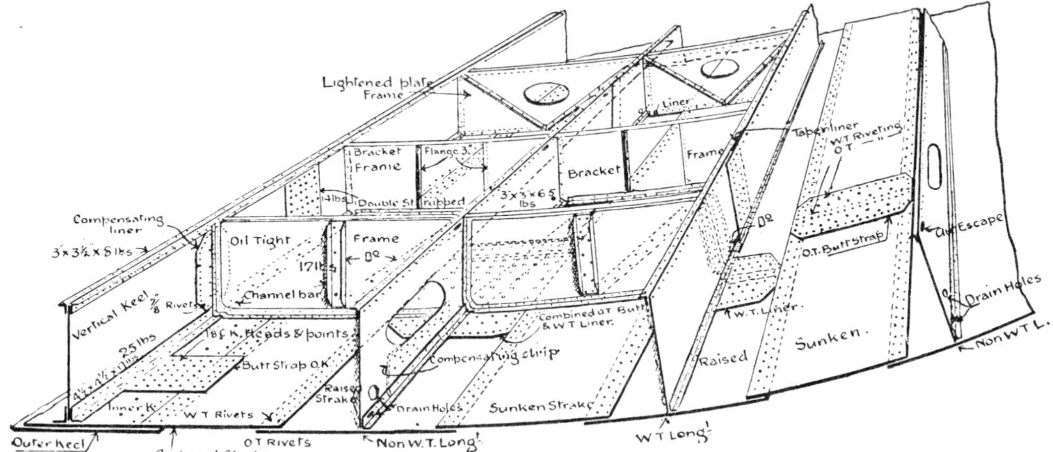

FRAMING WITHIN DOUBLE BOTTOM

intercostally between these longitudinal girders, their height being the same as that of the girders.

The next step is to fit a series of watertight bulkheads. Apart from a fore peak bulkhead fitted a few inches back from the stem (sometimes called a collision bulkhead) the number and position of the others will be dictated largely by the positions of the machinery and other equipment in the model. The shape of the bulkheads can be determined from the body plan, and a card template should be made to ensure that the tinplate when cut will fit close to the shell plating, to which it will have to be soldered. In larger models it will be advisable to fit some form of stiffening to the plate before fitting it in the model; it will, of course, have to be slotted over the longitudinal girders, to which it must be soldered.

If the bulkheads are fairly widely spaced, and you feel that there is a need for more hull stiffening, this can be done by the addition of some side frames at intervals between the bulkheads. Cut one edge of a strip of tinplate to a close fit to the inside of the hull plating — it is advantageous to make a card template first from which to cut the tinplate — and then trim it so that it is about ½in (12mm) wide, or less or more according to the size of the model, and solder in place. Great care must be taken when doing this to avoid any distortion of the hull.

It is more than likely that by now you will have 'run out of hands' and become equally short of fingers when trying to hold several parts together or in position for fitting purposes, long before you are ready to tack them in place with solder. I recommend that you invest in a number of Eclipse (or similar) button magnets. Place the piece concerned in position and hold it in place through the the hull plating by the crafty application of some button magnets on the outside of the plating — instant fingers with no danger of distortion of fragile parts!

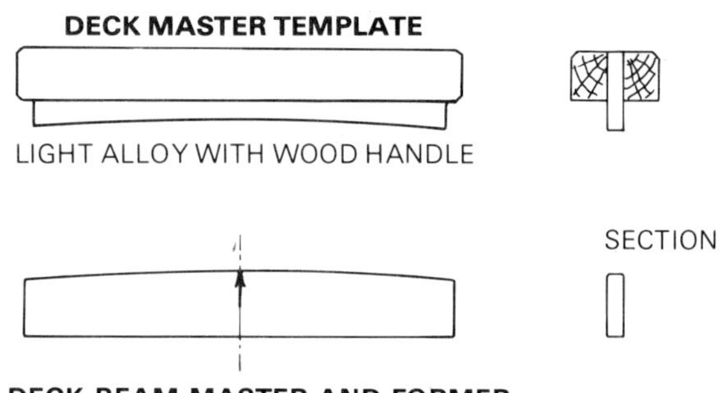

DECK BEAM MASTER AND FORMER
MILD STEEL PLATE (¼IN X 2IN X 12IN)

The deck plating, whether fixed or portable, will have to be supported by deck beams, so a word or two about these beams. First cut the material well oversize for the length of each beam, and mark a centre line on it. Make sure this is matched exactly to the centre mark on the deck beam former to ensure that when the edge has been turned over on the former and you come to cut to the length required, the maximum height of the beam above the gunwales will always be right on the centre line of the ship; remember that the camber is constant throughout. The number and position of the deck beams will require careful thought. There should be enough for strength and rigidity of the hull, and yet you must leave all major openings into the hull clear for access to the machinery and other equipment. Furthermore they must not be in the way of any parts of the superstructure which protrude below the deck. Hence the need to give some thought early on to their positions.

To stiffen the top edge of the hull, and also to provide a sound support for the decks, I fitted a deck shelf all round the inside of the hull. This was simply

Right: Typical of the useful illustrations which can be found in such technical publications as the *Manual of Seamanship.*

"ROYAL SOVEREIGN."—MIDSHIP SECTION.

A. Inner Flat Keel Plate.
B. Outer Flat Keel Plate.
C. Vertical Keel Plates.
D. Bracket Plates.
E. Longitudinals.
F. Outer Bottom Plating.
G. Inner Bottom Plating.
H. Longitudinal Bulkhead.
I. Air Space.
J. Longitudinal Protective Bulkhead.
K. Oiltight Flat.
L. Lightened Plate Frames.
M. Protective Side Bulge.
N. Bilge Keel.
O. Electric Lead and Pipe Passage.
P. 520 lbs. Side Armour.
R. Sloped Protective Deck.
S. Middle Deck.
T. Main Deck.
U. 240 lbs. Side Armour.
V. Zed Bar Frames.
W. Upper Deck.
X. Forecastle Deck.
Y. Deck Beams.
Z. Shelter Deck.

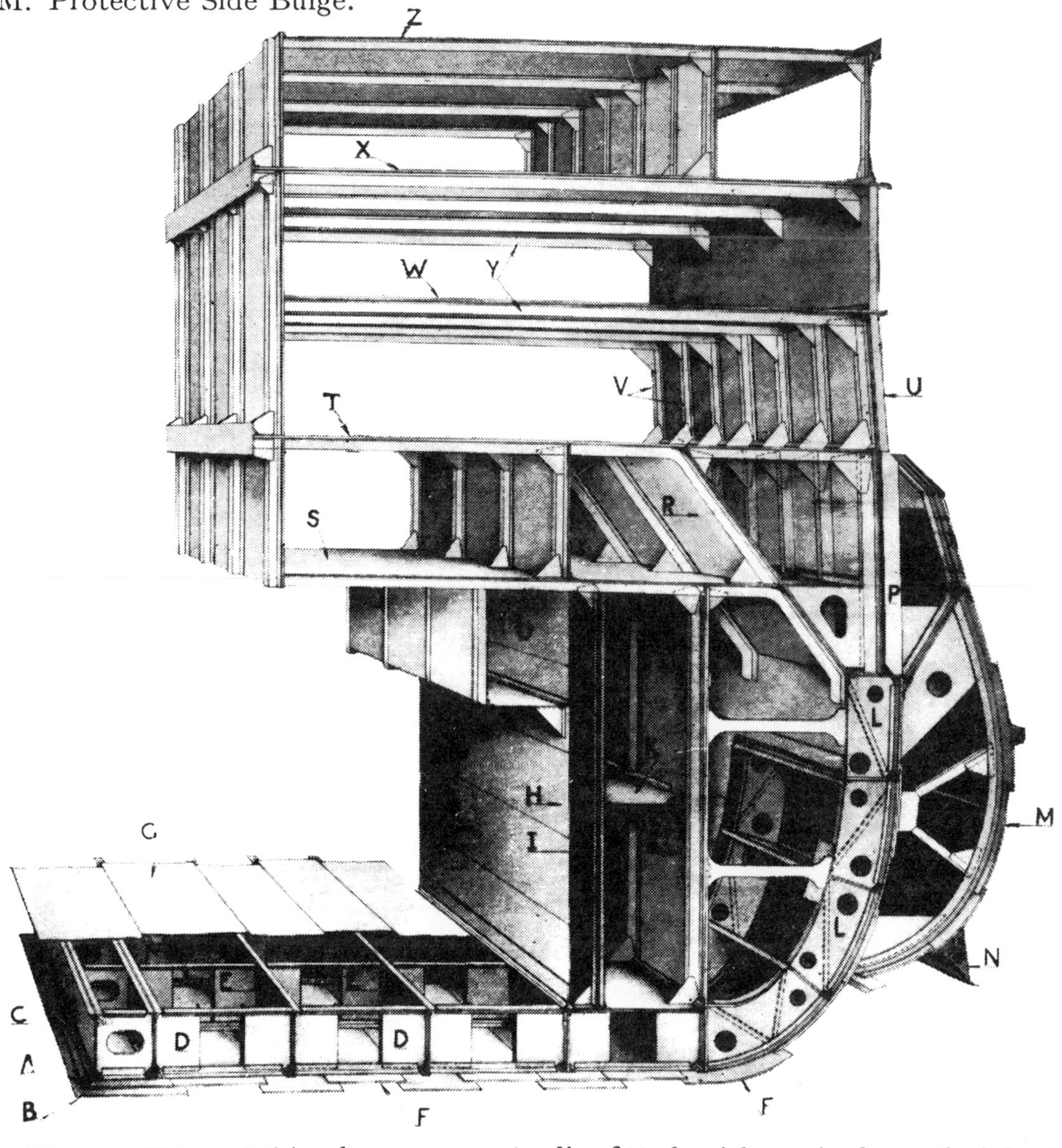

NOTE.—Ships of this class were actually fitted with a single vertical keel, instead of the two keels shown above. Two keels were adopted in later ships.

a 1in (25mm) wide strip of tinplate soldered horizontally to the inside of the hull about 1/8in (3mm) below the top of the plate. Eventually the decks, and thereby all the superstructure, are held to the hull by this deck shelf, so it must be well made, be a sound close fit to the shell, and be really well soldered. Once it is fitted, the deck beams can be added and soldered to the underside of the shelf, the horizontal flange of the beam being cut away in way of the shelf to provide a flush surface for the deck plating. The beams on *Pheasant* were about 5/8in deep, with a 3/16in flange turned over along the top (16mm x 5mm).

SEALING AND PROOFING THE HULL

Once the plating of the hull has been completed, all the permanent hull fixtures and fittings must be prepared and fitted into place so that the whole of the inside of the hull can be thoroughly proofed against corrosion. The outside can be left till later, but the internal surfaces will soon become impossible to reach, so the sooner it is done the better.

This proofing can be done in two stages. The first is the complete sealing and proofing of all that part of the hull which will be covered when the concrete ballast is added. It is easier to do this before the deck beams are added. The second stage, that of dealing with the rest of the inside of the hull, can only be carried out once all the fittings on the outside of the hull have been added, since many of these will involve some soldering on the shell plating. To return to stage one. The whole of the inside of the hull plating, including any wells which you may be intending to leave clear, must be treated up to a level at least ½in (12mm) above the proposed maximum height of the concrete. The method and materials for proofing are largely a matter of personal preference, but should be preceded by a general clean up of the area with a non-active degreasant to remove the major areas of flux from the surface and the corners. I have found that a cotton wool pad soaked in perchlorethylene, frequently washed clean, and used on the end of a stick will clean all but the most inaccessible corners. If you have used Fluxite this material will not prove harmful in tight corners, but being of a greasy nature will not assist in the adhesion of paint applied by brush or spray.

If you have paid attention to detail and tinned over any cutouts in the stiffening members — waterways for instance — then they should not provide any extra hazard. If you have not, or are unsure of any such exposed edges, then make sure that they are well proofed. So far as paint is concerned my preference is for two coats of good quality bare metal primer, applied by brush and allowed to harden thoroughly before a final application of a lead based undercoat. Colour is of no great importance here, but just as a matter of interest I used an aluminium coloured primer followed by a red oxide undercoat. The same procedure will be followed in stage two, once all the external hull fittings, as well as any internal ones, have been secured in place.

BALLASTING

Early on in the construction of the hull it is wise to pause and consider some of the much later requirements, so that you have a clear mental picture of what lies ahead. Eventually the model will require ballasting, which normally means carrying deadweight. My way round this is to put this deadweight to good use, and the method I have adopted with this form of construction does just that. The *last* operation in finishing off the hull will be to add a solid layer of concrete throughout her full length on the bottom plating. This really does work! The sand/cement mixture can be dosed liberally with small pieces of lead, which are easy to prepare, or other suitable bits of metal.

The mixture is made up and tamped into all the apertures and spaces between the lattice beam structure on the hull floor; where any interference with working parts is likely to occur, these should be kept clear. The concrete layer is built up carefully into all the inaccessible corners, and in particular should tuck in well into the forefoot, stem and sternpost areas. Once this process has gone off you will be astonished at the strength and rigidity for weight of the finished structure. But you must never lose sight of the fact that once there, though it will neither corrode, rot nor come to harm from water, salt or fresh, it is permanent. You cannot readily remove all or part of it, and it will be extremely difficult to fix anything to it, unless provision has been made in advance for so doing. Now you will appreciate the wisdom of pausing to consider what lies ahead.

The major part of Colonel Batchelor's notes ended at this point. With the construction of the basic hull completed, and with all the external fittings in place, he was intending to move on to describe the construction of the three major superstructure units, each on its specially prepared master. However, with no notes available for this next step, it is appropriate to finish this chapter at this point. Having mastered the techniques of working tinplate, no great difficulty should be experienced in building up a vessel's superstructure in this material.

Superstructure 4

by GIANCARLO BARBIERI

A close-up of the author's model of the modern Italian destroyer *Impavido*. Note the relatively 'clean' superstructure and the precison of the detail work. (Photo: Giancarlo Barbieri)

For the purpose of this chapter I am considering all those erections above the upper and forecastle decks of warships as 'superstructures', and I will cover also some of the other major items such as masts and funnels. If you study the plans or photographs of vessels built during the last ninety or so years you will notice that these erections vary from the simple hut-like conning positions of the early destroyers to the

complex structures of the battleships and cruisers of the 1930s and 1940s. Funnels range from those having a plain cylindrical form to the huge, trunked and often angled shapes of the above decades. It is the same story with masts — from pole masts and lightly constructed tripods carrying the odd platform, to heavy tripods carrying a number of houses and platforms, reaching the ultimate in complexity in the 'pagodas' fitted to Japanese warships just prior to WWII and to the *Fuso* and *Yamashiro* in particular. Today masts as such tend to be more akin to boxed-in towers, a development brought about in some respect by the need to provide a more substantial support for the multiplicity of aerials and other associated equipment required by modern communication, detection and weapon control systems.

At first glance these superstructures on a large vessel can appear to the modelmaker as a formidable and daunting problem. This need not be so. The key lies in having a good set of plans from which to work. The subject of plans has been covered in some depth in the first chapter but I would add here that, as far as superstructures are concerned, it is essential that the plans show each deck separately, and this goes for the platforms on the masts as well. There are drawings in which the only plan view of the decks is a single aerial or 'bird's eye' one of the vessel as a whole. In the case of older vessels such plans are of little use as they do not indicate the outlines of the individual decks and houses below the uppermost ones. Official plans are of the former category, as are some of the more reputable ones prepared specially for modelmakers. The layout of each deck or platform, as well as showing the position of all fittings, gives also the shape of the deckhouse(s) on it, and will include in many instances an indication of the doors, sidelights and other fittings on the sides of the house. The height of the house will be determined from the profile drawing and/or from any sections which may be on the plan.

As well as the principal decks and platforms there are often smaller platforms 'hung-on' to, or forming part of, a structure but at different levels to those just mentioned. Again there are other additions to houses, such as the blast screens or shields found on some destroyers.

Earlier I made some critical comments about 'bird's eye' view deck plans in relation to vessels having a multiplicity of decks, but in fairness I must add that this is not so relevant when considering many of the modern warships. With atomic fall-out in mind the present day aim of designers is to eliminate as many extraneous surfaces as possible. Thus we find deckhouses with rounded corners and top edges, and only a minimal presence of overhanging decks or platforms — all designed to reduce fall-out lodgement and to facilitate subsequent decontamination processes. So the single aerial view plan could provide the necessary information for many vessels of this type.

SUPERSTRUCTURE CONSTRUCTION

Construction breaks down into a series of basic steps. First there is the deckhouse itself, then there is the deck which, depending on the way you look at it, is either the one it sits on or the one covering its top. These are followed, as the case may be, by other houses and decks, or by minor platforms attached thereto, or such other items as blast screens. Whilst all this is going on you must bear in mind the fittings

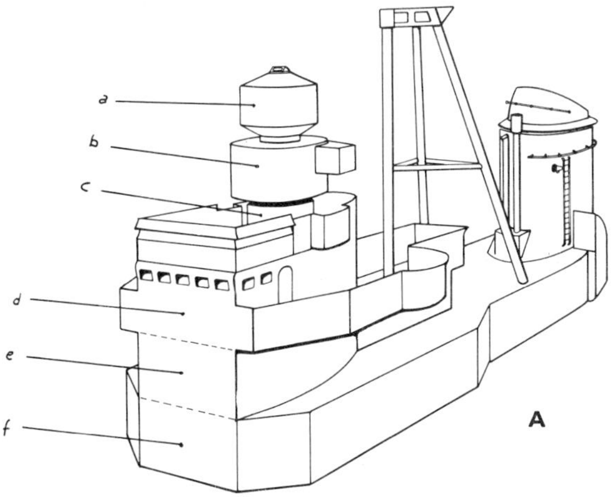

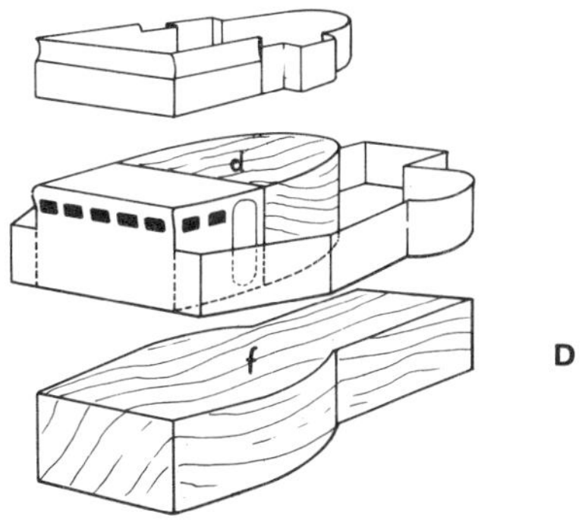

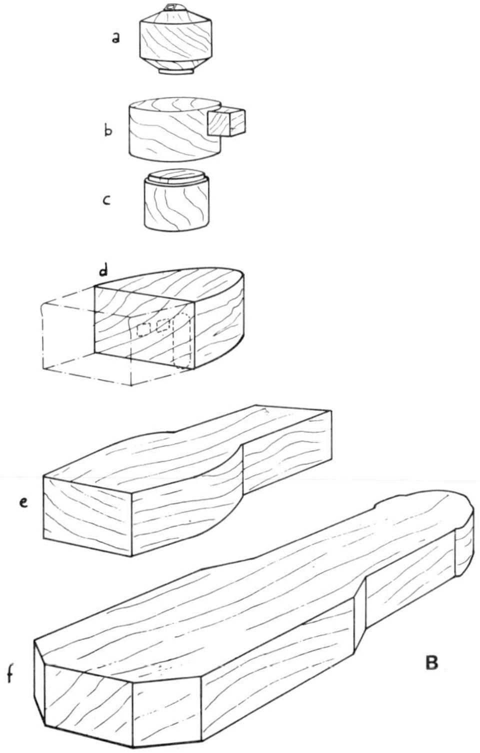

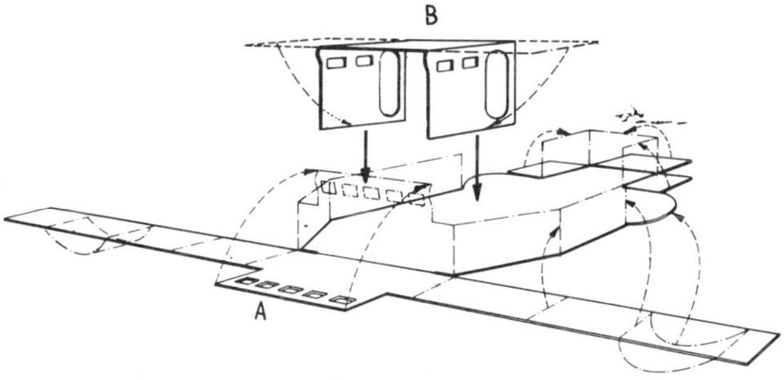

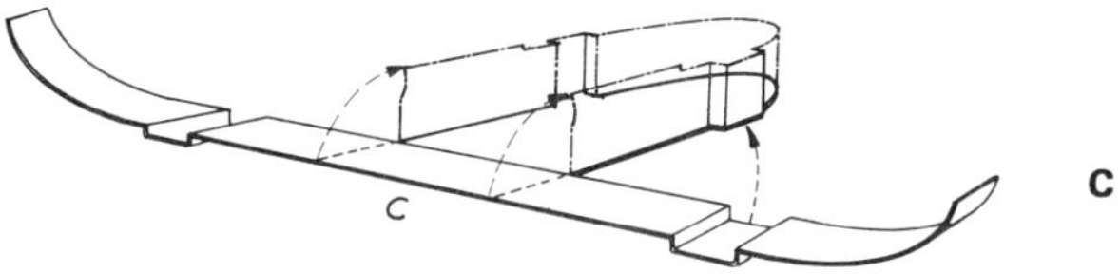

SUPERSTRUCTURE CONSTRUCTION

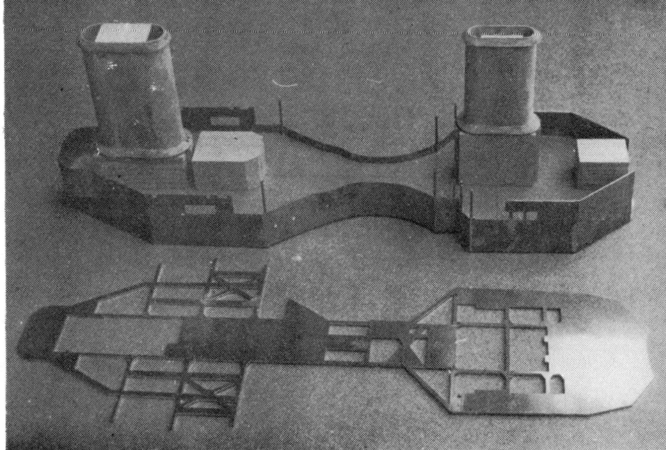

Opposite: An overall view of the *Impavido*. Built to 1/100 scale, it was the outright winner of the static section of the European 'Naviga' Championships in Vienna in 1974 and Como in 1976. (Photo: Giancarlo Barbieri)

Right: Superstructure for Brian King's 1/110 scale model of HMS *Dreadnought* in the course of completion. Although the principal material is metal this approach to superstructure could have used plasticard just as easily. (Photo: Brian King)

Overleaf: The author's drawings of *Pompeo Magno* show the value of good plans in superstructure construction.

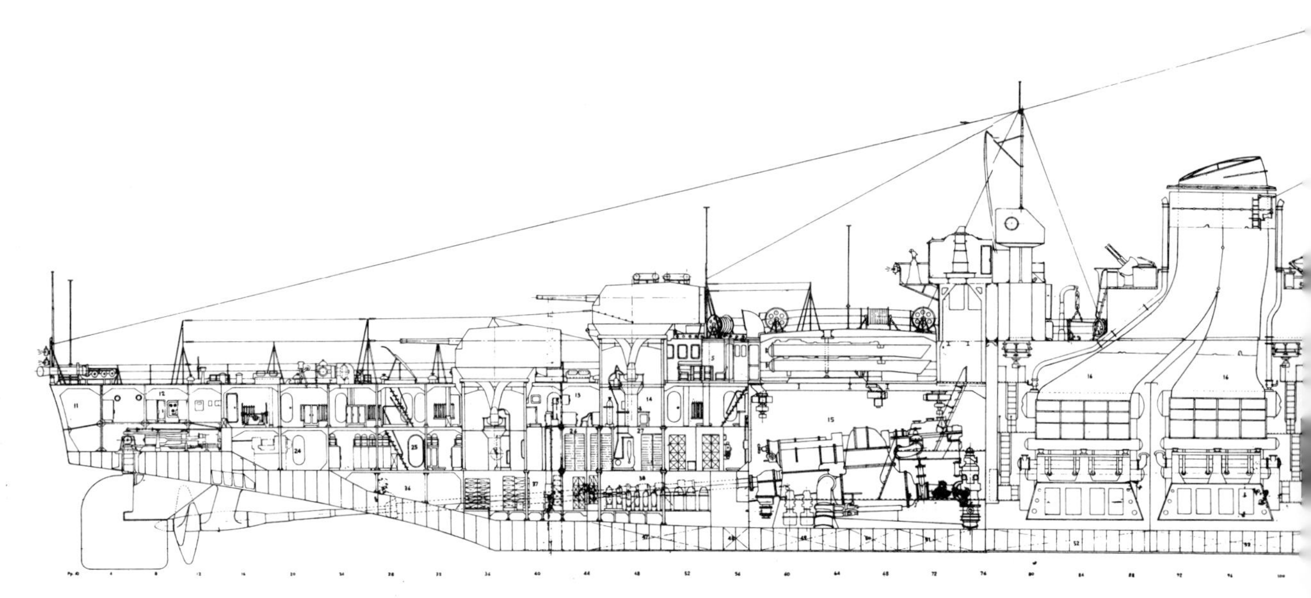

PLANCIA DI COMANDO

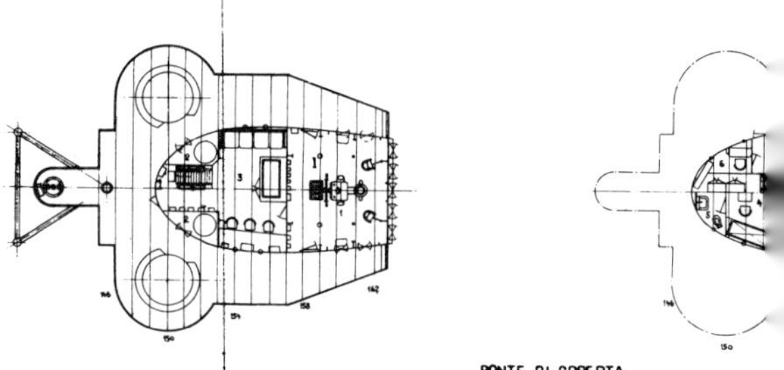

PONTE DI COPERTA

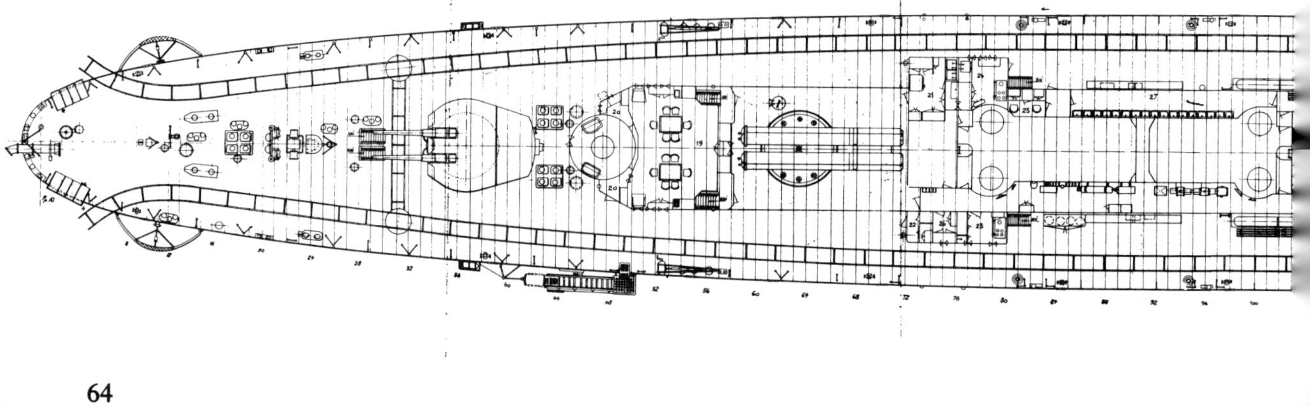

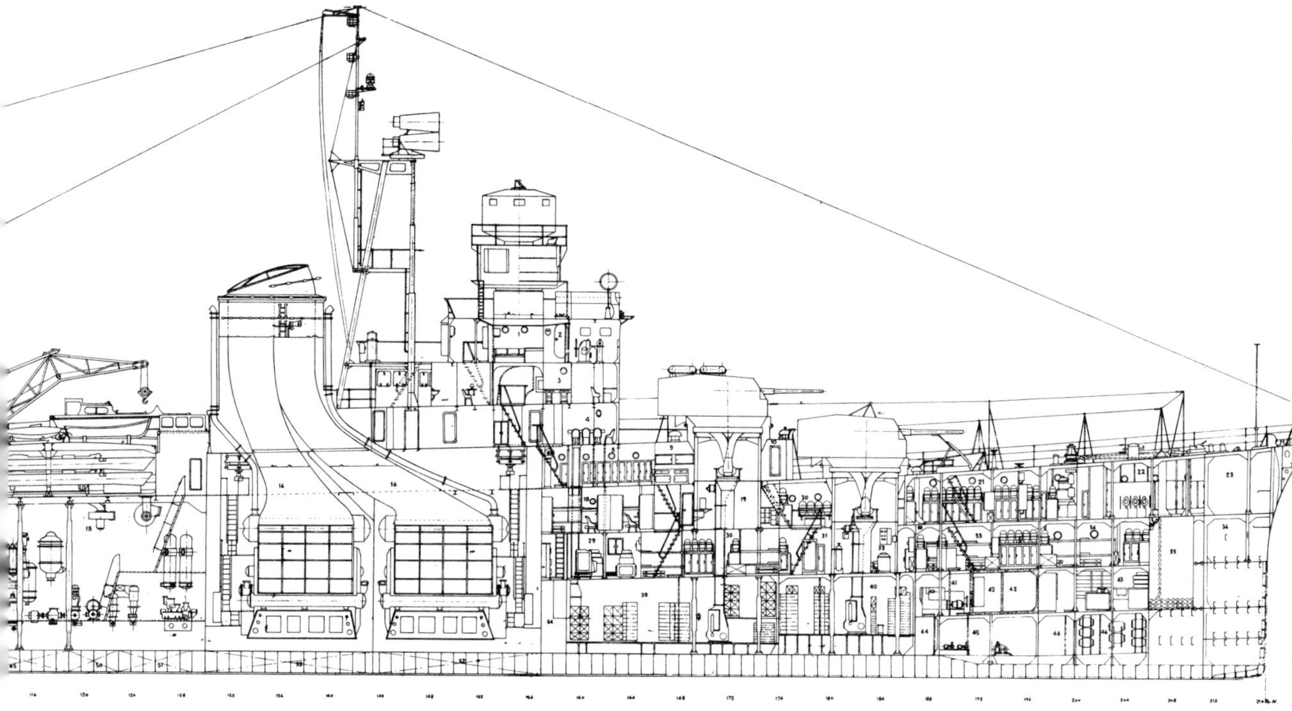

2ª TUGA

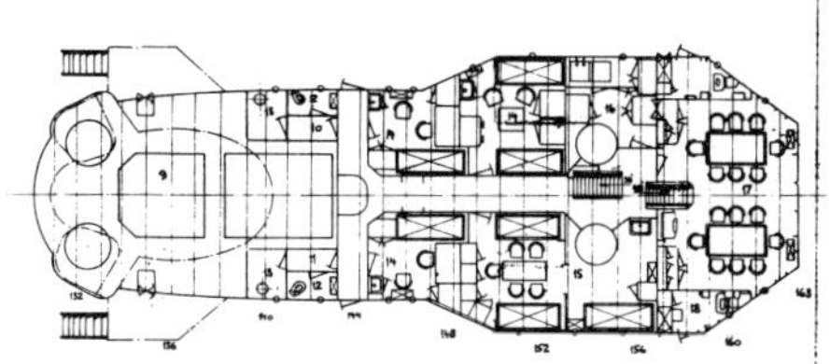

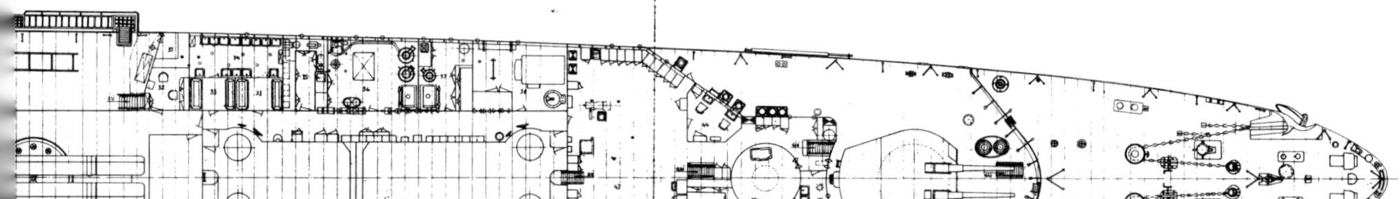

CONSTRUCTING BRACKETS

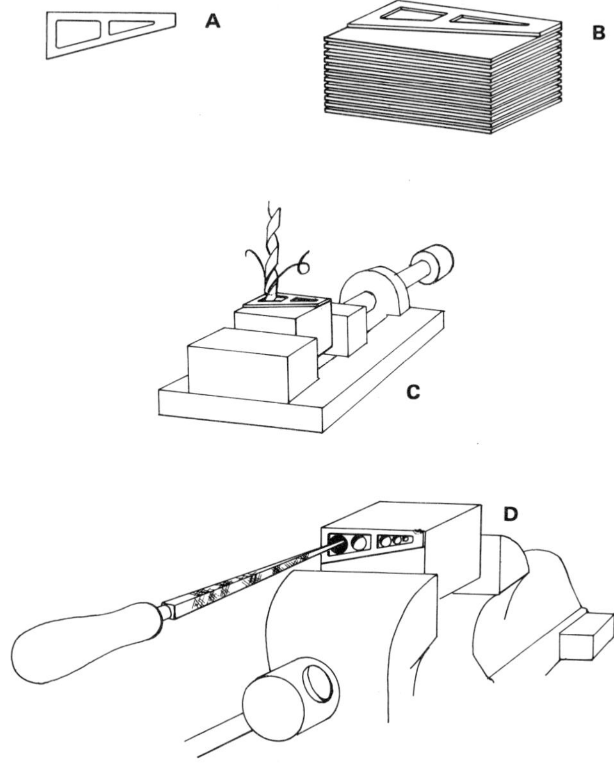

on the side of the houses, for these will often have to be added at an early stage in the construction, because later the place where they are to be attached will be inaccessible.

These in turn break down into a number of components. The deck on top of the house, if it projects beyond the house sides or ends, may well have beams and/or supporting brackets on the underside. There may be open rails round the periphery, in which case there will almost certainly be a narrow vertical plate fitted to the edge. If a bulwark or a splinter shield (zareba) is fitted this will have stiffeners fitted on its inside face — sometimes on the outside — and in some instances a wind deflector. Some platforms, depending on their position, may sit on a tubular support or be sustained by a system of pillars and brackets. These principles are illustrated with the accompanying diagrams outlining the construction of the complex forward superstructure of the Italian light cruiser *Pompeo Magno*.

DECKHOUSES

These can be solid or hollow. Much will depend on the scale and hence the size of the model, whether a working or showcase model, and upon the materials being used for its construction. In the case of small scale models plasticard is an ideal medium, and since the way to use it has been covered in another chapter, I would refer you to it to avoid unnecessary repetition.

On larger scale models I feel that, generally speaking, it is better wherever practical to make these of timber — unless it is a tinplate model — of hollow construction and with the outer surface covered with plasticard, which will give an excellent representation of steel plate. Where sidelights have to be fitted the wood in the immediate vicinity inside will have to be removed to allow insertion of the sidelight.

DECKS

Again, depending on the size of the model, the decks can be either of a suitable gauge of plasticard or of, say, thin plywood with a plasticard surface — except when it is a planked deck. To my way of thinking there is only one way of representing a planked deck, and that is to make it with individual planks. A scored deck, that is, one on which the planking has been represented by pencil or ink lines, or score marks on a plain piece of wood looks just what it is. On steel decks the strakes of plating can be represented by gumstrip paper on larger models, if the authentic detail, in the form of a deck plating plan, is available. The narrow plate round the edge, or the bulwark or splinter shield if there is one, can be of plasticard or very thin ply — metal in the case of a tinplate model. The stiffeners can be cut from narrow strips of the same material, and fixed in place on the underside or elsewhere as appropriate.

WINDOWS

The control positions of naval vessels have always embodied a number of rectangular windows in their design, but in recent years with the trend towards a high degree of total enclosure, some vessels appear to have quite a considerable area of glass in such positions.

On way of tackling this job is to cut a piece of clear acetate sheet to the full length and full deck-to-deck height of the space concerned, scribe on to it before shaping the outlines of the windows, fit in place if curved and then cover the area between the deck and the lower edge of the windows with a piece of thin plasticard, adding very narrow strips of thin plasticard to represent the divisions between the windows. The space behind the glass must of course be hollow, and on larger models this position should be fitted out with the appropriate instruments and furniture.

CONSTRUCTING BRACKETS

The superstructures of warships include a considerable number of diagonal brackets, supports and various kinds of strengtheners, which the

Right: A British 'Battle' class destroyer model. The bridge is not very different from the *Janus* shown later (14) but the single Mk6 director requires widespread use of perspex if it is to be modelled satisfactorily. Note the lattice mast and the details of the funnel — the flare at its base, the piping, platform and rigging stays. (Photo: John Bowen)

Below: The main radar aerial of the author's model of *Carlo Bergamini,* a modern Italian frigate. (Photo: Giancarlo Barbieri)

modeller often encounters. The following process shows how it is possible to make a large number (in this case 20) of identical pieces very simply. Using sheet brass of 0.2mm, make one piece ('A' in the relevant figure) to be used as a pattern or template. From the same sheet cut 19 pieces large enough to cover the template. Then whiten them with tin, arrange them one on top of the other with the pattern on top, and while heating them keep them pressed down firmly so that when they have cooled they will form one single block (B). Drill holes inside the perforations on the template (C). Then, using a file of suitable size, work round the inside of the template, making sure that the file is kept square (D), and then work round the outside. Once this operation is complete, heat up again and detach each piece. They will all be identical, as though individually made.

LATTICE STRUCTURES

Making lattice structures in metal may at first seem difficult, but the process can be simplified with a few easy tricks. Parts should be joined by soldering with tin, and the first rule to observe is to polish them thoroughly. If you wish to join brass wire or sections, they must be whitened beforehand with tin so that the surface is covered with a thin film.

These are essential preparations for joining metal parts if you are using an electric soldering iron as a heat source, but not to distribute the melted tin. It is possible to solder without using too much soldering material so as to produce a surface that needs very little finishing except for polishing greasy or corrosive soldering paste.

To make part of a lattice-mast or radar aerial first sketch the part to be made on to a wooden block (A in the relevant figure) and then arrange the main struts holding them on the board corresponding to the area marked out with small nails placed inside and out (B). Then cut the cross-pieces to measure, fix them to the

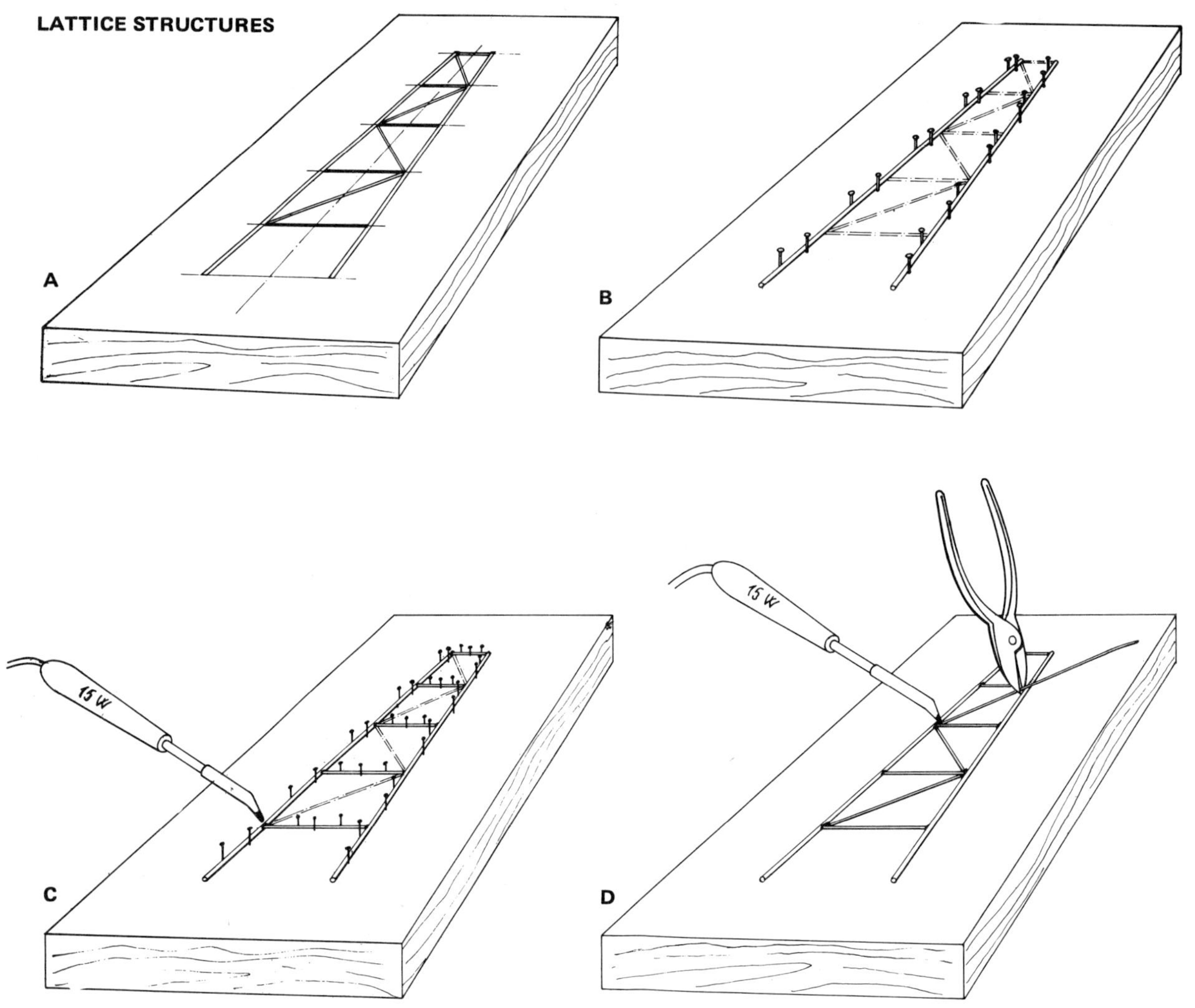

wooden board with the arrangement of nails and solder them to the struts with a 15-16 watt soldering iron and a small amount of tin (C). Put the diagonals in position using one length of wire for the whole diagonal; solder where necessary. Hold the other section of the diagonal in position and cut with small pincers, then press into its corner and solder into place (D).

PARABOLIC RADAR ANTENNA

It is clear that the process described so far is very simple, and it can be applied in many ways which will enhance the appearance of the models you wish to make. In particular it can be used for radar aerials, as with the following parabolic type. As indicated above, make a wooden mould according to the camber of the radar, and mark on it the exterior profile of the antenna and cross-pieces. Then attach a 0.4mm wire to the mould, forming the outline of the antenna, using only the nails placed inside and outside (A). Fix the cross-pieces, starting from the centre, using 0.2mm brass wire, suitably whitened with tin and curved to cover the template. Solder one end (B) then, pressing it onto the mould, cut the other end with the small pincers (C), soldering it to the external framework of the antenna (D). If this process is repeated as indicated, the parts already soldered will not come away because they will be cold and attached firmly to the structure.

FUNNEL CONSTRUCTION

The diagrams show the steps for modelling a typical funnel (1) of the Second World War period. In (2) parts A and B are shaped wood, with C being made from 0.2mm brass shim. The geometry of part C is shown in (3), the shape being formed from the bases of two cones on profile view (C2), and two interlinking circles in plan (C3): the final flat shape is

PARABOLIC RADAR ANTENNA

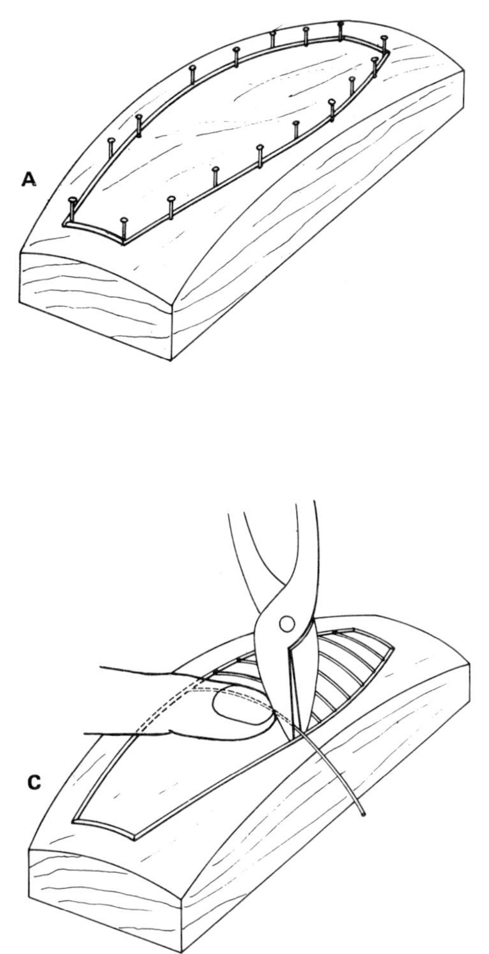

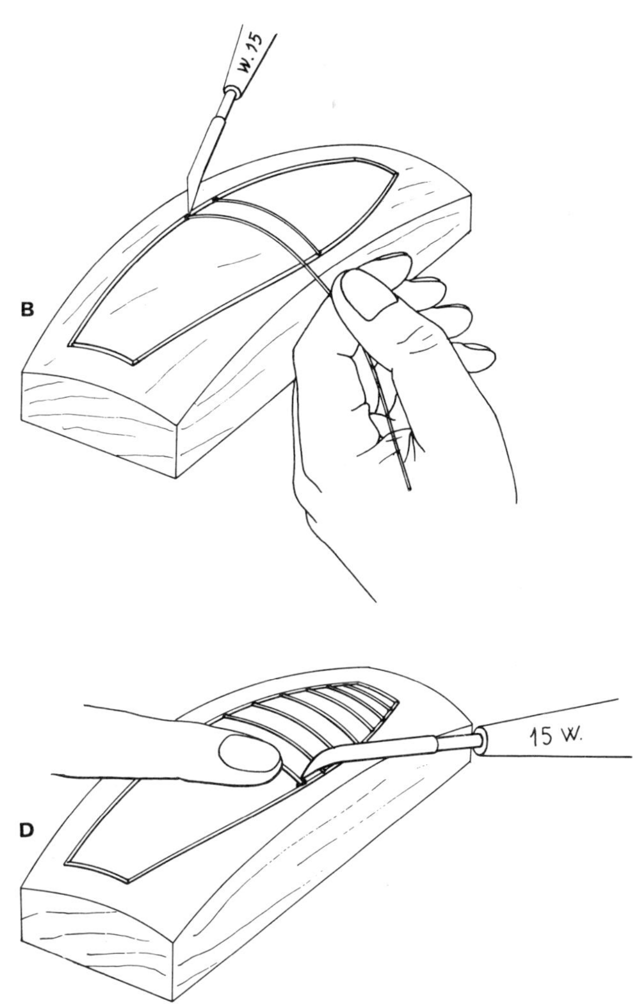

shown in C4. The funnel cap is also constructed of brass shim, by the method outlined in (4): to get the rake aft the cap is cut vertically, the pieces bent over, shaped and soldered.

Jackstays (5) can be made from brass wire of appropriate diameters, with staples twisted into stanchions. Holes are then drilled in the wood body of the funnel (6) and the completed length of jackstay pressed in and soldered or cemented (7). Steel access ladders can be made on a former as described for

Also from *Dreadnought,* the complex mainmast tripod is here shown broken down into a number of simple sub-assemblies. Part of the secret of superstructure construction is planning — if the apparently complicated ensemble can be divided into a series of simple pieces the modeller should have few difficulties. (Photo: Brian King)

lattice masts (8), and further use can be made of staples (9) for the footrungs.

ASSEMBLY

As many of the component parts of a superstructure should be assembled as practicable before being put in place. In the same way, as many of these parts as possible should be painted before assembly. Obviously there will be times when some of the deckhouses and platforms will have to be built up on the model, and I have in mind particularly those houses on the forecastle and upper decks. If finished or partly finished houses are added to these decks, remember to camber the underside of the houses. One way of doing this is to shape the top surface of a piece of scrap board to the camber of the deck, place a piece of sandpaper on this surface, and then rub the deckhouse along the length on the centre line until the correct amount of camber has been imparted to the end members of the house.

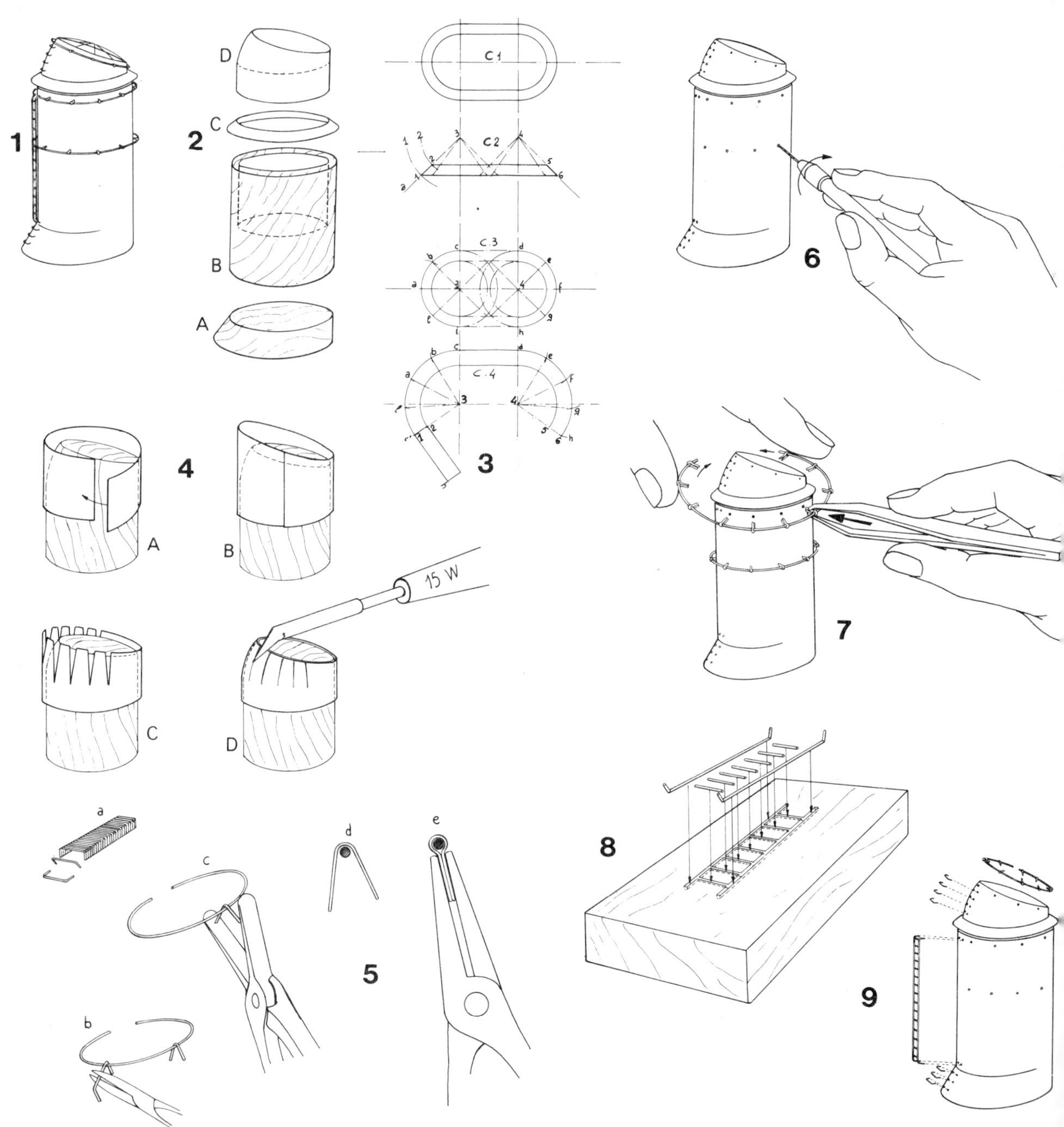

1

SUPERSTRUCTURE DEVELOPMENT FROM 1900

The United States battleship *Alabama* (1) seen here coaling at St Lucia in January 1908, was completed at Cramp's yard at Philadelphia in 1900. One of three vessels of this class, the twin side-by-side funnels bring to mind the somewhat similar British *Majestic* class of capital ships of the same period.

The superstructure is simple and typical of the period. Many of the platforms are supported over a greater part of their area by light vertical stanchions or pillars, a form of construction which does present the modelmaker with some problems if rigidity is to be obtained without falling into the trap of using overscale material to achieve the desired strength. This is particularly noticeable in the case of the platform abaft and above the top of the wheelhouse, where only a short length of its fore edge rests on the roof of the house. On the other hand the cranes do have solid, not lattice, jibs. Anyone considering a model of one of these vessels would do well to show it as it was during the earlier years of its service, for between 1909 and 1912 the tubular masts of this class were replaced by the characteristic cage masts found in many US vessels. Notice that the masts below the upper platforms are of appreciable diameter, and the circular platforms are supported by a number of brackets extending to their periphery. Above the upper platform it is a pole mast of much smaller diameter, with a separate topmast. The teak or mahogany wheelhouse would have to be built on the clear acetate principle mentioned previously, as it is such a prominent feature. (Photo: Conway Picture Library)

HMS *Dreadnought* (2), Brian King's 1/110 scale radio-controlled working model shows the typical superstructure to be found in the early capital ships. However, it can be broken down into easy-to-build

2

units, as can be seen in the earlier photographs. On this model the superstructure was made of metal. Incorporated into the boat deck piece are the supports to take the cradles for the steam picket boats, as well as those for the cutter stowed athwartships abaft the foremast. The funnels are similar to those on the *Howe* (13) and the mast is the usual robust tripod. Just above the searchlight platform is the fore control top, supported on a system of large triangular brackets, the construction of which is illustrated elsewhere in this chapter. (Photo: Brian King)

The development of cruiser superstructures between the wars (3-5) — USS *Trenton* (3), photographed at Yokohama in October 1928, was essentially a First World War design, with little superstructure and antiquated casemate mountings for part of her main armament. Also typical of the period are lattice searchlight towers, and the relatively light pole masts, with separate fidded topmasts and consequently rather elaborate rigging.

By contrast, USS *Pensacola* (4) has heavy tripod masts supporting searchlight platforms, lookout stations, the forward gun directors and even light AA platforms. With her sister *Salt Lake City* they were the first US 'Treaty' cruisers and one of the massive 8in gun turrets is visible in this photo. Heavy cruisers were designed to be able to operate self-sufficiently in a wide variety of roles, and this had its effect on the superstructure: heavy guns mean elaborate fire control apparatus for long range fire; reconnaissance and patrol work required aircraft, which needed space; flagship duties necessitated more accommodation, a larger outfit of boats and a crowded boat deck in consequence. Note the platform deck over the torpedo-tubes, to allow space to handle both the aircraft and the single 5in/25 AA guns. (Photos: CPL)

The *San Francisco* (5), a later heavy cruiser design, demonstrates the early war appearance of US cruisers. Although the later proliferation of light AA weapons is not yet apparent, the ship already sports gunnery radar. The bridge is a complex four-level affair with an armoured conning tower built into the front of the first deck. Note the elaborate shape of the wind deflectors on the bridge wings. Abaft the fore funnel is a lattice searchlight tower. The mast is a straightforward pole with rigging simplified to improve the sky arcs of AA guns. (Photo: USN)

The bridge and control tower of the German pocket battleship *Deutschland* (6) taken before the war. Unlike the neater tower bridge familiar from the *Graf Spee*, *Deutschland* was completed with an arrangement reminiscent of First World War practice, a number of platforms surrounding a stubby tubular 'mast'. Although providing suitable mounts for the various directors, rangefinders and searchlights, this form of bridge was short on accommodation, and exposed to the elements. Note also the necessity for a docking bridge wing (carrying the navigation lights) as German dreadnoughts with their small conning towers had required. (Photo: CPL)

The most noticeable feature of US battleship design down to the 1930s was cage masts, very obvious in this shot of *New Mexico* (7). This relatively light form of construction was supposed to be able to absorb tremendous punishment, but this proved to be untrue, since even a heavy storm was capable of damaging them. *New Mexico*'s forward superstructure is in three distinct sections: immediately abaft the turret, a heavily armoured conning tower with tiny slit sights; behind and above that a lightly built navigation bridge and pilot house; on the cage mast a spotting top. The secondary armament is mounted in deckhouse casemates, atop which most of the space is devoted to boat stowage. (Photo: *CPL)*

The US replaced its cage masts (usually) with heavy tripods, as in this fine study of *Pennsylvania*'s mainmast (8). Although the fighting top appears complex, because it is enclosed it is relatively simple to model. However, the platforms being open are more of a problem; nevertheless with detailed photographs such as this one, plus a good set of plans, the modeller should have few queries. The exposed motors of the cranes (on the platform at the base of the jib) are particularly interesting. Also of *Pennsylvania,* this bridge view (9) was taken during her refit at Mare Island, California shortly after she received minor damage at Pearl Harbor. Compared with *New Mexico* (7), the forward superstructure has been considerably expanded: decks now encompass the conning tower; the pilot house has become a fully enclosed bridge; the tripod has replaced the cage foremast and two large directors for the 5in AA gun are positioned on platforms supported by sturdy pillars; light AA and searchlight platforms surround the funnel. Although the secondary guns are still in

5

casemates, the 5in AA guns have been fitted with shields, and numerous light AA guns added. (Photos: USN)

Between the wars British warships also acquired more elaborate superstructures. *Queen Elizabeth* (10), seen here in 1930, and her sister ships underwent extensive modification, the two funnels being trunked into one, and the bridge structure extended. This view from sea level shows the overhang of the various bridge deck levels and the heavy bracket supports, while the core of the assembly is still the tripod mast. On British battleships of this period the armoured conning tower was still separate and, with its armoured rangefinder hood, is very noticeable. Amidships there is still very little superstructure except the enormous uptakes of the trunked funnel: note the heat shield to protect the bridge on the forward section of the trunking. The searchlights are mounted on towers enclosing the operator's position, the sighting ports being visible towards the bases. The boats are nested on the forecastle deck amidships and worked by a large derrick rigged from the pole mainmast. (Photo: National Maritime Museum)

The Japanese developed this form of bridge to its greatest heights — literally. This photo of *Hiei* (11) in 1928 shows an early stage of development with a British style structure built up of platforms around a tripod mast. The conning tower is still separate, there are searchlights on lattice towers abreast the forward funnel, and the funnels themselves do not yet show the bizarre trunked shapes later adopted. The Japanese eventually produced towering 'pagoda' bridge structures, best exemplified by *Fuso* and *Yamashiro,* where no supporting tripod was needed at all. (Photo: CPL)

Part of the upperworks of the German battleship *Bismarck* (12). This very large model, some 8ft (2.5m) long was built by H R Wilson of Surrey. The lower part of the superstructure can be built up from a number of separate units, but it is the section above this which is of particular interest. In place of the heavy tripod mast of, say, HMS *Hood* or the modified USS *Pennsylvania* class of capital ships there is a large control tower. The central core can be constructed as the basic unit, to which the various platforms are then added. This is another instance where a number of

OFFICIAL PHOTOGRAPH
NOT TO BE RELEASED
FOR PUBLICATION
NAVY YARD MARE ISLAND CALIF
RESTRICTED
1107-42
PENNSYLVANIA
BROADSIDE VIEW STBD. SIDE
MARE ISLAND, CALIF.

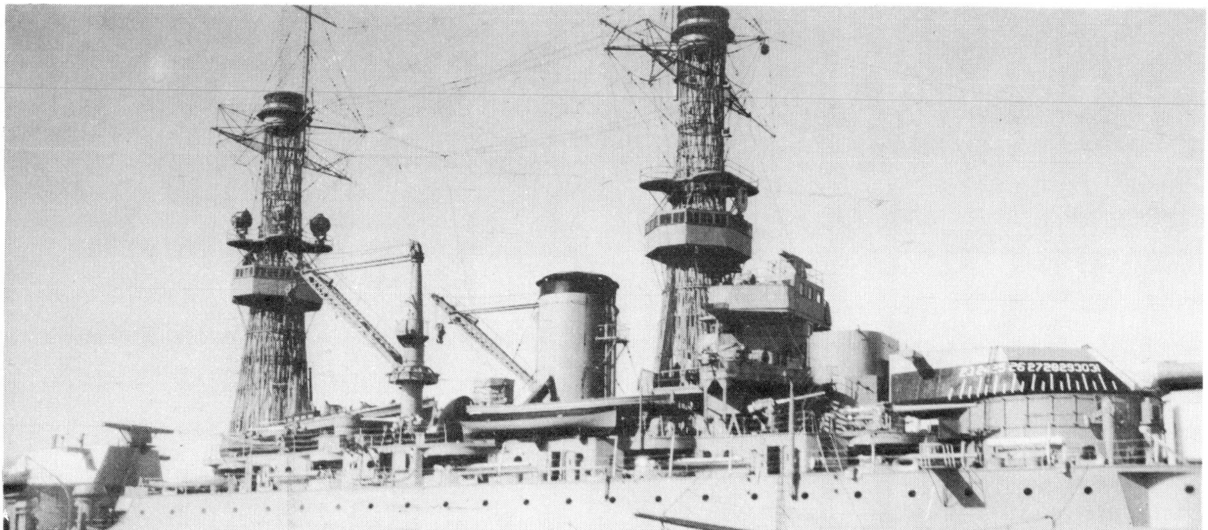

9

10

11

individual units can be built, be fitted in place and then removed for painting in their sub-assembled state before being fixed permanently in position — remembering of course to leave the fixing points clear of paint.

The funnel is a straightforward shape, but would have to be made in three sections — the base to a height of or level in line with the junction of the floatplane's wing and fuselage, the plain oval main body, and the shaped top part. The latter is somewhat similar in form to funnels found on a number of French and Italian warships. The searchlight platforms, though apparently of quite lightweight construction, are supported by a number of heavy brackets, which would have to be included. The omission of such small detail, because it seems to be hardly visible, can mar a good model; by leaving it out it makes the already lightweight platform look so fragile that one's immediate reaction is to feel that surely there must have been some additional supports to sustain the weight of the fittings it carries. (Photo: John Bowen)

The British abandoned the elaborate platforms-and-tripod structure with the simplified tower bridge of *Rodney* and *Nelson.* This was further developed into the truncated block bridge of the rebuilt *Warspite* in 1937, which itself served as a model for the *King George V* class. The forward superstructure of HMS *Howe* (13): this scale model is in the Museum of

12

Transport, Glasgow. A close study of the model will reveal that the assembly under the funnel is separate from that forward (or to the left) of the foremast. Both structures can be broken up into a number of separate units for constructional purposes at the level of the various platforms. This is a good example of the need to have a plan which shows each of these platforms or decks separately. The bulwark and splinter shields to the gun positions might present a slight difficulty because of the shaped top, which acts as a wind deflector. On a smaller scale model this top could be represented by turning over the upper edge of the bulwark material to 90° and then running a fine fillet of (waterproof) glue along the inside of the flange to simulate the cross-section.

Unlike so many of the funnels on capital ships those on the *King George V* class were a plain flat-sided oval in section with the standard Admiralty pattern cowl top. They are readily built up on a former having this cross section, the bands being added separately, as are the cowl top and the sirens, whistles, platform and access ladder.

The tripod mast, too, presents few problems since it passes through only one deck, the signal deck, and thus the modelmaker is spared the difficult job of working out the size of the openings to be cut in each deck when it is necessary to pass the tripod legs in an assembled state through a number of decks.

Much other useful information can be gleaned from this photograph — the different sizes of the signalling projectors, the stowage of the Carley floats, the close-range armament and its siting and supporting structures, ventilators, the aircraft cranes, the fixed athwartship catapult, and the accomodation ladder and the boat booms. (Photo: Museum of Transport, Glasgow)

Reference has been made to blast shields, particularly on destroyers, and the one shown here at the fore end of the forward gun platform of HMS *Janus* is typical (14): this 1/96 scale model was built by A M Hall. The purpose of such shields was to protect the crew of the gun in the lower position from the blast of the upper gun when firing ahead. The platework of the shield sloped upwards and the stiffeners, generally in the form of web plates and angles, were usually to be found on the upper surface.

The forward deckhouse and open bridge of this destroyer are typical of the period. Notice the number of ready-use shell racks along the edge of the forecastle and inside the guard rails to 'B' gun position. The twin 4.7in mountings, the quad .5in machine guns and the open bridge are particularly well detailed, the latter including among other equipment such things as the compass, pelorus, azimuth repeater and the binocular sights. (Photo: John Bowen)

The US destroyer *Fletcher* (15), on the other hand, had an enclosed bridge, in keeping with usual US

KGV 1940

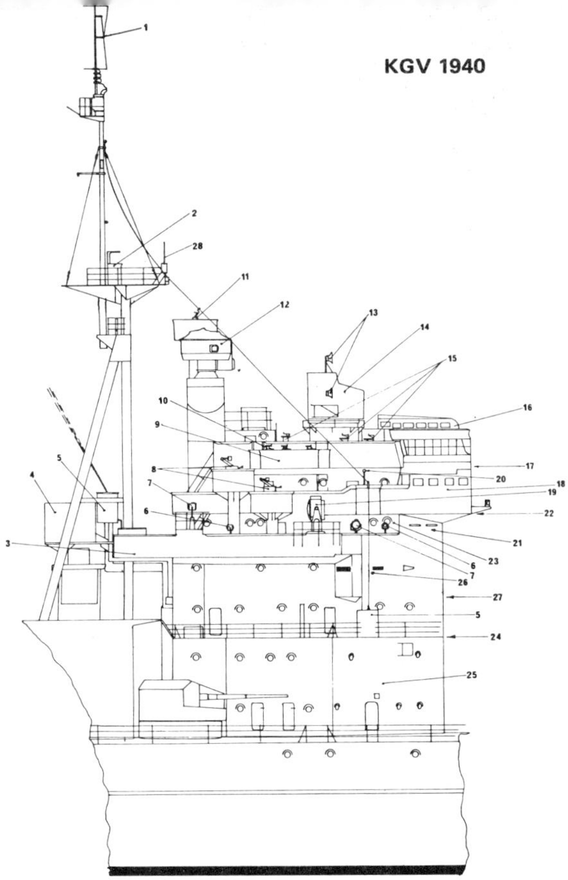

HOOD 1920
SHOWN AS IN 1932

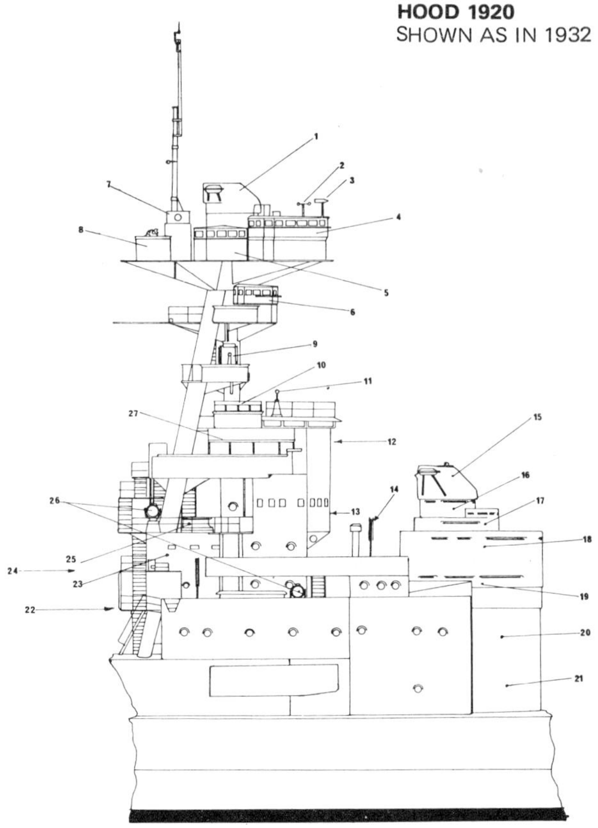

13

RODNEY 1928

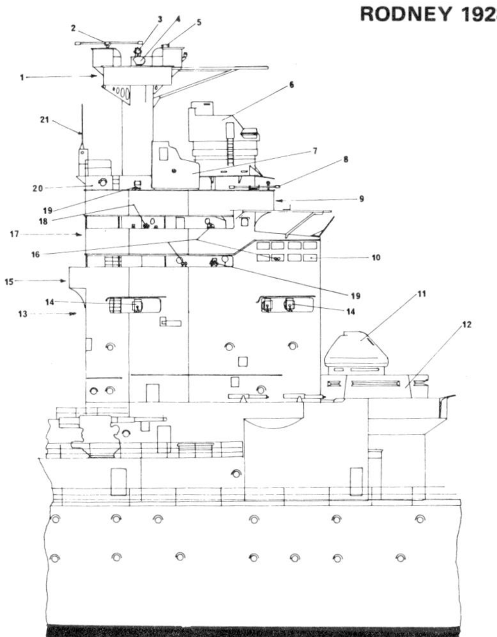

DREADNOUGHT

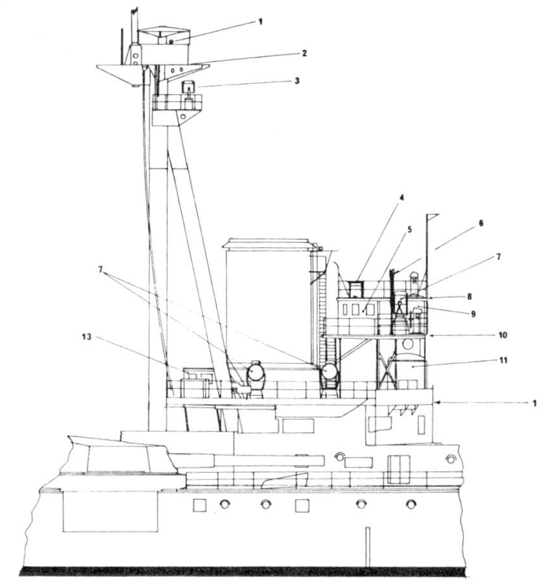

KEYS: KGV 1940

1 Tramsmitting aerial for Type 279 air warning radar
2 Crows nest
3 Signal (flag) deck
4 Radar office
5 W/T aerial screen
6 Signalling lamp
7 12inch signalling search light
8 Pompom directors
9 Air-look-out position (ALO)
10 ALO sights
11 Director for UP mounting on 'B' turret
12 HA/LA directors with 15ft range finders
13 Radar aerials for Type 284 gunnery radar
14 Main armament director control tower with 15ft range finder
15 Bearing sights for target indication star shell etc
16 Compass platform and chart house
17 Upper bridge
18 Admiral's bridge
19 44in search light
20 9ft range finder
21 Conning tower
22 Lower bridge
23 Chart house
24 No 1 platform (crew space etc)
25 Lower section of bridge containing stores, recreation space, galley etc
26 Surface look out
27 No 2 platform (officers' accomodation, navigating office and surface look out
28 Short range W/T aerial

HOOD 1920 Shown as in 1932

1 Main director control tower with 15ft range finder
2 Anemometer
3 Wind vane
4 Main armament spotting position
5 Secondary armament spotting position
6 Torpedo look out
7 9ft range finder (secondary armament)
8 Pom-pom director
9 36" searchlight
10 Searchlight control position
11 9ft Range finder
12 Compass platform
13 Admiral's bridge
14 Semaphore
15 Main armoured director control tower with 30ft range finder
16 Main armament control tower
17 Secondary armament control tower and Admiral's conning tower
18 Conning tower
19 Torpedo control tower
20 Signal distribution office
21 Intelligence office
22 Admiral's signal platform (flag deck)
23 Submarine look out
24 Conning tower platform
25 Secondary armament director control tower
26 24" signalling searchlights
27 Torpedo control platform

RODNEY 1928

1 AA Control platform
2 12ft High angle range finder
3 Bearing sight
4 High angle director
5 Dumaresq
6 Main director control tower with 15ft range finder
7 Secondary armament director control tower with 12ft range finder
8 9ft range finder
9 Director platform
10 Compass platform
11 Revolving armoured director hood
12 Conning tower
13 Searchlight platform
14 18" searchlights
15 Captain's bridge
16 Bearing sights
17 Admiral's bridge
18 Torpedo sights
19 Searchlight control
20 High angle calculating position
21 Short range W/T aerial

DREADNOUGHT

1 9ft Range Finder
2 Fore top
3 24" Searchlight
4 Chart Table
5 Chart House & Captain's Cabin
6 Semaphore, Port and Starboard
7 36" Searchlights
8 Compass Platform
9 Wheel House
10 Navigating Platform
11 Conning Tower
12 Flag deck
13 Admiral's Sea Cabin

practice. This 1/384 scale model by Eric Dyke reveals the basically simple superstructure layout of a war-standard design, the bridge having only a flag deck and a compass platform: US destroyers were flush decked, and the midship deckhouse is continued aft to form a base for the torpedo-tubes — in a destroyer in a seaway, the weatherdeck is often awash and this would hamper the operation of the tubes if they were so placed. The funnel is of oval cross-section but has a complex shape at its base. (Photo: John Bowen)

14

15

Funnels at first glance may appear to be relatively simple shapes. However, few are devoid of some form of exterior fittings, as in this view (16) of the French super destroyer *Le Triomphant*. Prominent are the steam whistle and siren with their associated piping and valves, access ladders, handholds, and a rail around the circumference of the funnel, which has a complexly shaped funnel cap and is rigged with rigid steel stays. The fore funnel also carries aerial spreaders, but in this class of vessel there was no mainmast and consequently the after funnel carried a large array of communications aerials. (Photo: CPL)

Because of operational requirements the superstructures of aircraft carriers were of necessity large island blocks sited to one side of the flight deck, and often with an abundance of small platforms springing from the main structure, as in this photograph of HMS *Indomitable* in March 1943 (17). It will be seen that the major part of the island could be built largely as a single unit, the various platforms then being built and fitted in position. The necessity of making those areas with a considerable number of windows as hollow structures complete with internal fittings is very apparent here. *Indomitable* at this time had just completed a major refit in the USA which included the installation of new radar. The centimetric Type 273 navigation and surface warning set is mounted on a platform at the fore end of the island in its distinctive octagonal protective 'lantern', and on top of the island, forward of the director, three of the four pompom directors can be seen with their Type 282 radar. The main director has Type 285 (turned upwards) and the main mast carries Type 79. (Photo: CPL)

The forward superstructure (18) of the author's model of the modern Italian destroyer *Impavido* illustrates very clearly the main points about the design of modern warships — the uncluttered decks, smooth surfaces with rounded corners (and radiused deck edges too), and here only one essential overhanging deck, the bridge wing. On these wings note the shape and form of the wind deflectors, with the convex face plate and the long tapered bracket plates; compare them with those on, say, similar British vessels.

There are other interesting features to be observed — the supports for the whip aerials, the guard rail stanchions each with its supporting stay, and particularly the design of the watertight doors, semicircular at top and bottom, with the locking mechanism operated by the large central wheel.

Although at first glance this would appear to be a comparatively simple unit to construct, closer inspection will reveal some potential problems, such as the split level control position, the radius edges meeting three ways at some corners, and the awkward little alteration in shape at the after end of the topmost house under the foremast. This is one of those instances where the suggested method of facing with plasticard needs considerable skill and care, especially as those compartments with windows will require to be hollow. (Photo: Giancarlo Barbieri).

Typical of the very latest British superstructure practice. When this model (19) of HMS *Broadsword* was built no ships of the class had actually been completed. A Type 22 frigate, she represents the first all-missile major warship class in the Royal Navy, although they retain two single 40mm Bofors for use against small craft. The most notable feature of the simple superstructure blocks and the straightsided hull is the absence of scuttles: together with decks relatively free of obstruction, this facilitates the ship's ABC (atomic, bacteriological and chemical) defences. Warships can now be fought from completely sealed 'citadels' deep within the ship, and in the 1960s 'prewetting' was introduced whereby all the topsides are sprayed from an elaborate network of sprinklers to reduce the effects of ABC fall-out.

This ship has no compass platforms, the only open areas for navigation being the bridge wings and these are sealed off from the bridge with heavy doors. However, the platform also mounts the 6-barrelled 'Corvus' rocket launcher (with flare launcher) which is a last ditch defence against anti-shipping missiles, and the Bofors mentioned previously. The Type 22s carry the 'Sea Wolf' anti-aircraft and anti-missile system fore and aft and the director is visible forward of the foremast: it will probably be covered with a plastic radome in service.

The enclosed foremast, developed from the old lattice mast, is common in many navies. Indeed some navies, including the USN, developed combined masts and funnel uptakes. These 'macks' (masts-and-stacks) have been abandoned in most steam or gas turbine ships since the effect of heat and dirt on

17

delicate electronic equipment simply repeated the First World War problems of smoke interference with spotting tops. Although the foremast still carries old-fashioned signal halliards (note the flag locker at the base of the mast), it is almost entirely given over to radar and ECM (electronic countermeasures). Equipments. Immediately forward of the funnel, the two domes are the terminals for the SCOT satellite communications system.

After being reduced, or even eliminated altogether, in 1950s designs, the funnel once again seems to be growing in size. Usually the reason is the adoption of gas turbine propulsion. Gas turbines require enormous quantities of air, and first generation ships have large and prominent air intakes, often in the superstructure. However, in some designs those intakes are being built into funnels in the traditional way, thus increasing the volume of the casing. Furthermore, in gas turbines considerable heat is generated and 90 percent of this must be exhausted through the funnel, where the effect on the electronics can be disastrous — hence the adoption of funnel 'wings' or split funnel ships like the new Canadian 'Tribals'. This is why the British destroyer *Sheffield* was completed with temporary 'ears' to the funnel, pending further developments, and why the US *Spruance* class have their funnels en echelon at the sides of the superstructure rather than on the centreline. *Broadsword* demonstrates the latest British thinking, with sponsons from the funnel proper to deflect heat either side of the mainmast.

The new close-range triple 21in tubes for anti-submarine torpedoes are visible aft of the motor launch. (Photo: John Bowen)

Guns and gun mountings 5

by PETER HODGES

The weapons of a surface warship are not only the outward and visible sign of her offensive and defensive capabilities, but also very largely dictate her physical dimensions. There are naturally exceptions to this general rule — notably in specialist vessels like monitors — but even with an aircraft carrier, whose main armament is her aircraft, the number of machines and their range determine her eventual displacement.

In most warship classes, the gunmountings appear

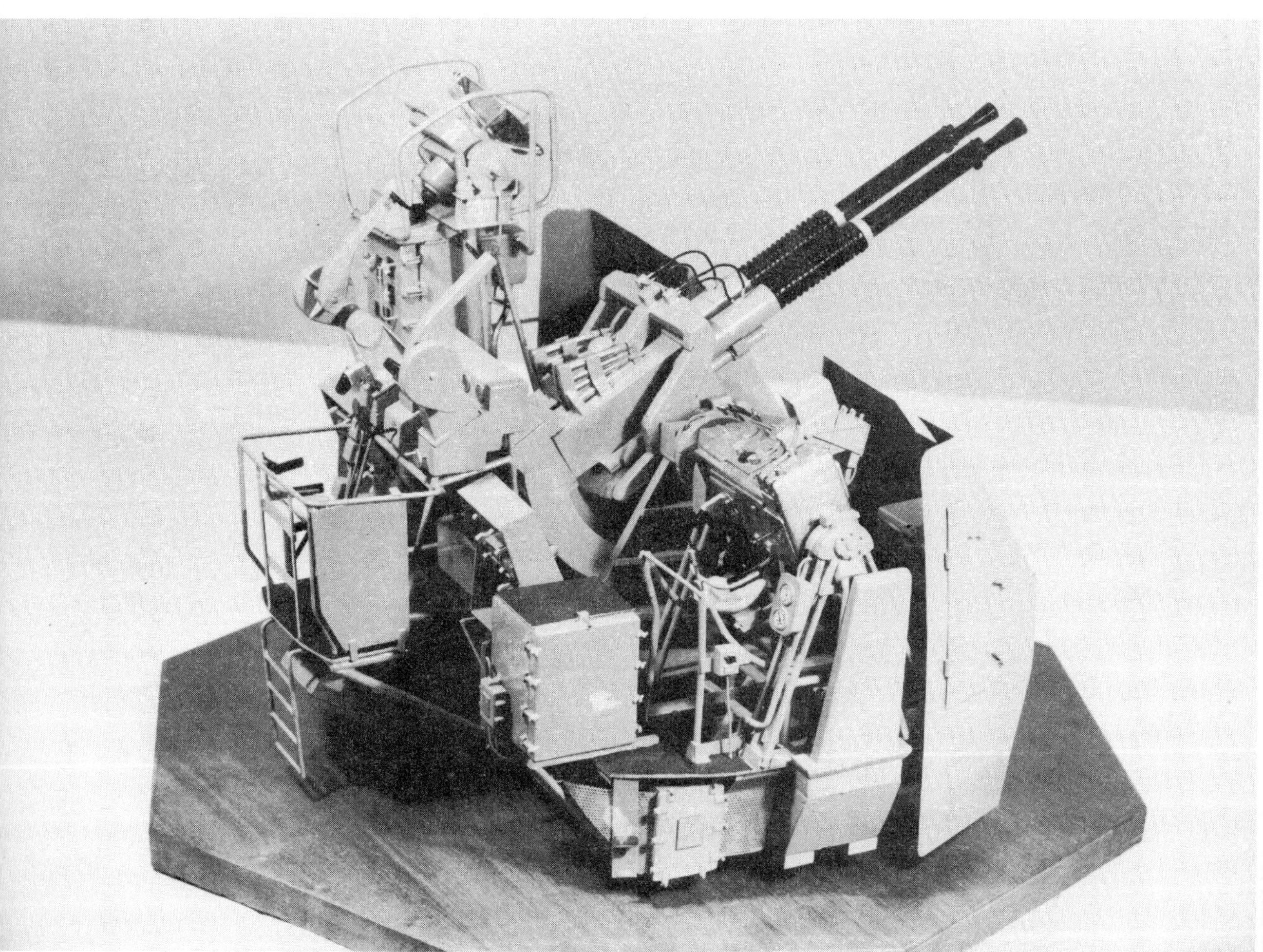

Opposite: One of the most complex mountings any modelmaker is ever likely to tackle, the twin 40mm STAAG Bofors as mounted in British vessels of the 1950s — an exquisite model. (Craine Collection, CPL)
Right: The parts of a gun demonstrated by this 12pdr HA/LA (High Angle/Low Angle) on a Mk IX 'central pivot' (CP) mounting. (MoD Navy)

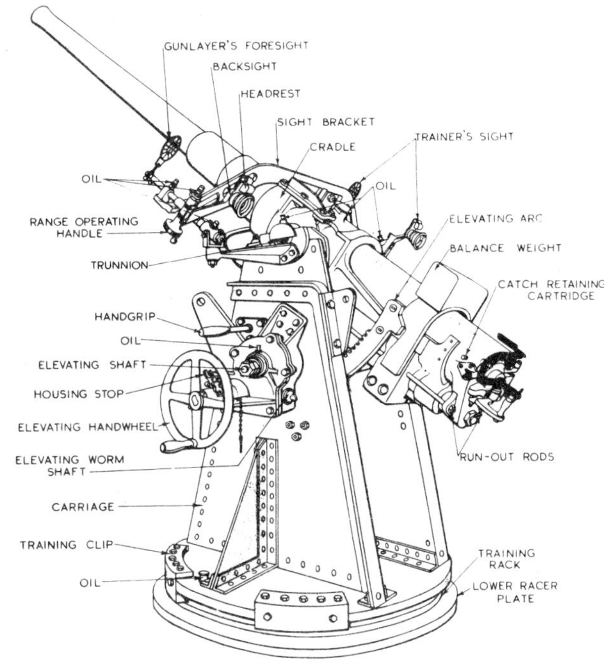

in multiples in the one hull; and further, identical guns and their associated mountings may be fitted in a very wide range of ships of differing ship classes and differing ship types: and this multiplicity of gun barrels and wide-spread mounting fitting presents the modeller with special problems.

Each barrel of a particular calibre must be of identical dimensions in each mounting; each mounting must be of identical shape; and these criteria must be followed if that mounting is to be found in models of *other* ships.

GUN BARRELS

The manufacturing process of a gun barrel is one of considerable complexity but happily, from the modeller's point of view, it is only the outward appearance that is of concern. Clearly, for large scale models, the work of producing tapered and stepped barrels can only be undertaken in the lathe, following normal turning practice; and naturally, the ideal is to get every barrel identical — but there are some minor short-cuts that can save time and material. It is most important to 'match-up' individual barrels in a particular mounting, but small differences between mounting and mounting often go undetected. Thus, supposing that the model is to have twin mountings in 'A' and 'B' positions and a second pair at 'X' and 'Y', then 'A's pair should be identical, 'B's should be identical and closely dimensioned to 'A's, with a similar comparison aft. It may well be that 'Y' does not compare too favourably with 'A', but it will take a keen eye indeed to detect the difference — assuming, of course, that it is not glaring.

For barrels that project about 3 inches from the gunhouse in modelled form, good results can be obtained using conventional commercial dowel rod set into the chuck of a pistol drill held in a vice. Inevitably, one gets the indentation marks of the chuck on the dowel, but these can be hidden within the gunmounting structure and are of no consequence. Achieving like tapers is more difficult and needs careful caliper work, but 'step' positions are easily marked with a pencil — and after all, dowel is inexpensive and is fairly quickly worked, so that not much is lost if a barrel is spoilt (usually as it is almost finished!). 'Matched pairs' (or matched 'quads' for the stout-hearted who take on a *King George V* or *Richelieu* class battleship) are even more important as the accuracy of production diminishes.

A final point on gun barrels. Unless one is working in metal on the lathe, never try to drill a hole into the muzzle to represent the bore. The chances of getting it dead on the axis are very remote and in dowel, there will almost certainly be a ragged edge, if not a complete split. Better schemes are either to turn a tampion solid with the barrel and to touch it in with gold or bronze to represent the ship's crest, or simply to cover the muzzle with a 'muzzle cover'.

GUN MOUNTINGS

This very term has a number of synonyms and — rather like 'galleon' — can be difficult to define accurately. For many years, however, the British have followed the practice of defining the *gun mounting* as the total entity of rotating structure carrying the guns, and extending downwards in a 'trunk' to the shell rooms and magazine.

This construction appears at deck level as a

gunhouse or *turret* and in large warships its trunk may be surrounded by a *barbette* of armoured steel set in the ship's structure.

Semi-enclosed mountings of smaller calibres are protected by a spray or splinter *gunshield* of varying shapes and size and nowadays in the Royal Navy, *turret* is used (loosely) to describe a totally enclosed gunhouse, while *mounting* refers to an open or partially shielded weapon.

Two important questions have to be answered by the modeller before he undertakes gun mounting production. The first is, does he intend to make his gun moveable in training (or traverse): and the second, does he intend to make his gun moveable in elevation? Both motions entail considerable extra work, but the modeller must decide whether, on display, he may either invite the viewer to examine the accuracy of his weapon alignment: or proudly say 'the turrets train, and the guns elevate'. It may be, if he is very skilled, that he can combine all attributes, but whether the game is worth the candle, only he can decide. Moveability in my view is mere play value and is far outweighed by accurately aligned, fixed weapon equipment.

GUNHOUSES

From the foregoing, the reader should understand that this term implies a totally enclosed structure housing the gun barrels, and in the model what matters is as follows:

1 The gunhouse must be identical to other similar gunhouses in the same ship.

2 The gun barrels in a multi-barrelled mounting must as near as possible be identical, following earlier guidelines.

3 The barrels must be parallel to the centre line of the ship, when the gunhouse is set exactly fore-and-aft.

4 The barrels must be set at identical heights in the horizontal plane.

5 The barrels must project to identical distances from the front face of the gunhouse.

6 The barrels must be at the same elevation.

Now these points may appear obvious (once they are read); but nevertheless, each must be given the most careful attention, for an error in any one will, in the modeller's eye, if not in others', stick out like the proverbial sore thumb.

GUNHOUSE PRODUCTION

Just as it is possible to make up gun barrels in more than one way, according to one's resources and to the chosen scale, so is it possible to produce gunhouses.

At first sight, this may seem an ideal opportunity to resort to solid modelling techniques but nothing, in fact, could be farther from the truth. The problems of cutting out and shaping four identical structures from

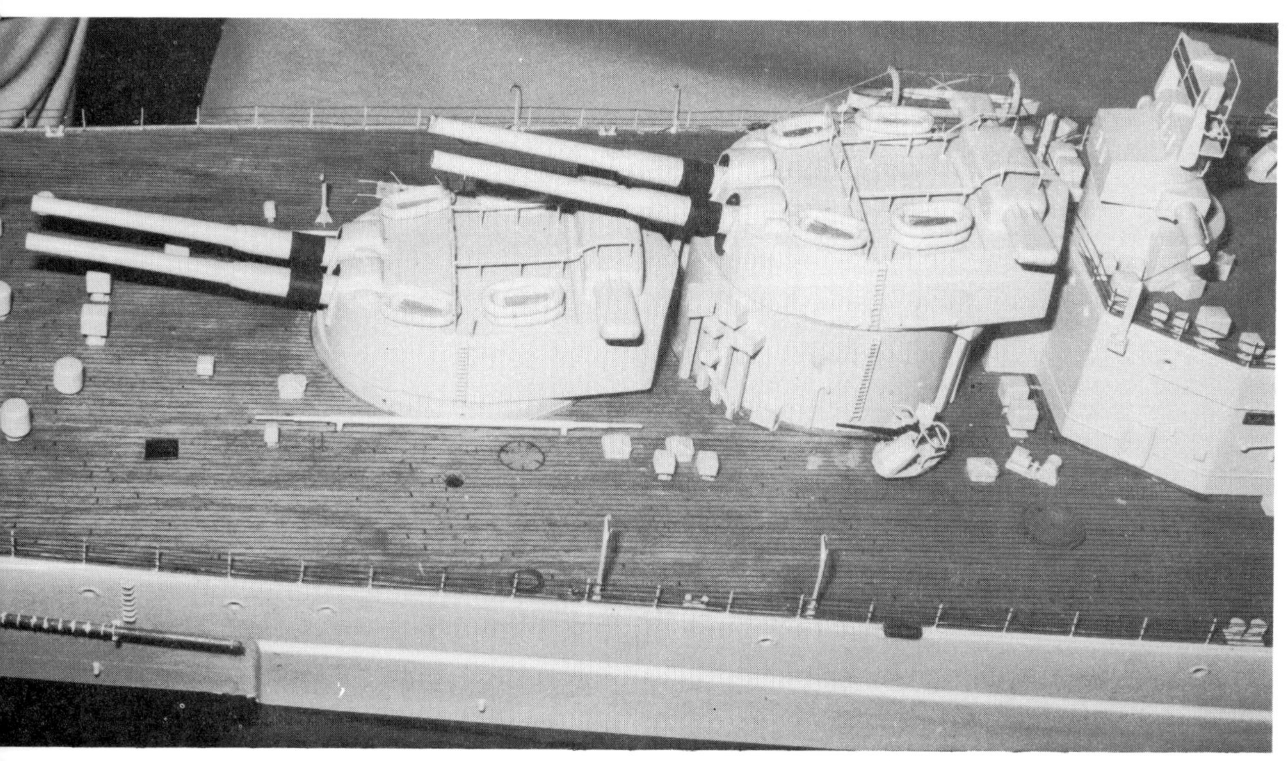

Opposite: The complex shape of big guns — the forward 15inch turrets of a large 1/96 scale model of *Vanguard.* Note also the turret rangefinders.
Right top: A variety of US weapons on Eric Dyke's 1/192 scale model of the destroyer *Fletcher.* The main armament guns are two of five 5inch/38 calibre singles in enclosed base-ring mounts, between which is a twin 40mm Bofors Mk I and single 20mm Oerlikons can be seen in the weatherdeck zareba. The quintuple 21inch torpedo-tubes and depth charge throwers are also visible.
Right bottom: By way of contrast the 18 ton 10inch MLR (muzzle loading rifle) on pivoting slide carriage of the British 'Rendel' gunboat *Fidget* of 1873. The model, by Ray Cattle, is 1/48 scale.

any kind of solid material are such that even the most skilled would be hard pressed. Most gunhouses have a front face that slopes backwards and it may, in addition, be curved in plan, so that the difficulty of setting the barrels into it hardly needs explaining. Not only is the front face angled towards the roof but very often the sides are similarly angled, while the gunhouse plan view may reveal that it is octagonal in shape.

Building up a gunhouse from sheet material, on the other hand, solves these problems; and further, gives its own satisfaction in that, to some degree, it follows prototype practice. Now 'sheet material' is a broad term and can, of course, mean anything. Indeed, I have built German military tank turrets of very complex shape from stiff white card with complete success, but personally favour commercial white sheet polystyrene. This is available in a wide range of thicknesses from 5 thou to 40 thou, and polystyrene strip from .5mm x .5mm up to .5mm x 2mm is also marketed by firms specialising in plastic kits.

This material has many merits. It has a naturally smooth finish, its cuts easily and can be worked with a file. Joining with the conventional polystyrene cement gives a very strong structure and several thicknesses can easily be built up into a block.

Equally, one could use thin ply, or sheet metal, but the basic procedure will remain the same. Let us examine it, assuming that polystyrene has been chosen.

Marking out. White polystyrene sheets are produced in about A4 paper size and have dead straight edges so they can be pinned to a drawing board and the 'working drawing' completed on them in pencil. This, of course, is very useful because a scale drawing can easily be transferred to the plastic, and mistakes can be erased as readily as on paper.

Now because the intention is to ensure that each gunhouse is identical — and supposing that four twin mountings are needed — the following two rules must be observed. (1) *Always* mark out, cut and complete sufficient similar parts for each mounting (eg make all the required gunhouse floors) at the same time. (2) *Always* mark out, cut and complete *one extra part.* This is the 'master' to be retained so that should the same mounting be needed in the future on another model, it will be identical with those of the first. Make a note on the additional part in pencil — 'Gunhouse Floor, 6in Mk XXIII' — so that it is easily identified.

Building up the Structure. (The figures relevant to this procedure are neither to a particular scale, nor are they of a particular mounting, and are intended solely to illustrate the principles.) The first part to mark out, cut and true-up, is the gunhouse floor. This should be of 40 thou material, which is strong enough for even the largest scales.

This part is *not* drawn to the true size, but is undercut on every edge by the thickness of the side

6 INCH VAVASSEUR BROADSIDE MOUNTING, ABOUT 1885

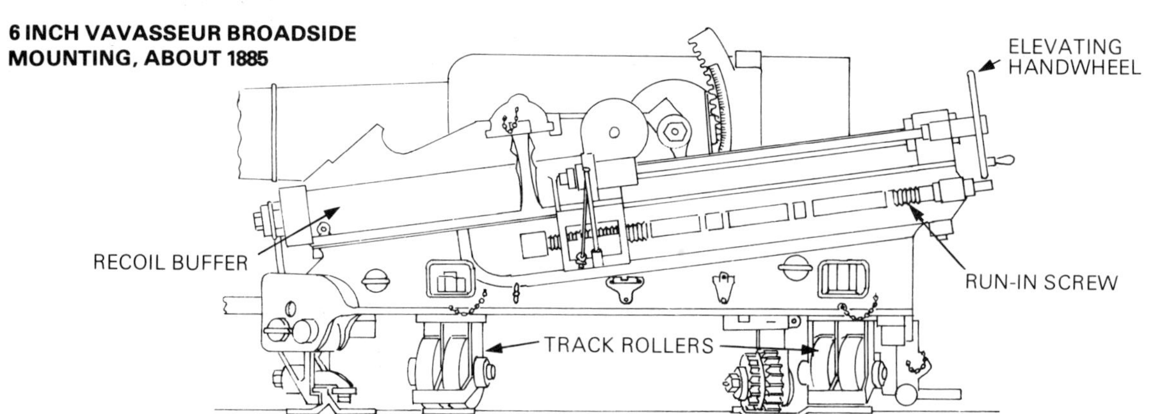

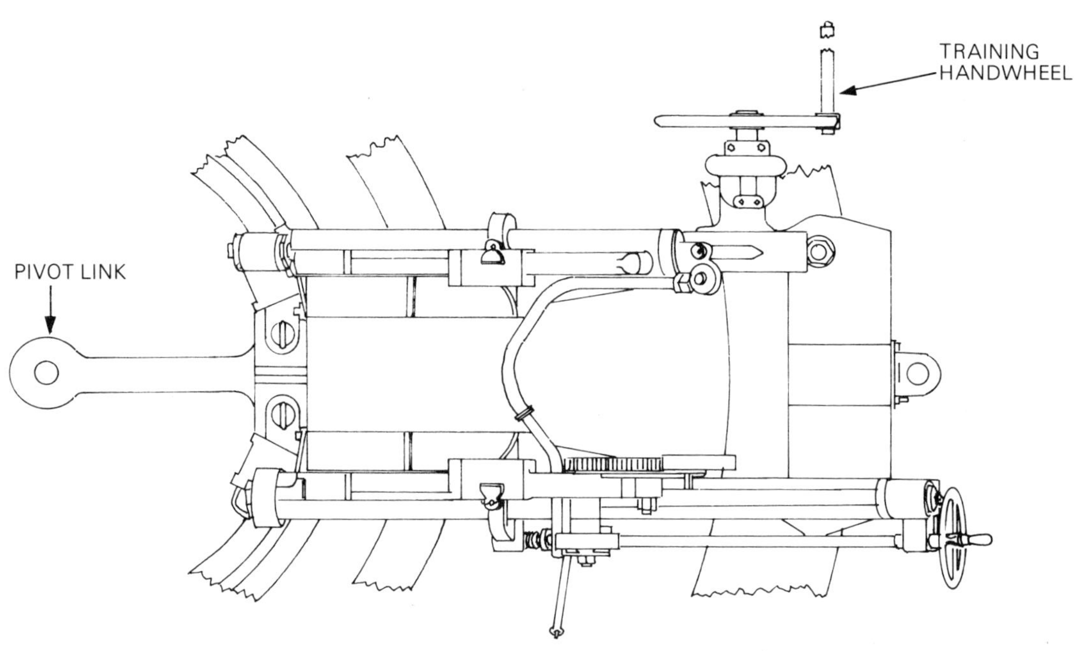

16.25 INCH BARBETTE MOUNTING, HMS BENBOW, 1885

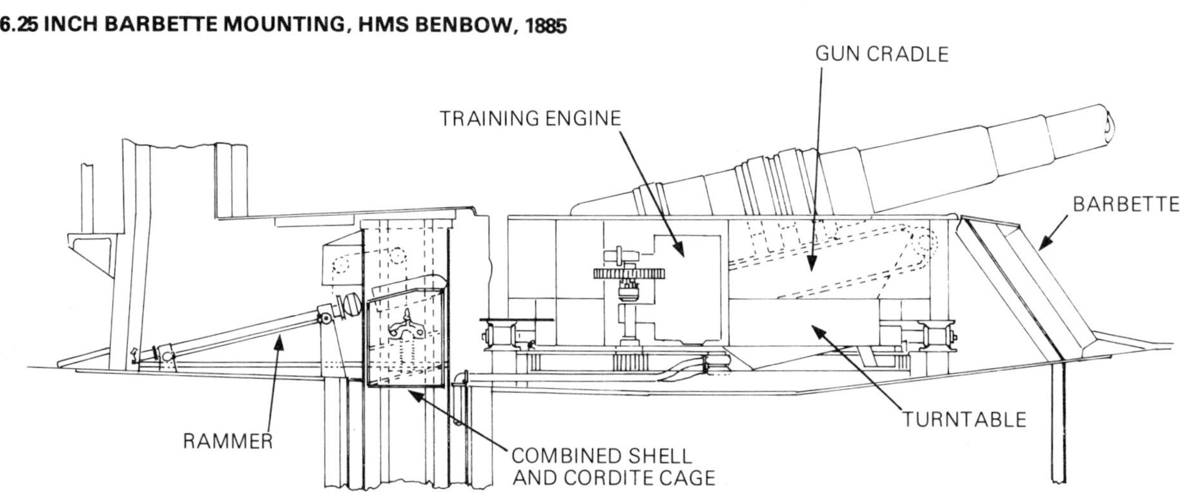

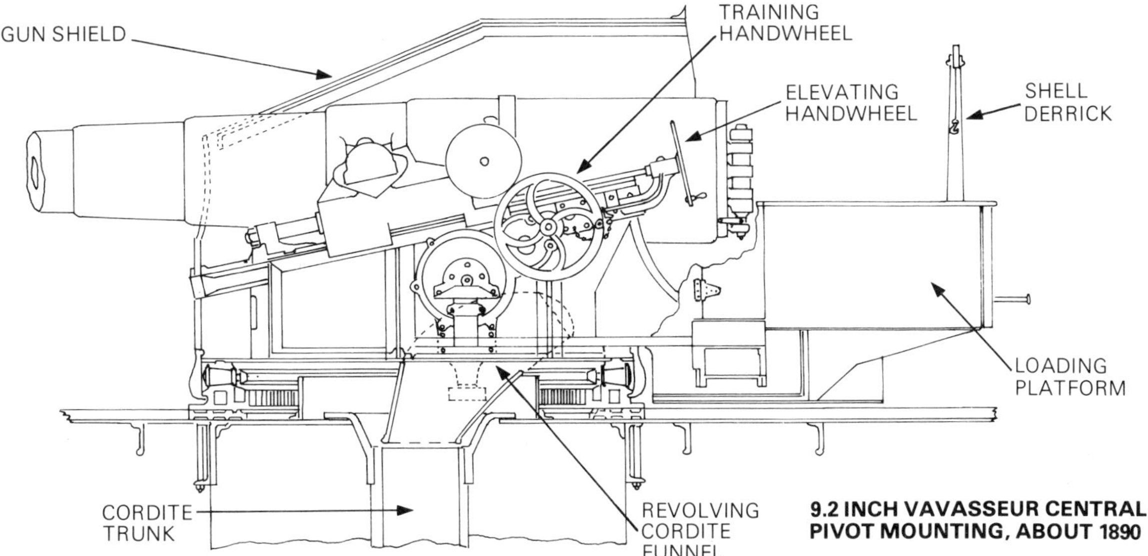

9.2 INCH VAVASSEUR CENTRAL PIVOT MOUNTING, ABOUT 1890

plates, front plate and rear plate. If these are all flat surfaces, then we can use the same 40 thou plastic for them in which case, of course, each floor edge will be undercut by 40 thou in the transferred working drawing. But in our imaginary gunhouse, the rear plate is curved and will only be 10 thou thick, so this *rear* edge needs less undercut.

When the transfer from the scale drawing is complete (when one can scale up or down as necessary) and while the plastic sheet is still pinned to the drawing board, accurately mark the centre of rotation and draw a centre line through this point, followed by the centre lines of the gun barrels and the other important alignment lines. Cut out the gunhouse base (plastic will snap easily and true along a sharp cut against a steel straight edge) and bring the dimensions to the finished (ie undercut) size. Drill a hole through the centre of rotation point and a second hole at a convenient point elsewhere on the centre line. These holes should be very small — sufficient only to be able to accept a sharp pencil point.

Using the finished first floor as a pattern mark around it with a pencil on the plastic sheet to give another four floors (remembering one is for 'store'). Each of these will thus be slightly oversize. At the same time mark the two holes with a sharp pencil, and cut out the four floors. Open out both holes in the original floor with a larger drill to some convenient size of BA bolt, and similarly drill each other floor.

Clean off any swarf left from drilling, lay each floor upon the other and bolt all together through both holes. This will ensure that there will be no rotary movement. Set the group of floors in a hand-vice, and bring the four down by fine file to the dimensions of the first.

Take all the alignment lines to the edges of the first floor and mark them on the edges of the others on both sides. Unbolt the five (now identical) floors, pick up the edge alignment marks on the four 'repeats' and draw them in. Mark *Floor Top* on the surface of each floor and bevel the finished edge to suit whatever slope the side, front and rear plates may have. It is better to *over* bevel since any gap will fill with cement in due course. (If one is distracted half-way through bevelling a particular floor, it is easy to reverse it and put a bevel on the wrong way, hence the 'Floor Top' reminder.)

The gunhouse floor is now ready to receive the guns and because it will be totally enclosed, all internal detail is omitted. Some heavy calibre guns have a 'blast bag', and this sleeve-like fitting effectively hides the passage of the barrel through the front face port. However, many have a mantlet plate, shaped as the segment of a circle whose centre is the trunnion axis, and this is the type drawn. A hole has to be drilled through the mantlet plate before it is curved to shape, and because it seriously weakens it, it is best made of light tinplate.

The safest way of dealing with this item is to make a simple wooden jig curved to the right radius. Cut a strip of tinplate wide enough to seal the port in the gunhouse and drill it to give a neat fit around the barrel at the correct distance from the muzzle. Snip off the tinplate leaving sufficient below and above the gun, and form the mantlet plate around the jig, taking care that it does not distort near the weak area of the hole.

Slip the mantlet plate over the muzzle and then, using the jig as a template, cut out two stiffeners and cement them to the gun body immediately behind the mantlet plate on each side. This design includes a short stub tube — the end of the non-recoiling cradle, in fact — which projects out from the mantlet plate and in which the barrel recoils. In large scale models this can be made from a tinplate sleeve, soldered along the seam underneath and on to the mantlet plate, but in smaller scales it is easier to simply bind a paper strip around the barrel, close up to the mantlet plate, starting and ending the binding under the gun barrel. Carry out this assembly on all the gun barrels (plus the 'spare').

Returning to the gunhouse floor, the guns now have to be correctly positioned, and the following procedure will ensure accuracy, the principle being to set the inboard part of the barrels into two simple supports. Mark the centre line on a sheet of, say, 20 thou plastic and on each, strike the gun centre lines exactly as has already been done on the gunhouse floor. Mark a line at right angles and drill two holes to suit the diameter of the inner part of the barrels. Below and above these two holes, mark a line the distance down from the hole-centre to the scale trunnion height. This is the 'trunnion support' and to one side of it, on the plastic sheet, draw in its end elevation. Using a protractor, strike down a line from

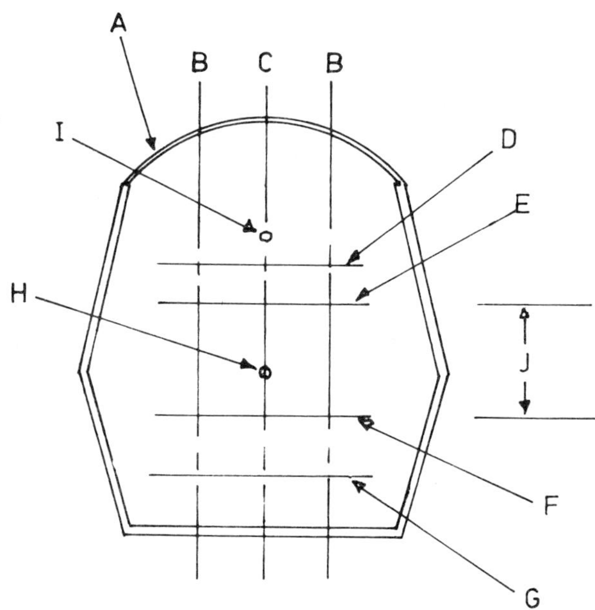

GUNHOUSE FLOOR

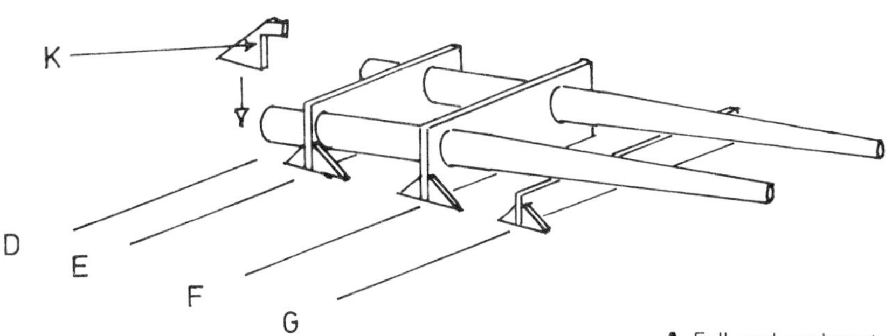

SCHEMATIC OF BARREL POSITIONING PROCEDURE

A Full and undercut profile **B** Gun centre line **C** Gunhouse centre line **D** Breech end line **E** Rear support **F** Trunnion support **G** Glacis support **H** Centre of rotation **I** Auxiliary alignment hole **J** Support spacing

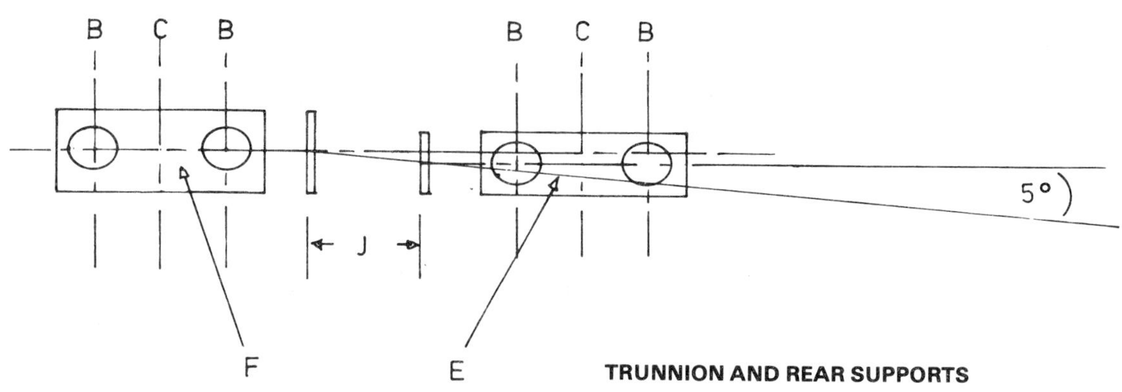

TRUNNION AND REAR SUPPORTS

the horizontal centre line to suit the stowage angle of the gun (5° elevation is common) and at some convenient distance mark a second elevation. This is an end elevation of the 'rear support'. Next to it, draw a front elevation, using the same centre line dimension and drill two similar holes. Clearly, they have dropped with respect to the holes in the trunnion support by the equivalent (in this case) of 5° provided that the distance is maintained, so mark this distance on the gunhouse floor to the rear of the trunnion support line. From these two master supports as many repeats as are required can be made following the procedure adopted for the gunhouse floor. Cement the trunnion and rear support onto the floor, aligning them to the marked centre and athwartships lines, slide the barrels into the support holes until the breech-ends align with the breech-end line and cement into position. (It may be necessary to chamfer off the underside of the barrels in the rear.)

Then, make up finger stops for the breeches, and stiffen up the front and rear supports with webs made from scrap. Finally add a glacis support immediately in front of the mantlet plates. The floor is now set into position on the barbette. A pin through the centre rotation hole will allow the mounting to train and it can be permanently secured by another pin through the second alignment hole. The next step is to cut and position the internal vertical webs which will support the sides, front and rear, and also the roof. Again, these must be undercut to compensate for the 40 thou floor and whatever thickness is used for the roof.

When it comes to the side plates, there is an extra requirement; to prevent the gunhouse looking lopsided, the angle of *opposite* side plates must be the same. Therefore, the webs are made in left and right pairs. The slope is set at an angle to the edge of the plastic sheet after this has been pinned down on the drawing board and squared with the T-square. Parallel lines drawn across the slope-line and spaced to internal webs height thus automatically give identical 'mirror images' for the left and right hand sides of the gunhouse. When parts become smaller like this, it is a good plan to mark them in a code — say *'A' F L* — to signify *'A' mounting Front Left Web,* and it should be done *before* the parts are cut out.

Because it is difficult to clamp up a large number of these webs in the vice, they need accurate cutting out. For this reason, firstly, make them from about 10 thou plastic sheet which a modelling knife or a single edged razor blade will cut straight through and, secondly, make several extra spares. These webs are cemented to the floor, flush with its bevelled edge and vertical to it. They are easily stiffened up with right-angle scrap plastic supports. The number of webs is a matter of choice, but at least one is necessary to support each plate. One at the front and rear centre lines is important, although in triple mountings the front web becomes a pair, set wide enough apart to clear the centre gun between them.

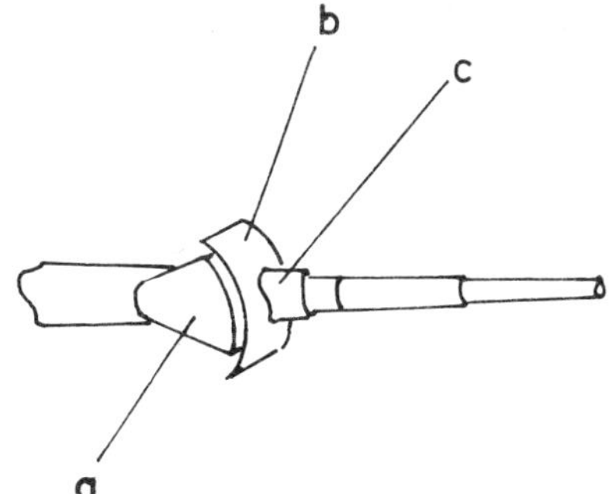

GUN BARREL ASSEMBLY

a Mantlet plate cheek support **b** Mantlet plate **c** Non-recoiling cradle tube

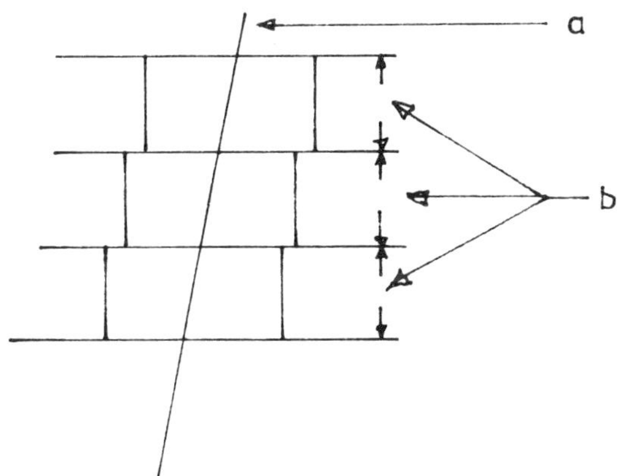

CONSTRUCTION OF SUPPORT WEBS FOR GUNHOUSE SIDE PLATES

a Side plate slope angle **b** Internal gunhouse floor-to-roof dimension

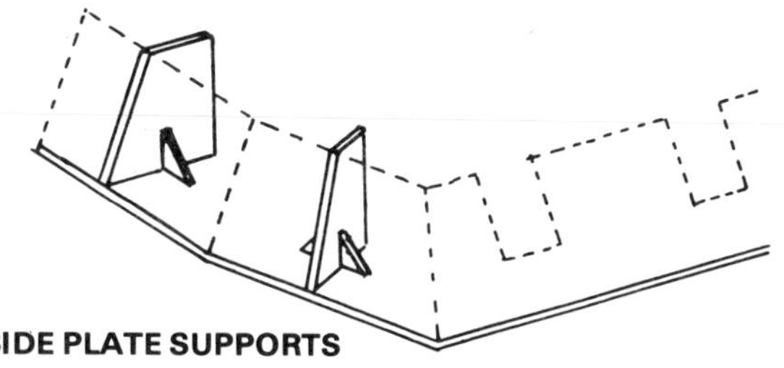

SIDE PLATE SUPPORTS

The gunhouse roof is next cut out and undercut exactly as was the floor and is cemented to the top of the webs. Then the rear plate is fitted, oversize for depth at top and bottom, followed by the front plate slotted for the barrels, using the fundamental centre lines. The slots should be undercut on the bottom and on each side by the thickness of the glacis and the side filling pieces. Trim down the front plate to the roof and floor levels, fit the glacis plates, resting on the internal glacis support and then the side cheeks.

(The mantlet plate jig can be used as a template for the side cheeks.) Make these pieces oversize for length and file them flush when they are in position.

Finally, plate up the sides, again filing down the edges flush with the gunhouse roof and floor, and bevelling vertical joints where necessary. If the undercutting has been accurately done the gunhouse will be restored to its true outer dimensions.

BARBETTES

The barbette is a non-rotating circular wall of armoured steel which is set between the underside of the rotating gunhouse and carried downwards below the armoured belt to protect the trunk, its ammunition hoists and the gun mounting machinery.

In most classes, little of this structure appears above deck level and it is thus easily made as a solid disc from any convenient material. It is important to include a central hole (and a fore-and-aft centre line) for eventual alignment to the deck and to receive the centering pin of the gunhouse. There is usually a weathering 'skirt' on the underside of the gunhouse floor overlapping the barbette and this may be either turned solid with the barbette itself, or added later as a wrapped-round strip.

Even when a gunhouse sits on a tall barbette, as in 'B' mounting of the Japanese *Takao* class cruisers, it is more practical to model it solid, than to attempt to construct a hollow circular drum.

Procedurally, it is easier to treat the barbette as part of the gunhouse than to fit it to the hull in the first instance. It makes work on the gunhouse easier and also provides a rotating 'adjustment' for perfect fore-and-aft alignment.

OPEN AND SHIELDED MOUNTINGS OF MEDIUM CALIBRE

The amount of detail that can be shown on these depends to a large extent on the scale and totally open mountings are the most difficult because everything is revealed.

Fortunately, however, most have gunshields of one kind or another, and these can be built in the same manner as the enclosed gunhouse. Often, 'sided' AA batteries on large warships are trained outboard in their stowed position when little, if anything, of the internal detail is visible.

Centre line guns on destroyers, on the other hand, need more attention and the relevant figure shows a typical side elevation. These guns are muzzle-heavy, but are counterbalanced in the rear and the easiest way to get the stowage angle correct is to make up a plate gauge and to trunnion the gun, following prototype practice.

A filling-piece is then cut to suit, on which the barrel rests. Note that the angle is to the mounting

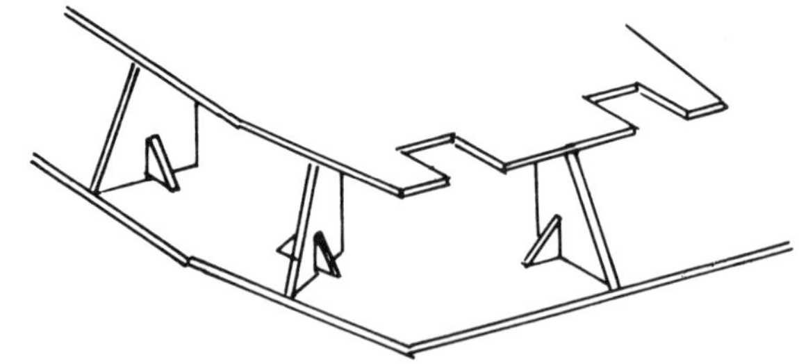

FRONT PLATE SUPPORT AND TURRET ROOF

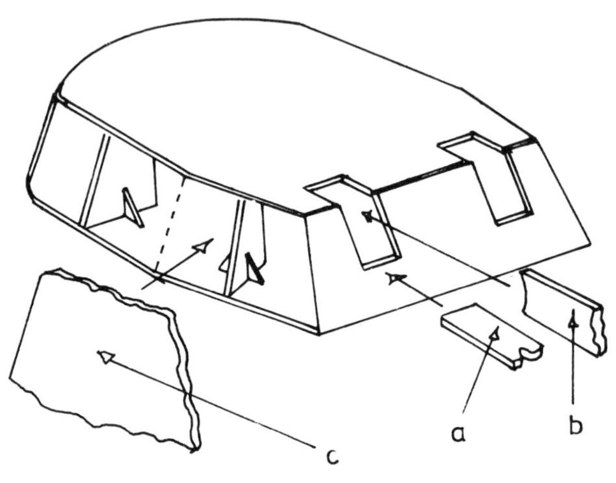

a Glacis plate **b** Gunport side cheek **c** Front left side plate

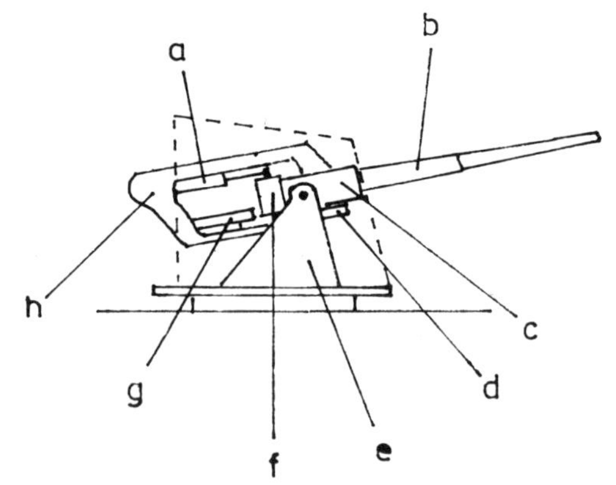

TYPICAL OPEN-SHIELD MOUNTING

a Recuperator cylinder **b** Jacket **c** Cradle **d** Recoil buffer cylinder **e** Trunnion support **f** Breech ring **g** Loading tray **h** Balance weight

Right: A very fine model of the quad 2pdr pompom, aboard Dave Sambrook's 1/96 scale 'Tribal' class destroyer *Ashanti.*
Below: The 4.7inch Mk XVIII destroyer mounting was typical of the designs of the 1930s. This is a gunshop photo before the gunshield was fitted. (MoD Navy)

floor, and *not* to the deck (which often follows an upward sheer, especially on the fo'c's'le): and the angle must take into account the taper of the barrel.

CLOSE RANGE WEAPONS

These may be totally open, or may have partial splinter shields, but in the scales likely to be adopted by the modeller, they are quite small when scaled down.

Only the fundamental features should be attempted, but alignment of multi-barrels is most important. The British 8-barrelled 2pdr is clearly one of the most complex equipments and one of the figures shows a method of construction.

Below: One of the most advanced and complex naval mountings of WWII, the twin Bofors Mk IV (Hazemeyer) presents difficulties to the modelmaker, especially since it is unshielded. (MoD Navy)
Right: A neat pair of Hazemeyers on a model of a 'Battle' class destroyer.
Opposite: The greatest 'scatter gun' of all time, the 8-barrelled Vickers 2pdr pompom, another challenge to the modeller. (MoD Navy)

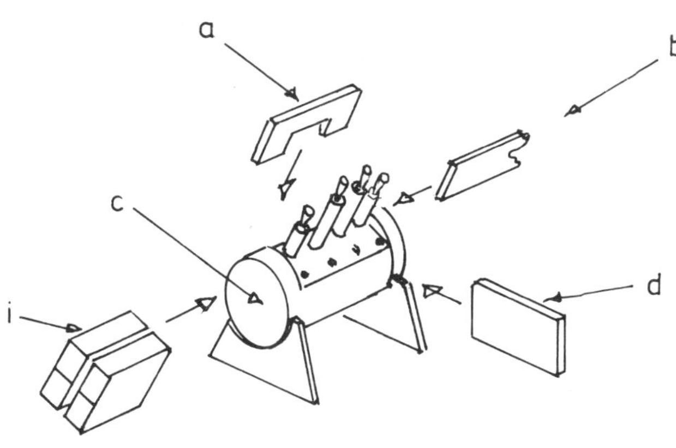

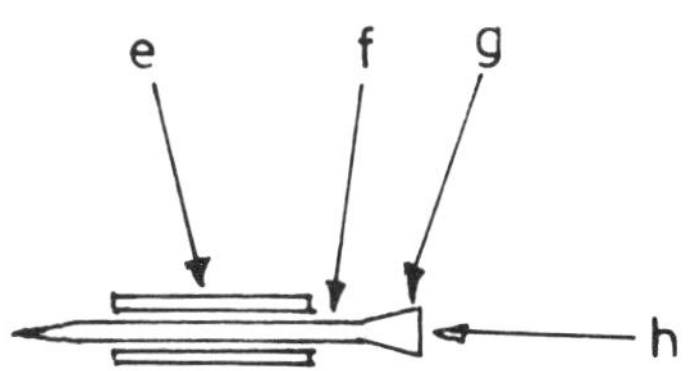

MULTIPLE 2 pdr construction
a Barrel-stagger gauge **b** Barrel vertical spacing gauge **c** Dowel cradle **d** Barrel lateral spacing gauge **e** Barrel lateral spacing gauge **e** Jacket from fine cable plastic sheathing **f** 'Bare-metal' chase **g** Flame guard, painted black, with red muzzle **h** Barrel from panel pin **i** Right hand ammunition hoppers

LIGHT WEAPONS

This term embraces a wide range of machine guns and their like and it is difficult to do other than generalise on their construction because so much depends on scale. A 20mm Oerlikon barrel is about one inch diameter at the muzzle, making it, of course, only 10 thou in 1/100th scale, so that one is already looking towards something like fuze wire as a suitable material. Few are able to model a capital ship in this scale and may be working to something like 1/125th or even smaller: but under such circumstances, don't omit these weapons. Model them simply in the most practical material even if they are, in fact, over-scale. Personal experience has proved that 8-barrelled pompoms with 5 amp fuze wire barrels can be included even in 1/1200th scale without looking unsightly.

DIRECTORS

The design of directors is as variable as that of the gun mountings they control and ranges from heavily armoured Director Control Towers closely resembling gun-less mountings, to shallow, open-topped circular bins. They are inherently smaller than their associated mountings and, depending upon scale, may be solidly modelled or built up, following gunhouse practice.

Sometimes, open AA directors are covered with a 'pram' style hood and this can cut out all the internal detail. Even in large scales the outward appearance can be admirable. Alternatively, they can be in the open state and include basic details.

GUNNERY RADAR AERIALS

Again, these are very variable and range from the 'cheese', which is the simplest to model, through the modern saucer-shaped scanner, to the WW II 'Yagi' or 'fishbone' array, each progressively more difficult to model. The hollow saucer shape is best left flat on the face (which makes production easier) but the 'Yagi' array reflector can be well modelled by making up a simple trough and fitting 'fishbone' aerials through prepared holes.

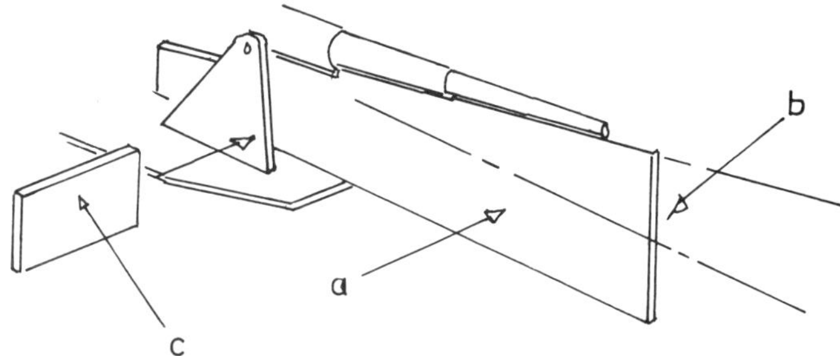

ELEVATION PLATE GAUGE
a Gauge cut to barrel profile **b** Stowage angle **c** Filler-piece across trunnion supports

TORPEDO TUBES

The overall length of a conventional 21in upper deck torpedo-tube was of the order of about 30ft, and how

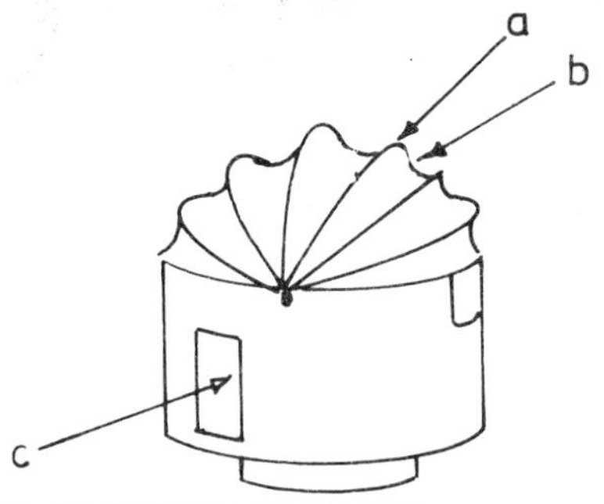

SOLID-MODELLED DIRECTOR
a Semi-circular webs **b** Filler, dressed with rat-tail file **c** Access door in closed position

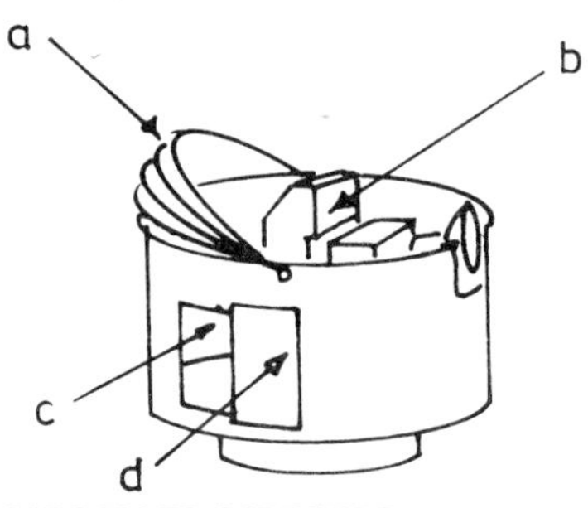

OPEN-MODELLED DIRECTOR
a Stack of open web hoops **b** Basic internal detail **c** Cut access in director side **d** Set door in open position

much detail is incorporated is not only a matter of scale, but also of position.

Groups of tubes in multiple mountings are prominent in many destroyer classes, but in cruisers the mountings are often under a shelter deck, when it is acceptable to detail only the outboard and visible tube and reduce such niceties on the inboard tubes.

Unlike gun barrels, torpedo-tubes are of thin-wall structure, and are frequently fabricated in flanged sections, bolted together. There may be several tube sections terminating in the outer one, known as the 'lip end'. This is chamfered on the underside to allow the torpedo to plunge into the sea as it leaves the tube, and must be modelled as a tube rather than in solid material, whatever the scale, unless one is down to plastic kit sizes. A very nice touch can be obtained by making the tube appear loaded. This is done by turning the tube solid, but terminating it in a torpedo of reduced diameter. Flanges can be incorporated at the same time and finally a hollow lip-end slid over the tube. Bringing the torpedo nose to a finished surface and painting it red (as a 'war-head') *before* fitting the lip-end gives an excellent appearance on the completed unit.

TYPICAL BRITISH DIRECTORS OF THE 1940s & 1950s

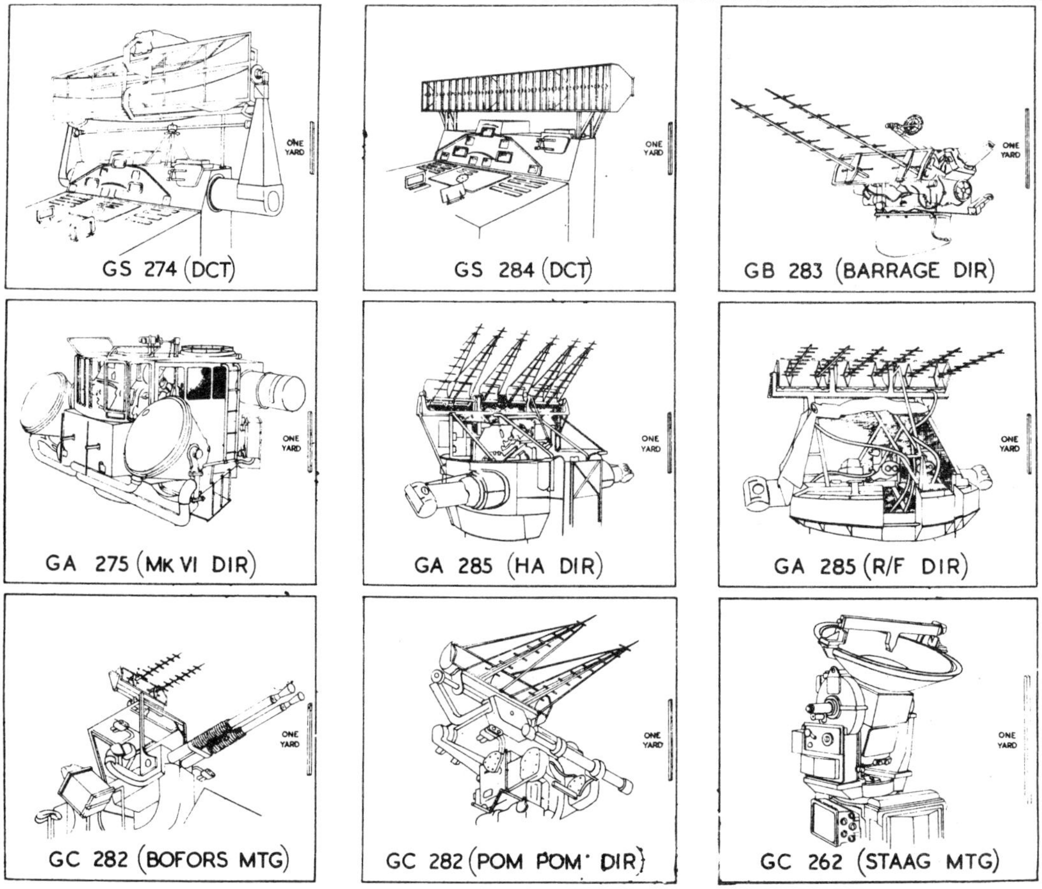

ONE YARD

GS 274 (DCT)

GS 284 (DCT)

GB 283 (BARRAGE DIR)

GA 275 (MK VI DIR)

GA 285 (HA DIR)

GA 285 (R/F DIR)

GC 282 (BOFORS MTG)

GC 282 (POM POM' DIR)

GC 262 (STAAG MTG)

(MoD Navy)

The pre-war Vickers .5inch machine gun mounting in which much faith was placed. It proved to be virtually useless against even early WWII aircraft and was easily surpassed by a single 20mm Oerlikon. (MoD Navy)

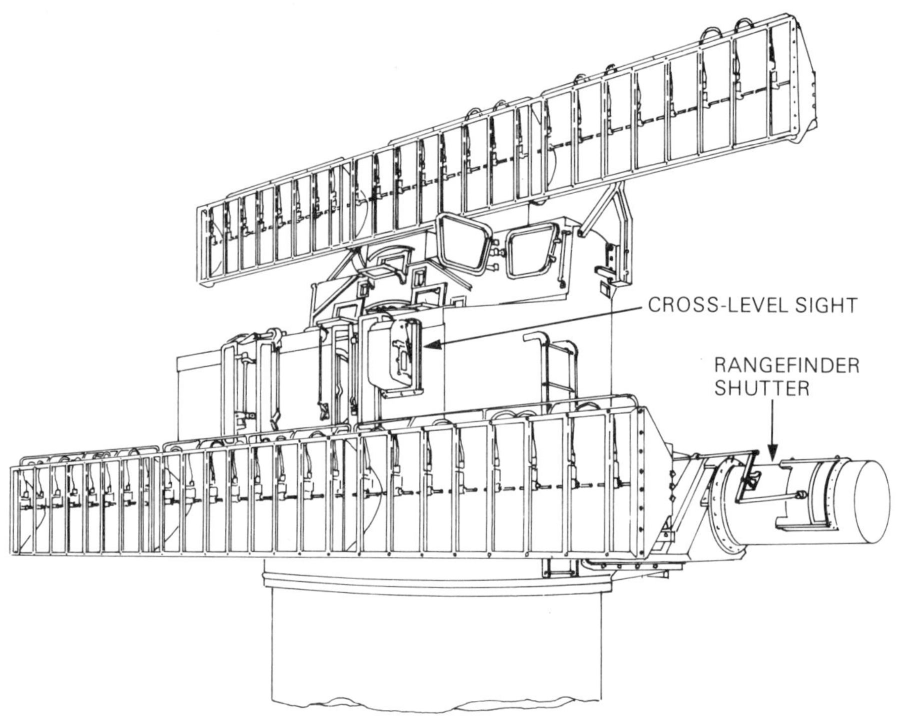

BRITISH CRUISER DCT WITH EARLY RADAR 284 AERIAL

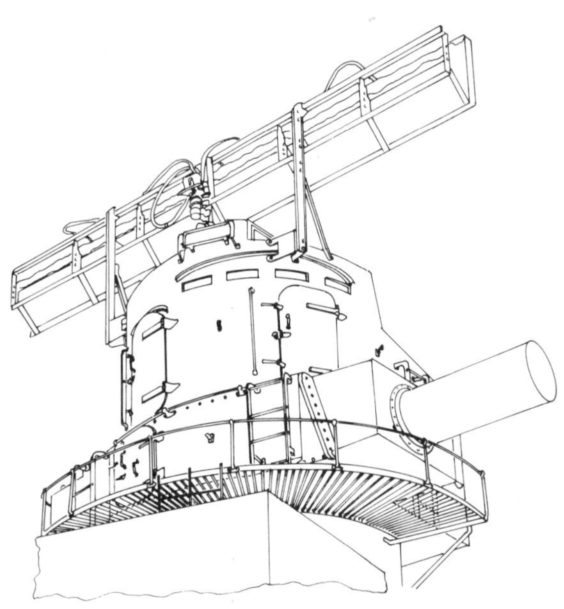

BRITISH CRUISER DCT (REAR) WITH FIXED RADAR 284 AERIAL, ABOUT 1943

Above: The 20mm Oerlikon was itself obsolete before the end of WWII and its mounting was adapted for heavier calibre guns. This is the stalwart Vickers 2pdr Mk VIII on the Mk XVI mounting. (MoD Navy)

Right: The American Mk 37 Director supplied to the British under wartime 'Lease-Lend' (together with its associated fire control computer). Both were superbly engineered and were held in the highest regard in the Royal Navy. (Anthony Peters)

Below: The twin 20mm Oerlikon Mk V mounting with the side plate of the aimer's cab removed to show the 'joystick' or 'scooter' control column. This mounting had hydraulic powering and was designed to give the high slewing speeds necessary to combat fast-flying aircraft at close range. (MoD Navy)

Torpedo-tube mountings are almost always open — although some have 'dustbin' control positions, with or without lid. They are much more simple devices than gun mountings and consist of a pivoted turntable on which the tubes are secured, surrounded by a skirt to protect the rollers. An explosion vessel shaped like a gas cylinder bottle is fitted to the rear of the tube, with a simple breech at one end.

Tube mountings are rarely other than hand-worked and generally have a training shaft straddling the tubes and terminating in hand cranks. The shaft is

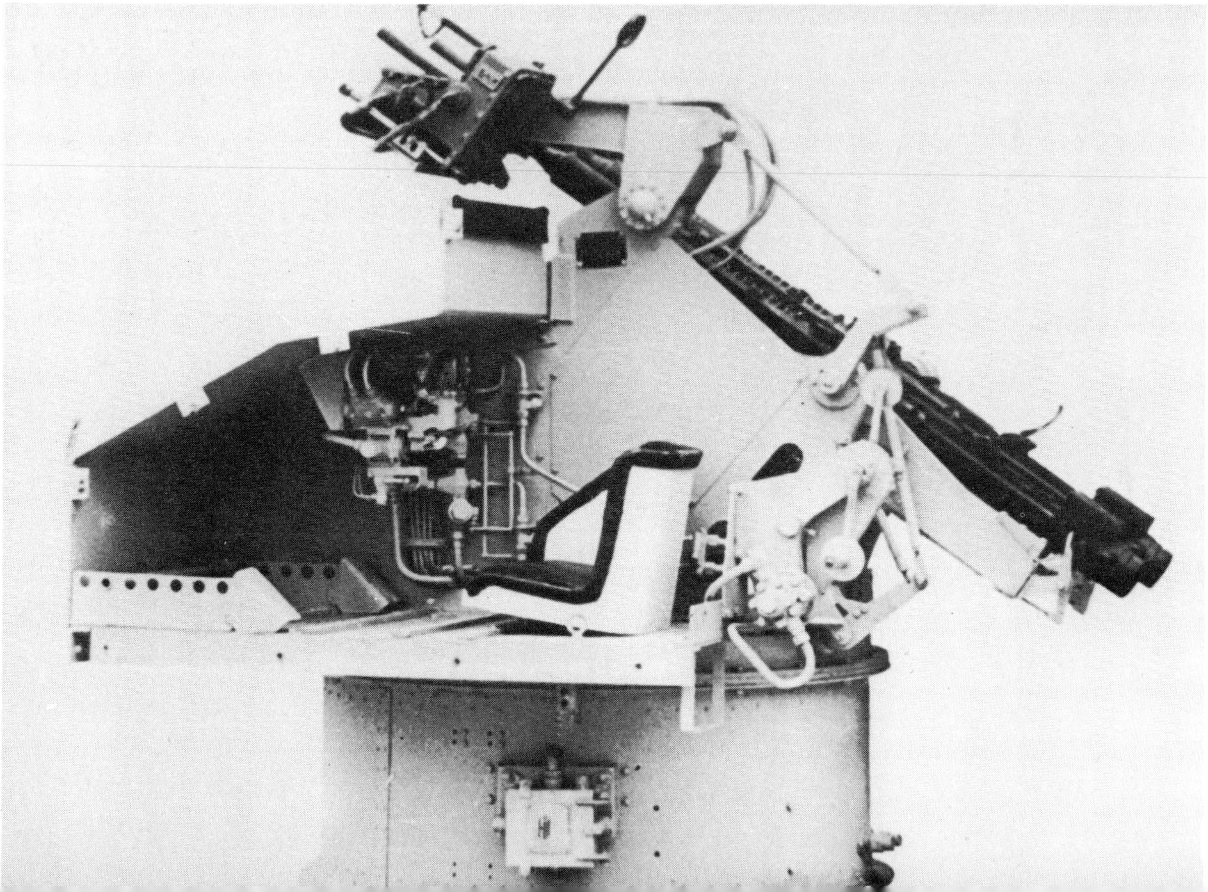

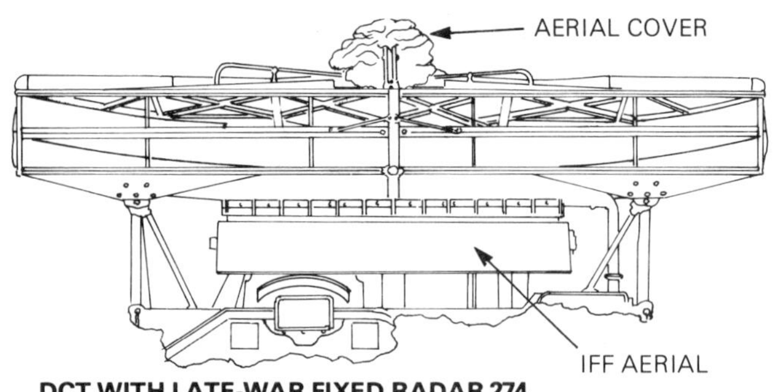

DCT WITH LATE-WAR FIXED RADAR 274 AERIAL AND IFF

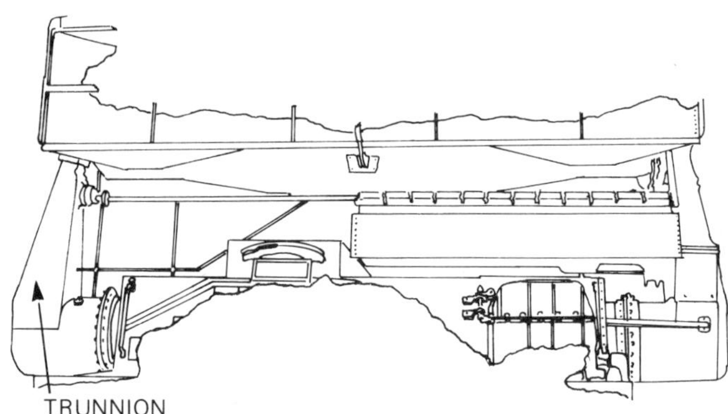

DCT WITH FINAL STABILISED RADAR 274 AERIAL AND CO-AXIAL IFF

HACS MK IV DIRECTOR, ABOUT 1943

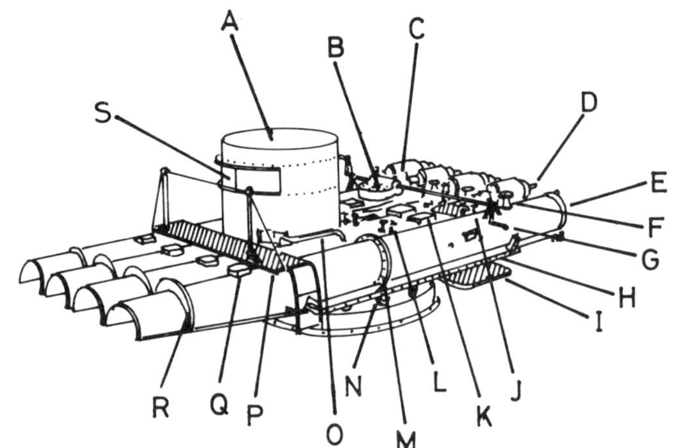

THE QR MK VIII* TORPEDO TUBE MOUNTING**

A Enclosed blast screen, housing Torpedo Deflection Sight and percussion firing levers. (Access door in rear) **B** Transfer gearbox to training pinion shaft **C** Explosion chamber **D** Cordite valve **E** Rear door **F** Set gyro angling handwheel **G** Tube training handcrank **H** 'Tube feet' girders, supporting torpedo tube **I** Trainer's platform **J** Set torpedo running depth handle **K** Distribution box for tube heater circuits **L** 'Top stop' and spring catch holding torpedo **M** Flange securing Rear and Lip Ends **N** Training roller **O** Cable trunking to Operator's position **P** Servicing platform **Q** Access flaps for torpedo pistols **R** Stiffening flange over Lip End **S** Sighting port shutters

easily made from wire appropriate to the scale and a nice touch is to add the brass hand-grips, using the yellow plastic insulation from fine electric wire. Always ensure that the rear door of the tube is domed, rather than flat.

The various tube fittings are simple but must be aligned tube-to-tube and it is best to complete the basic mounting and then add the fittings to a squared line marked across the top of the tubes themselves.

AIRCRAFT CATAPULTS

These devices vary considerably in both position and appearance. In early days of naval aviation they were often mounted on top of large calibre gunhouses, although re-siting the recovered aircraft — which were of course float-planes — often had to be done by a derrick.

Between-wars cruiser classes almost always included an aircraft catapult, usually on a turntable, and with an aircraft recovery crane (which doubled as a boat crane) close alongside.

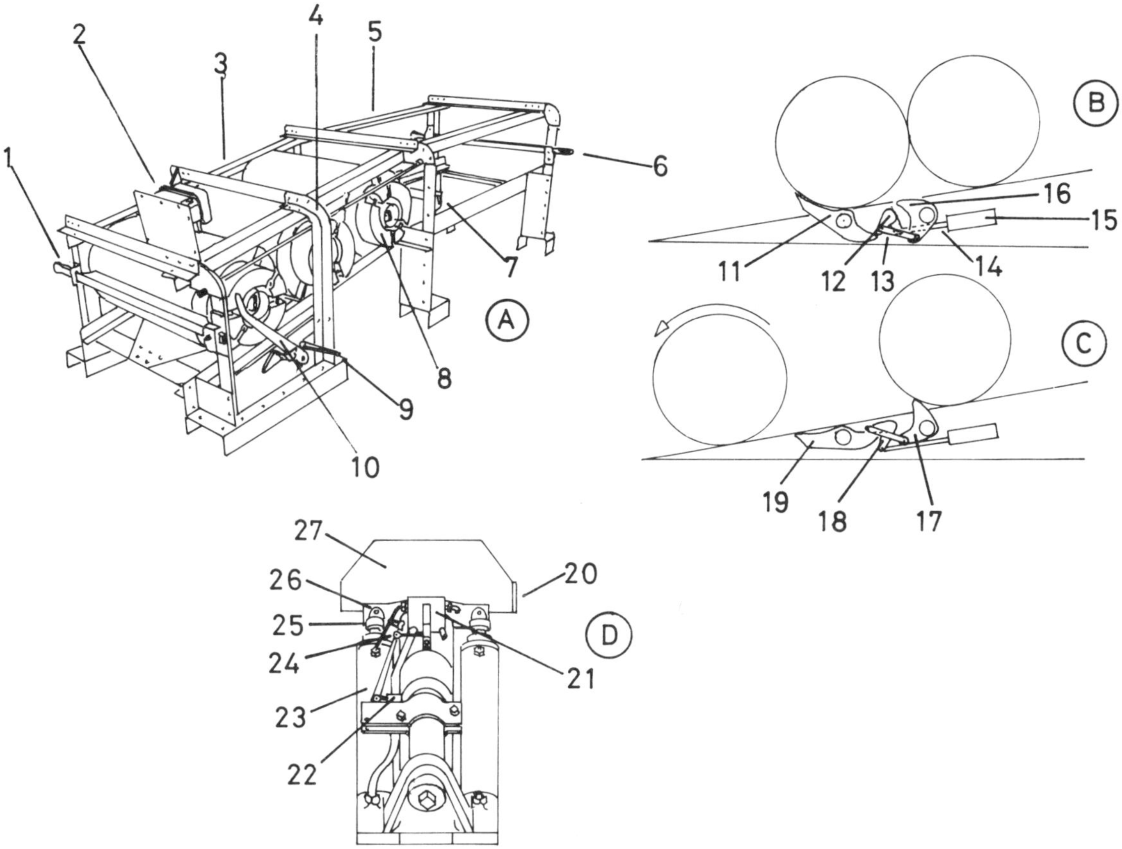

Depth Charge Discharge Arrangements

A 6-charge port rail
1 After stop-bar **2** Depth charge order receiver **3** 10 degree downward slope **4** 'Stand-out' of girders to clear ballast weight of heavy DCs **5** 1½ degree downward slope **6** Inboard stop-bar **7** Middle stop-bar **8** 150 pound ballast weight of heavy charge **9** Trap gear safety lever **10** Trap gear manual release lever

B Schematic of trap release gear
11 Rocking lever, holding outer depth charge **12** Actuating lever, holding rocking lever up **13** Link **14** Piston rod **15** Hydraulic cylinder **16** Resetting lever

C One charge release
17 Resetting lever, holding second charge **18** Actuating lever, moved by piston to release rocking lever **19** Rocking lever, depressed by weight of outer charge

D Depth charge thrower, Mk IV
20 Stop plate **21** Hydraulic buffer header tank **22** Hydraulic cylinder **23** Left hand buffer **24** Firing lever **25** Buffer piston **26** Cross-head **27** Depth charge tray

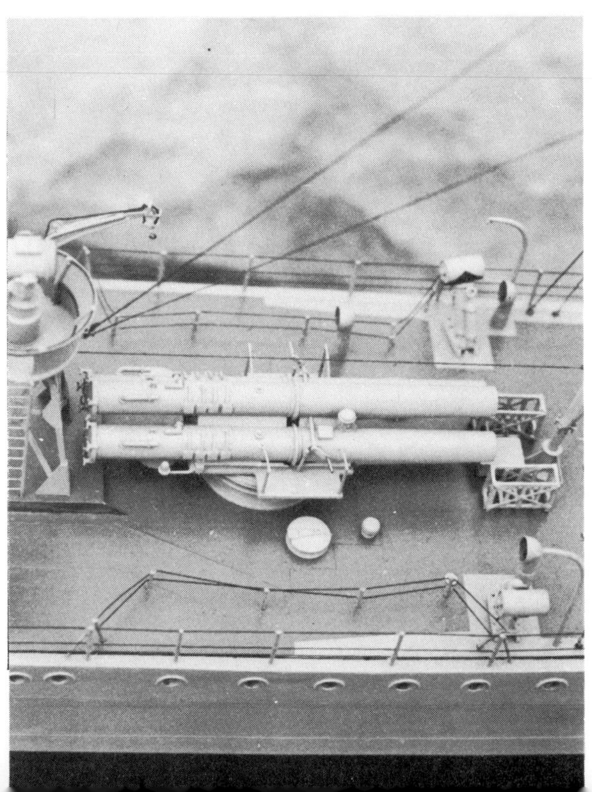

The after triple 21in torpedo-tubes and depth charge throwers on Don Brown's model of *Vendetta,* a British 'V & W' class destroyer.

These catapults were of girder construction, rather like a crane-jib, and it should be said immediately that it is worth any amount of extra work to model them thus, rather than make them 'solid', even if the lattice-work is reduced in complexity. (Polystyrene is a superb medium for such work and using it I have built lattice masts in 1/600th scale with excellent results.)

TYPICAL CATAPULT CONSTRUCTION AND CABLE LEADS

a Truck retracting - retarding cables **b** Aircraft release hooks **c** Shock absorbers **d** Wheeled truck **e** Truck launching cable **f** Anchor point for retracting cable **g** Anchor point for launching cable **h** Hydraulic or pneumatic cylinder on turntable **i** Piston rod **j** Sliding cross-head **k** Twin independent pulleys on cross-head (lower arrow indicates direction of movement to launch)

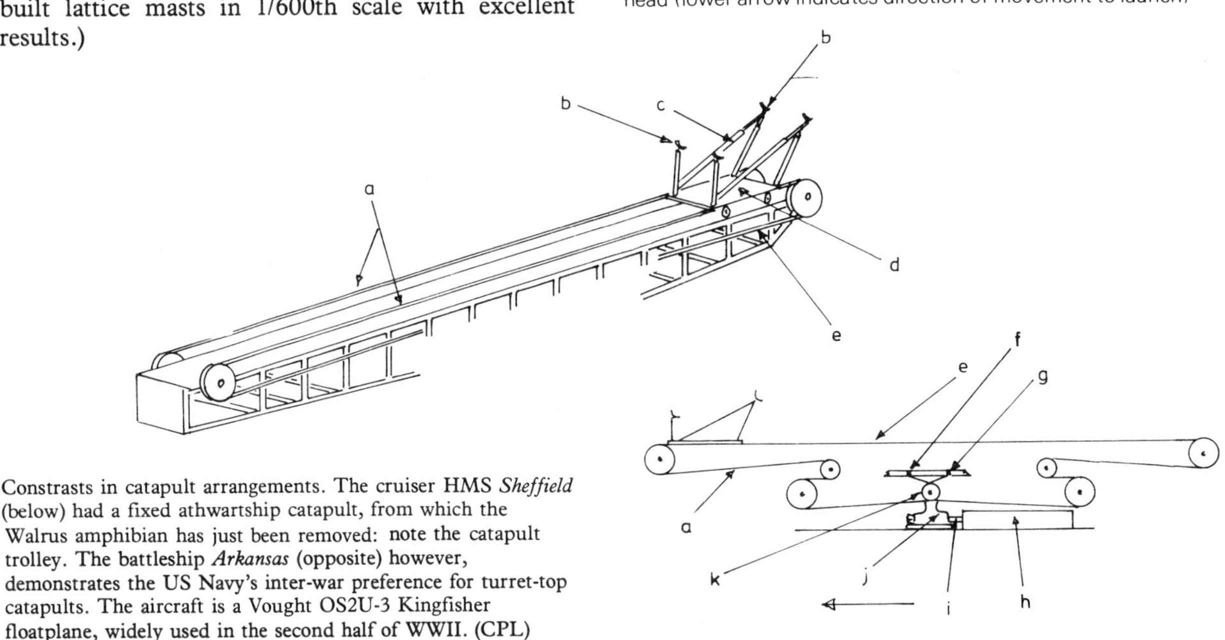

Constrasts in catapult arrangements. The cruiser HMS *Sheffield* (below) had a fixed athwartship catapult, from which the Walrus amphibian has just been removed: note the catapult trolley. The battleship *Arkansas* (opposite) however, demonstrates the US Navy's inter-war preference for turret-top catapults. The aircraft is a Vought OS2U-3 Kingfisher floatplane, widely used in the second half of WWII. (CPL)

A wheeled truck, like a inverted four-legged table, carried the aircraft and ran on trackways on top of the catapult structure. The truck was connected by cables to the launching power unit which might be either hydraulic or pneumatic.

Some classes — notably the British *King George V* class battleships and the *Town* and *Colony* class cruisers — had an in-built beam catapult between the funnels which revealed only the cables, truck and trackways, making for easy modelling; and it is worth pointing out that the aircraft in these classes — normally a 'Walrus' amphibian — could only be launched to starboard, since this was the direction of catapult thrust.

In aircraft carriers, whether with hydraulic- or steam-powered catapults, there was little or no restriction on the length of the single trackway, through which a sliding 'shoe' moved. A wire strop hooked to the shoe and to the aircraft literally slung it into the air.

PAINTING

In general, the paint scheme of gunhouses and directors follows that of the parent ship including, where applicable, the camouflage scheme (when the roof was often painted to 'deck colour' paint). Barrels may be similarly treated, but are sometimes black in smaller calibres — 4.5in and below — and in British close range AA weapons it is common practice in peacetime to paint the inside of conical muzzle 'flame guards' a bright red. Moving parts, like the recoiling chase and the mantlet plate are *not* painted and are left as lubricated bare metal, as is often the muzzle band — except in wartime. The inside of gunshields is normally painted white and the British practice is to paint all oscillating parts — like the elevating mass, the loading trays and so on — a signal red.

SOURCES

The weapon equipment of a warship is subject to considerable change throughout her active life and modelling a vessel at a particular period in her lifetime needs the most careful research. Total reliance cannot be placed even on such draughtsman as the late Norman Ough, who often depicted an incorrect barrel 'stagger' in multiple pompom mountings and sometimes included close range AA weapons that were totally inconsistent with the ship class (see Chapter 1).

However, the majority of his work (which was taken from the offical Admiralty 'As Fitted' drawings) is excellent and gives a wide range of gun mountings, directors, torpedo-tubes and so on. Museums are a superb source, particularly in ship building centres,

The importance of good reference photos cannot be over-stated. For example, these two close-ups of the Seaslug missile director (below) and its complex twin launcher (opposite) would be invaluable to anyone modelling a first-group *Devonshire* class DLG. (CPL. All uncredited photos by John Bowen)

where the shipbuilder often presents a model of one of his productions.

Contemporary photographs are invaluable, especially in showing the multitude of close range weapons which were added to all classes during World War II; and the ability to *recognise* particular weapons is well worth developing.

Other centres which may provide help in serious research into British weapon equipments are the Naval Historical Branch at Whitehall; The Priddy's Hard Weapon Museum at Gosport, Hants, and the Director General Weapons (Navy) at Bath, and other addresses can be found in Chapter 1.

In conclusion, remember that weapons are the raison d'etre of the warship; everything else is subsidiary to them. Even if their modelled portrayal is slightly out-of-scale or slightly incorrect, provided they are all identical in appearance and alignment, they will serve the modeller as well as did their real-life counterparts serve those who maintained, controlled and manned them.

Deck fittings 6

by DON BROWN

It is in the area of fittings that the modeller can display his skill and ingenuity to the widest extent, since the scope of the items to be produced is legion, and they are such an important feature in the final appearance of a model.

Perhaps because of their variety they are the items for which accurate information is most elusive; drawings are produced for the modeller giving reasonably accurate details of hull and basic superstructure shapes but, with the possible exception of the late Norman Ough's, none appears to offer a reasonably comprehensive range of drawings of fittings. The other major source of drawings for the modeller, official 'as fitted' drawings, are excellent to show the location and overall size of fittings, but the item concerned is usually indicated in a very basic manner as the draughtsman knows that separate detailed drawings of the units will be prepared; but these latter drawings are not usually available.

For these reasons it is essential to obtain photographs in order that accurate model fittings can be manufactured. Obviously photographs of your chosen subject are to be preferred, but photographs of other vessels of the same class, or indeed similar classes of the same period, can be most useful.

TOOLS

I feel, at this point, a brief word about tools would not be out of place; most modellers possess, or are well aware of the uses of, small pin vices, drills, needle files, etc, but some other tools not quite so popular are most useful. The first of these is a piercing saw, being a light frame similar to a small fretsaw which can take a variety of blades, again similar to fretsaw blades, all of which, down to the finest, are intended for cutting metal. For fine sawing, where a piercing saw is too big to use, a jeweller's slitting file is most useful; this is a thin blade some 3in long and $\frac{1}{4}$in wide with fine toothed edges.

To hold delicate items, a small hand vice is indispensable; these can be obtained with jaws no more than 5/8in wide and can, of course, themselves be held in a bench vice if both hands are required for working on a piece. Finally, a pair of spring bow dividers is an excellent tool for scribing and setting out small work pieces.

WEIGHT-SAVING

In the construction of working scale model warships, particularly destroyers, it is imperative to keep the weight of all superstructure and fittings to an absolute minimum in order to achieve stability; whilst not so essential with other types of vessel of a larger displacement, it is desirable. It is much better to have to ballast a model down to her marks rather than have a model which sits too low in the water or is so tender that she does not perform in a realistic manner on the water. Generally speaking brass fittings should be avoided, unless for some reason it is important that components be soldered, or you require the fitting to be polished. Not only for reasons of weight, but also because I find aluminium alloys nice to work I recommend their use wherever possible for fittings. Even then, hollow construction with sheet metal should be employed wherever possible, rather than solid construction. It is not usually considered practical to solder aluminium, but parts may be put together satisfactorily with an epoxy resin adhesive. I am often asked if it is not difficult to produce small fittings which are not smeared with surplus adhesive when using an epoxy resin; of course, one keeps the amount of adhesive used down to a minimum, but there is a time during the setting of the adhesive before it has become rock hard when surplus can be cut away and the fitting be cleaned up before being put aside for the final set.

With most fittings it is simpler, and the results are cleaner, if the fittings or sometimes even part of a fitting, are painted before assembly. To this end, and indeed to facilitate repainting or repairing, I recommend that fittings be bolted on to a model and not permanently fixed. For this purpose 10 BA or 12 BA studding can be cut to a suitable length and fixed to the back or underside of a fitting for securing in place with a small nut. Box spanners are made for these small sizes but since they are usually of fairly bulky proportions the ends should be turned down in the lathe in order that they may be used in restricted locations. Fittings generally fall into three groups, according to the best method of construction, or type of material used; sheet metal fittings, wire fittings and turned fittings. In the following paragraphs examples of these types are given which, although they describe

Below: A very good example of the 'reference' type photograph. There is a wealth of detail here and shots of this quality and type are of inestimable value to the modelmaker: the cruiser USS *Honolulu* at Mare Island, California, January 1942. (Photo: USN)

D69

Opposite and above: HMS *Vendetta,* a 1/96 scale *V & W* class destroyer by Don Brown. This model is notable not only for the standard of craftsmanship but for the amount of detail incorporated in the multiplicity of fittings included on this 39in (1 metre) working model.
(Photos: John Bowen)

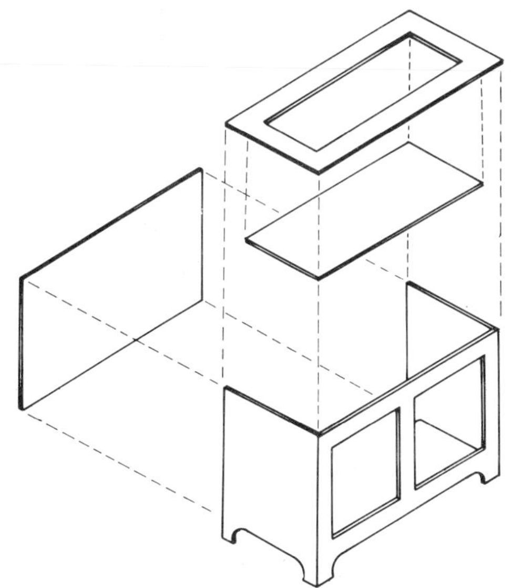

LOCKER (FIRST TYPE)

specific methods which I have found satisfactory, are really intended to illustrate the general approach to any fitting you may find it necessary to make.

SHEET METAL FITTINGS

A simple sheet metal fitting which adds greatly to the appearance of a model is the watertight door. Here the door is cut to shape with the recessed panels cut out and mounted on a back plate which projects all the way round the door to represent the frame. Whilst not altogether satisfactory at small scale, at larger scales the recessed panels only should be painted with a fairly thick paint which will produce a coved fillet around the edges of the panel; then, when the whole is painted with a fine paint of the correct colour, the panels will appear dished as in fact they are.

One of the most common fittings on warships are ready-use ammunition lockers; they occur in many different shapes, and two typical examples are described below. For all lockers where two or more of a given size are required a block should be filed up from scrap metal for bending the body around to obtain uniformity.

The first type of locker usually backs onto the superstructure and comprises a front and two ends bent out of thin flat sheet, the bottom edges being filed away to form feet, the panels cut out with a piercing saw trimmed up with a needle file and

FREE STANDING LOCKER

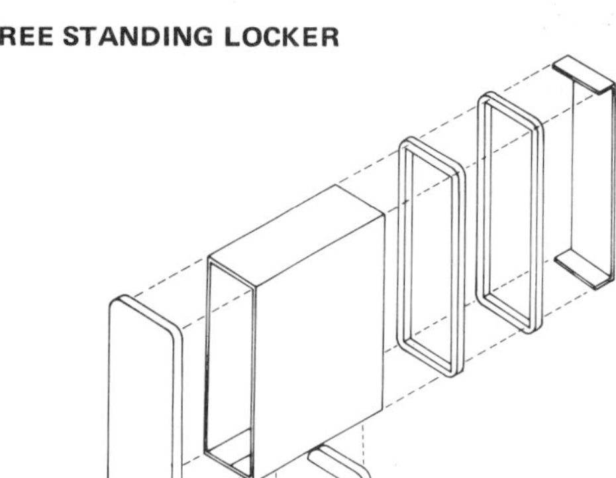

CIRCULAR HATCHES

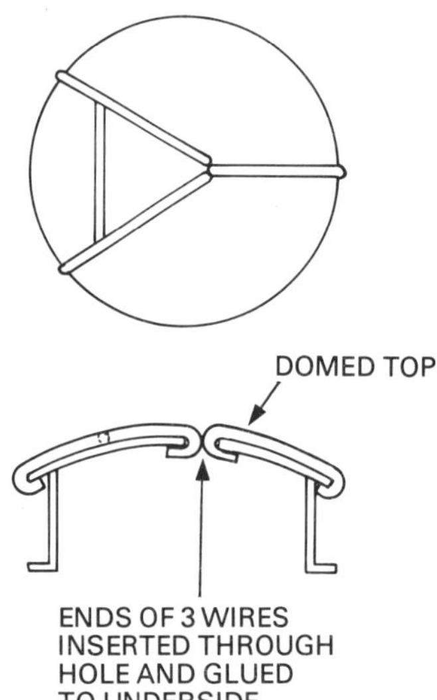

Opposite: Another model which catches the eye for detail work, particularly on the many close range weapons. The American cruiser USS *Tucson* at 1/32in = 1ft scale (1/384) by Eric Dyke.
(Photos: John Bowen)

backed by a further piece of sheet glued into place to form the panels. The top is similarly constructed and glued on with a small projection all round. Meat lockers can be made in similar manner, but with nylon mesh, cut from a coffee strainer, in place of the flat panels.

The second type of locker is best made as a free standing unit with fixing stud projecting on the underside; the top, bottom and sides are again bent up from thin sheet with a 'U' shaped panel glued in flush to form one end. The other end is cut from fairly thick sheet and glued on to project all round. The intermediate ribs are formed from metal of the same thickness as the larger end panel, a rectangular hole is cut and filed up to be a snug fit over the body of the locker, after which the outside is filed down to the same size as the larger panel. Small strips are finally glued across the bottom to form feet.

Flag lockers can usually be constructed in a similar manner to ready-use amunition lockers and look most attractive if, instead of being made with the front canvas covers down, they have a small 'egg crate' of aluminium strips inserted to represent the pigeon holes for the flags.

Rectangular deck hatches also follow the previously described construction but the circular hatches on the weather deck of a destroyer are worthy of mention. If a suitable piece of tubing or an eyelet is not available for the base it is necessary to turn one in the lathe, in which case it should be complete with a small flange on the base end. The slightly domed top is formed by placing a small piece of sheet metal over the end of a suitably sized tube and then lightly hammering the dome end of a bifurcated rivet over the hole to shape the sheet; after filing circular, it is glued on to the top of the base ring. The uniquely shaped hinge can be formed by glueing three lengths of copper wire into a hole drilled through the domed top; after the glue has set they are bent down onto the top and the outer ends bent under the projecting edge to secure them. Finally, a short cross piece of wire is glued into the 'V'.

WIRE FITTINGS

Stanchions are one of a number of items which cannot be suitably made from aluminium. For larger scales a common method is to bend up half round brass strip over a former to form stanchions similar to hair grips, but with half round projections on each leg to form holes for the rails. For 1/8in scale however I consider these stanchions to be rather clumsy, and prefer to use 28 thou brass pin wire; a slit is cut in the end using a pin vice as a saw guide and small notches are cut with two or three strokes of a piercing saw on the side of the stanchion for each of the intermediate rails. Uniformity of the location of these slits is

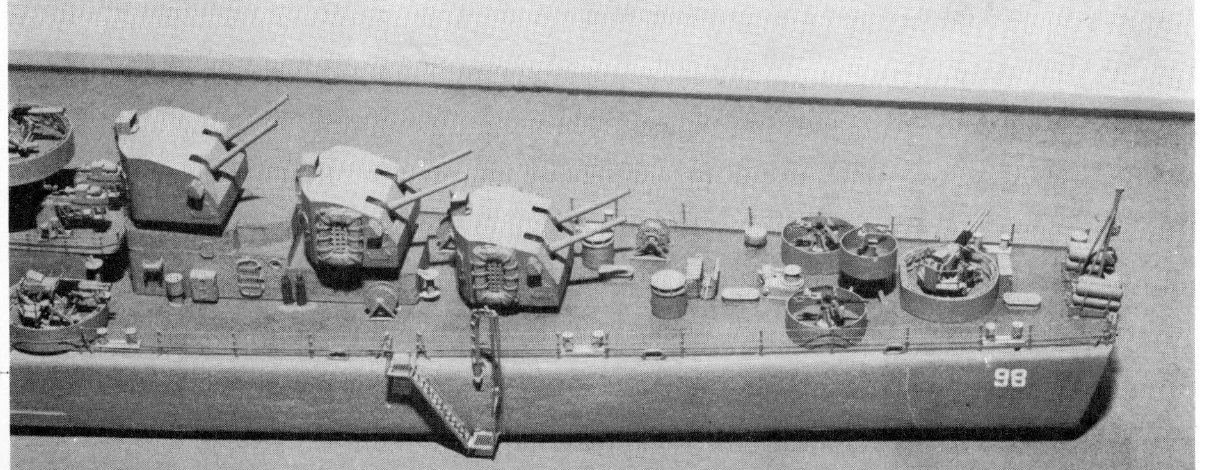
98

ensured by using short lengths of tube cut as gauges to regulate the amount of wire projecting from the pin vice, and then cutting the slit tight up against the jaws. Finally a notched piece of plate should be cut to use as a jig for setting the stanchions to an even height in holes drilled in the deck.

Rails can be thick nickel wire (say 9 thou for 1/8in scale) soldered into the slits using wet cotton wool around the base of the stanchion to prevent damaging the glued joint of the stanchion into the deck. This type of rail, however, has the disadvantage that it is easily damaged if hit, and tends to stretch when bent. On a working model I find nylon fishing line makes a more satisfactory rail; it can be fixed under slight tension with one of the rapid setting cyanoacrylate adhesives, and has the advantage that it recovers if knocked or stretched.

One item which looks most attractive, particularly if made in polished brass, is the hand rail around the superstructure, and it is not as difficult to construct as it may appear at first. The brackets are again made out of hard brass pin wire. I use 40 thou for 1/8in scale and it is necessary to drill a hole through the wire for the rail, say 25 thou or 28 thou. This is done by filing a slight depression across the wire with a round needle file to form a surface on which the drill can be started and, holding the wire in a pin vice and using a fine numbered drill in a second pin vice, it can be drilled through. The first four or five attempts may be unsuccessful, the drill either running out completely, or running so far off centre as to be useless. However, one suddenly gets the knack, and thereafter only about one in four are unsatisfactory. The end brackets, of course should not be drilled right through and it is sensible to make them first since, if by mistake you do drill through, then they can be used as intermediates.

The next step is to shape the bracket. Using a washer of thickness equal to the clearance required between handrail and superstructure, and with a temporary pin through the hole, the bracket is positioned in the lathe chuck and then shaped with a needle file. The edge of a half round file forms the neck very nicely, and the round head is then simple.

Access or cat ladders are another variation on wire working. Having decided what size the strings of the ladders should be, say 20 thou thick and 40 thou wide, a somewhat wider strip, about 60 thou wide, is cut off the edge of some 20 thou brass sheet with a piercing saw, having previously made a fairly deep scribe line down the centre of the strip. After cutting off two lengths, somewhat longer than required, a hole is drilled through on the scribe line near one end in the location require for the first rung (say 15 thou for 1/8in scale). Since a lot of work with a fine number drill in a pin vice is necessary, this may be a suitable place to mention that a large drawing pin, placed in the outer end of the pin vice, not only prevents a sore hand but also gives one much greater control of the pressure exerted and hence cuts down the number of breakages. One drill of each of the finer sizes is useless; if you have one drill, you break it first time, but if you have a package of ten, the first one lasts for ages!

To get back to the ladder — your spring bow dividers should now be set to the centres of the rungs and, placing one point in the hole already drilled, the position of the next hole is marked and drilled, and so on, for the full length of the string. The two strings are now put together and fixed with a small dab of solder on each end and using the first string as a jig, the second is drilled; the outsides of the holes on both strings are next countersunk to provide a recess for the solder fixing the strings, and lastly the two are unsoldered, ready for assembly.

I like nickel wire for the rungs; unpainted it resembles steel, but if you intend to paint the whole ladder, brass can be used. The rungs are cut somewhat longer than required from wire the same diameter as the drill, and the two end rungs are inserted through the holes in the string. Using small blocks to maintain a parallel width between the strings, the end rungs are soldered on the outside. Make any adjustments necessary to get the whole square and parallel, and then solder in the remaining rungs.

At this stage the ladder looks very crude, and I start to tidy it up: it is first rubbed on the face of the file, turning over side for side and end for end frequently, until the strings are brought down to the required width (in this case 40 thou). Next, holding the strings in a small hand vice, the projected ends of the rungs are carefully cut off and the string once again rubbed on a file to finish off the outer face.

There are many items of equipment on a warship constructed from metal angles, from lattice masts down to depth charge rails; the larger items are perhaps best made from brass angle and the smaller from aluminium angle, but a combination can be very useful. Taking depth charge rails as an example, the two sides can be constructed separately from brass angles soldered together over a wooden former, and to prevent melting these joints when adding the cross framing between the two halves, these latter members should be fixed with an epoxy adhesive.

Perhaps a word about the fabrication of small angles would be useful. I have found it practical to produce angles down to 25 thou x 25 thou of 9 thou substance. Vice jaws are not usually sufficiently accurate to bend over; I use two lengths of 1in x $\frac{1}{4}$in bright mild steel fitted with nuts and bolts to form a clamp. The piece of the metal to be bent is clamped between the steels leaving a strip projecting slightly wider than the required width of the angle flange, and this is bent over with a further length of steel the full length of the clamp; by bending the whole length in this manner in one operation it prevents stretching the metal of one flange which, if it occurred, would result in a curved length of angle difficult to straighten. After removing the sheet from the clamp the required width of flange is scribed on the turned edge with dividers, and the surplus cut off with a piercing saw. Using a piece of metal of a thickness equal to the desired inside dimension of the angle, the sheet is held down on a block with this metal and the flange filed down flush. The other flange of the angle is then scribed, cut off the parent sheet, and filed up as before. On very small angles it is rather difficult filing up this second flange but with patience, and a small ledge formed on the support block as a stop to push against, it can be achieved. This may sound a rather laborious method of producing angles, but the result is vastly superior to that obtained by trying to bend metal where one or both of the flanges have been previously cut to width.

HAND RAIL BRACKETS

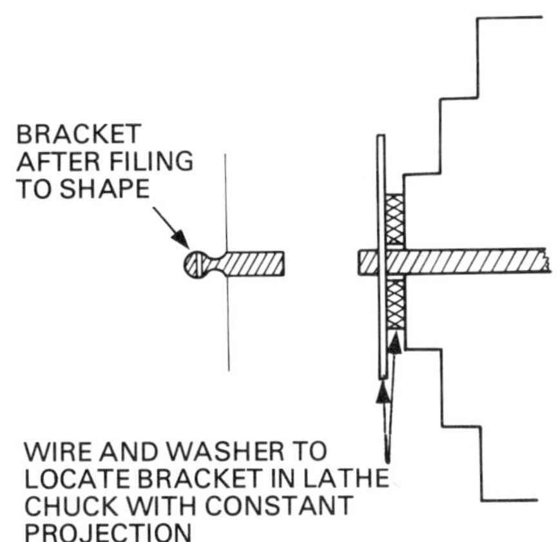

ACCESS LADDERS

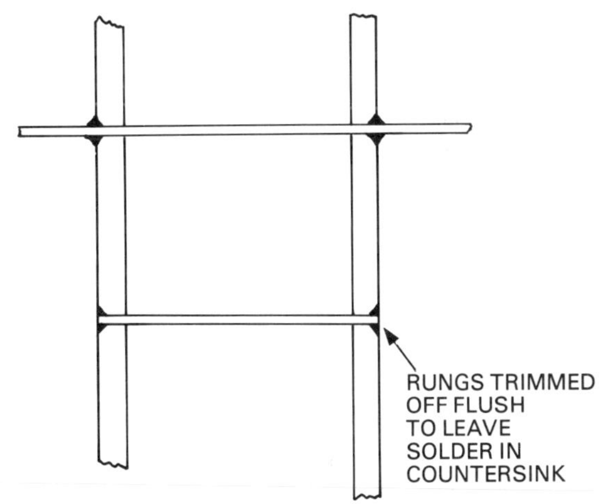

TURNED FITTINGS

A considerable number of fittings, such as mushroom vents, W/T trunks, pelorus, standard compass, etc are best made by turning in the lathe. I like to work from one end of a piece, making separate pieces to fit together rather than cutting grooves; a fairly simple example is a small gun or searchlight pedestal.

Composite recessed shapes, such as occur in a capstan, are again simpler to build up. The rectangular pockets in the top for the ends of the capstan bars can be produced by filing notches in the edge of a thick disc and then adding thinner top and bottom discs, projecting slightly or flush, dependent on the result required.

Warping drums are similarly constructed; a core is turned, slit vertically at regular intervals, and finished off with a disc top and bottom. The chain gypsy requires five pieces — a central spacer, two star shaped washers, and two plain discs.

Depth charges illustrate a useful combination of turned and sheet metal work. They should be cut from lengths of slightly undersized rod with the ends turned down to leave a small raised boss in the centre to represent the fuse; small sinkings or rings may be added at this stage to represent the lifting rings. To complete the depth charge a wrapping of very thin sheet (say 5 thou lithoplate) slightly longer than the body, is glued on. This sheet is nipped with pliers to make a close fit around the body and should be held with strong clips until the glue has set; finally, the surplus sheet is trimmed off. If carefully carried out the joint can be very difficult to detect but in any case the depth charge should be mounted with the joint concealed. The depth charge thrower itself is built up from turned pieces with filed up brackets and base plates.

BOATS

Ships' boats provide a complete change in construction from other types of fittings, and are most varied. All types of boats of clinker construction can be made over a carved mould which, for preference, should be in two halves. It is obviously more satisfactory to carve the mould in one piece, and I therefore dowel two small blocks together. When done in this manner the joint line is most useful in getting the keel and stem straight.

The two halves are planked separately with overlapping strips of gummed paper, the strips being

CAPSTAN

CAPSTAN	DIA. (thousandths ")	THK
SHAPED TOP WASHER	370	20
WASHER NOTCHED FOR CAPSTAN BARS	350	40
PLAIN WASHER	370	10
SLOTTED WARPING DRUM	280 to 350	200
PLAIN WASHER	370	20
"STAR" GYPSY WASHER ϕ	260	30
SPACER	125	30
"STAR" GYPSY WASHER ϕ	260	30
PLAIN WASHER DRILLED AND FITTED WITH WIRE PAWLS	370	40
PLAIN WASHER FIXED TO DECK	445	20

ϕ NOTE: CORNERS OF "TEETH" TO BE SLIGHTLY ROUNDED

turned round the end of the mould and stuck to the back to secure them. After completely planking one side it should be given one or two coats of thinned varnish to stiffen it up, after which the turned back ends are trimmed off flush with the flat side of the mould, and the half shell can then be removed. In fact, this is the most difficult part of the procedure, even though the outer part of the mould may have been well waxed. I usually find it necessary to jiggle about with a strip of fuse wire to part the shell from the mould without damage. It has been suggested to me, although I have no personal experience of the idea, that a layer of aluminium kitchen foil, or plastic film, can be used to prevent the paper from sticking to the mould.

After the two half shells have been made, it is necessary to cut out a combined keel and stem and stern (if the boat has no transom) from a piece of aluminium sheet. This unit should be cut to the profile of the inner line of the keel etc, and no attempt should be made at this stage to cut to the outer profile.

The two halves of the shell can now be glued to the keel member with one or two small dabs of glue; when satisfied with the location, and after the glued dabs have set, a small continuous fillet of glue can be run full length inside. However it is important to use an epoxy resin, or similar glue, as one which shrinks or exerts any pull may distort the shells.

A narrow strip of veneer can now be glued in for the gunwale, and gummed paper ribs stuck in between gunwale and keel; although sometimes less than 1mm wide, these ribs add tremendously to the strength of the boat.

The boat may now be fitted out and thwarts etc added. It is at this stage that one appreciates not having cut the stem and keel to profile since the boat

DEPTH CHARGE AND THROWER

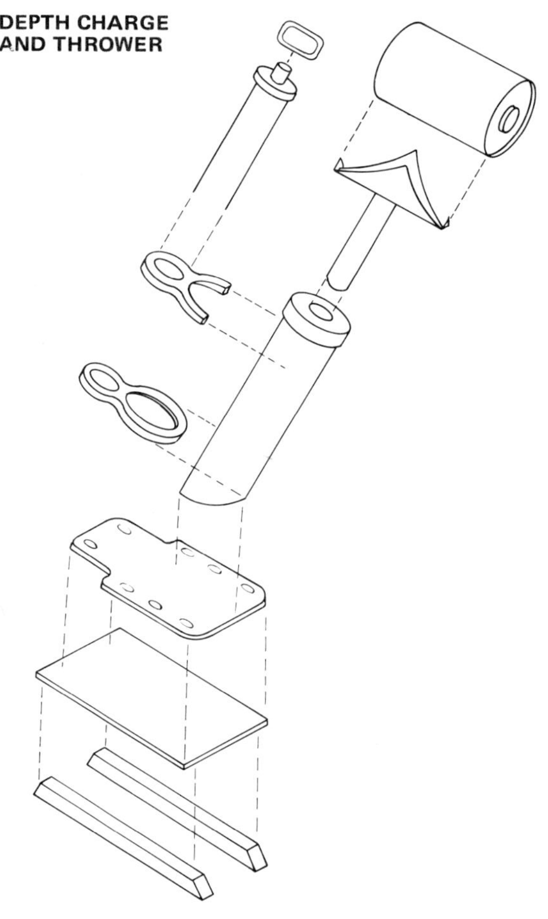

Opposite top: The importance of including as much detail as possible in open bridges is seen here on Jack Bidgood's 1/40 scale working model of the Ghanaian corvette *Kromantse*. (Photo: John Bowen)

Bottom: The open bridge of the 'Weapon' class destroyer HMS *Battleaxe* showing — as well as major items like the compass and pelorus — how much equipment was placed inside the bulwarks. (Photo: Conway Picture Library)

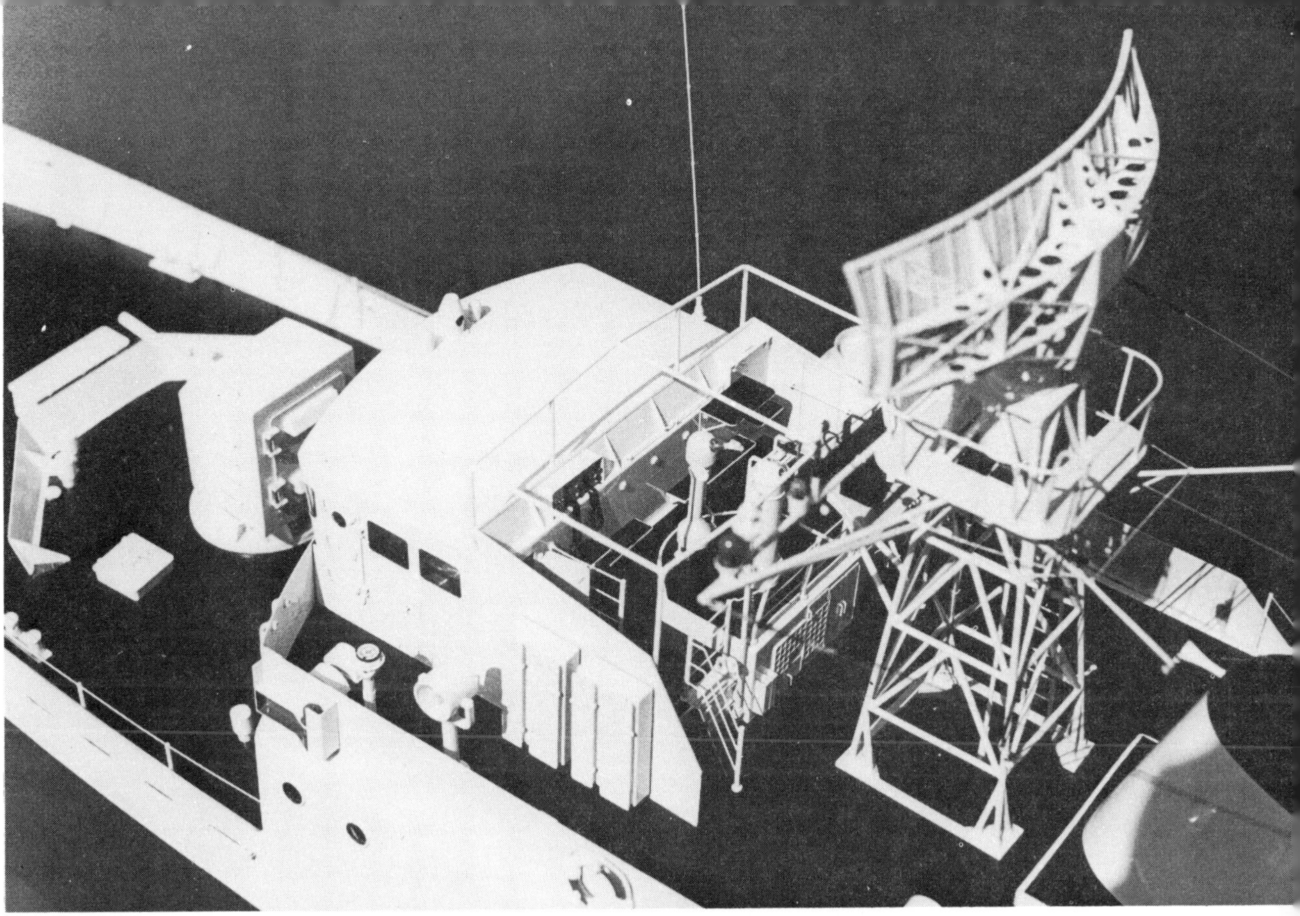

may be held in a vice by the surplus material of this component.

Gratings can be added to the bow and stern or in the bottom, as appropriate; these may be cut from a fine brass petrol filter gauze, the wires of which have been filed slightly flat on the upper surface. It is not necessary to attempt to file them completely flat, since painting tends to even things out and the result looks flat.

Finally, the keel stem and stern unit may now be cut with a piercing saw and filed up to the outside profile and, if appropriate, hand grip bilge keels may be filed from the edge of a sheet of aluminium and glued on.

Hard chine motor boats can be built up of sheet on frame, as is the more traditional method for larger models, the frame being constructed from 0.8mm plywood, and the sheet sides from veneer; other materials could, of course, be substituted.

One method I have tried for the Admiral's barge type of boat with a number of separate cabins and cockpits, is to cut a deck from thin sheet aluminium with the necessary holes for cabins and cockpits; the planks and coverboards are then laid on this deck in different veneers, and rubbed down smooth. Cockpit and cabin sides in aluminium, with the windows cut

Above and opposite: Note the boat stowage, ready-use ammunition lockers for the 0.5in multiple machine guns, and the detail on the four-barrelled pompom and on the after conning position on this 1/96 scale working model of the 'Tribal' class destroyer HMS *Ashanti* by Dave Sambrook.
(Photos: John Bowen)

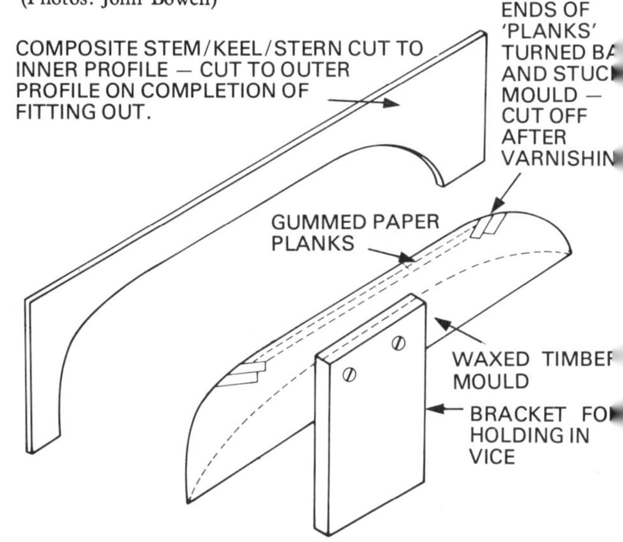

SHIPS BOATS

out, can then be glued in place to the underside and top deck. When the necessary internal shape has thus been completed, small blocks of wood are glued around the cockpits under the deck unit, and subsequently carved to the shape of the hull.

The appearance of motor boats is usually enhanced with a polished brass shaft and propeller and deck fittings. Fairleads can be cut from the edge of brass sheet with a piercing saw, and cleats made in a similar manner to that previously described for the superstructure handrail brackets.

CARLEY FLOATS

Whilst talking about ships' boats, it is possibly a suitable place to consider the Carley floats. I know many people construct them from plastic tube but I find that the tube, particularly on smaller floats, tends to kink on the bends so I have reverted to my all-purpose material — aluminium.

A simple core is made to the internal size of the float; this may merely consist of two lengths of metal rod dowelled together, side by side. This core is placed in a vice, trapping an aluminium knitting needle of suitable diameter between one side of the core and the vice. Using a blow lamp in one hand to soften the knitting needle, and pliers in the other, it is wound spirally round the core, keeping the needle in tension with a strong pull on the pliers all the time. However it may be necessary to use in addition blocks of wood to press the needle tight against the core. After cooling, the spiral is cut across the windings to produce a number of links, which are easily flattened to form individual floats.

The bottom grating is built up from narrow strips of aluminium and is laced in position with cotton. To locate this lacing and the various life lines, I find it necessary to drill a small hole through the knitting needle at each of the major intersections for the lacings to pass through. With a little thought you can device a sequence to execute the lacings a section at a time on alternate sides, which completes most of the rope work in two circuits of the float.

DAVITS

Radial davits are fairly simply formed from wire, tapered at the head if necessary, with the ends split in order that a fine wire ring may be soldered in position. Quadrant davits, however, are not quite so simple. Since I have been unable to find a suitable 'H' section metal, I settle for a 'T' section, using TT scale model railway track, filing the web and flange to thickness and width required with a square section file. The 'T' section is now bent to profile round a former to ensure that all are to a constant shape, with the web of the 'T' to the outside so that it is stretched rather than compressed on the curves. The 'H' section can now be completed by soldering a narrow strip of brass to the outer edge of the web.

The jibs of torpedo davits vary considerably in shape, and a slight variation to this latter method can be used for those which are constructed from a shaped plate web with angle stiffeners top and bottom. Two webs are cut from sheet brass and held about 1mm apart with tightly fitting brass dowels; strips of brass are then soldered on top and bottom to the pair of webs and filed up on the external facings to leave the require projection of the top and bottom angles. The piece is then cut full length between the webs into two halves, and the top and bottom plates filed flush with the inside of the web.

DETAIL WORK

In the previous descriptions I have purposely refrained from mentioning the ironmongery or mountings which should be added to fittings, since they are common to many items and must be added to make the fittings look interesting and give that true scale impression, rather than leaving the item to be generally representative of the prototype. This is the stage of construction where photographs are essential, since this type of information is very rarely shown on drawings.

The types of items I have in mind are hinges and fastenings on lockers and hatches; crank handles on winches and torpedo tubes; hand wheels on cable stoppers, guns and bridge equipment and so on.

Small catches, and the smaller sizes of hinges, can be represented by tiny 'L' shaped pieces of wire (say 15 thou for 1/8in scale) glued on; in the case of hinges, however, the wire should be hammered flat. The more prominent catches on watertight fittings with butterfly nuts can be formed by holding a piece of brass pin wire in a pin vice and slitting the end with a piercing saw, using the jaws of the pin vice as a guide in a similar manner to a mitre block. A length of fine wire is then soldered into the bottom of the

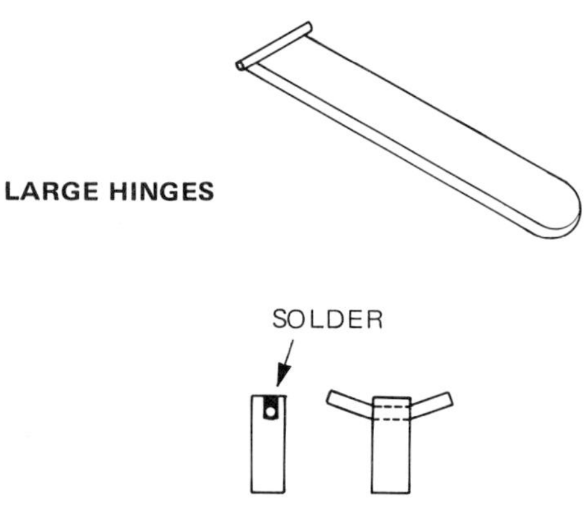

Right: A 1/384 scale model of the American destroyer USS *Fletcher* by Eric Dyke shown in full camouflage (which gives the paintwork on the model an erroneously heavy appearance). As with his USS *Tucson* model note the detail on the close range weapons, and on the torpedo-tubes, control tower, watertight doors, and depth charge throwers.
(Photos: John Bowen)

slit. To ensure uniformity in the length of the projecting ends of the wire, a hole should be drilled in a piece of metal the thickness of which is equal to the required projection and, using this metal as a gauge, the wire can be cut off flush with one side with a slitting saw.

The larger hinges for lockers and other fittings are made from narrow strips of brass or copper shim with a piece of wire soldered across at one end and cut off, leaving both ends projecting slightly, as previously described for the butterfly catches.

Holding down bolts around the base of binnacles, depth charge throwers, gun and other mountings etc, are made by slightly shouldering a length of wire; a shoulder, 2 thou deep, is quite sufficient. This wire is then placed through a close fitting hole in the base plate which has been countersunk on the underside. The wire can then be soldered or glued in position, depending on the material of the base plate, the countersinking forming a space in which a small amount of solder, or glue, is retained after filing. Finally, the top is filed down to leave a bolt of the required height using a piece of sheet metal with a hole drilled in to pass over the bolt as a gauge for the height.

Crank handles are made in a similar manner to holding down bolts, the spindle and handle being made from shouldered wire, and the crank from a strip of sheet metal. This strip, of course, is not filed down to width until the spindle and crank have been soldered in and filed up.

Wheel handles can be made in two ways. By the first method a small cross is filed from thin sheet metal and a brass ring soldered around the arms, one end of this ring being bent up at the joint if a handle is required.

The second method for the smallest of hand wheels again uses the pin vice as a saw guide; the end of a short length of pin wire (say 28 thou) is slit, and a short piece of 15 thou hard drawn wire soldered into the slit. The work is then returned to the pin vice and tightened up with the cross wire set down between the jaws, and a second slit is carefully cut through across the cross wire and spindle at right angles to the first, once more using the jaws as a guide. A second cross wire is soldered in, without unsoldering the first wire, by pushing the spindle through a close fitting hole in a block of wood and then taping or stapling the two ends of the first cross wire to the block before attempting to solder the second cross wire with a quick dab of the soldering iron. A hole is now drilled in an aluminium plate and the radius of the rim

88

Opposite top: The simple layout and sparcity of fittings on early warships is seen in this model of the old armoured cruiser HMS *Monmouth* (1901), 1/96 scale, by Ray Cattle.
(Photo: John Bowen)

Bottom: In contrast to the *Monmouth* is this model of one of the Royal Navy's latest ships, HMS *Broadsword,* a Type 22 Frigate, showing the sophisticated detection equipment and clean lines of modern naval construction. 1/96 scale model by T Johnston.
(Photo: John Bowen)

scribed on with spring bow dividers. The spindle can then be inserted through the hole and pulled down until the cross wires rest on the sheet, in which position they can be cut to the scribed radius by steady pressure with a very sharp knife. This work piece is then returned to the wooden block and the rim is soldered on, holding and covering three ends of the spokes with a small piece of timber, whilst the fourth end is soldered. No doubt the experts will cringe, but for this type of soldering I find a dirty soldering iron ideal; if the whole of the bit is dirty, except for an area a little larger than a pin head at the tip edge, you will find that the iron will only hold a tiny amount of solder and your work will not be swamped, which is one of the most frequent calamities when soldering tiny items.

VISUAL GLOSSARY OF FITTINGS

ANCHORS AND CABLES

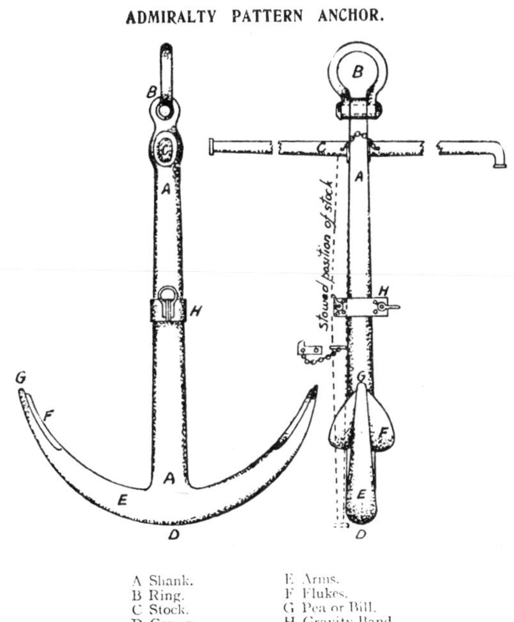

The standard pattern of anchor used by the Admiralty before and during WWI, but superseded by the stockless anchor. Its size depended on that of the ship on which it was fitted.

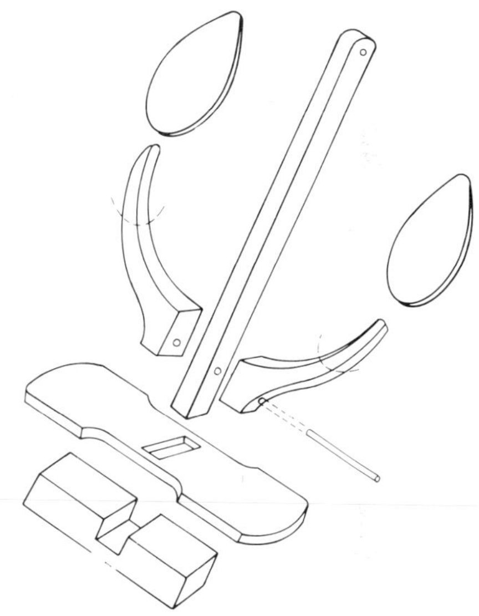

An exploded view of the author's method of constructing a stockless anchor; the D-shaped shackle fitted at the top of the shank has been omitted from this sketch.

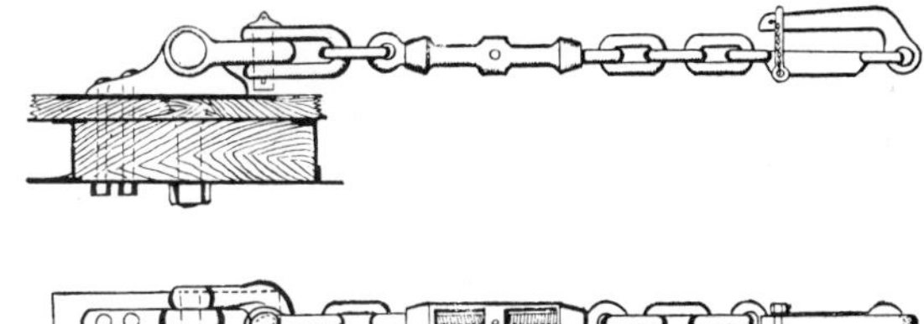

A stopper such as this, tensioned by the bottle screw, was used for heaving and securing stockless anchors close into the hawse pipes.

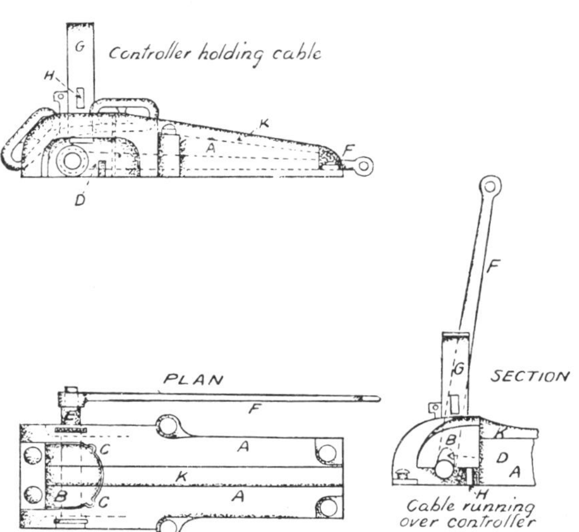

The bow stopper was used to hold the anchor cable as it was being hove in link by link. Of very solid construction, it varied in size depending on the size of chain cable being used. They were usually fitted abaft the inboard end of the hawse pipes.

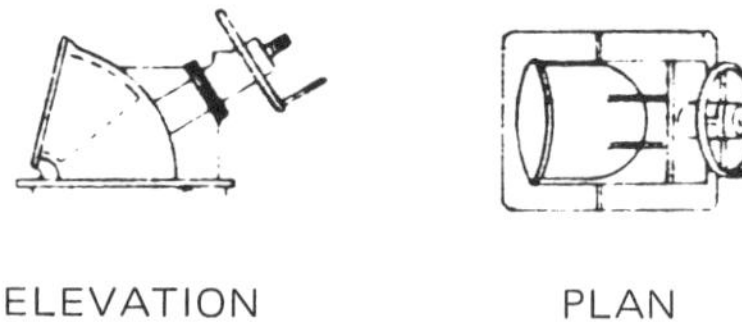

On leaving the cable holder the cable passed through the deck pipe to the chain locker. Of very solid construction, this type incorporated a compressor.

Left: The 1/48 scale model of the battleship HMS *Howe* in the Museum of Transport, Glasgow. This gives a good idea of the arrangement and fittings on the forecastle of a battleship of the WWII era. Points to note are the bollards and fairleads, the chain stoppers on the stud link anchor cables, the paravanes stowed on the after side of the forward breakwater, the wire rope reels and the planked deck.
(Photo: Museum of Transport, Glasgow)

BOLLARDS AND FAIRLEADS

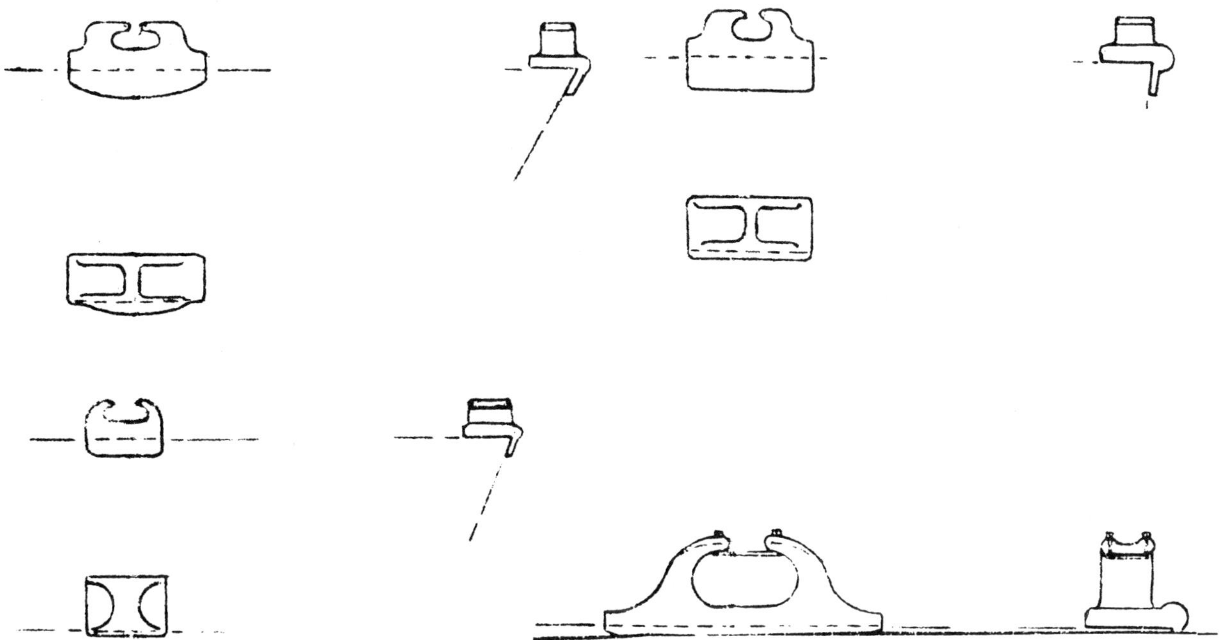

Different styles of fairlead. These have been designed to be fitted on and over the edge of the deck. Other types can be seen in the photographs. They are all heavy castings and their size again depends on the duty and the class of ship to which they are fitted.

SECTION THRO P.V. FAIRLEAD

BOW FAIRLEAD.

P.V. FAIRLEAD.

JACKSTAFF

P.V. FAIRLEAD

BOW-FAIRLEAD

SECTION

ELEVATION OF BOW FAIRLEAD

The bow fairlead for a battleship; note the bolted closing plate, and also the smaller fairlead for the paravane wires.

CAPSTANS AND CABLE HOLDERS

Section through capstan.

Side view.

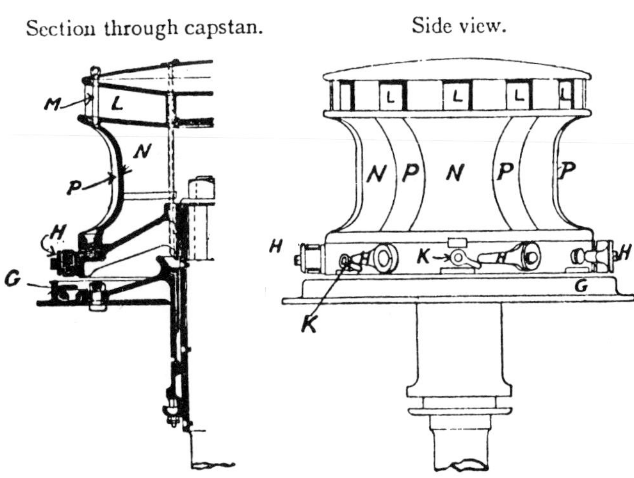

An electric capstan of the type fitted to capital ships of the WWI period. N is the cast steel barrel, and the whelps P are cast on it. The pawls H are shown on their toe rests K, but when turned over they engage with the teeth G on the base. L is the recess in the capstan head to take the shoes of the capstan bars, which are held in place by the pin M.

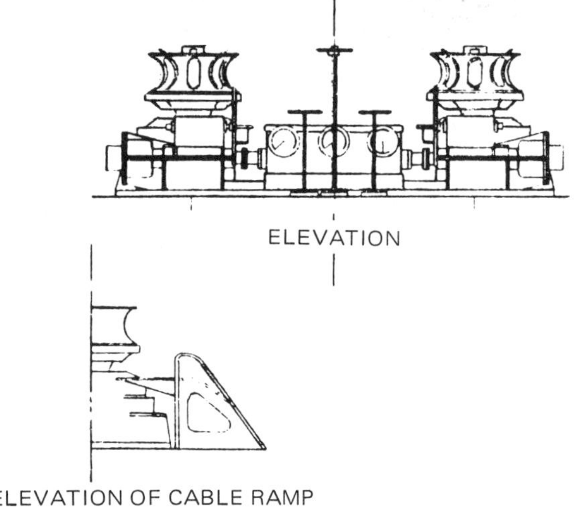

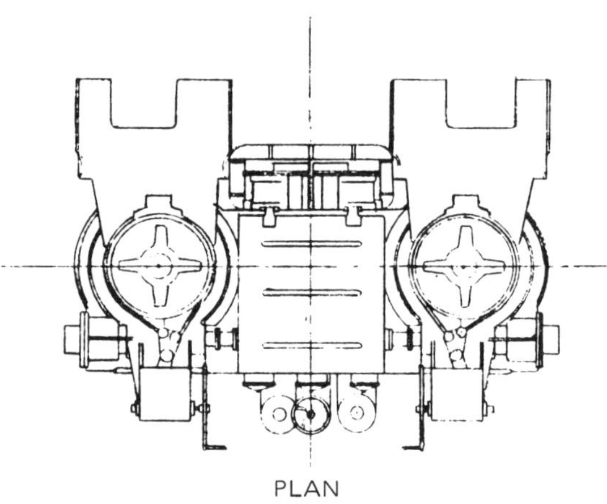

This twin barrel steam capstan, as found on later destroyers, also has a cable holder below each capstan barrel.

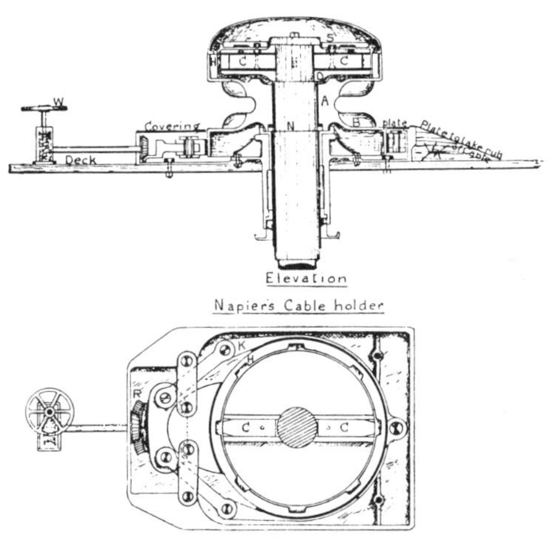

The Napier type cable holder found on the larger vessels. The cable passes round the very solidly constructed drum, each link fitting into the snugs at A and B.

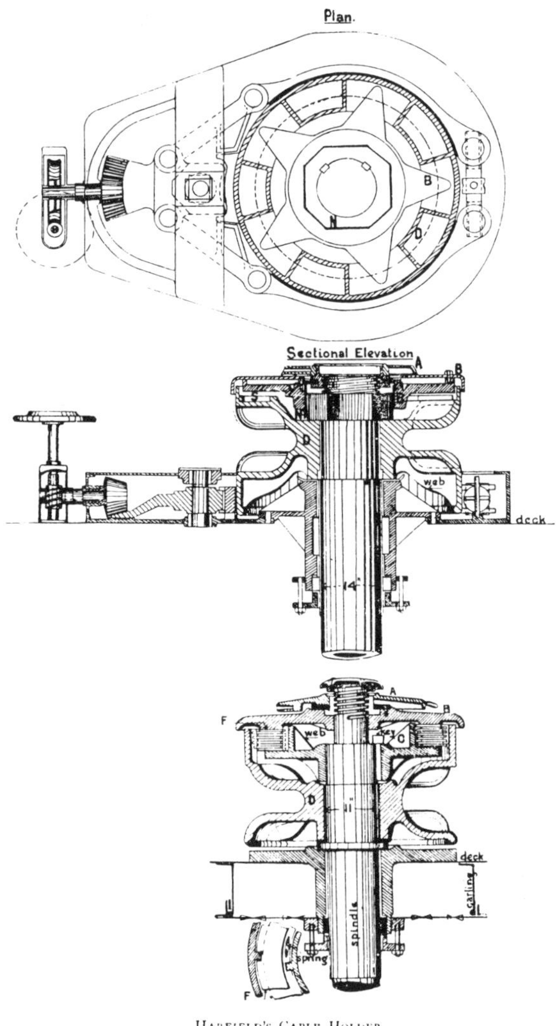

A different pattern of cable holder, the Harfield; the cable lies in the snugs as in the Napier holder.

Opposite top: The forecastle of Dave Sambrook's model of HMS *Ashanti*. Forward of the breakwater the deck is of steel with footstrips to provide a measure of grip. The anchor cables pass to the chain locker through chain pipes fitted with compressors.
(Photo: John Bowen)

Bottom: A most useful photograph showing details of two of the steam picket boats on the super-dreadnought HMS *Thunderer*. Note the detail of the heel fitting of the main boom.
(Photo: Conway Picture Library)

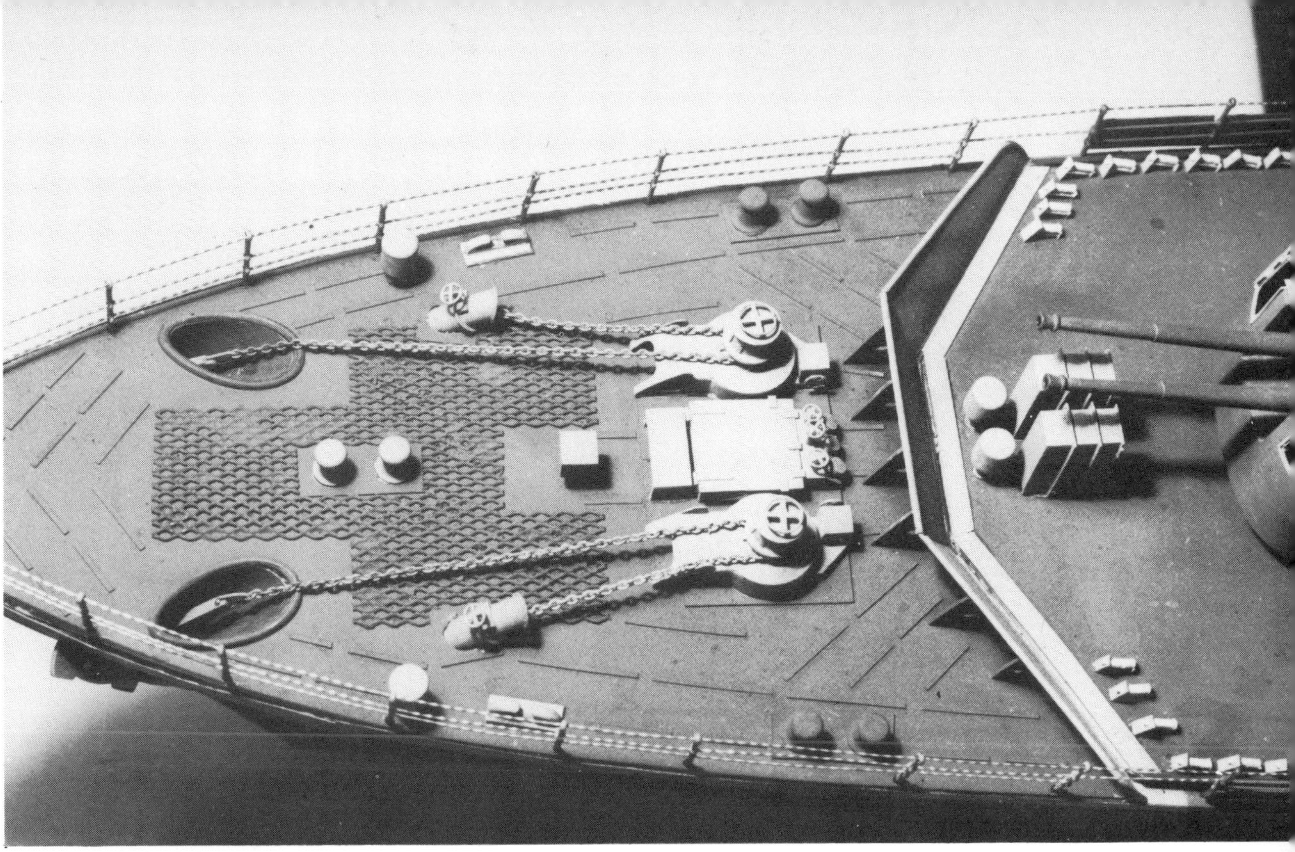

CARLEY FLOATS, BOATS AND LIFESAVING EQUIPMENT

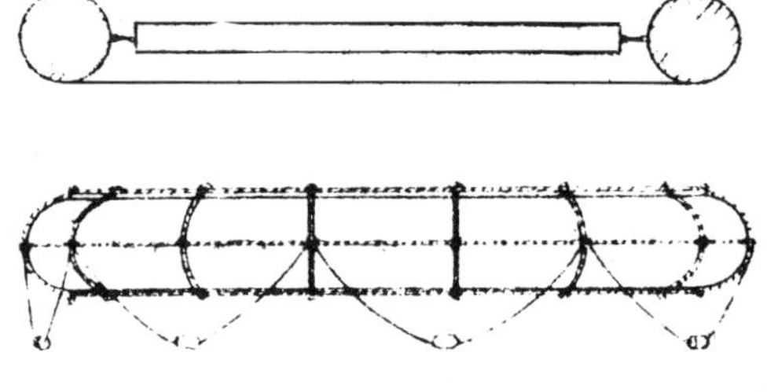

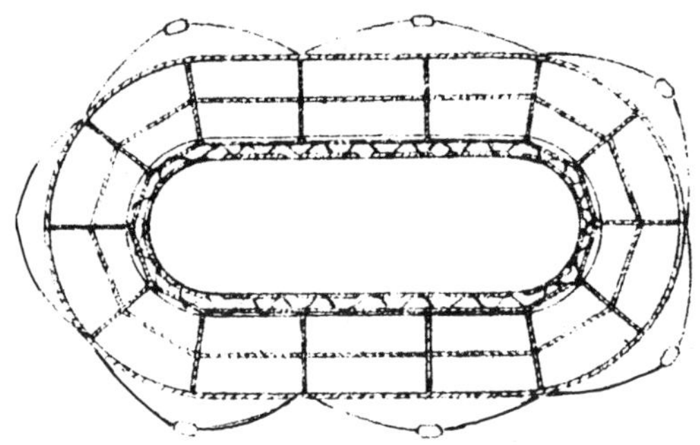

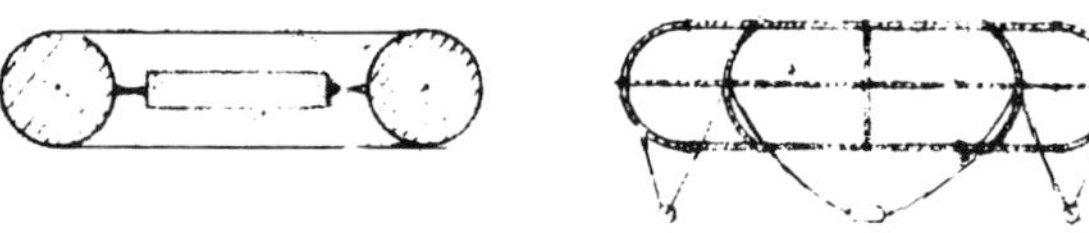

A typical carley float. The length is about 10ft, the width about 5ft 6in, and the body is about 15in diameter. The 'floor' is secured to the body with lashings.

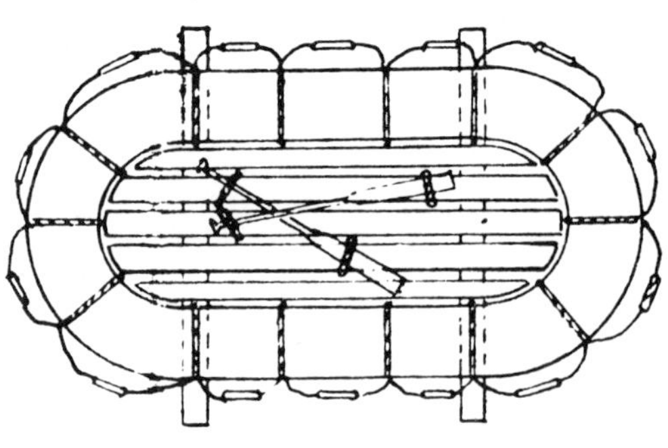

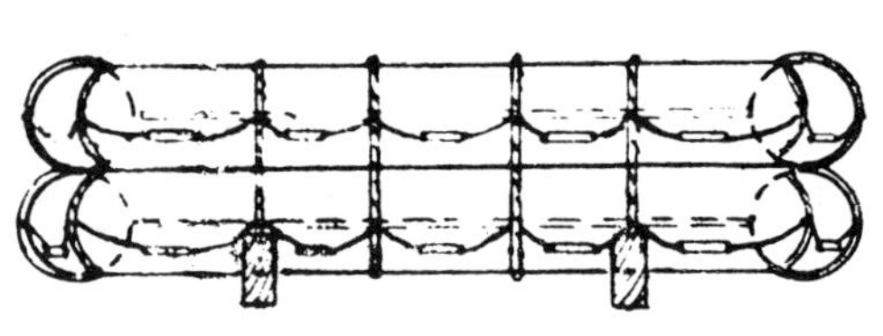

A double tier set of carley floats stowed on wood chocks.

The 56ft steam pinnace was carried by dreadnoughts and other capital ships. Much useful data about the construction of these wooden vessels is shown here.

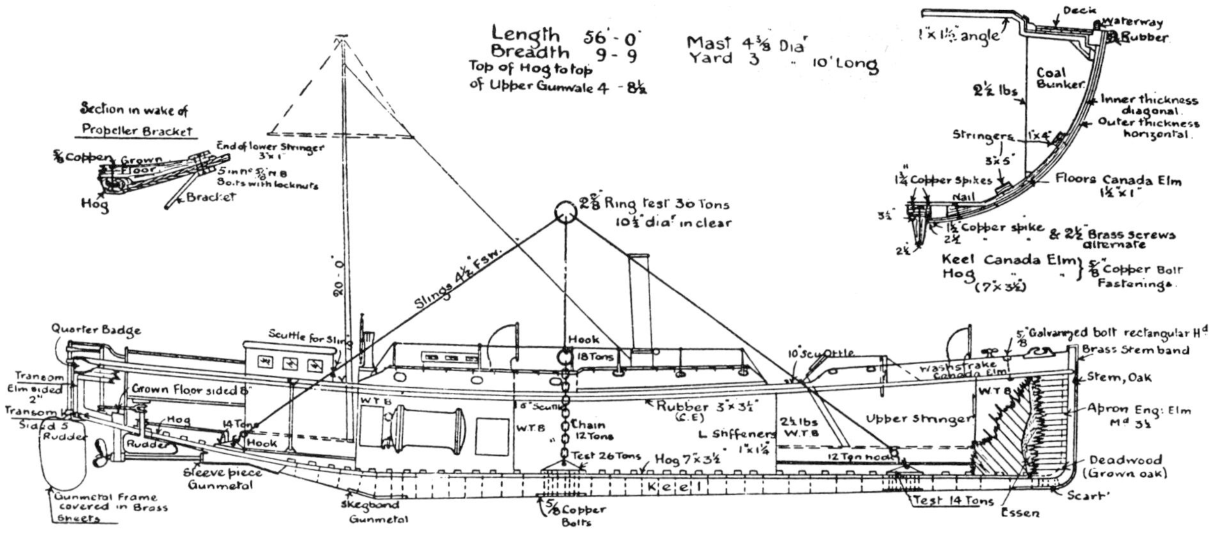

STEAM PINNACE.

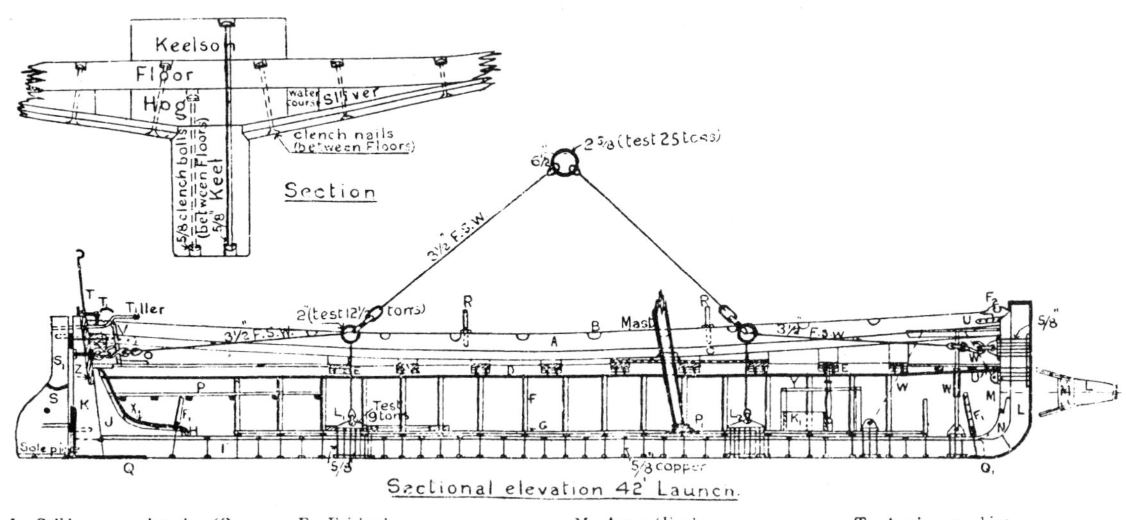

A. Solids or washstrake (C elm).
B. Shutters or poppets.
C. Gunwale (C. elm).
D. Rising (C. elm).
E. Portable thwarts (red pine, except in wake of mast, where they are of oak).
F. Floors (C. elm).
F_1. Grown floors (oak).
F_2. Fairlead.
G. Keelson (C. elm).
H. Hog (C. elm).
I. Keel (C. elm).
J. After deadwood (oak).
K. Sternpost (oak).
K_1. Cable locker.
K_2. Cross-piece.
L. Stem (oak).
L_1. Lifting or sling plates.
M. Apron (E. elm).
N. Fore deadwood (oak).
O. Sternsheets.
P. Seat.
P_1. Mast step.
Q_1. Skeg band.
Q_2. Stem band.
R. Lumber irons or crutches.
S. Rudder.
S_1. Rudder cheeks.
T. Awning stanchion.
T_1. Pump lever.
U. Steel breasthooks.
V. Steel quarter knees.
W. Bottle screws for supporting gun stand.
X. Tail pipe of pump.
Y. Platform for working gun.
Z. Transom (E. elm).

Another of the boats carried by capital ships was the 42ft pulling and sailing launch, the construction details of which are shown in this sectional elevation. The rig was a loose-footed gaff mainsail, and a foresail.

The carvel-built 30ft cutter, a pulling and sailing boat, was carried by many classes of warship, and there is much useful information about their scantlings in these two sections.

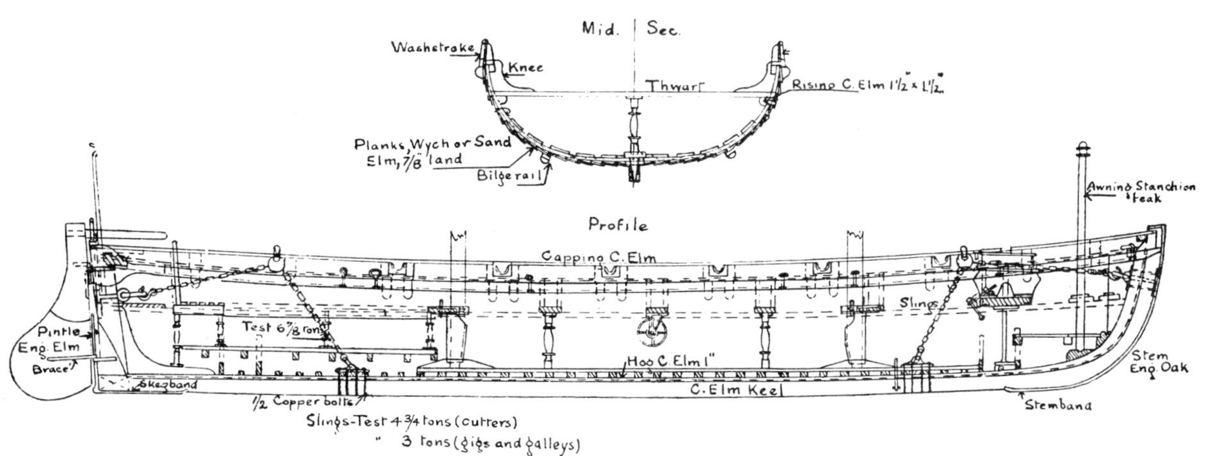

CUTTER.

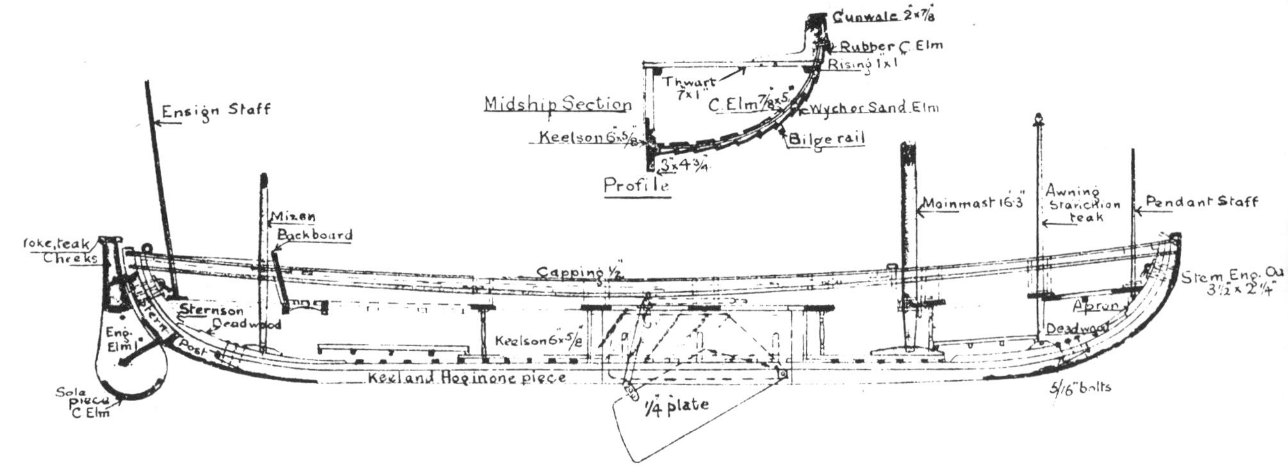

The design of the 27ft clinker-built whaler has altered little over the years, and it is to be found on most warships.

Below: The boat stowage arrangement on a battleship — the arrangements have changed little over the decades, just some of the boat types and the design of the handling gear. The 1/96 scale model of HMS *Vanguard* was built by Alec McFadyen. (Photo: John Bowen)

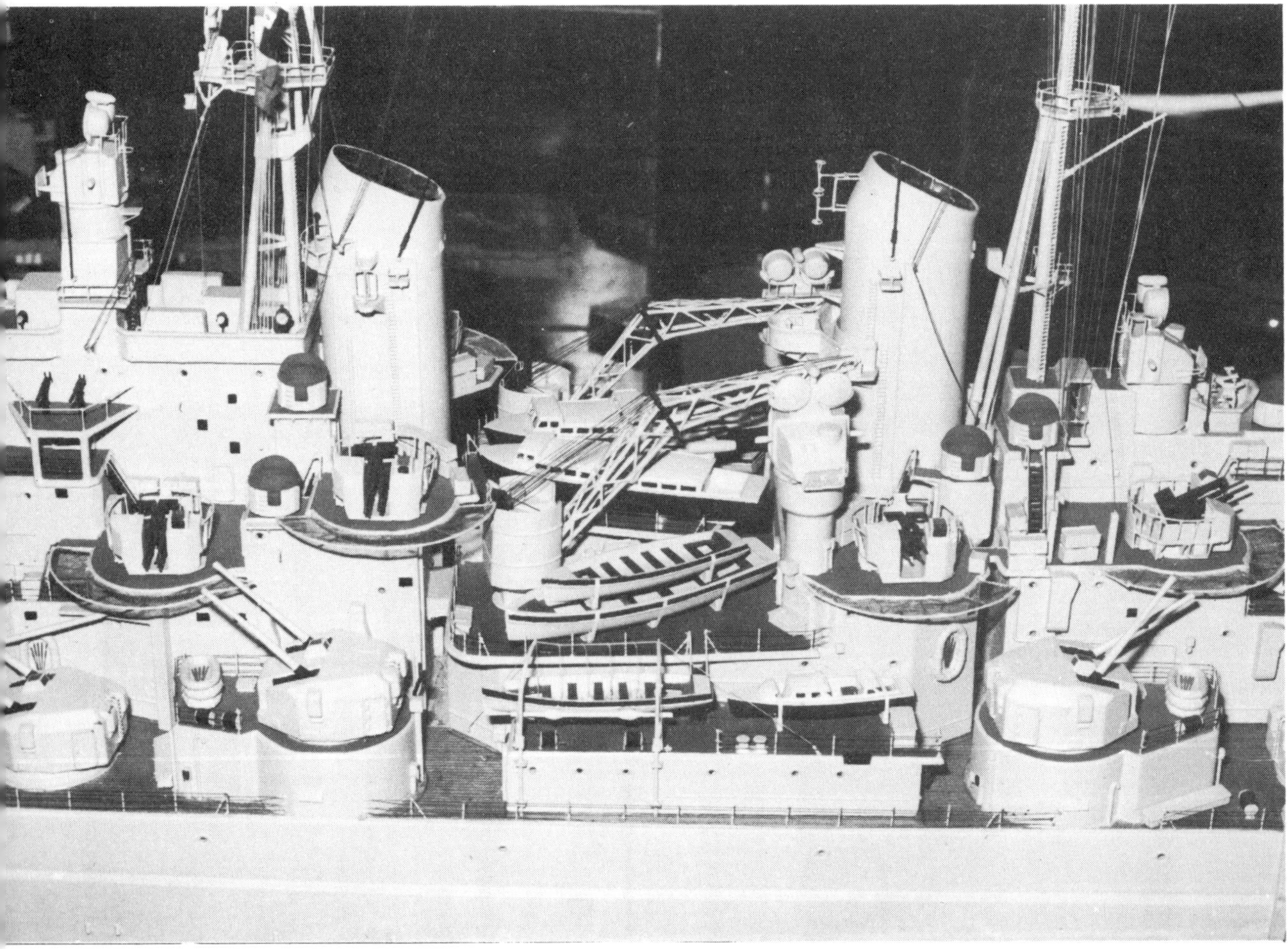

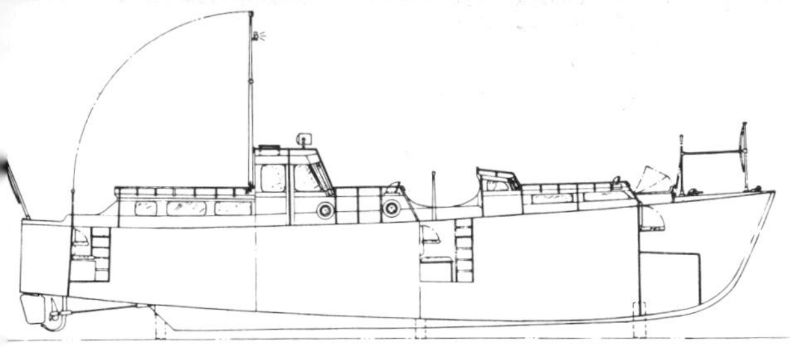

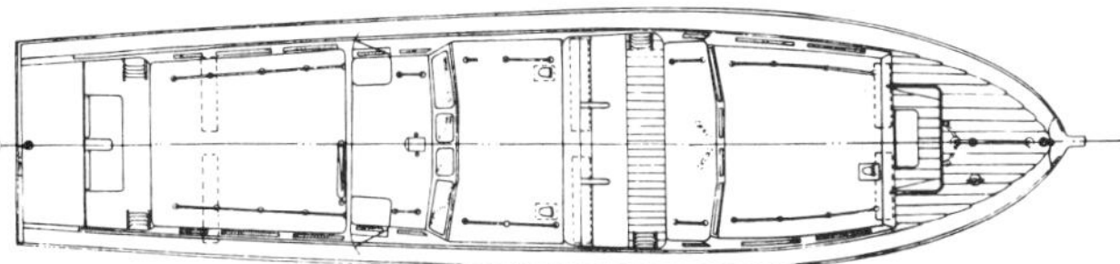

The 45ft motor picket boat replaced the steam pinnace. There is a good deal of brightwork about the cabin tops and metalwork on deck. They were usually of diagonal construction.

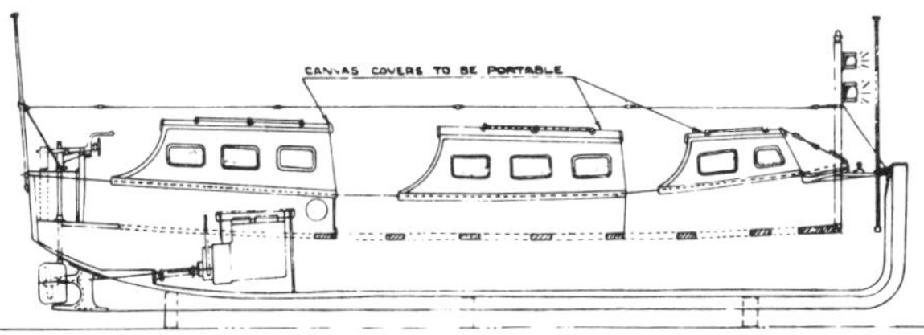

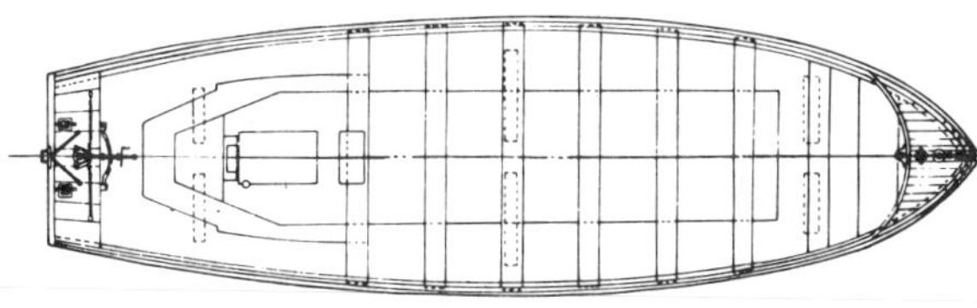

The 36ft motor pinnace was to be found on the larger warships from the 1930s onwards. As with the motor picket boat, there was a considerable amount of brightwork on the cabin tops. Generally of carvel construction.

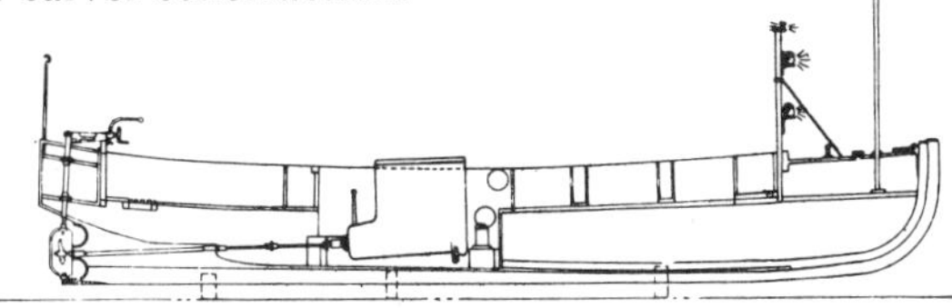

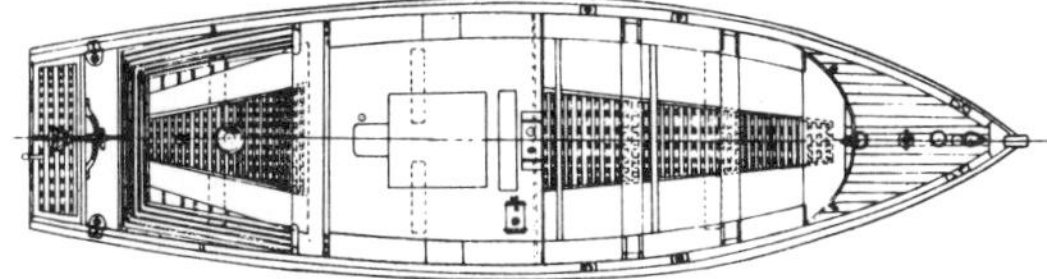

The 32ft wood motor cutter was a useful general purpose boat: from the modelmaker's point of view one of the most prominent features is the number of gratings fitted to the boat.

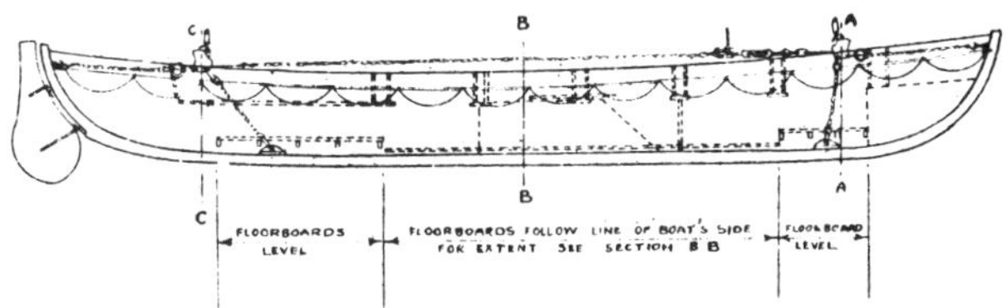

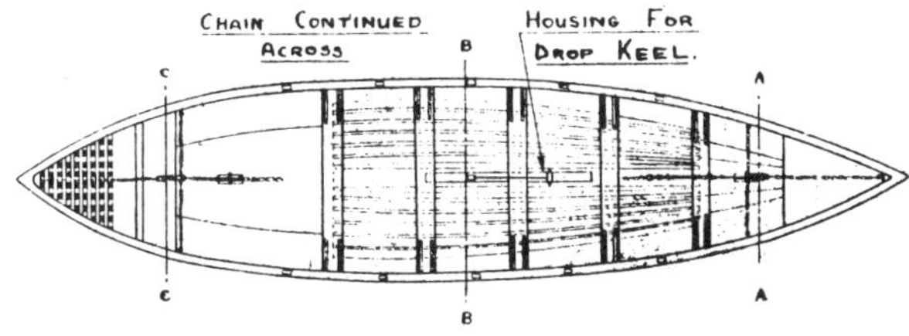

More details of the 27ft whaler. A very prominent feature of these boats is the sheer line and the shape in plan view — the latter requiring very careful attention if an otherwise good representation is not to be spoiled.

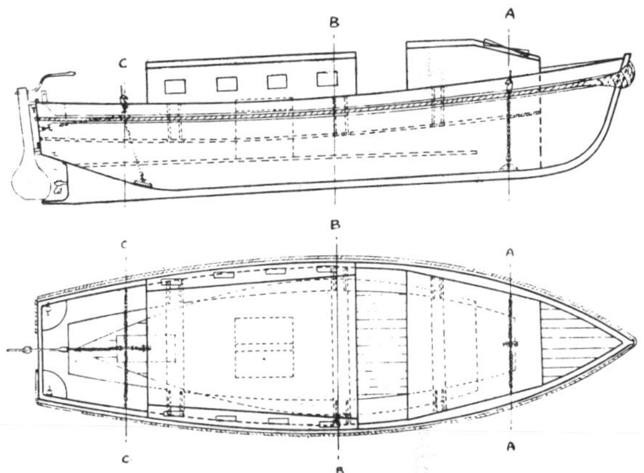

Although not indicated in this modelmakers' plan the 25ft motor cutter was a clinker-built boat. It was to be found on most classes of warship.

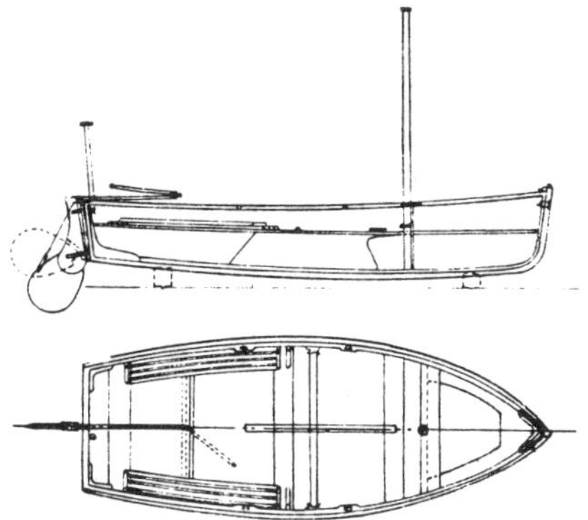

The 14ft sailing dinghy was a clinker built boat stowed either on chocks, as shown here, or more often on a small trolley.

CLINKER BUILT BOAT

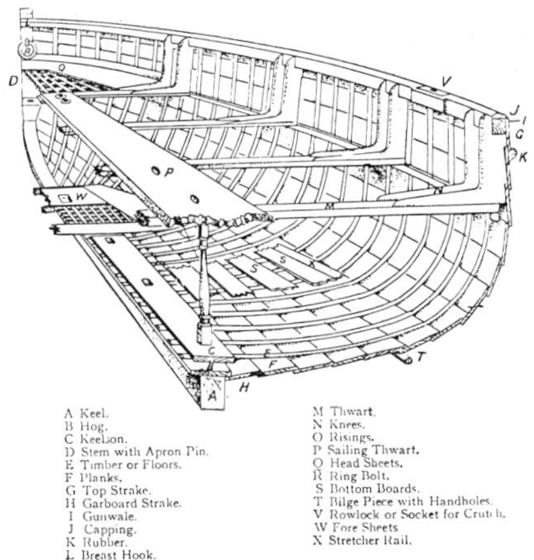

CARVEL BUILT BOAT

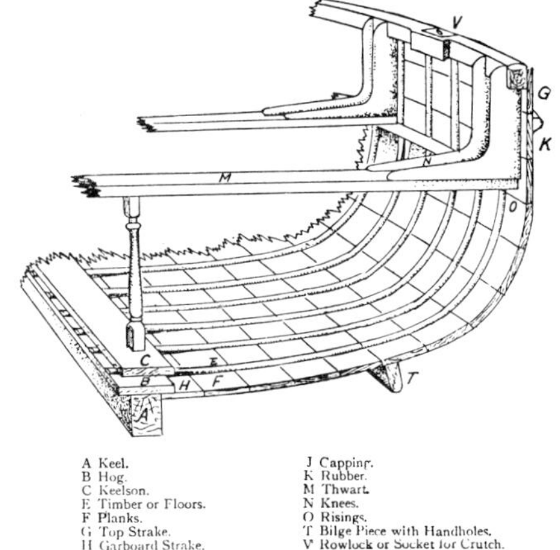

DIAGONAL BUILT BOAT

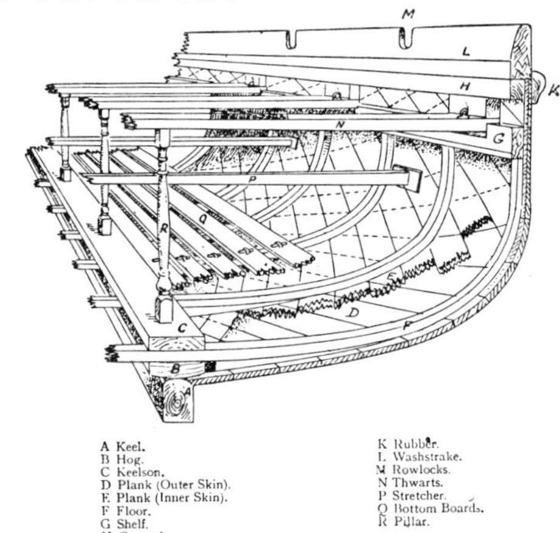

These three sectional views show much useful detail of the three types of construction adopted for the ships' boats.

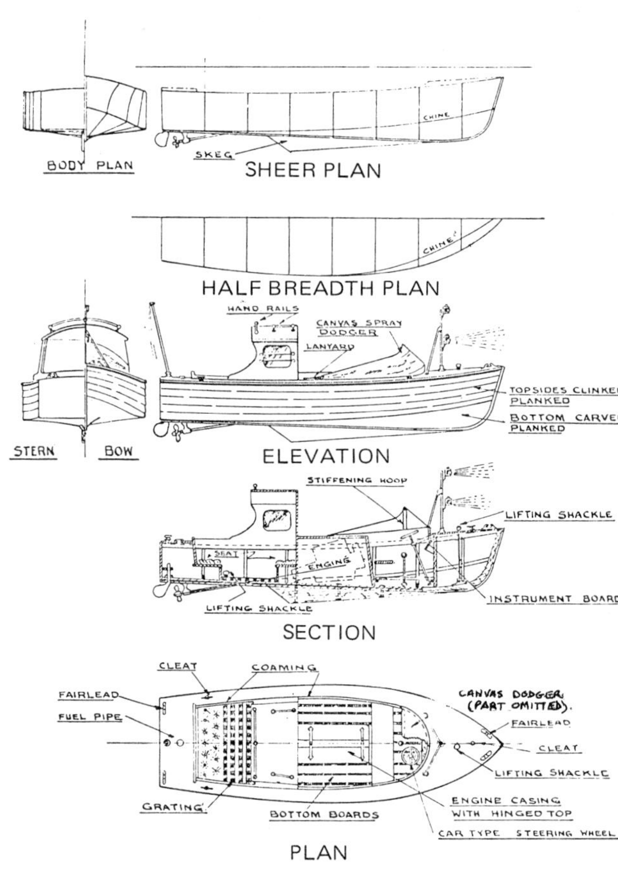

The 16ft fast motor dinghy was unusual in that it embodied both clinker and carvel construction in its hull.

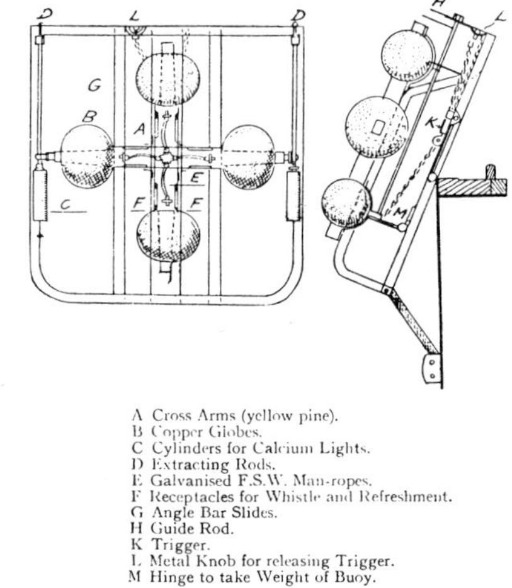

Before more sophisticated equipment became available warships were fitted with these night lifebuoys carrying self igniting calcium lights. The whole apparatus was about 6ft square and was carried in a quick release stowage fitted on the ship's side at deck level.

DAVITS AND DERRICKS

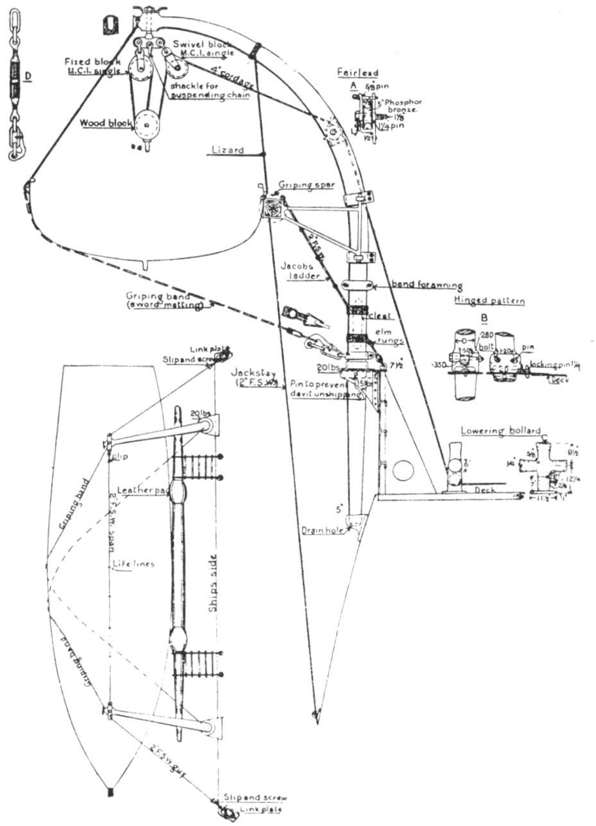

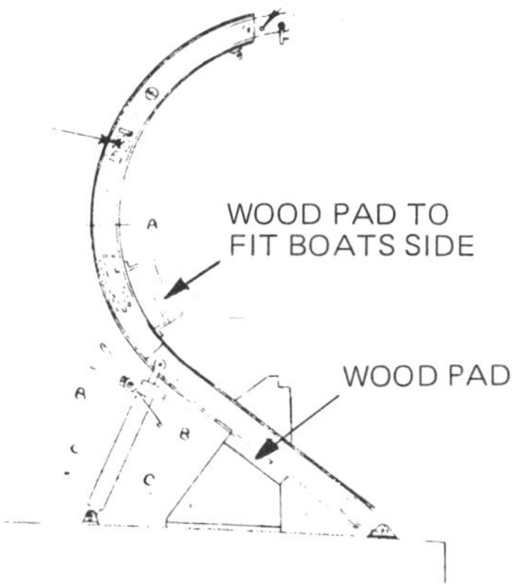

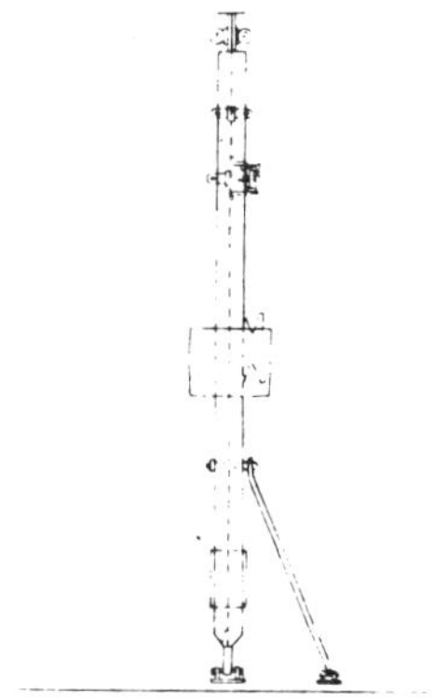

This davit is typical of those fitted on destroyers carrying a 25ft motor cutter. The davit itself is of I-section steel, and is turned into the outboard position by the operation of winding gear. When in the inboard position the weight is taken on the wood pad mounted on a steel supporting bracket welded to the deck plating.

Among the many details of the fittings for this radial type davit, note the alternative for the hinged type. This one is shown fitted outside the bulwark and on a vessel with a sharp tumblehome.

Below: Part of the boat stowage arrangements on a capital ship of about WWI. In the foreground the foredeck of two steam picket boats with, beyond, a pair of hinged radial davits. Note the supports for the griping spar and the fittings at the davit head. The object at top right is the bracket to take the head of a derrick when stowed.
(Photo: Conway Picture Library)

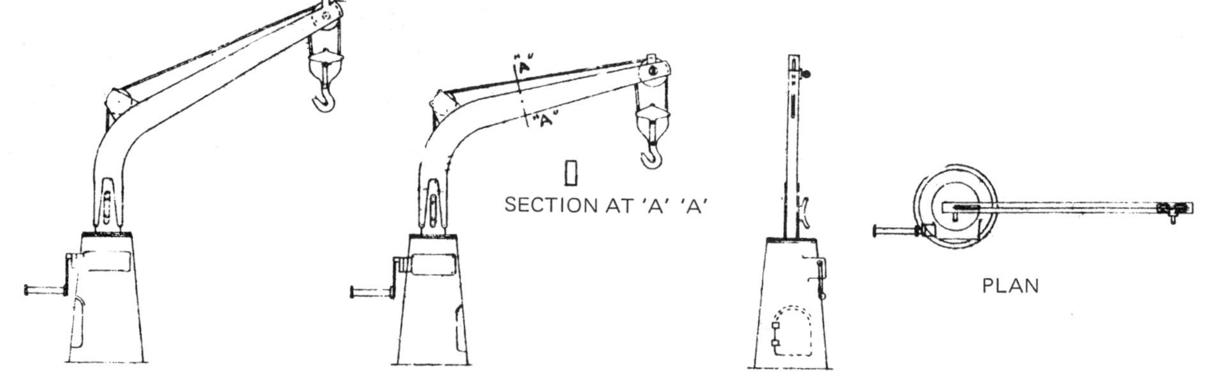

FRONT ELEVATION FRONT ELEVATION END ELEVATION

Two variations of the torpedo loading davit found on destroyers adjacent to the torpedo tubes; the difference lies in the angle of the jib. The jib is of rectangular cross-section, is of steel, with the upper sheave set into the end of the jib. The lifting wire passes inside the jib below the lower sheave, to a drum set within the conical steel base.

GUARD RAIL STANCHIONS, RAILS, AND FLAGSTAFFS

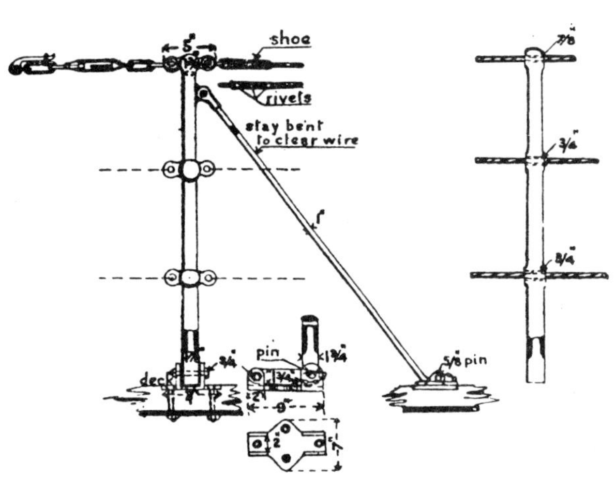

The guard rail stanchions are possibly the one fitting on a warship model most often incorrectly represented. They are not rigid upright fittings, but are designed to be readily turned down when clearing for action. The heel of the stanchion is L-shaped, and is set in a shoe fastened to the deck; there are two fastenings for the stanchion, one a bolt and the other a pin. By removing the pin the stanchion can be turned down, wherever possible in a fore and aft position. The guard 'rails' are flexible steel wire rope, passing through the balls on some stanchions, and secured to others by small bottle screws and slip hooks. The stanchions taper from bottom to top.

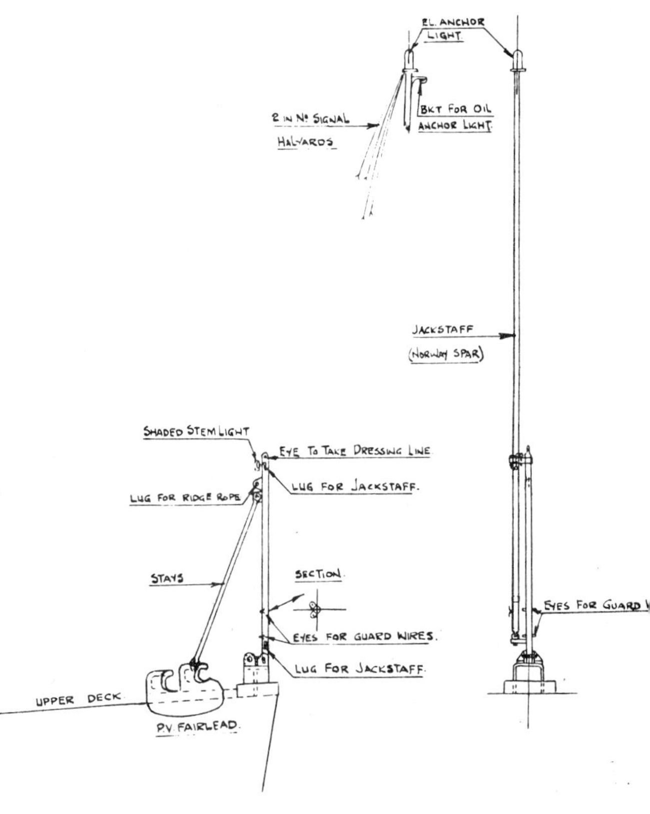

This is a typical set-up for the wooden jackstaff fitted at the stem head of one of the last of the battleships to be built. The jackstaff itself is secured to the steel tripod arrangement, the main leg of which stands in a heel fitting set on a low stool, whilst the supporting stays are attached to the paravane fairleads. The whole assembly can be hinged down in the same way as the guard rail stanchions.

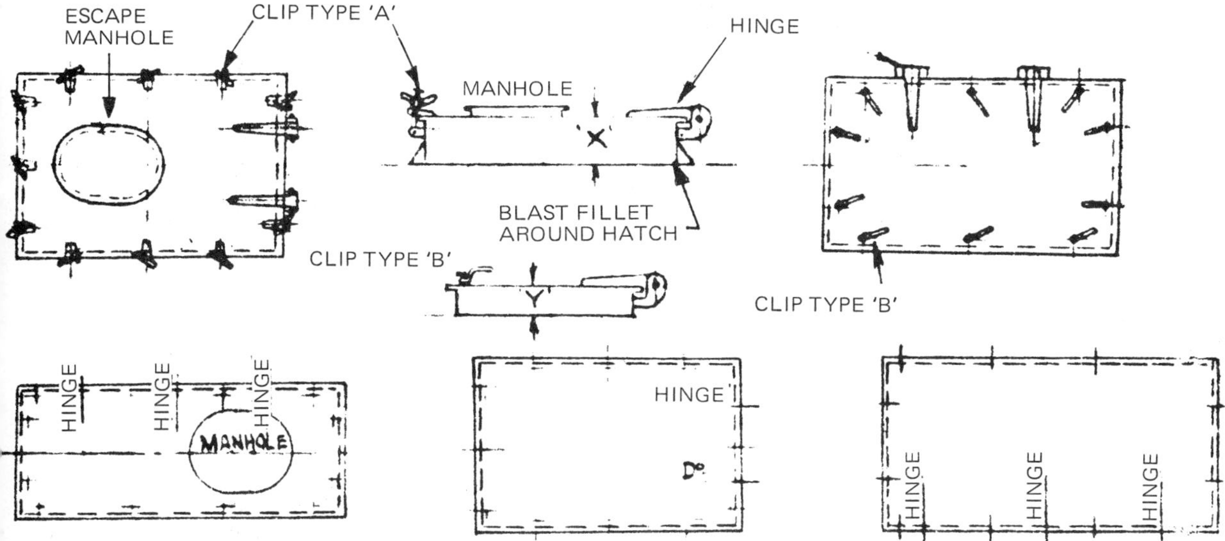

The watertight hatches fitted to warships vary considerably in shape and size, though the basic design is generally the same. Those shown here are rectangular, others may have rounded corners, and others again may be circular. Where they have to be opened from below, they are fitted with the 'B' type clip shown. Those intended to be opened from above only have the toggle type clip. The edge of the cover is flanged down, and this flanged edge stands clear of the hatch coaming. They are always of steel construction.

METHOD OF FASTENING HINGED W.T. SCUTTLES.

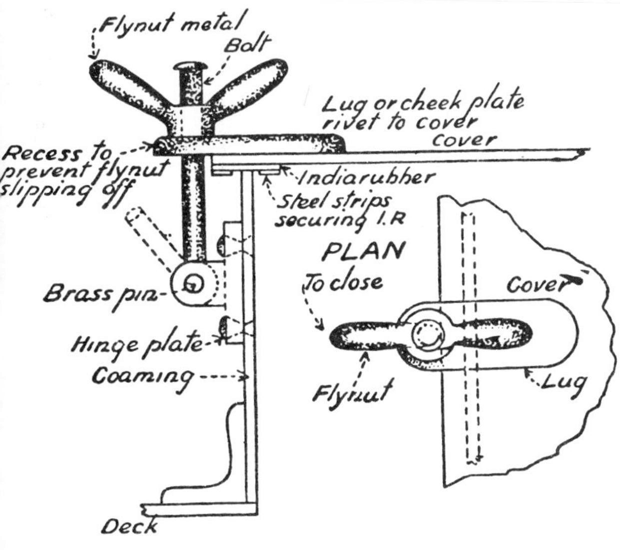

A typical detail of a toggle type scuttle clip. In this case the scuttle is shown without a flange to the lid.

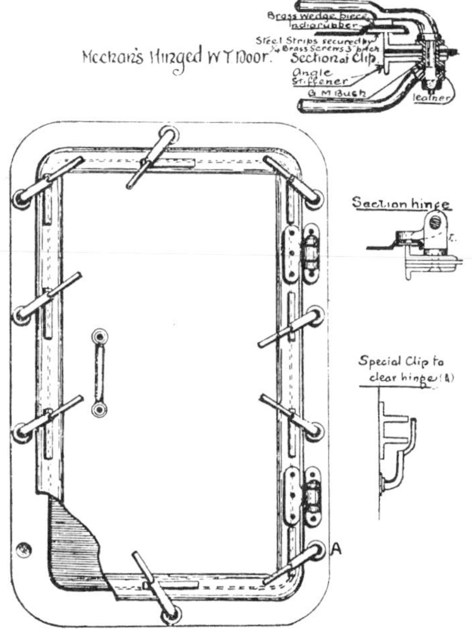

The design of hinged watertight doors has changed little over the years, except that nowadays they have three swaged, or recessed, panels formed in the main panel for strength; this can be seen in some of the photographs. Note the shape of the special clip to clear the hinges.

SKYLIGHT

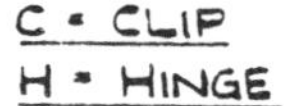

PLAN

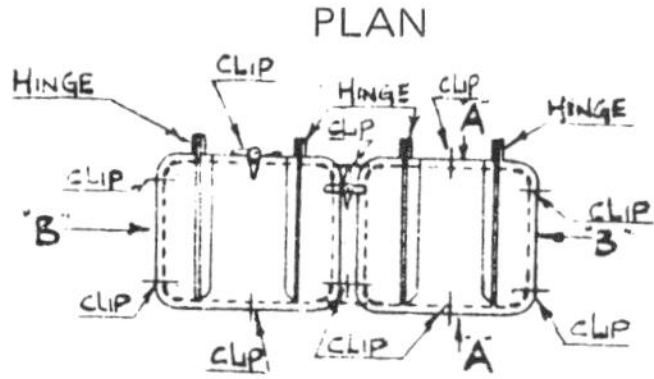

SECTION AT 'A-A'

SECTION AT 'B-B'

PLAN

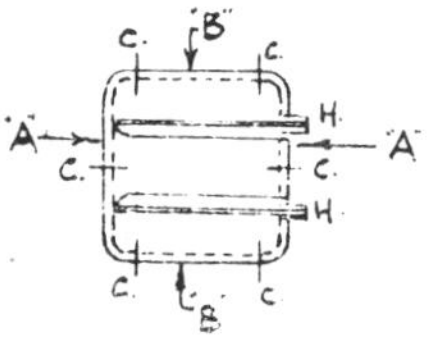

'B' C. C. 'A' H. 'A' C. C. H C. C 'B' C

SECTION AT 'A-A'

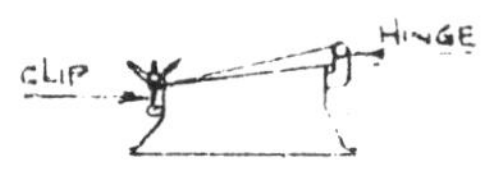

SECTION AT 'B-B'

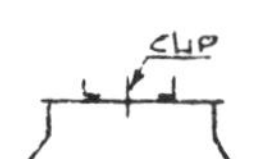

Skylights of this type were generally to be found on capital ships. Note the hinges, with the long arm running across the full width of the cover.

REELS AND WINCHES

Cordage reels, used for the stowage of ropes, were often fitted to the sides of deckhouses, and this is the type shown here on this special modelmakers' plan. The reels and brackets were of steel.

'A'

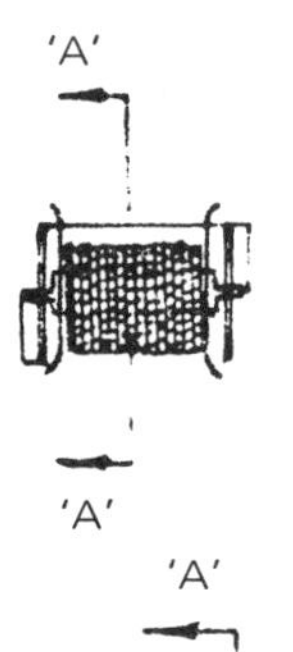

'A'

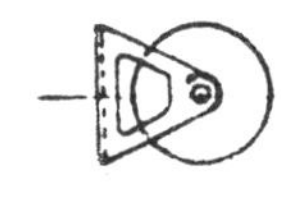

DETAIL OF WHEEL AND BRACKET

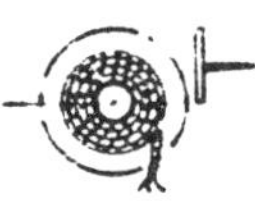

SECTION AT 'A-A'

'A'

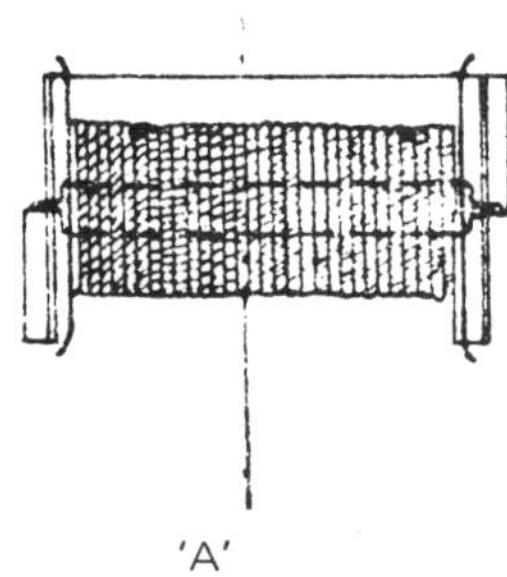

'A'

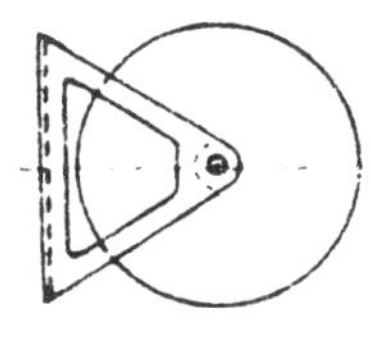

DETAIL OF WHEEL AND BRACKET

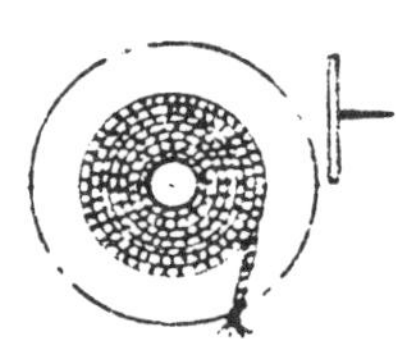

SECTION AT 'A-A'

ELEVATION OF DRUM

'A' 'B'

'A' 'B'

WIRE TO BE WOUND
ROUND DRUM

ELEVATION ON 'A-A'

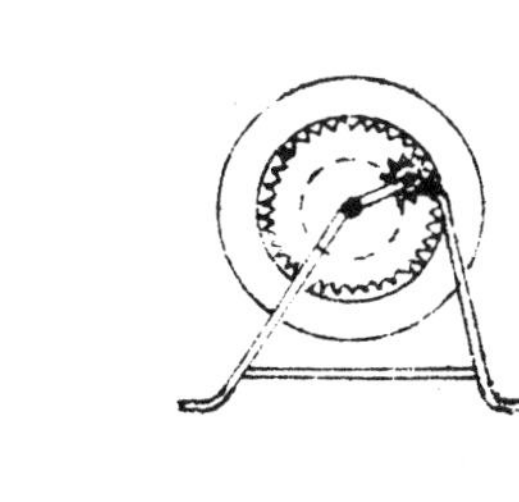

ELEVATION ON 'B-B'

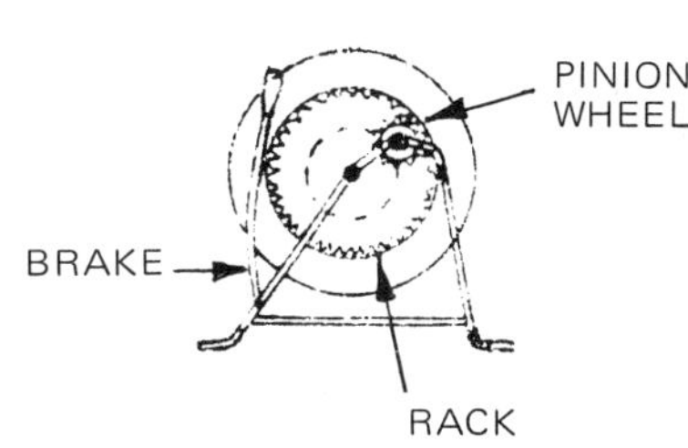

Typical reels for the stowage of wire ropes. These are of the geared type for the heavier sizes of wire. These again are special modelmakers' plans. The reels and stands are of steel.

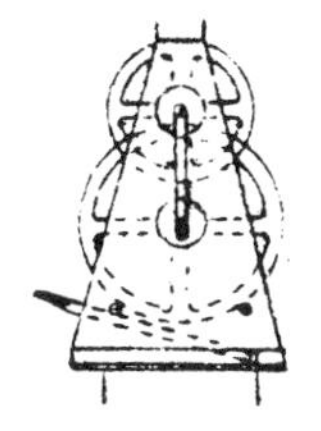

END ELEVATION

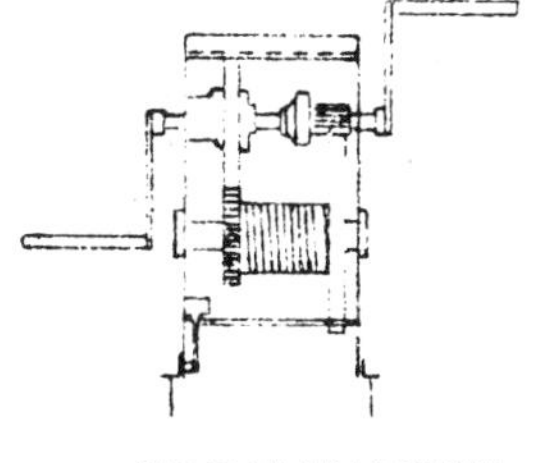

SIDE ELEVATION

A typical torpedo loading winch, as found on destroyers.

VENTILATORS

Whereas the older warships carried large numbers of prominent cowl ventilators, modern ventilation systems require far fewer, and smaller, types mainly of the designs shown here. They are of steel, with wire mesh over the intake opening.

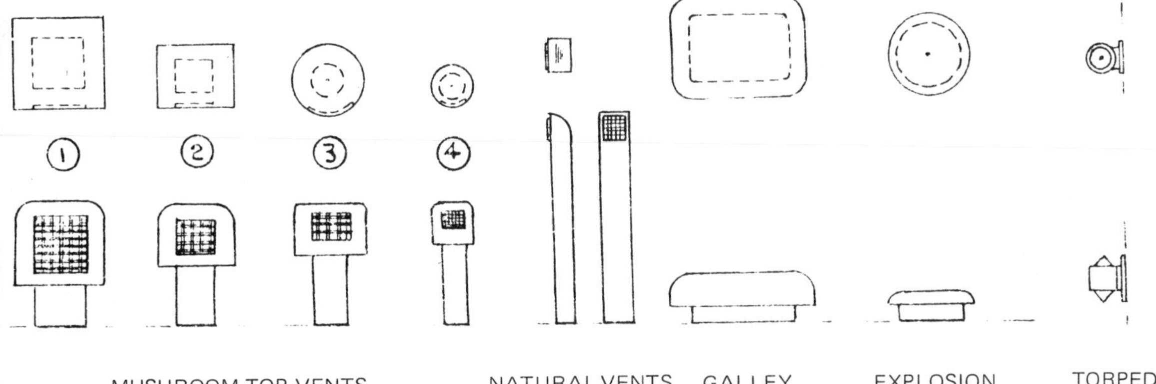

MUSHROOM TOP VENTS   NATURAL VENTS   GALLEY VENT   EXPLOSION VENT   TORPEDO VENT

Warships in miniature 7

by LARRY SOWINSKI

The sight of a large formation of warships plowing through the sea has always impressed me. Therefore, as a model builder, I set my sights very early and worked towards a single goal — a large number of constant scale waterline models. However, I failed to appreciate that my level of skill would improve to the point where my early attempts would be completely incompatible with recent models. My self-imposed standard was to build numerous realistic models that looked good from 18 inches away, at or above museum quality levels. Gems of detail (which could only be appreciated as seen through a magnifying glass) had to be considered irrelevant. And then there are just too many magnificent warships I have yet to build. While I have seen endless models of the *Constitution* or *Cutty Sark,* I have never even heard of one scratch-built replica of the *Ramillies, New York* or *Nashville.*

The choice of my bastard scale was based solely on an initial model that happened to measure out 516 feet to one foot. While not the smallest miniature scale, the size enables a large collection to be stored in a relatively small space.

A step-by-step 'how to build' is fundamentally worthless unless you can discriminate between what to use and what to ignore. I hope that some of the following will be helpful in aiding warship modelers to greater success, and with this in mind I have decided to show in the illustrations some of my earliest and poorest work with the belief that this will encourage novices to keep at it.

TOOLS

There are many exotic tools and aids which can be useful — however, I have found that only a handful are actually necessary.

Lots of razor blades, preferably single edged, are essential, as is a pair of pointed tweezers (with gripper teeth). Few tweezers come with a decent point on them, but you can easily grind down the points yourself. The pointed tweezers are intended for detailed work and picking up thin pieces of styrene or strathmore card. They are not intended for heavy work.

A steel T-square is very helpful and time saving. Wood or aluminium squares are not very practical for the straight edges will get nicked if used for cutting. A steel T-square will last a lifetime and can be used both for drawing and cutting. I prefer a 30in T-square for the majority of my work. Occasionally, I also use a small steel triangle for cutting.

Several good camel hair paint brushes are essential. My most prized brushes are 000 fine point brushes which are used exclusively for detailing, lettering or fine touch-up work. I use Winsor and Newton's (they are expensive) and always reshape all brush tips (with my lips) after they have been cleaned and before I put them away. The camel hairs should all come to a perfect point. Chisel shaped brushes are handy, but not essential to my needs. It never ceases to amaze me how badly some modelers treat their brushes — and then wonder why their paint finishing is poor, or why they cannot cut a line. Never lay down a paint-saturated brush without first cleaning it, even if you are only going to be gone for a few minutes. When applying a lot of paint with the same brush, I make a practice of cleaning it every five minutes or so. Get

Top right: There isn't a destroyer built that I don't like — however, the WW2 'Tribals' were especially handsome. The first model clearly shows the appearance variations between the 'Tribal' design and its predecessor. The models are (front to back): *Inglefield, Eskimo, Huron, Sikh, Tartar* and in pre-war appearance, *Mohawk* and *Afridi.*

Bottom right: One of the many models I had built as a child was something that 'looked like the German cruiser *Admiral Hipper*.' I completely rebuilt the model as an experiment to test the effects of plastic body filler on larger and small portions of flat and curved surfaces. Experiments were also made with weathering and battle damage techniques.

several cheap brushes for 'junk' work — glueing, etc.

I find 'push pins' are very handy, primarily to hold small objects. While the pins have sharp points, the wide base allows the modeler to use them as a handle during painting. Furthermore, this base being flat, after you have finished painting the pinned object, simply stand it on the pin's flat base and allow to dry without having to touch any of the wet paint.

'C' clamps are necessary to ensure permanent bonding. At least two each of small, medium and large 'C' clamps will do initially. Never place a clamp directly on the two wooden pieces being joined together (the steel clamps will leave indentations). Sandwich a length of flexible wood between both contact points of the clamp and the joined pieces: this will absorb any damage. This procedure should also be followed when working with a vise.

Gouges and flat wood chisels are needed for hull shaping. The curved chisels (gouges) save a lot of time when working bow flares. The flare is a feature of hull work which novices tend to ignore or botch up. Toothpicks are one of my most useful tools. They can be quickly worked to various shapes. I use them constantly for applying dabs of glue. Cut off a flat end and dampen the tip with saliva. This will enable you to pick up the smallest pieces of strathmore or styrene and apply them directly to a pre-glued position on the model. Naturally, various grades of sandpaper and drills are also essential.

MATERIALS

While soft woods are easier to work, hard woods produce sharp corners and fine grain. However, since everything gets covered with paint, the grain is not a serious consideration (unless the wood has an open, unworkable grain, eg balsa). Working sharp corners comes with practice. White pine and basswood are used for hulls, turrets, mounts, stacks, deck houses and boats. I favour basswood over pine. Balsa has some limited, but handy applications. When used for deckhouses, it must be completely covered with strathmore card. Strathmore card is basically just stiff paper. It is sometimes referred to as bristol board. However, I prefer the strathmore brand because I know that its 100% rag content is reputed to have the same life expectancy as wood. Strathmore comes in two finishes, smooth and kid (slight pebble) — I prefer the former. It is available in several

Above: The three push pins show how easily small objects and details can be painted (without handling). The three superstructures exemplify three different materials. **Left:** pine built island of *Ticonderoga,* some bulwarks have been added, as well as wind deflectors. **Centre:** Basswood island of a modern *Intrepid;* the deck levels have not yet been glued together. **Right:** The balsa bridge of *New York.* Strathmore has yet to be added to all exposed balsa bulkheads. Note the balsa used for the 01 deck (upside down on the hull). The matching 01 balsa casemates have already been covered with strathmore and worked into the basswood hull. The *New York* will eventually carry a 3 color camouflage pattern.

Top right: Four of 12 German 'Narvik' class destroyers which were all built at the same time.

Bottom right: The German battlecruiser *Gneisenau* displays some of those traits common to all my early models — mediocre workmanship, lack of detail and obviously inadequate research material.

Top left: Early models of the British battleships *Duke of York, King George V* and *Anson.* All were built at the same time.

Centre: The French light cruisers *Montcalm* and *Gloire* were built at the same time as a post war *Georges Leygues* (not shown). The anchors were put on wrong!

Bottom: The French cruiser *Montcalm* with destroyer *Le Terrible* in the background. They are crude compared to my current standards and ability.

thicknesses, from one to five ply. For my scale, I use one ply for gun tubs and bulkheads, and two or three ply for decks and bulwarks. A high grade, transparent artists' tissue is also used for covering certain problem areas. Styrene plastic card is magnificent for small details from ammunition boxes to the complete construction of 40mm or 5inch open mounts (except for wire barrels).

Nylon fishline can be used for heavy bollards, depth charges and some types of torpedo tubes. I use 30, 40, 50, 60 and 70 pound test line. The fishline cuts very cleanly with a razor blade. Thin slices of 70lb line then become the wheels on carrier aircraft, scuttles, etc. Hairline copper wire is the basis for all railings, ladders, radar antennae and some rigging Heavier copper wire is used for light caliber gun barrels, yard arms, lattice work, bracing on so on. Stainless steel wire is used for untapered masts, tripod legs, yard arms (which are intended to carry signal yards) and light to medium caliber gun barrels. Major caliber barrels are usually turned from wood, brass or built up around stainless steel.

Ordinary nylon sewing thread is used for most of the rigging. It must be stretched by hand prior to application or else it will stretch by itself after it has been on the model for a time. A slight curve can be worked into this single filament thread, but this must be done with a great amount of care. I have yet to find a completely successful rigging material. I try to keep the amount of 'strings' on a model down to a minimum.

White resin glue is used for most of the wood-to-wood bonding. Ambroid cement is heavily relied on for joining strathmore, metals and fishline to wood. Plastic cement and/or solvent is reserved for styrene-to-styrene, wood or strathmore bonding. Orange shellac takes a long time to dry, but it is well worth it. I use it primarily to bond the hairline wire together to form railings, ladders, radio and radar antennae. Ambroid cement is generally used to mount the assemblies to the model. The rigging is also usually bonded with shellac.

My primary paint is Testors dope (lacquer). Most people find it hard to use. However, I 'broke in' with it and prefer the results I get from it, doing all the tinting, color mixing and flattening myself. My colors now include about forty different tints, shades and values. White is added to all colors to scale them down. Each color is stored in a 4oz bottle. Every couple of months I give the entire batch a thorough stir and if necessary add thinner to a bottle of color that seems a little too thick. If this is not done periodically the paint will jell and then it is worthless — do not bother to try to save it. I use Pactra flat enamel for detailing; it is compatible with lacquer as long as it is on top of it.

PREPARATION

The very first step is research. Find out as much as possible about the warship you intend to bring back to life in miniature form. It often pays to search out several ships at a time. Look for plans, photographs and any books which can be helpful. Some navies, particularly the US, were constantly modifying and up-dating their ships. If you can avoid it, do not guess. I speak from very sad experience and some of the enclosed photographs bear testimony to this.

When I first began serious modeling, there was next to nothing available in the way of plans and photographs, and what was around was usually poor or inaccurate. The same pictures seemed to appear in every naval book. All of that has now dramatically changed as interest in the subject has grown. If necessary, beginners can depend on any volume of the 'Ensign', 'Ship's Data', or the 'Man o' War' series to get a combination of plans, large photographs and paint schemes. The chances are likely that you will not be able to get a set of plans on the ship you intend to build. Settle for any plan of a ship from the same class, and make use of photographs to point out deviations.

There are many commercial plans now available, though most of them are usually drawn to a very large scale. You could take the time and trouble to scale down, but I do not bother. I simply have the entire plan photocopied down to my scale. It may have to be done in two or three steps, if the original is very large. The quality of the plan may well suffer, but you can always refer back to the original. (Keep in mind that it is against the law to copy a plan that has been copyrighted). After the plan is down to your scale, place a piece of tissue paper (tracing paper) over it and make those corrections, using photos as a guide, which are appropriate to the ship you intend to build. Do this for each deck level, as well as the hull plan

and profile. This is where a T-square comes in handy. We will constantly refer to this corrected tissue and plans as we go along.

THE HULL

Select a piece of wood which is larger than the extreme hull dimensions. Take the hull profile tissue, rub graphite (pencil lead) on the back of it and transfer the sheerline to the wood block by tracing round the outline. Do this to both sides taking care to get both outlines in alignment. Chisel down the sheer and sand smooth. Work in the camber at this time. This takes some practice, but once you teach yourself how to handle the tools, you will be surprised how quickly you can cut the sheer on a number of destroyer hulls. Draw a centerline on the top and bottom of the hull and trace off the main deck plan and the waterline plan. Rough cut the excess away and sand smoothly up to the traced lines. I do not use cross sections, but I recommend that you use them. The bow flare is then rough shaped with a gouge. Any tumblehome or stern shaping is usually done with flat chisels. Then everything is sanded down to the final hull form. I constantly check the shape by eye as I go along, matching the hull with the similar hull angles in the photographs. The entire hull is then completely sealed with sanding sealer. The initial coats are very thin. Several coats are applied with much sanding in between, to work out any imperfections. After a final seal, begin painting the hull. All my paints are very thin and I also sand between coats. I prefer six or seven light coats as opposed to one or two heavy coverings.

When applying a camouflage pattern always start the lightest colors first. I draw the pattern lightly on the hull with soft pencil after the entire hull has been completely covered with the lightest color. Then lightly place transparent tape over the pencil lines. Pick the tape up and put it, back down, on a piece of glass. The tape has picked up some of the pencil pattern. Simply cut along the line and match up the appropriate pieces of tape to the pencil pattern that remains on the hull. Burnish down only that edge of the tape that must block the paint from seeping under. Follow the same painting procedure. After the paint is dry, remove the tape. Pick up any excess tape adhesive with a 'rubber cement pick up'. Any hull details or protrusions are added *after* the hull is completely painted. They are then touched up with the appropriate colors.

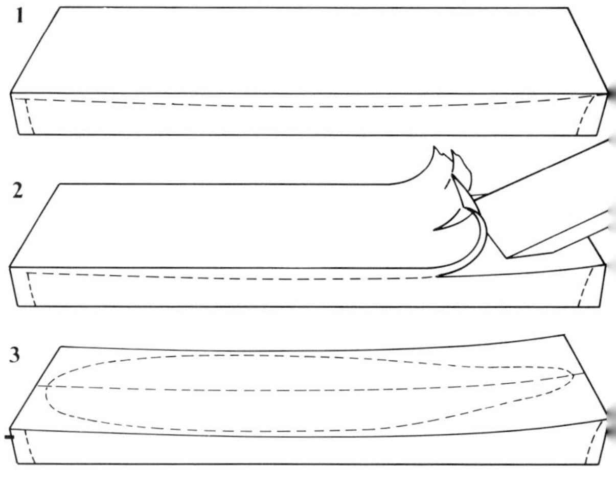

SHAPING HULLS

1 TRANSFER PROFILE TO BOTH SIDES

2 CHISEL OFF EXCESS, TAKING CARE NOT TO GOUGE BELOW PENCILLED SHEER. SAND TO FINISH

3 DRAW CENTERLINE TOP AND BOTTOM, TRACE WATERLINE AND MAIN DECK OUTLINE. CUT OFF EXCESS, SHAPE AND SAN

Left: The Japanese *Yamato* was built some time ago. Her sister, *Musashi* was built at the same time. Due to inaccurate drawings, a number of major mistakes were unknowingly incorporated, primarily in the shape of the pagoda. Both models have since been corrected.

Right: Eight *Baltimore* class cruiser (US) hulls in various stages of shaping. Note the pencil centerline, the main deck outline, and the waterline outline (the fourth hull is upside down). The sheerline has been shaped on all but the last block of pine. Hulls 3 and 4 were cut down from very early and larger hulls (I don't throw anything away).

Centre: Partially completed models of HMCS *Snowberry* and HMS *Legion.* The corvette's after deckhouse follows the curvature of the deck. This was accomplished by laminating. The *Legion* model has yet to be finished; her camouflage colors have to be completely reworked.

Bottom: Three models are currently under 'active' construction. Front to back: battleship *New York,* carrier *Intrepid* and carrier *Ticonderoga. Intrepid*'s hanger (pine) will be completely covered with prepainted strathmore.

TRIPOD FOREMAST AND SUPERSTRUCTURE ASSEMBLY OF USS NEW YORK

EACH DECK LEVEL IS SPOT GLUED INTO POSITION. THE CENTERPOST HOLD IS THEN DRILLED COMPLETELY THROUGH

THIN WIRE IS THEN USED TO APPROXIMATE THE POSITION OF THE TWO TRIPOD LEGS, THROUGH SMALL HOLES. ONCE POSITION IS CORRECT, TAKE DECKS APART, DRILL HOLES TO CORRECT DIAMETER AND REASSEMBLE TO MAKE SURE EVERYTHING LINES UP PROPERLY

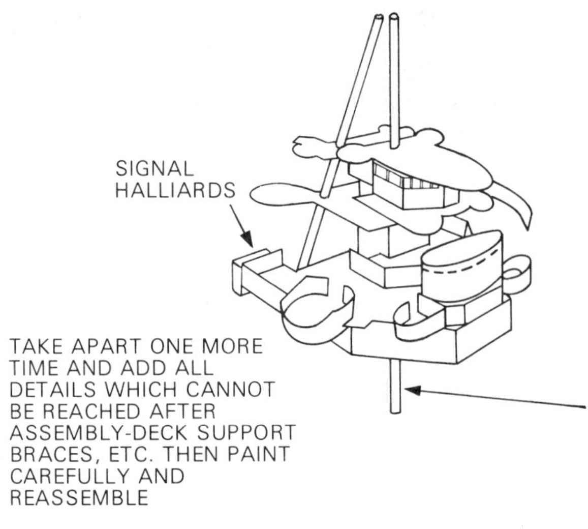

ALL VERTICAL BULKHEADS AND BULWARKS ARE ONE PLY STRATHMORE, PREPAINTED BE[illegible]E FINAL ASSEMBLY

ENTIRE ENCLOSED BRIDGE IS HOLLOW, NO GLASS WINDOWS, JUST ONE PLY BRACES – THIS ENABLES CONTINUOUS PAINTING WITHOUT FEAR OF HITTING A PANE OF GLASS WITH EXCESS PAINT

STAINLESS STEEL POST GOES THROUGH THE ENTIRE SUPERSTRUCTURE INTO THE HULL TO GIVE STRENGTH TO AN OTHERWISE VERY FRAGILE ASSEMBLY

RAILING, LADDER AND RADAR ANTENNA JIG

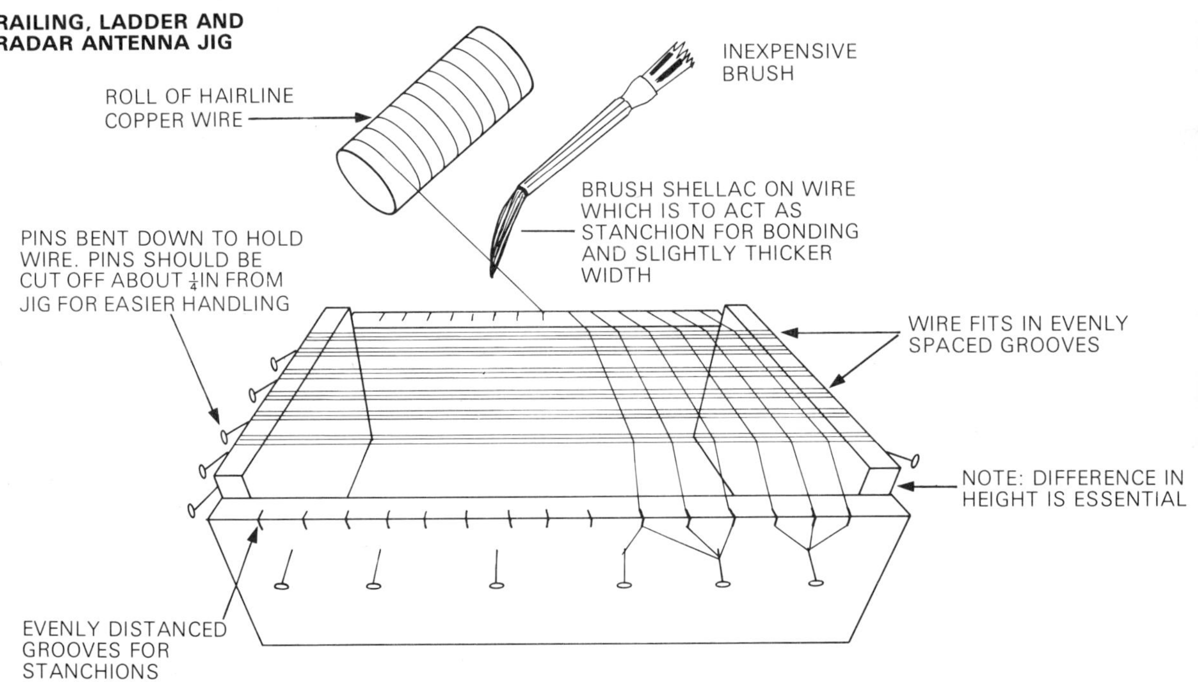

METHOD FOR SHAPING SHIP'S BOATS

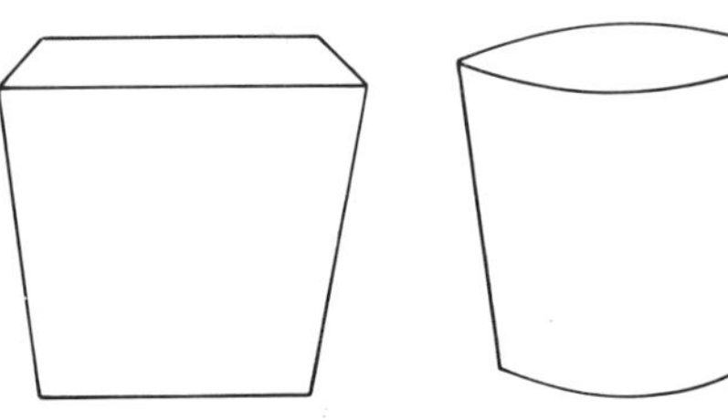

1 BLOCK CUT TO OUTSIDE DIMENSIONS OF 26FT WHALEBOAT

2 BOW AND STERN ARE SHAPED FIRST

3 NEXT SHAPE SHEERLINE TOP AND BOTTOM, THEN GOUGE OR DRILL OUT INTERIOR OF BOTH AND CUT OFF

4 CUT OFF A LITTLE MORE THAN YOU NEED ON EACH HULL

RAZOR

5 SHAPE THE BOTTOM OF EACH CUT OFF HULL WITH A RAZOR BLADE, SAND T(A FINISH, SEAL, ETC

6 INTERIOR CAN BE LINED WITH FITTED STRATHMOR (ONE PLY) TO HIDE ANY IMPERFECTIONS THEN USE TWO PLY FOR SEATS, A BLOCK OF STYRENE FOR ENGINE COVER, ETC

SUPERSTRUCTURES

The superstructure deck tissue tracing is transferred onto a piece of 2 ply strathmore and cut out. Here, the steel T-square saves a lot of time. The decks are then glued to preshaped basswood, pine or balsa. The balsa must be completely covered with tissue or 1 ply strathmore, then painted. The basswood or pine must be sealed and painted using the same hull techniques.

SHAPING PARTS

None of us has enough workbench time to devote to our models. However, there is much wasted time in our daily routine that can be put to good use. I always carry a couple of small 'parts' boxes around with me. When the time avails itself, I then put myself to work, shaping ship's boats, turrets, mounts, aircraft fuselages, or wings. Another box will be filled with shaped parts which have several coats of sealer and must be sanded. This kind of work can be done almost anywhere — the beach, on a train or at the in-laws. It is easy to see how several dozen ships can be in the works at the same time.

Below: Three US models in early stages of construction: the destroyer *Wainwright,* the light carrier *Monterey* and the fleet carrier *Ticonderoga.* The plan has been stated down to my scale. Note the partially worked twin 5in mounts in the foreground.

RAILINGS, LADDERS, ANTENNAE

While they may seem like worlds apart, railings, vertical ladders and rectangular radar antennae all employ the same method of construction. Rectangular 'boxes' were constructed for each (one for railings, one for ladders and one for each different type of antennae). The short sides were cut approximately 1/8in higher than the long side (dimensions about 3in x 5½in). Working tissues were then made of the items to be built. Measurements were carefully marked off and transferred to the respective sides of the 'box'. The marking off and grooving of the slots for the ladder rungs became too nerve-racking, so I simply 'eye-balled' their respective positions. Pins were pushed in all four sides of the 'box' and snipped off about ¼in from the base. Hairline copper (.0005) was then worked over the high sides, fitting into the indentations. Make sure that everything is uniformly taut. The wire is then laid perpendicular (across the low sides). This requires just the right amount of pressure: too little will cause warping, too much will cause compressing and pinching of the previously laid high wires. Before each low strand is laid over, it must be coated with orange shellac.

When laying the ladder rings (on the high sides), make sure that you are relaxed and at ease; half way through you may be ready to pull your hair out.

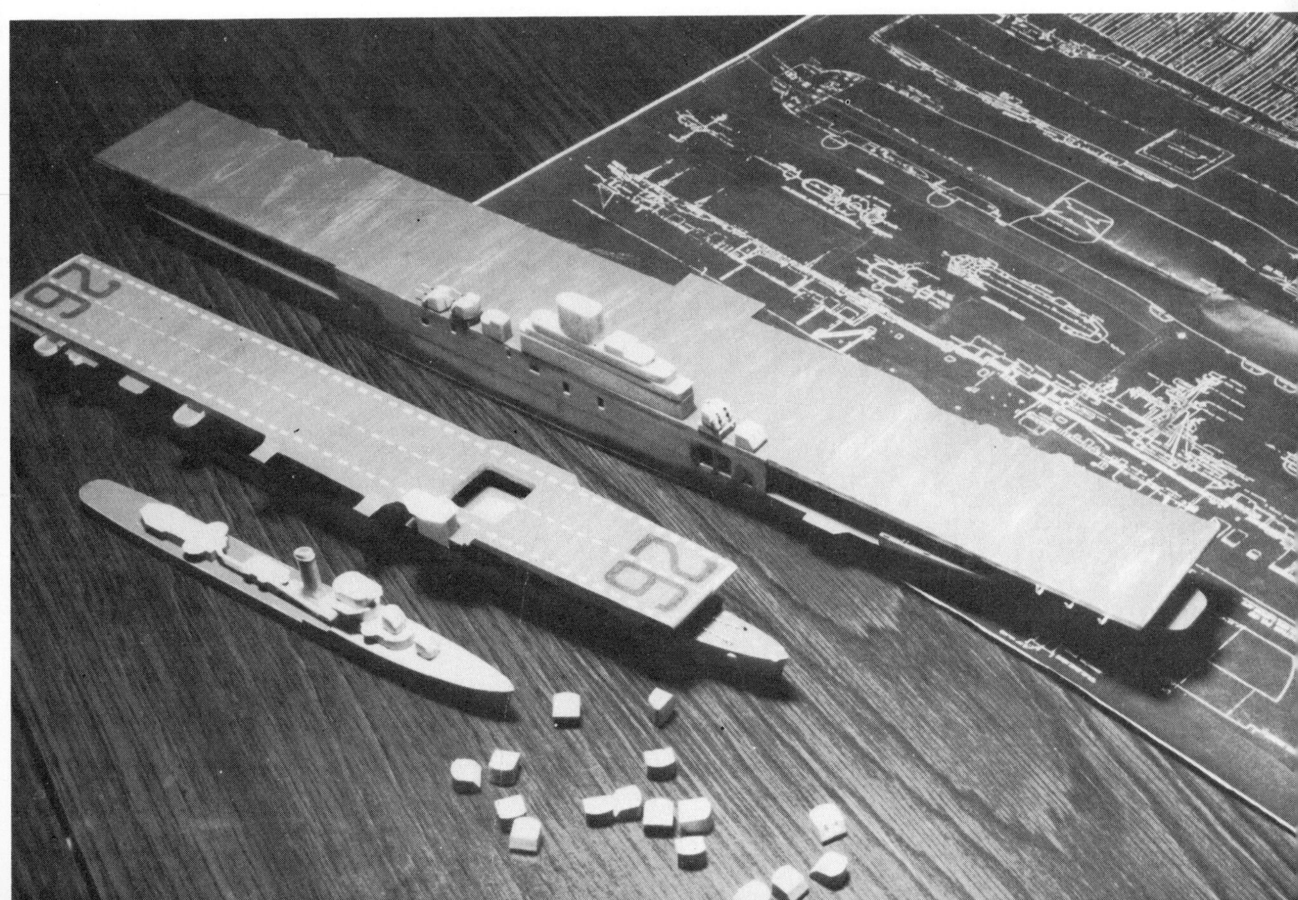

"TONE" as in
scratch built
by L.

Top left: French battleship *Richelieu*, before addition of railings and ladders. The coarse radar antennas were never replaced because of the concern about damaging the rigging.
Centre left: A very early model of the Japanese cruiser *Tone* next to an elaborate *Richelieu*. Everything is wrong with the cruiser: workmanship, proportion, sealing, painting, etc.
Bottom left: The *Yorktown* was the last model completed before I started adding railings, ladders and detailed radar antennas to models. Expect for the antennas, railings and ladders were added later. The *Yorktown* model is shown prior to their installation. The fake water is made from kitchen cellophane wrap (Sarum Wrap) cotton, flat white paint, and high gloss blue spray paint.
Below: The recently completed *Intrepid* in front of a very early HMS *Ark Royal*. The 'Ark' was completely built by 'eye' and has several obvious major errors.
Bottom: USS *Lexington* (CV-2) with biplanes lined up for inspection. With all 84 planes topside the flight deck is completely full.

However, once you are finished with this job, you will have over one hundred ladders.

Before removing the completed 'mesh' of wire from the box, lightly paint the entire mesh with a medium gray paint. Use a razor to cut along all four sides and remove this mesh in one piece. Flip it over and paint the other side. Place the mesh, its railings, ladders or antennae on a piece of glass and cut away any excess. Then cut off whatever you need — very carefully.

Circular radar antennae Each one has to be done individually, but this can move rather quickly despite this. Shape a round dowel just a little smaller than the outside diameter of the antenna. Then wrap a length of copper wire tightly around the dowel a dozen or so times and slide off. I use a sharp finger nail clipper to

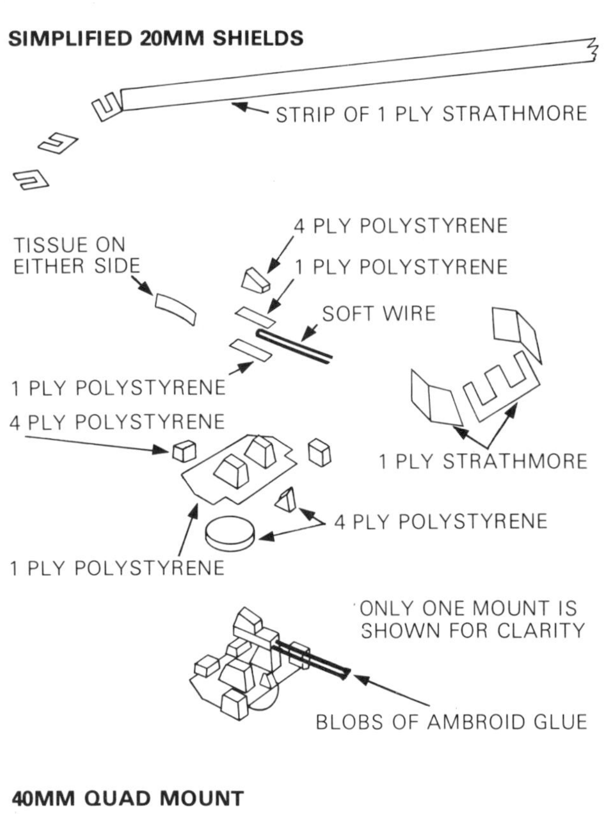

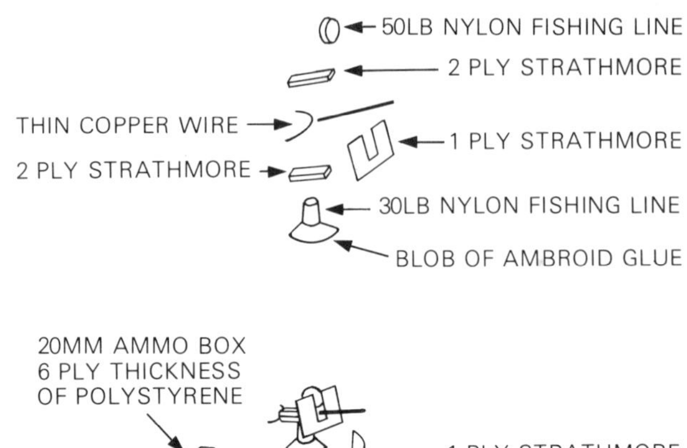

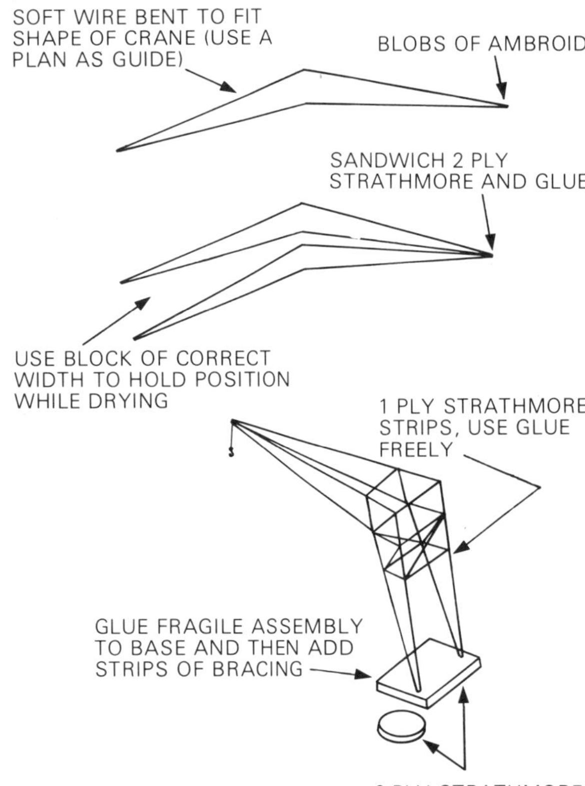

cut it up into individual perfect circles. I then use Ambroid to join 3 or 4 circles. After they dry, I cut a matching number of half circles and glue perpendicular to the full circle. One end is glued directly over the full circle's joint. Six quarter circles are then cut and glued, equidistant on either side of the half circle. Use the glue sparingly.

DOORS AND BULWARKS

Doors are simply measured and cut off a length of one ply strathmore card which has been previously cut to the height of the ship's standard doors. Before the individual door is cut off, the top and bottom corners of the exposed edge are rounded off. Thus only two corners have to be rounded on the now hard-to-handle individual door.

Bulwarks are almost always made from one ply strathmore. In a number of limited cases, I also employ an equivalent to a one ply thickness of polystyrene card, but I find that the strathmore is stronger, more stable, less transparent and can be bent in any direction even after it has been glued. The only reason that I ever use polystyrene is because of its always very clean finish (never any burrs). Also strathmore has the advantage of continuous flexible bending (without heat). Once glued, strathmore bonding is always much stronger. This is especially true for very small details.

DIFFICULT DETAILS AND ASSEMBLIES

Often, there just is not any easy way to build some things, especially delicate see-through cranes, radar antennae, lattice and cage masts. They take a lot of

Below: The US cruiser *Wilkes-Barre* as prepared for exhibition. Unfortunately, some of the rigging was damaged during the show. The irregularities in the camouflage shapes were matched as closely as possible to the actual design as painted on the actual ship in the summer of 1944.

Bottom: Close up of *Lexington*'s island. The heavy build up of glue, to adhere the rigging has been corrected on later models by using shellac or thinned Ambriod.

time and patience. You must make the decision whether or not you are ready to tackle them. Your most indispensible tools will then be your fine pointed tweezers, lots of patience and a positive attitude. Keep in mind that the only difference between gluing down one very small piece or 300 pieces is just time. Your handy 'reduced to your scale' plan will be especially useful to quickly check your details for correct size and position. Remember, especially if you are a beginner, it always looks harder than it actually is.

FINISHING

Unfortunately, I have been able to give you in this chapter less than a tenth of what you need. Anything

Above: The US carrier models already built and ready to be installed in the 'Aircraft Carrier Hall' at New York's *International Aerospace* and *Naval Memorial Museum.* They are (front to back): *Intrepid* (CV-11), *Yorktown* (CV-10), *Monterey* (CVL-26), *Franklin* (CV-13), *Lexington* (CV-2) and *Wasp* (CV-7). (All photos: Larry Sowinski)

that is wood, no matter how small, must be sealed, sanded and painted. Whenever bonding anything to an already painted surface, scrape away the paint and sealer so that you have exposed the raw wood, or strathmore, or whatever.

Very small fittings will have to be carefully painted after they are glued to the model.

Railings, ladders and radar antennae are lightly painted with lacquer which has not been flattened (Ambroid cement will adhere to original Testors dope). Ambroid must be handled carefully because it will mar any lacquer finish. White glue, on the other hand, can be wiped or washed off. Excess plastic cement can be picked off lacquer after the cement is dry.

CONCLUSIONS

If a model 'goes wrong' and you cannot fix it, go on to another one. We learn much more from our mistakes — and the best craftsmen make mistakes; however, they usually do not talk about them. What had initially begun for me as a rewarding hobby has grown into a total way of life. Time has become precious and must be used as efficiently as possible. Now I am building warship models for a very worthwhile purpose. A non-profit organization, Odyssey In Flight, Inc, is preparing the International Aerospace and Naval Memorial Museum. The complex will be housed on board the historical aircraft carrier USS *Intrepid*. My models will be used to portray naval history, warship evolution, worldwide warship comparisons, and famous and classic warships. The constant scale and convenient size makes a collection such as mine ideal for these purposes.

Working models 8

by COLIN GROSS

DESIGN CONSIDERATIONS

If it is intended to make a model operational several factors should be considered during the design phase.

The first, and most important, is the finished size of the model. Initially you must decide what you intend to fit to the working model ie, propulsion system, radio control, special functions such as working turrets etc, since the more you intend to fit to the model the larger it will have to be. Although it is often possible to fit a large amount of equipment into a very small volume, the finished weight of the model must be kept within that of its displacement. The actual finished weight of the model can easily be

Below: The author's model of the Russian circular ironclad *Novgorod* is some 14in in diameter, and shows that unusual vessels can also make very interesting models.

Left: HMS *Fidget.* This 1/48 scale radio controlled model of a gunboat of 1873 was built by Ray Cattle. It shows that it is possible to build a working model of a shallow draught vessel to scale; in this case the draught is just on 1½ inches. The hull is of glass fibre, and the plating has been represented by using gumstrip paper.

found by weighing the parts which you intend to fit. It is also easy to calculate the displacement of the model, if the actual displacement of the full size vessel is known. The calculation is simple: multiply the weight of the full size vessel by the cube of the scale to which the model is to be built. For example, if the full size vessel displaced 1000 tons, and the model is being built to a scale of 1/96, the model's displacement will be:—

1000 ÷ (96 x 96 x 96)=0.00113 tons ie, 2.53lb or 1.14kg.

If the expected weight of the model is greater than this figure, the best course of action would be to build a slightly larger model. If special functions, such as working turrets, have been included in the design they could be removed from the model to lighten it, or the draught of the model could be increased, though the finished model will no longer be true scale. A few years ago it was the accepted practice to increase the draught of a scale model, due to the heavy batteries (for both propulsion and radio control) and the large electric motors which were then available, in order to produce a scale model with a reasonable length. With the introduction of modern lightweight motors, and high power/weight ratio batteries, there are now very few occasions when the draught of a model will need to be increased.

If the displacement of the full size vessel is not known an approximation of the model's displacement can be calculated using a block coefficient. First the length and breadth of the model (at the waterline) are multiplied together, and this result is multiplied by the draught of the model. The overall result is then multiplied by the block coefficient chosen from the following list:

Block Coefficients (typical)	
Destroyer	0.51
Cruiser	0.55
Corvette	0.62
Battleship	0.63
Liner	0.64
Tanker	0.80

This gives the expected volume of the submerged portion of the hull and since 1cc of water weighs 1gm (1 cubic inch weighs 0.57oz) the expected displacement of the model can be calculated. For example, if a model corvette has waterline dimensions of 60cm x 9cm and a draught of 4cm and its block coefficient is 0.62, its expected displacement would be 60 x 9 x 4 x 0.62 x 1=1339gm. In Imperial units this becomes approximately 24in x 3½in and a draught of 1½in giving a displacement of 24 x 3½ x 1½ x 0.62 x 0.57=44.52oz.

However since this figure is an approximation, the actual weight of the model should be kept lower, say 1200gm (40oz), thus allowing 139gm (4½oz) spare for ballast to trim the model to its waterline.

With the size and weight of the model known the position of the access hatches to the inside of the model should be planned. Remember that, if possible, access should also be provided to the top of the rudder post, and that any of the working parts of the model should be capable of being removed from the hull through the access hatches. In general any hatch system with a raised coaming will be more than adequate in terms of waterproofing. If however, you have to operate your model with waves breaking over the decks, the hatches can be completely waterproofed by taping a piece of celluloid over the entire hatch area, using a waterproof adhesive tape (such as Sleek Surgical Tape), prior to fitting the outer hatch or superstructure into position.

In addition to the main access hatches on the model, other small openings in the hull may be required. These are best disguised by making an entire locker removeable, for example, or opening a doorway. To retain the hatch on the model, the simplest method is to locate it over its raised coaming and let its own weight hold it in position. In the case of hatches without coamings, some form of locking system will be required, and this should preferably be operated from only one or two places. A good solution to this is to use a moving gun turret or torpedo tube mounting to operate the locking levers.

The main point with all hatches however is that the better they are fitted and located to the model, the more waterproof they are likely to be.

The final point to bear in mind while designing the model is the positioning of the major items within the hull. Obviously the main criterion is that the model must float level and to the correct waterline, but attention must also be given to its stability. The position of everything except the permanent ballast is to a large extent determined by the openings in the hull, since access to the working parts of the model is essential for maintenance etc. The height above the keel of the heavy items will govern the stability of the model in roll, whilst their disposition fore and aft will govern its performance in pitch.

In general these items should be kept as low as possible in the hull, as this will give the model its maximum stability. Furthermore, keeping them together, while maintaining the correct waterline, will allow the bow of the model to rise quickly when meeting a wave. In practice, it is possible to move the ballast from this central low position in order to lessen the model's stability (or 'stiffness') and give it a more realistic performance, but this can only be done by trial and error when the model is operating.

PROPULSION SYSTEMS

There are three basic forms of motive power. In their order of suitability for the average working model, these are electricity; steam; internal combustion (petrol etc).

Hybrid models using, for example, IC and electric motors with clutch systems, have been used successfully, but in general their complexity outweighs their advantages.

IC Engines

This type of motor has the advantage of providing the highest power output over a prolonged period of time. For short term use of 5 to 10 minutes, electric motors can be as powerful but will occupy a larger hull space. The normal diesel, or glowplug style motor can provide about $1\frac{1}{2}$hp per 10cc (0.6 cubic inches) of capacity at about 15 000rpm. However the vibration they cause could well be troublesome for a good scale model, and the noise from even a very well silenced motor is just not right for the majority of models. The fuel can also cause problems with the paint and plastic fittings of the model. This type of motor is thus best suited to large scale fast vessels, such as MTBs, although electric propulsion would be a better choice if the reduced running time is acceptable.

Petrol motors tend to be relatively slow running and a good deal less noisy with less vibration, but they are not generally available in small sizes, for example, less than 15cc (0.9 cubic inches), and their complexity tends to make them unsuitable for the average

HATCH LOCKING GEAR

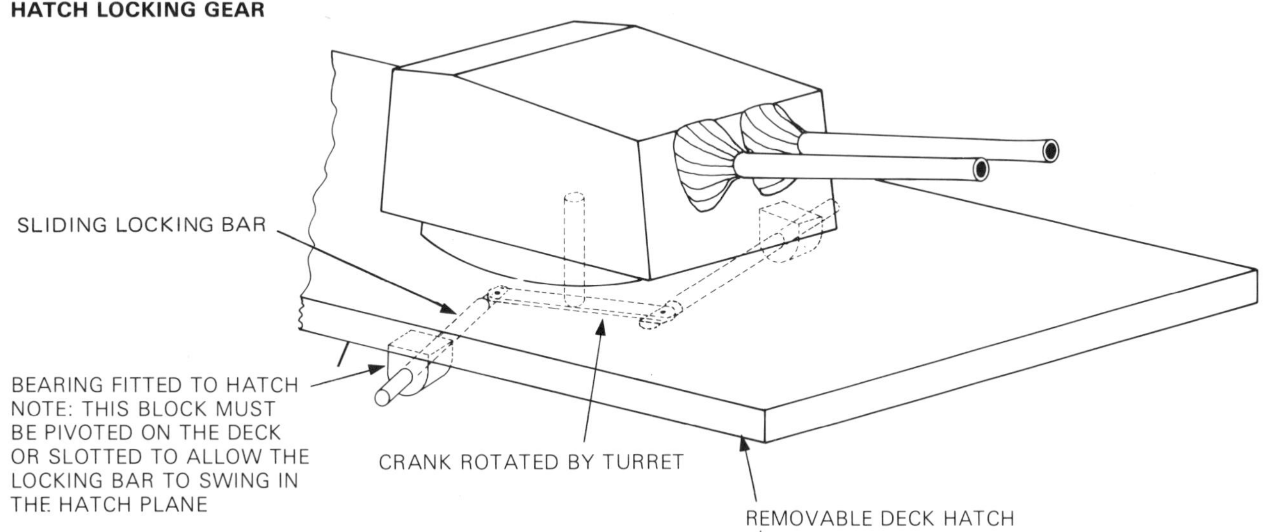

Right: Tony Broad's live steam model of the destroyer HMS *Cygnet* (1898) is over 6ft long. The model was built with straight running competitions in mind, but is completely to scale. It was placed 5th in its class in the European Championships at Kiev in 1977.

Below: Because of the noise problems, IC installations, such as the one shown here in this Air Sea Rescue Launch, are not so frequently seen in scale models these days.
(Conway Picture Library).

Bottom: A typical steam plant layout, this time in a plank-on-frame model of a launch.
(Conway Picture Library)

modeller. They can be used to advantage in very large models but as with all IC engines a gearbox will be needed to give astern operation of the model.

STEAM ENGINES

In the past few years steam engines have begun to appear in good scale model vessels, and with the increasing availability of complete engine/boiler systems their popularity is likely to continue to grow. Their biggest problem so far as scale models are concerned is that of heat damaging the model. To a

large extent this can be overcome by suitably lagging the boiler and steam pipes, together with keeping them as far away as possible from the deck and superstructure of the model. If radio control is fitted it must obviously be kept as far away as possible from the boiler to avoid overheating it.

Small double acting oscillating engines are perfectly capable of propelling models up to about 75/90cm (30/36in), but they are not self starting, so if stop and reverse functions are required, a suitable clutch and/or gearbox system will be needed.

For larger models the slide valve engine of two or more cylinders is normally used, and reversing gear is often fitted on the valve gear. However this style of engine is relatively complex, and any boiler should not be tackled lightly; in fact the modeller who is intending to use this type of steam plant will be well advised to read up as much as possible on the subject beforehand.

ELECTRIC MOTORS

By far the most popular propulsive system for the scale model is the electric motor and battery system. Besides having none of the disadvantages of the previous two engine types, it has several advantages of its own. The most important of these is its simplicity of control, and reversing; no complicated mechanics or gearboxes are required and, unlike steam or IC engines which require frequent oiling and cleaning, the electric motor can be left unattended for long periods. The main decision when using electric motors is the choice of batteries, there being three main types.

Dry Batteries (primary type). This is the type of battery normally used in torches and radios. In general is not of great interest to modellers since the cost of buying replacements will soon exceed the initial cost of a rechargeable battery pack. However, in small infrequently used models they can be a good source of power.

Lead/Acid Types. Until recently this type of battery was used in nearly all electric model boats. It had the advantage of being relatively cheap, and of giving a reasonable power output for its size. The main disadvantage of the lead/acid cell is that it must be stored in a charged condition and if ignored for a period of several months it will often start to decompose and thus be ruined. However, if properly maintained the lead/acid battery is still a very good source of power.

Nickel Cadmium Types (nicads). In the past few years these cells have become much cheaper to buy and are now about the best power source for the average electric model. They generally have a longer life than lead/acid types, require vertually no maintenance, and can supply very large discharge currents for short periods, which makes them ideally suited for fast electric models.

Special Notes On Batteries. In many models batteries are connected in parallel to increase the running time of a model.

In most cases the switch 'A' is ignored and the On/Off switch fitted at 'B'. Since the two battery voltages are often marginally different, although the model is switched off one battery will always be discharging into the other. As a result the total battery

Above: This beautiful 1/96 scale model of the destroyer HMS *Vendetta* by Don Brown, is electrically driven and radio controlled. It shows that fine and tricky detail can be incorporated in a true-to-scale working model.

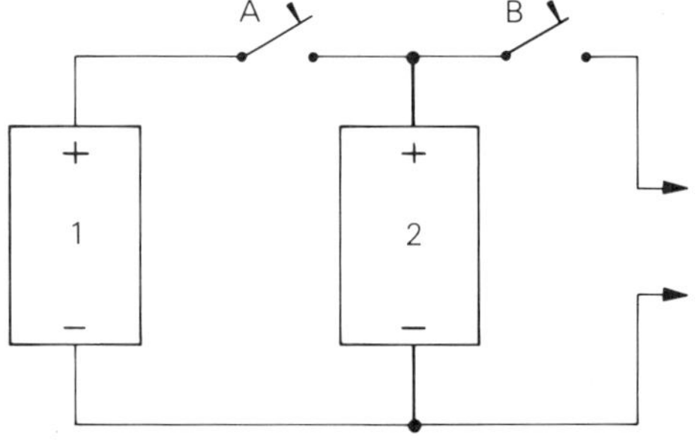

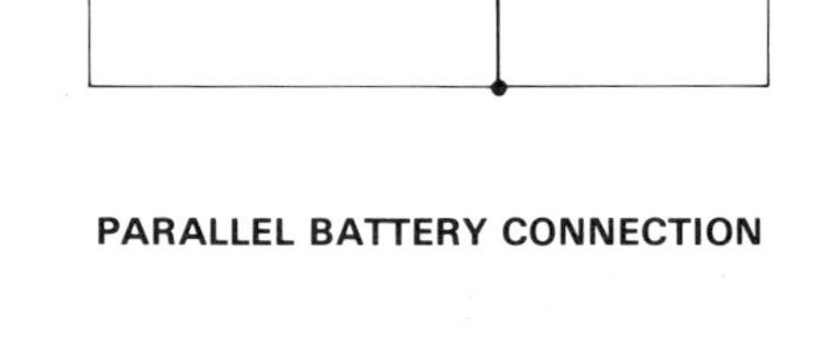

PARALLEL BATTERY CONNECTION

capacity, and thus the running time of the model, will be reduced. Using a double pole switch to switch both 'A' and 'B' will overcome this. Whenever possible the best solution is to use only one battery of a sufficient capacity.

When batteries are used in series, they must be of equal capacity (eg, all be 2Ah). If they are not, the cell or battery with the lowest capacity will become discharged before the others, and will then be charged in reverse if power is still taken from the system. As a result the cell will be damaged.

The final point on electric power is that of using wires and switches of sufficient rating. In systems using high currents (above about 5Ah) power is often wasted in the wiring. In this case the wire should not be of the type used to wire up radio circuits. The same applies to switches used in motor circuits. If the switch is too small its contacts will at best be damaged each time the switch is operated, and they may even weld together, making it impossible to switch off again.

PROPELLERS

The propeller system on a model should, as with the rest of the vessel, be scale. This one basic rule can always be applied, thus giving the model a propeller with both the correct diameter and number of blades. However to achieve the desired performance both the rpm and the pitch of the propeller can be adjusted, (the same applies to paddle wheels where the wheel is made to scale, and its rpm increased). From the requirement of adjusting pitch, it follows that the propeller is best made from brass. The propeller can be bought from one of the manufacturers who advertise in the model press (and who will often construct to your requirements) or built as described later in this section. If a plastic propeller is used it should be roughened with wire wool, painted and varnished to improve its appearance.

Since the size and appearance of the propeller is scale, it follows that the number of propellers fitted and their position should also be scale. The best solution to powering multiple propellers is to use a separate motor on each shaft. This will allow each propeller to run at a speed at which it can do most work.

On a vessel with a multi-shaft layout the propeller 'B' will be operating in the water stream from 'A'. As a result the load on its motor will be less than that on 'A's motor, and so it will speed up. The higher speed of propeller 'B' will thus ensure that it still does its fair share of the work.

As stated this is the best solution. With slow moving models, or those where optimum efficiency is not required, it is perfectly acceptable to drive both propellers 'A' and 'B' from the same motor, or indeed all four propellers from one motor. The tunnelled propellers fitted to some types of river gunboat (and Q-ships) also function satisfactorily in model form, for as soon as the propeller has made a few revolutions all traces of air will have been pumped from the tunnel. The only type of propeller system which may give trouble when built to scale is the surface piercing propeller as fitted to some coastal motor boats. In this case the only solution will be to experiment with the pitch of the blades until the model behaves in a satisfactory manner.

PROPELLER CONSTRUCTION

The following is one of the many possible ways of constructing a brass propeller.

1 Using a lathe, turn the outside diameter of the propeller boss to about twice the length of the finished boss.

2 Drill and tap the boss with the thread appropriate to the size of your propeller shaft.

3 Turn the shape of the propeller boss leaving between 1mm to 3mm (0.04 to 0.12in), depending

Above and top: Two stages in making a simple brass propeller, the first showing the two prepared blades and the slotted boss into which they will be soldered, and the other the job completed with the blades correctly shaped.

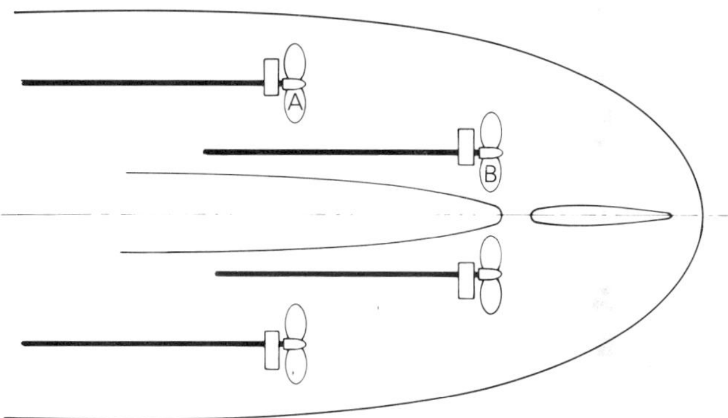

MULTIPLE SHAFT ARRANGEMENT

PROPELLER BOSS ROD – TURNED TO SIZE AND TAPPED

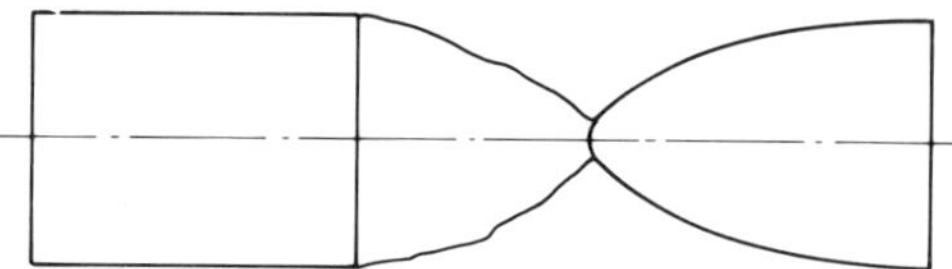

PROPELLER BOSS TURNED TO SHAPE BUT NOT PARTED FROM ROD

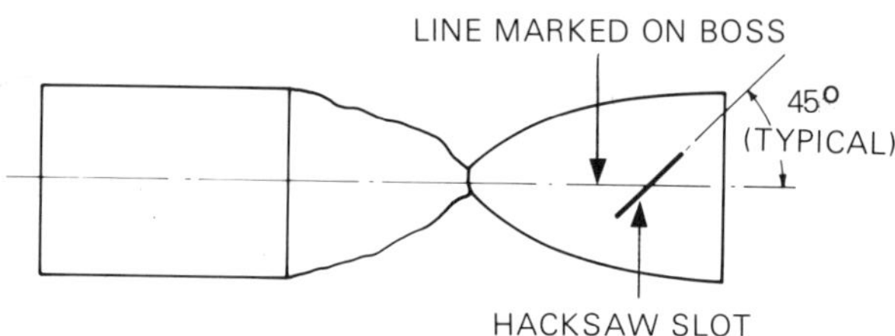

NOTE: THE SLOT IN THIS SKETCH IS FOR A LEFT HAND PROPELLER. REVERSE THE DIRECTION OF THE GROOVE FOR A RIGHT HAND PROPELLER

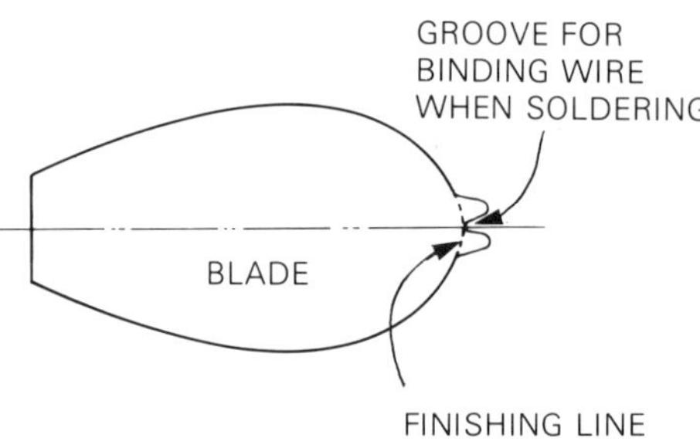

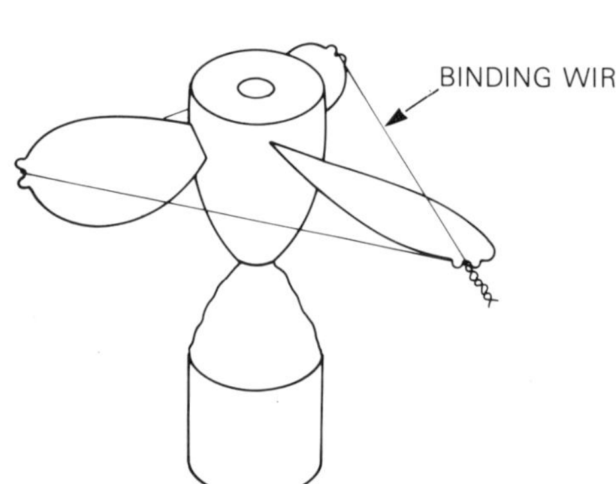

METHOD OF SECURING BLADES TO BOSS WITH WIRE READY FOR SOLDERING

upon the diameter of the boss, joining the boss to the rest of the rod.

4 Mark along the axis of the boss the centre line of each blade; this is best done while the boss is still in the lathe. Use the tip of the turning tool and the cross slide to mark a line across the end face of the boss. This gives a reference for two blades. With four blades rotate the lathe chuck through 90° and repeat the operation. For three and six blades use the jaws of the three jaw chuck to give a reference for marking the boss. Mark the end of each line lightly along the outside face of the boss.

5 Remove the work piece from the lathe and with a hacksaw cut a small slot across each of the marked lines for the rest of the blade.

6 Cut a thin card template for the shape of the blade and offer it up to the boss. Adjust the shape of the card until the blade is correct, and then use it to mark out the required number of blades on brass sheet. Each blade should be cut out as shown. Once the propeller has been completed the two 'ears', formed to retain the binding wire during assembly, must be cut off.

7 Clean all the parts thoroughly for silver soldering and assemble each blade into the boss and then bind with thin copper wire as in the sketch (remember to assemble the blades the correct way round if they are asymmetric).

8 Once everything is set up make a final check for symmetry and then silver solder the blades to the boss (soft solder may be used but is mechanically weak). When cool remove the wire and trim the blades to their correct shape.

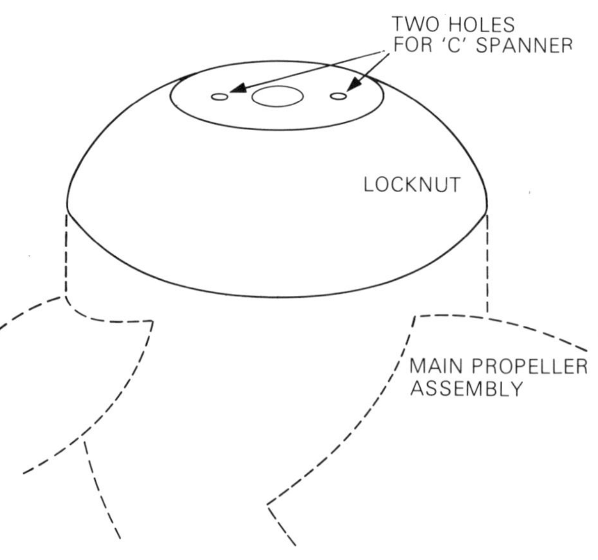

PROPELLER LOCKNUT

Above: Another unusual model, a radio controlled LCT complete with tank. The ramp could be lowered when the model beached, and the tank driven ashore. This electrically powered model was about 36 inches long.

Right: Submarines as working models are still a comparative rarity, but there is a growing interest in building such models: a British *U* class, by Steve Kirby.

9 Cut off the boss from the stub and mount it on a thread rod in the lathe for machining the point. The entire propeller is then cleaned and finished as required.

10 For propellers with a boss diameter greater than about 6mm ($\frac{1}{4}$in) it is best to machine a special locknut to fit the propeller to the shaft. This gives a better appearance than the normal propeller nut but does require construction of a 'C' spanner to fit it.

SPEED AND POWER

The formula for calculating the 'scale' speed of a model based upon a known prototype is:—

$$\frac{V}{v} = \sqrt{\frac{L}{l}}$$

where V is the speed of the prototype in knots, L is its length in feet, l is the corresponding length of the model in feet, and v is the speed of the model in knots.

Alternatively the same answer will be obtained by multiplying the speed of the prototype by the square root of the scale factor of the model. For example, if a model of a vessel having a speed of 30kts is built to a scale of 1/100 the scale speed will be :—

$$30 \times \sqrt{\frac{1}{100}} = 30 \times 0.1 = 3\text{kts}$$

Although this is an accurate figure for the model's scale speed (being based on Froude's law of comparative speeds), it can only be a guide to the modeller, since other factors — wind, waves, ripples on the water — can affect this model's performance. Often the only way to overcome this is to increase its speed slightly — but not to the extent that one so often sees of the model of a normal 20kts prototype charging across the pond at a scale speed up to 70kts!

The best and most practical solution to this problem is to adjust the speed of the model until the wave pattern it produces matches that of the full size vessel. In free-running models this can be achieved by adjusting the pitch of the propellers, and varying the voltage supplied to the motors. With radio controlled models it is always advisable to have excess power available and to use a speed controller to set the actual speed of the model.

SIZE

The problem of how big the motor should be is always one of the most difficult when building a working model. One solution is to try and look at similar models and their performances, and then use a similar size of motor installation. Even if you cannot find a vessel of similar type to your own, this method can still provide a useful guide.

The majority of scale model warships tend to be of the displacement type, so we shall concentrate on this type. As a guide however, a 100cm (40in) MTB style of vessel should be capable of planing on the power provided by either a 5cc (0.3 cubic inch) diesel or glowplug engine, or about 250 watts of electric power (the Ripmax Bullet or 2 Cyclone 15s).

The majority of steam propulsion systems will either be purchased complete, or built from plans, and in both cases the supplier will normally recommend the size of hull in which it should be used.

With the large number of electric motors now available it is obviously not practical to list all the types suitable for any one model. The power rating of the motor however can be used to define the power requirements of some typical models. Power = Voltage x Current (measured when motor is running at its correct output).

The voltage and current at which a motor should be operated are often supplied with the motor. From practical experience the following results are typical:

Corvette	60cm (24in) = 10w
Frigates & Destroyers	90cm (36in) = 25w
Battleships	150cm (60in) = 50w
Landing Craft	140cm (55in) = 40w

To a first approximation, doubling the size of the model will require about three times the power to produce a scale speed. When multiple propellers are involved the power should be split between them in direct proportion to the propeller's size. For example, with four equal propellers it would be best to fit four motors, each of one quarter the total power, although if required the propellers could be geared to either one or two of the motors (two motors would each equal half of the total power).

Since the total motor current will be known it is also possible to calculate roughly how long the model will run before the batteries become flat. Batteries are rated in Ampere Hours (Ah), so a battery quoted as 4Ah will be able to supply 4 amps for almost 1 hour. However in practice, because of the way batteries are specified and the chemical reactions inside them, they will not last as long as this simple calculation would suggest.

PROPELLER SHAFTS

The first requirement with any propeller shaft is to obtain a piece of material (preferably silver or stainless steel) that is not only the correct diameter but absolutely straight. The various parts of the shaft and tube assembly can then be constructed.

On vessels such as corvettes where there is no exposed shaft the construction is identical except that the shaft has only two bearings and the propeller assembly replaces the thrust block fairing. Starting at the propeller end, the shaft is threaded for the propeller and its lock nut. This thread should not extend inside the 'A' frame bearing. The bearing in the 'A' frame can be made from brass etc, but a PTFE bearing pushed into the frame will give a better life. It is important that the propeller does not push on the 'A' frame but that the thrust from the propeller is taken on the thrust fairing. For this reason the fairing must be firmly secured to the shaft either by a grub screw or by a pin through the shaft, although the latter is difficult to remove for maintenance.

The bore of the tube should be about 2 to 3mm (0.08 to 0.12in) larger than the diameter of the shaft and have a bearing of about 3 shaft diameters in length at each end. These bearings can be built up from concentric pieces of tubing, or turned on a lathe, and should be a good running fit on the shaft before being soldered into the tube. To keep the system waterproof, the tube is filled with grease, either by removing the shaft, or preferably through a grease point fitted on the inboard end of the tube. On very large models it is possible to fit 'O' rings to keep the bearings waterproof but in general these are not required. The method of aligning the tube and 'A' frame has been described in another chapter.

GEARBOXES AND COUPLINGS

Gearboxes are normally used for connecting the drive motor to one or more propellers, but they may also be used for other applications, such as gun turret rotation. The basic requirements of a good gearbox are:—

1 A rigid mainframe to keep the gears in correct mesh.

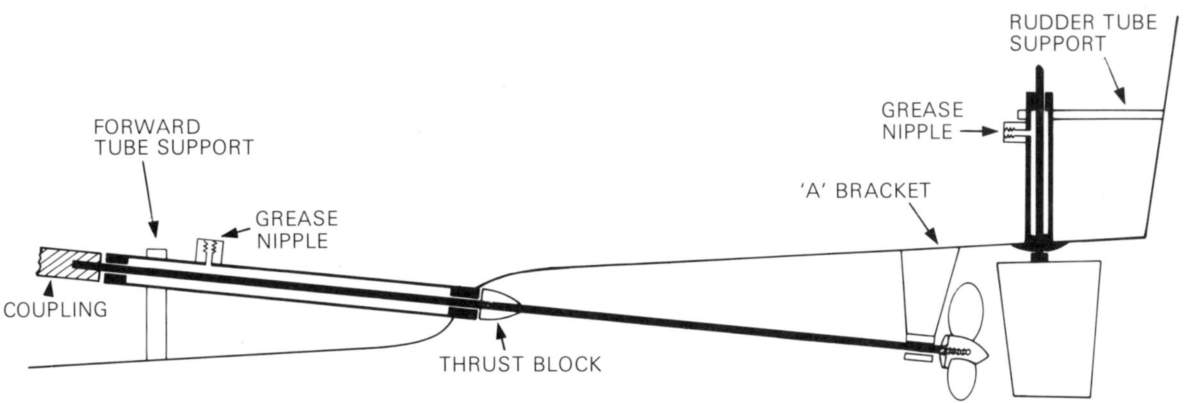

STERN GEAR

2 Accuracy in manufacture to set the gear mesh correctly.

3 Gears of sufficient size for the job.

In addition some thought should be given to the lubrication of the gears, especially in high speed, heavy duty systems.

In low power models (up to about 20w) multiple fall pulleys and rubber driving belts can provide a very simple solution.

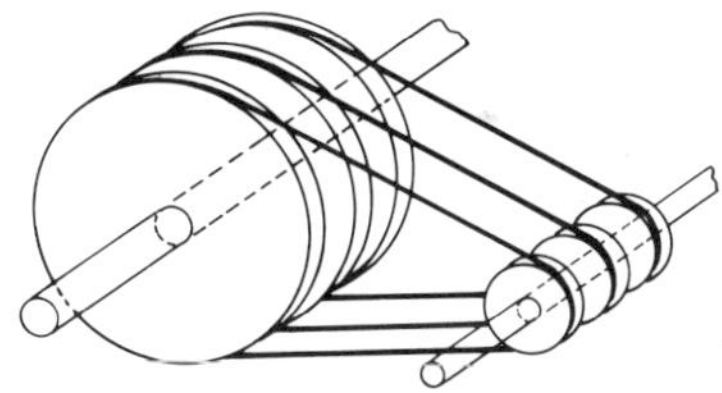

ARRANGEMENT OF MULTIPLE PULLEYS

The system is obviously capable of being used in larger models although with heavy duty drive belts the diameters of the pulleys tend to become excessive. An alternative would be the toothed belt, but these are not always readily available.

For linking multiple propeller shafts together chain drives become useful, but as with pulleys the sprocket size tends to be excessive, especially if ratios above 3:1 are required. Chain drives obviously require less accuracy during construction than gearboxes, but care must be taken to obtain the correct tension on the chain — usually achieved by the inclusion of an adjustable chain tensioning sprocket.

In the majority of cases, however, when a motor is not directly coupled to the propeller shaft a conventional gearbox will be used.

Many gearboxes built by modellers, especially those intended for special functions such as operating gun turrets, fail to function properly due to the

Above: The author has referred to powered gun turrets, and here is his method of constructing such a working turret for a *Leander* class frigate. The standard cable connectors on the left of the top plate give an idea of size.

Left: A composite gear and chain drive by the author for a twin screw installation. The left hand gear is driven from a worm gear on the starboard propeller shaft. Note the inner hatch frame into which celluloid is taped for total waterproofing.

mainframe distorting under load. When finished it should be impossible to twist the input and output shafts out of their original alignment. If twisting is possible additional stiffening will be required.

The correct meshing of gears is essential but is also difficult to obtain. With the majority of gears used by modellers the correct spacing for the gears will not be available, but can be measured as follows. Using the lathe turn two spindles, one for each gear, to a good sliding fit in the boss. One end of each spindle should be turned to a point. Place the gears on a flat surface and space to give a very small amount of backlash.

This job is easier if the lower ends of the spindles are of equal diameter, since they may then be held in a vice. The correct gear spacing can then be measured between the points of the spindles. When the spacing of all of the gears in the train have been measured the gearbox can be marked out for drilling. The final point on meshing concerns layshafts.

The layshaft is subjected to a leverage which will tend to turn it end over end. If the spacing between the bearing is short, or worse, if the shaft is fixed and the gears run on it, this leverage may well move the gears out of their correct parallel alignment, therefore layshaft bearings should be as far apart as possible.

Obviously it is difficult to give sizes for gears, since their applications are very diverse. However as a general guide the first priority is the tooth size, which should be sufficient to transmit the required power without breaking. The width of the face of the gear will also affect the load capability, and for most boat drive trains, gears with a face width of less than 2mm (0.08in) should not be considered. A further advantage of the large tooth is that it is generally easier to set the correct mesh of the gears.

As a last point on gearboxes mention should be made of the shaft bearings. These should not normally be made of aluminium (it is generally too soft) and their length should not be less than the diameter of the shaft they carry.

For joining the various shafts together the double universal joint is recommended. These are readily available in model shops and can couple shafts with both linear and angular displacement (the angular displacement should not exceed about 20° to 30° per joint). Their disadvantage over the ball and socket coupling is that access is required to disconnect them to allow shaft removal, and this should be borne in mind when choosing a coupling system. Bellows and flexible plastic couplings are also available but their

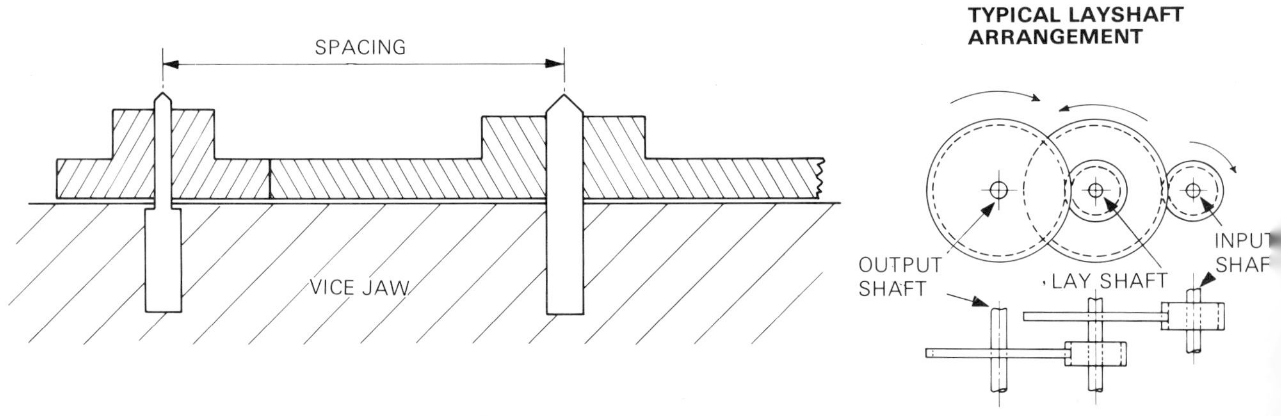

MEASURING THE SPACING OF GEARS

ability to cope with misalignment is generally less than other types.

RUDDERS

Once the rudder blade has been built and secured to the rudder post, it is mounted in the hull in a tube similar to that used for the propeller shaft. Although some modellers use a tube which is a sliding fit on the rudder post, these tend to corrode quickly and so cause problems with stiff rudder operation. A grease filled tube is a much better proposition.

For the majority of warships the rudder will need to be larger than scale size if a reasonable turning circle is required. This is especially true if the rudder is not directly behind a propeller. If an oversize rudder is not acceptable the best solution is to make a rudder shaped 'box' which can be clipped over the scale rudder when the model is to be run.

Normally a rudder need only be moved about 40° to 45° each side of neutral. Any movement beyond this will decrease the turning circle only marginally, but also will cause a considerable amount of drag, thus slowing the model.

On multi-screw vessels it is also possible to connect a switch which, when the rudder is on full throw, will cut off the power supply to the motor on the inside of the turn thus reducing the turning circle. A better solution, whenever practical, is to fit a separate motor and speed control for each side of the vessel, thus giving good manoeuverability even when going astern.

Above: Top and bottom views of a 'one-piece' radio installation by the author. Three servos and radio batteries can be seen on the left. The speed controller at right centre has main on-off switch and special function switching from the third servo.

RADIO CONTROL

The question most often asked by the newcomer to radio control is 'Can I build it myself?' Unfortunately the answer is generally 'No' since there are very few kits available, and even fewer good designs have been published. The biggest deterrent however is the cost. To build an outfit from scratch will often cost almost as much as buying the finished article (this is analagous to buying all the parts of a full size automobile which would cost more than the complete machine). Assuming that you are intending to build further models and that you may want to fit them with additional functions, such as separate controls for port and starboard motors, gun turret training gear and so on, it is best to buy a multi-channel outfit.

The high initial outlay for this type of equipment can be reduced somewhat by purchasing only two servos to go with a 4 channel set in the first instance. In addition several manufacturers will add extra channels to your radio at a later date, although this should be checked before purchase. When you are ready to instal the radio into your model the following points should be borne in mind.

POSITION OF COMPONENTS

Ideally all the components of the radio control system should be mounted as far away as possible from the main drive motor and batteries. In many cases it is possible to mount the entire radio control system on one sub-chassis, which is an enormous advantage when it comes to servicing and general maintenance. An added bonus is that it is very easy to transfer the entire system to another model. Care must be taken however to ensure that the servos can operate their respective controls, and that the linkage runs are both mechanically and geometrically correct.

In all cases try to mount the whole of the radio control above the bilges to avoid bilge water (some day they will inevitably become wet). If all else fails at least mount the receiver and its aerial as far as possible from the main drive motor.

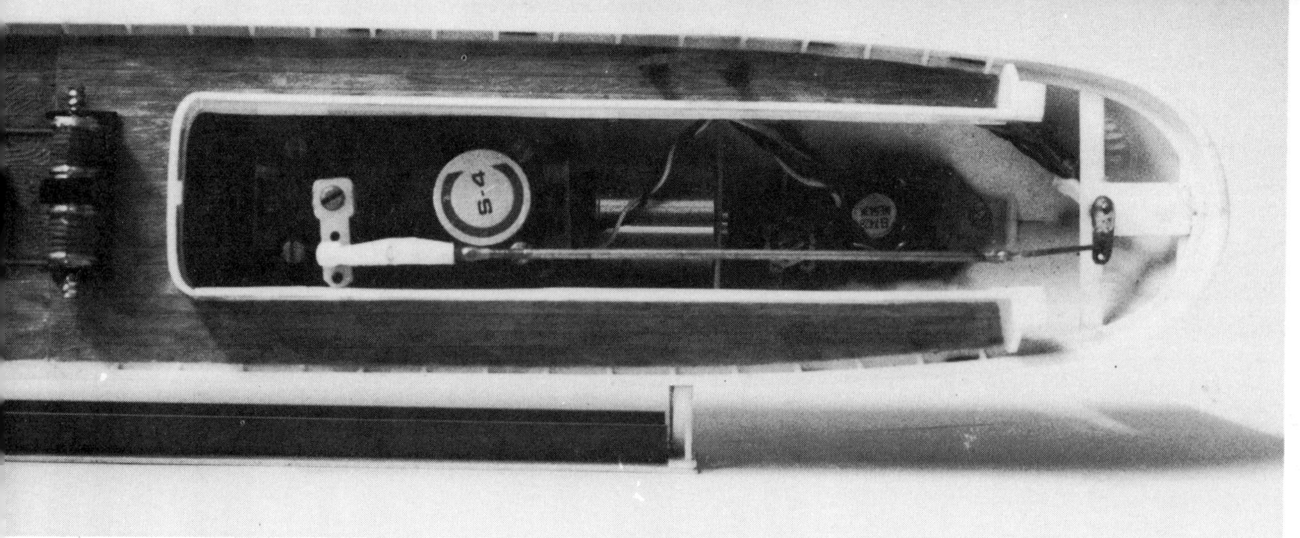

LINKAGES

The linkage from the servo output arm to whatever it controls is a very important part of the model and should be treated accordingly. For complete precision in control it must be rigid — for example, it must not be possible to deflect the rudder without the servo moving. For long control runs either Bowden cable or tubular push rods should be used, the ends being fitted with suitable servo links. The connection to both the servo and rudder arm (or whatever) should be made in such a way that no slop is introduced into the system, and commercial links are made for this purpose. Metal to metal contact should be avoided if possible since this can be a source of radio interference, unless the parts are joined together with a wire earthing strap.

When the servo and whatever it controls are at their central position, the linkages should be at 90° to the control arms. The reason for this is explained with the aid of the sketch. If the servo and rudder arms are initially at 'B' and 'B' the rudder is central at 2. If the servo moves 30° to 'A' the rudder arm moves the rudder to position 1, a movement of 53°. Moving the servo the other way from 'B' by 30° will only move the rudder to position 3, a movement of 36°. As can be seen the rudder takes up a different angle each side of centre for the same movement of the servo. Unless the effect is required, the linkages should be set at 90° to the control arms. When using a servo to operate a switch or any control that has end stops to its movement, it is important that the servo can still reach its full travel as controlled by the transmitter. If this is not permitted the servo may stall and its motor or amplifier could be destroyed.

AERIALS

The majority of warships have large quantities of 'rigging' amongst which the aerial wire can be hidden, preferably by making it part of the rigging. Aerials in the vertical plane are most efficient and in all cases should be between 30-100cm (12 to 36in) long, the longest being preferable. If possible the finished length of the aerial should be the same as that originally supplied with the radio since the radio was originally tuned with this length of wire. The finished aerial should be as straight as possible and must be electrically insulated from the rest of the model. If plug connections are used they must be tight to avoid interference problems.

ELECTRIC MOTOR CONTROL

There are two basic methods of controlling electric motors. The first is to use switches to provide forward

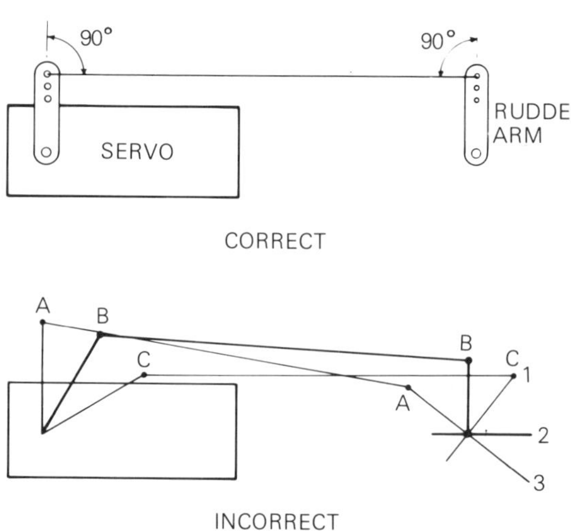

SERVO LINKAGE GEOMETRY

Left: The interior of a small model (it was about 16in long) showing the rudder control gear. The receiver and battery were stowed in a compartment at the fore end.
(Photos: Authors collection and J L Bowen)

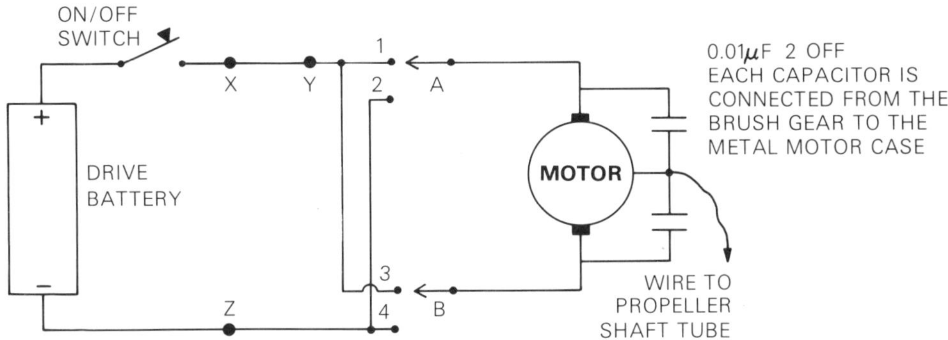

BASIC CONTROL CIRCUIT

FOR PERMANENT MAGNET MOTORS ONLY
SEE TEXT FOR WOUND FIELD MOTORS

and reverse, and possibly an intermediate fixed speed from a tapping on the battery. The second and most preferable is to use a speed controller. A basic circuit for forward and reverse switching is shown which also incorporates a method of interference suppression which should be fitted to any electric motor used in the boat. If the motor has a plastic case, join the two capacitors to the propeller tube only.

The on/off switch should always be inserted in the circuit and switches 'A' and 'B' control the operation of the motor.

With permanent magnet motors the circuit is wired as shown. With switch 'A' at 1 and 'B' at 3 the motor is off. If switch 'A' is on 2 and switch 'B' on 3 then current flows from switch 'B' to switch 'A' and the motor runs. If switch 'A' is on 1 and switch 'B' on 4 then current flows from 'A' to 'B' and the motor runs in reverse.

With wound field motors having a series field coil, the coil would replace the piece of wire linking 'X' to 'Y'. If it has a parallel field coil it would join 'X' to 'Z'. In both cases the rest of the circuit would be identical.

To save battery power, however, it is best to arrange the motor switching servo to operate the on/off switch in order to avoid current flowing in the parallel field coil when the motor is stationary.

If a commercial speed controller is used it will come complete with instructions for its wiring; alternatively if a home made speed controller is used the information from which it was constructed will show its wiring.

OPERATING THE MODEL

Once the model is completely finished with all the equipment installed, the batteries should be charged ready for testing the model. Initially all of the functions of the model should be tested with the model on the workbench. With any new model fitted with radio control its operation should also be tested with the transmitter about 200m (or 200yd) from the model. If at this range the servos 'jitter', or the model is not under full control, additional radio interference suppression will be required.

With these checks complete, and the propeller shaft and rudder tubes packed with grease, the model should be placed in the water and checked for static trim and stability. Any ballast which is used for a final adjustment should be fixed in place before the model is released for its first run. After this run any adjustments to speed, stability or rudder movement should be made and the model retested.

The most important point about operating the model is that it should be run at a speed which gives the correct scale appearance whilst moving and if, as was suggested, a radio controlled model has been fitted with more power than required for 'scale speed' this should only be used for emergency manoeuvres.

Warships in plastic 9

by ROGER CHESNEAU

Plastics are without doubt among the most useful materials that the warship modeller can turn to, and for versatility one particular plastic stands head and shoulders above all others — polystyrene. This material can be cut, sawn, sanded and otherwise shaped with great ease, it can be bonded simply and effectively, it provides a first class surface for the application of enamel paints, and it is extremely cheap. Its major drawbacks are its fragility and its lack of rigidity, making it something less than ideal for delicate parts of models, but the fact that it can be moulded, both under pressure and, more especially, under the influence of heat, gives it an all-round capability that is hard to match. These properties have been responsible for the introduction and continuing success of the plastic construction kit, which has provided millions of people with the means to produce a simple model of an aeroplane, a vehicle, a ship, a figure, a locomotive — indeed, almost anything that they could wish for.

Unfortunately, there are still very many people who look no further than the contents of the box and regard plastic kits purely as toys for schoolboys. Admittedly, this is their prime function, but there can be much, much more to plastic modelling than gluing together pre-formed parts provided by a manufacturer. Many of the skills employed for handmade wooden models may not be required for building in plastic of course, but on the other hand scales are generally small and the time required to complete a model can be relatively short. So the latter is useful as part of a constant-scale collection that can be fairly rapidly built up, does not occupy too much display space and is instructive for purposes of comparison between individual subjects. It is also probably true to say that the plastic model appeals to those whose main concern is the end product rather than the methods used to achieve it.

Above: A typical kit layout, Tamiya's HMS *Prince of Wales* at 1/700

THE PLASTIC KIT

There are over a dozen companies currently producing plastic warship kits in five major countries — Japan, Great Britain, the USA, France and Italy, and in addition one comes across the odd product originating in Eastern Europe. The subjects portrayed are principally those connected with the Second World War, although the modern US Navy is fairly well represented; there are some post-war French, British and Russian vessels, and one or two pre-war ships have been translated into plastic kits. There are plenty of battleships and carriers to choose from, rather fewer cruisers and destroyers, and a handful of submarines and torpedo boats, but subjects such as minesweepers and monitors have yet

The Japanese MTB *PT-15*, built from Tamiya's 1/72 scale kit. This is an example of one of the larger scale, well detailed, and more expensive kits. It is also one of the few plastic ship kits with provision for motorisation.

to be tackled by the manufacturers, presumably because they constitute too big a commercial risk.

Scales are many and varied, but the largest ranges appear in 1:72 scale: mostly torpedo boats, though a corvette kit is being designed as these words are written; 1:400 scale: a large range of French types, some of the larger German vessels of World War II, and two recently-established series depicting Italian and British warships; 1:600 scale: a fair sized range with a good variety of subjects; 1:700 scale: the most popular scale in terms of different available subjects, with well over a hundred kits, of which more than eighty are of Japanese warships; 1:720 scale: a small and old-established range, but one which has recently been selected by an Italian manufacturer for a brand new series of kits, and 1:1200 scale: depicting larger vessels and regaining its popularity with wargamers. There are also a good number of kits, mostly of US origin, produced to 'odd' scales, but as manufacturers these days are electing more and more to work with established scales, these are becoming harder to find. A series of some half-a-dozen kits of Royal Navy warships, produced to 1:500 scale, should also be mentioned.

Working models, equipped with motors and sometimes with provision for radio control, are to be found at the upper end of the price range. The standard product is a static display piece, those scaled at 1:600 and over tending to be supplied with a complete lower hull, and those in smaller scales tending to be waterline models. The typical kit will cost around £1.50 ($3.00) and consist of two hull halves, separate weather decks, the larger superstructure components, funnels, etc, as port and starboard halves, separate platforms, the larger gun mountings each in four or five parts and smaller mountings each in one or two, masts in several pieces, and individually moulded anchors, capstans, boats, davits, rafts, searchlights, and so on, plus a rudder, propellers, and a couple of trestles on which to mount the completed model. An instruction sheet will present a potted history of the subject vessel, give a clear indication of how the various parts of the kit should be fitted together, and include a generally quite inaccurate two-view painting guide. The whole thing will be packed in a colourful and attractive box featuring some dramatic artwork on its lid and indulging in some self-congratulatory remarks along the sides.

Hyperbole aside, the plastic kit has a great deal to offer the serious warship modeller provided he regards his purchase more as the raw material for his model and not merely as a three dimensional jigsaw puzzle. Although moulding techniques are improving all the time, and although manufacturers are paying much more attention to accuracy and detailing than they did in the past, the commercial kit is subject to severe limitations, these occuring in three main areas — an inability or an unwillingness to obtain totally accurate data, problems involved in the moulding process and, above all and in part responsible for these, the cost of the finished product. The amount of work the modeller puts into his plastic kit will always be a matter of personal choice, but clearly if he wishes to produce a realistic, detailed model, considerable modification will need to be made to, and a good deal of extra detailing incorporated into, the basic components supplied.

TOOLS AND ADHESIVES

Modelling in plastic is a relatively 'clean' hobby requiring little work space and is therefore very much an armchair or at most kitchen table affair. The essential equipment is very basic, although these days there is available a wide range of tools which has been developed specifically for the plastic modeller, the majority of which can, however, be regarded as useful but not entirely necessary.

The first requirement is a modelling knife or scalpel for detaching the kit components from their 'sprues' or runners, general trimming, scraping, and so on. Although it is possible to spend a lot of money on a sophisticated tool with several varieties of blade, a simple knife with a detachable convex blade is quite adequate and costs only 20p or so. A pack of emery boards for rough shaping is a good investment, as are a couple of mouse-tailed files, particularly the round and half-round type. Some fine grade (400) wet-and-dry paper, cut into 1in squares, is needed for general cleaning up, with finer grades for more precise and final surface preparation. An American product known as Flex-i-Grit, unfortunately not widely available in Great Britain, is ideal for the latter task, although English Abrasives' Crocus Cloth is a good alternative.

A tube of filler is also an essential purchase, since ill-fitting parts and shrinkage resulting from the moulding process are inevitable features of plastic kits. Fine-grained proprietary brands such as Tamiya Putty or Green Stuff are the best available (though by no means cheap), but Fine Grain Polyfilla is more readily obtainable and does the job almost as well. A well-worn pointed nail file is useful as a spatula.

Other essential tools are a pair of pointed tweezers, a pin vice with a selection of jewellers' miniature drills and a fine-toothed saw plus, of course, a range of good quality paint brushes. Sellotape is useful for clamping parts together whilst they set, and plasticine is invaluable as a mounting for small components when they are being painted.

Turning to adhesives, the plastic modeller is fortunate in that he requires only one basic material, and it may come as a surprise to some to discover that this is not a tube of cement. The latter is rather too clumsy and wasteful for detailed work, and a much more satisfactory product is liquid cement such as Slater's Mek Pak. This is very clean and simple to use and merely requires two adjoining parts to be held tightly together, either between the fingers or by using strips of sellotape, and the liquid to be brushed along the joint in one quick stroke. The joint is bonded by chemical reaction and is 'welded' set within a minute of so. For the rare occasions when non-compatible materials need to be fixed together, epoxy resin provides as effective a bond as any other adhesive.

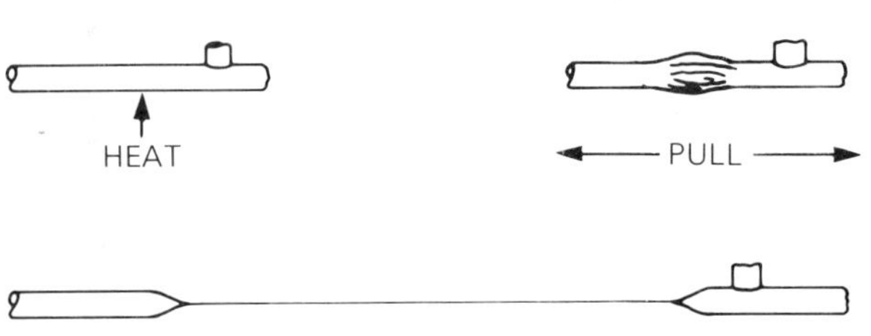

STRETCHED SPRUE' OR PRODUCING POLYSTRENE FILAMENT

ACCESSORIES

The growing popularity of modelling in plastic and its increasing acceptance as a serious adult spare-time activity has led to the introduction of a wide range of accessories, the three most basic of which are extremely handy for the warship modeller. These are popularly referred to as card, rod and strip, and consist of polystyrene in the form of flat sheets, fine rods and thin strips in a variety of gauges ranging from 0.005in upwards. Bearing in mind the properties of the material mentioned in the first paragraph of this chapter, it is easy to appreciate how wide is the scope of these accessories.

One extremely useful material is what can best be described as polystyrene filament, which costs absolutely nothing as it can be produced from the unwanted runners to which the component parts in a plastic kit are attached. A length (about 2in) of runner is heated over a flame until it becomes virtually liquified at a point half way along its length. The heat source is removed, one end of the runner is taped securely to a rigid surface, and the other end is drawn slowly and steadily away, thus producing a thread-like length of plastic. Some practice is required to perfect this technique, but with experience quite prodigious lengths can be produced, 20ft or more being easily attainable, and it is also possible to produce different thicknesses of filament by varying the speed at which the plastic is drawn out. The value of 'stretched sprue', as it is often called, for representing masts, yards, rigging, etc, will be readily apparent.

Commercially-made components for plastic models are not obtainable as individual accessories, but as the kits are relatively inexpensive it is well worth investing in some to use purely as a source of spare parts such as ships' boats, gun mountings, reconnaissance aircraft, searchlights, capstans and life rafts. Familiarity with different kits will indicate which are likely to be the most fruitful in this respect.

CONSTRUCTION TECHNIQUES

There are very thin lines in plastic warship modelling between building a kit, modifying it, converting it, and producing a scratchbuilt model. All kits have to be modified to a greater or lesser extent, whilst correcting and improving a poor kit often amounts to a major exercise in remodelling which involves the production of a great many scratchbuilt parts. For convenience, basic preparatory and constructional procedure will first be outlined, ways of modifying and improving kit models will then be discussed, and finally some consideration will be given to detailing and scratchbuilding techniques.

Plastic kits produced by the major companies are manufactured by a process known as injection moulding, by which polystyrene granules are forced under great pressure into steel moulds. The granules reach the individual moulds via a number of channels cut into the steel, and one moulding frame will, of course, carry many parts, each of which is attached to the frame by one or more spigots. The moulds are normally in two halves, although three-, four- or even five-way tools are being used more and more, and the plastic frame is released when ready by means of ejection pins which physically push it out, helped along by a releasing agent. This manufacturing process immediately endows the plastic kit with a number of inherent and mostly unavoidable flaws which require the attention of the modeller before construction can begin.

The fact that the component parts are formed in two moulds mating together means that each will have a seam somewhere around it where the moulds have met. This can normally be removed by touching it out with abrasive paper or a sharp blade, but occasionally, when for example the moulds are worn and the two faces have not met precisely, the plastic seeps along the joint and results in wafers — known as 'flash' — attached to the parts, which need to be trimmed off. Another common feature of kits which have been in continuous production for several years without having their moulds renovated is bad register, caused when the moulds do not align perfectly. This is a more serious problem and can involve a good deal of preparatory work on the part of the modeller on each component before it can be used.

Traces of releasing agent are often to be found on kit parts, appearing as an oily substance, and these must be dealt with by carefully washing the plastic in warm water to which have been added a few drops of liquid household detergent. The marks caused where the ejection pins have made contact take the form of small circles which may be raised, recessed, or flush. Where possible, manufacturers usually ensure that these are inconspicuous on the completed model by positioning them on the reverse sides of parts or on the runners, but now and then they are to be found on exterior surfaces, sometimes unfortunately resulting in a loss of detail. Although not always readily accessible, these marks should be disguised if possible by filling, sanding or scraping.

More difficult to correct, and frequently to be found on cheaper kits, is excessive taper. Quite obviously, the moulds for plastic kits must be tapered to some degree to permit ejection, but many manufacturers have nowadays so refined their techniques that the taper is virtually undetectable. However, there are still those whose products lack this refinement, presumably on grounds of economy, and the older the kit (irrespective of who the manufacturer is) the more serious this problem

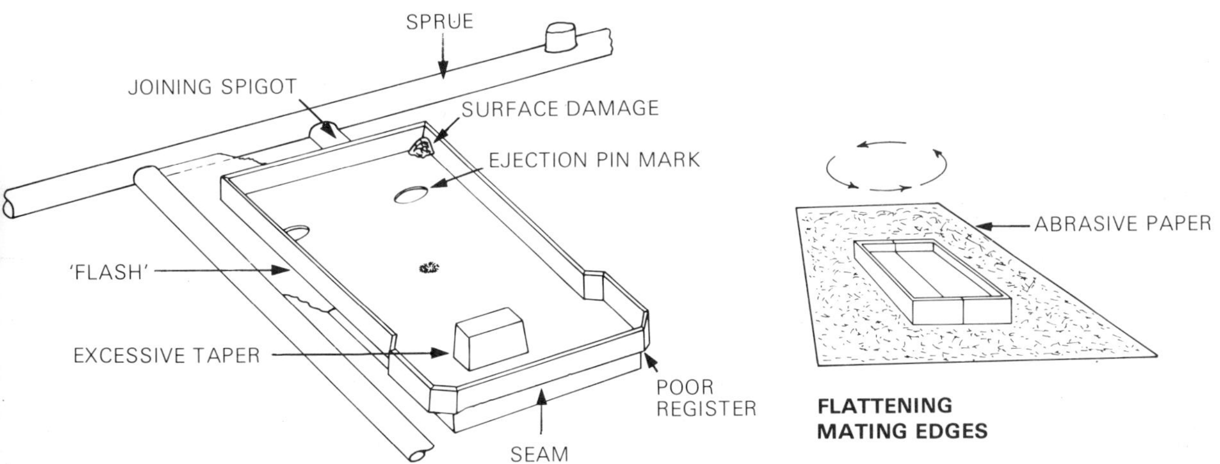

FLATTENING MATING EDGES

FLAWS IN KIT MOULDS

generally is. Methods of tackling it will be considered later.

Lastly, blemishes may occur on the surfaces of parts for two other reasons. One is where the face of the individual mould has been damaged, and this will result in lumps of plastic being formed on the finished component. The problem can usually be dealt with by removing the unwanted plastic with a blade or file, although some intricate work may be called for if the flaw occurs in an awkward place. The other type of blemish is more common, even with brand new kits, and takes the form of dimples, found where a relatively thick piece of plastic has been moulded and caused by shrinkage during cooling where an air bubble has become trapped inside the mould. Curing the fault is generally straightforward and can be achieved by using filler.

The various parts of a kit should be removed by cutting them from the runners, never by breaking them off, and the spigots should be carefully cleaned away with a file or with abrasive paper. Kit instructions vary with each manufacturer as regards the sequence of assembly, some advocating the construction of all sub-assemblies such as funnels and gun mountings as a preliminary, and other suggesting that one starts with the hull and then progresses in turn to the weather decks and superstructure. Generally speaking, it is best to build a plastic model from the keel up; sub-assemblies can be constructed as and when convenient, bearing in mind the painting requirements of the finished model.

The Japanese range of 1:700 scale waterline kits is unique in that the hulls are produced as single units on an expensive four-way tool and incorporate the bulk, and in some cases all, of the weather deck areas. The forecastle deck is sometimes a separate item carried back as far as the foremost barbette, a feature designed to obviate problems of shrinkage around the bows. The one disadvantage of this approach is the presence of a joint across the forecastle deck which may be difficult to eliminate without affecting the surrounding detail, but otherwise one only has to add the base to complete the assembly of this unit.

American and European kits are moulded more conventionally with the hull in two halves and the weather decks in one separate piece, or perhaps two if the ship in question happens not to be a flush-decker. This is one area where component fit is rarely as good as it might be, but there are ways of improving the situation. After the hull halves are cemented together, the deck unit or units should be trimmed where required, placed in position, and then taped securely to the hull at intervals along its length. Liquid cement is then allowed to run along the exposed joints (but *not* beneath the tape), and when the assembly is set the tape can be removed and the joints given a further coat of cement for additional strength.

Detailing such as breakwaters, cables, hatches, vents, skylights and bollards is normally moulded integrally with the weather decks, and fairleads are frequently already attached to the hull halves. In small scales such as we are dealing with here, it is rarely practicable to provide such items as separate components, although there is no need to mould the lower superstructure screens and barbettes as part of the weather decks, a practice which fortunately is now beginning to disappear. Some deft painting by the modeller is therefore necessary, and this should be undertaken before any further structures are added.

Any small fittings such as cable holders are best painted and positioned at this stage, before the superstructure is tackled. Construction procedure here will vary from kit to kit but will generally involve the fitting together of many parts of relatively complex shape. Filler may well be needed along joints, even if at first glance they appear good. A simple test is to smear some fine wet-and-dry paper over the surface. The plastic has a natural sheen which is removed by abrasion, and so any cavities will retain this sheen as the paper passes over, and inspection afterwards will reveal the areas to be filled. Excess filler can generally be removed by using wet-and-dry paper lubricated with water, although awkward angles may more satisfactorily be tidied up by carefully scraping it away. All areas where filler has been used should be sealed with a single coat of liquid cement prior to painting — this will also settle any dust that is present. Hairline gaps are sometimes better dealt with by using gloss enamel paint instead of filling compound, the excess being wiped away with the finger immediately afterwards.

Painting of all major superstructure assemblies should be completed before they are added to the model. It is important to remember that polystyrene cement will not be very effective on painted surfaces, so it may be necessary to scrape some of the paint away if it has strayed on to an area where other parts

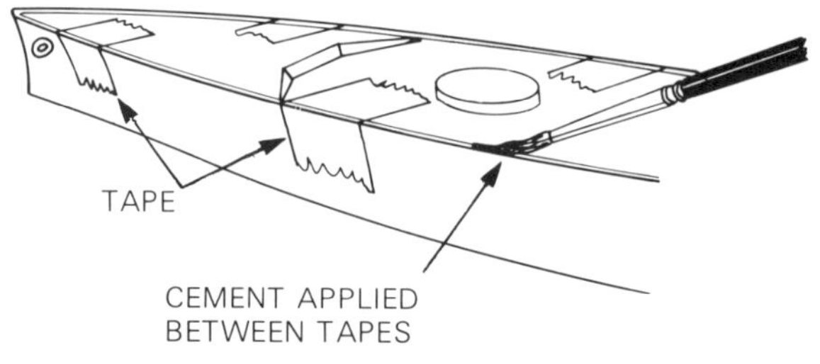

ATTACHING WEATHER DECKS

are to be fitted. It is also vital to ensure that the paintwork has throughly dried out before the various sub-assemblies are fixed in position, otherwise it may wrinkle and peel when it comes into contact with the adhesive.

To achieve a really good joint, it is again helpful if the larger structures can be taped firmly in position before the cement is applied. Perfect locations should thus be ensured, and any gaps that may occur can be closed up before a permanent fixture is made. It is sometimes advisable to flatten off the mating edges of an assembly which is composed of parts joined vertically. This can be done by wiping it firmly and evenly on a large piece of abrasive paper which has been secured to a level surface — any irregularities are thereby cleaned off.

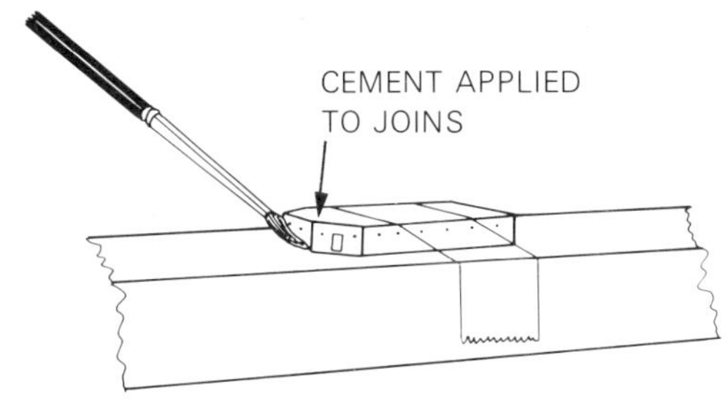

ATTACHING SUPERSTRUCTURE COMPONENTS

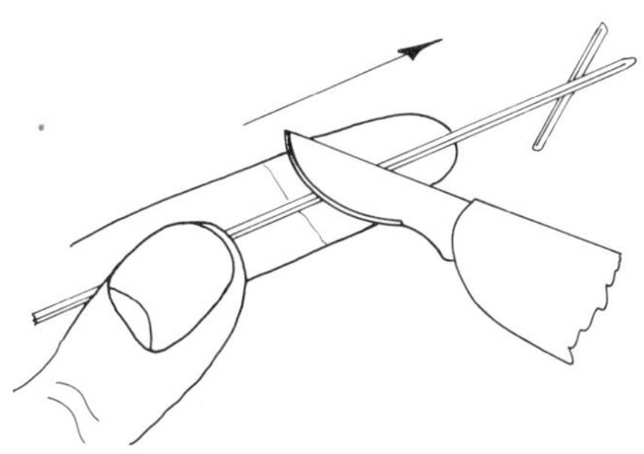

REMOVING SEAMS FROM FRAGILE PARTS

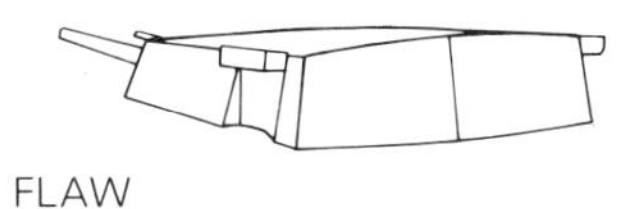

MOULDING FLAWS ON GUN TURRETS

Masts and yards present few problems, but they often have noticeable seams and, being fragile, are prone to breakage. The seams are best removed by scraping rather than by filing or sanding, and the parts should be supported with the finger during the cleaning-up operation. Gun barrels need similar treatment, whilst turrets with moulded-in rangefinders will generally require attention with filler and file where the rangefinder overhangs the turret sides because of the complexities of the ejection process.

Smaller components such as directors, searchlights and boats are usually provided as single units and are sometimes difficult to handle because of their size. Fine pointed tweezers are especially useful here, both for gripping the parts whilst they are being prepared and for positioning them afterwards. Locating holes for these parts are frequently oversized on older kits, due to wear on the moulds, and if this presents a problem the holes can first be filled with cement and the part pushed home after a few minutes when the cement has partially set. Any gaps still evident can be touched in with a spot of paint.

IMPROVING THE KIT

So far, all that should have been achieved is a neatly assembled plastic kit, and we now turn to ways in which the basic model may be improved and detailed.

Whilst all plastic kits are necessarily very simplified and omit very many of the smaller details, it is also true to say that they invariably contain inaccuracies. Dimensionally, and in general configuration, they tend to check out reasonably well, but the majority have several irritating and unnecessary errors, such as a missing anchor cable, a misplaced gun mounting or a wrongly shaped platform. One common failing of the plastic kit is a confusion over detail configuration, resulting in a hybrid model showing features appropriate to different periods of the ship's career. The 1:700 kit by Tamiya of *HMS Prince of Wales,* for example, represents the ship as she appeared after July/August 1941 but includes the earlier UP director between the forward HACS directors, whilst Airfix's *Prinz Eugen* features the circular AA platforms on 'B' and 'C' turret crowns, which were fitted towards the end of her period of service, but 20mm quadruple guns instead of single 40mms to fit on them.

Kits of sister ships are often released in pairs to utilize common components, and it is not unusual to discover three or four different kits from the same basic moulds. The extreme case is when a kit is simply re-boxed — a kit of *Scharnhorst* might suddenly appear as *Gneisenau* overnight, as it were — but most manufacturers at least recognize the fact that sister ships are never identical twins and provide alternative parts as appropriate. The trouble is that

they rarely make a thorough job of it, sometimes no doubt because of the costs involved, but also on occasions because they haven't done their homework properly. As an example, the *Prince of Wales* kit referred to above serves as the basis for a late-configuration *King George V* model which quite properly provides a different close-range armament, revised boat deck, new masts, etc, but the hulls are identical, with no doors on the quarters or blanked-off scuttles for *KGV*. Again, 1:700 kits for early-state postwar *Ark Royal* and *Eagle* models using common components are produced by Fujimi, but no account has been taken of the differences in shape of the flight deck, and one moulding serves for both vessels. Whilst the first instance is perhaps excusable on economic grounds, the second is so basic and incurs so much work to rectify the faults that one wonders how thorough the manufacturer's research has been.

In view of the foregoing, then, and assuming one is striving to produce a reasonably accurate model, it is necessary to check out a kit as much as possible, first identifying any major outline inaccuracies, and then progressing to the smaller details.

The hull may be supplied as a one-, two-, three- or

Above: The German heavy cruiser *Prinz Eugen*. This Heller 1/400 scale kit was slightly modified in order to show the ship in the colour scheme adopted for the dash up the English Channel. The rails were added by the *in situ* method; the stanchions, rails and rigging are of stretched sprue.

Opposite top: The German battleship *Scharnhorst*, 1/700 scale by Tamiya, well researched to include the differences from the sister ship *Gneisenau*.

Centre: Tamiya's 1/700 *Gneisenau*. Compare with *Scharnhorst*; the aircraft are about ¾in long, with hand painted markings.

Bottom: HMS *Nelson*. Apart from some slimming down of the masts, this model was built from the kit as supplied by Tamiya; 1/700 scale.

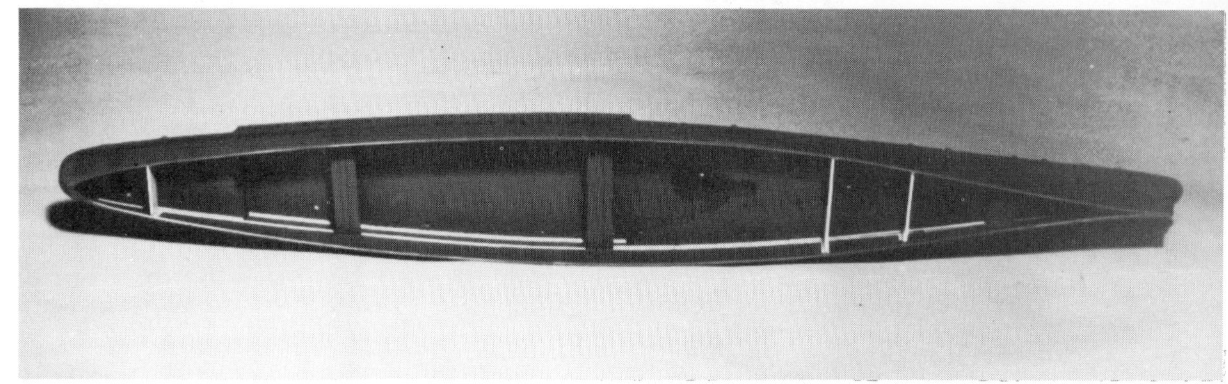

even four-piece moulding, may be full, waterline, or offer the option of either, and may or may not have all or part of the weather decks moulded integrally. The writer is of the opinion that small-scale warships look more effective if they are displayed as waterline models, and therefore some surgery is required where the complete hull is provided. Such kits usually include a moulded line along the boot topping, and this can be used as a guideline when the lower hull is removed. A razor saw is the best tool for the job, but a heated knife is quicker if not as neat. If the model is to be displayed underway in a 'sea', the cut must be made well below the actual waterline so that the boot topping can be exposed at intervals along the hull, and for the same reason it will often be necessary to deepen the hull of a kit that is provided as a waterline model by adding a layer or two of plastic card below the base and shaping it to the ship's contours. Hulls modified by reducing them to waterline configuration will usually require some sort of internal bracing with scrap plastic card.

Scuttles are usually represented in kits either by raised circles or as circular recesses, and of the two the latter are preferable, since although technically incorrect they make painting a lot easier and look effective enough in small scales. Where raised detail is furnished, it is possible to open out the scuttles by using a fine drill. Egress vents along the hulls of submarines are generally very poorly defined in plastic kits — at best they are shallow recesses and at worst they are shown by shapeless blobs. Time-consuming but very necessary work with a drill and a rounded file is required to give these features their proper appearance.

Hulls provided as port and starboard halves may demand some attention around the stem, which is frequently far too blunt. Such work should only be tackled when the two halves have set completely, which means at least twelve hours after they have been cemented together. Hawsepipes are nearly always satisfactorily depicted, though on occasions

Above: The French battleship *Richelieu*; this was originally a full hull, but has been cut along the waterline, which has necessitated the introduction of some internal stiffening as shown: scale 1/400.

the cables themselves are moulded directly on to the hull, and if so are best removed and replaced with individual items.

Plastic kits are renowned for manufacturers' gimmicks, but fortunately there are not too many atrocities that can be committed with regard to warships. Despite the continuing improvements in accuracy that kit models have shown over the years, one irritating feature persists, and that is the portrayal of planked decks by means of prominent, longitudinal raised lines that, scaled up to full size, would be something like six inches high. Whatever the scale of the model, these should be removed by sanding or scraping, taking care not to damage the moulded deck fittings. Because of the latter, it is extremely difficult to substitute more authentic planking effects, and it might be worthwhile building completely new weather decks from plastic sheet, as planking can then be scribed, inked on, or even built up from individual strips of plastic, without too much difficulty before the fittings are added. This is certainly worth considering if the fittings are poorly defined, and absolutely essential if they suffer from excessive taper or if the kit has another common fault — too prominent a deck edge.

The thickness of the plastic used in moulding the hull often results in a ridiculously overscale edge to the deck, and the hull/deck joint is frequently poor as well, needing a good deal of filling and smoothing. In addition, the spurnwater is almost always absent, because of course it lies along the joint. The appearance of the model may quite dramatically be improved by chamfering the inside edges of the upper hull, making a new deck from plastic card, and adding a spurnwater from fine sprue filament after the joint has been cleaned up.

The problem of excessive taper means, in the case of moulded fittings, complete removal and replacement by new parts. Breakwaters and bollards are common casualties here, and improved versions may be fabricated from strip and rod. Barbettes even suffer, but these are usually sufficiently robust to withstand filing and sanding to eliminate the fault. Barbette taper quite naturally means that the diameter of the barbette will be correct only at one point on its circumference, so a thin piece of card wrapped around will sometimes be needed to restore accuracy. Fairleads, chafing plates, hatches and vents can all very easily be made from odd pieces of plastic card, whilst cable holders and capstans, never realistic if moulded directly on to the decking because of ejection requirements, may be fashioned from sprue of suitable cross-section.

Several manufacturers have the policy of providing guard rail in strip form with their kits, and one wonders why they bother. The limitations of production techniques make it quite impossible to mould rail of anything like scale thickness except, perhaps, for the larger 1:72 scale torpedo boats. However, although by no means an easy task for small-scale warships, it is perfectly possible to make and fit guard rails that will look reasonably realistic on the finished model. The rails may be produced in one of two ways. For very small-scale models (1:600 or less), it is probably better to build up a grid of stretched sprue, fix it by brushing liquid cement over all the joints, and detach and fit strips as required. With larger scales, stanchions of stretched sprue may

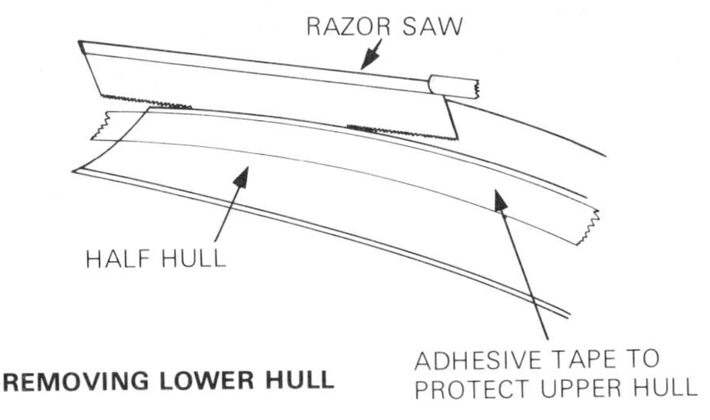

REMOVING LOWER HULL

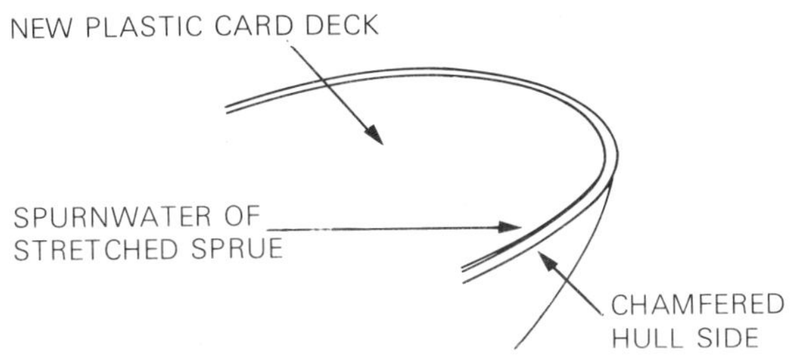

IMPROVING THE WEATHERDECK

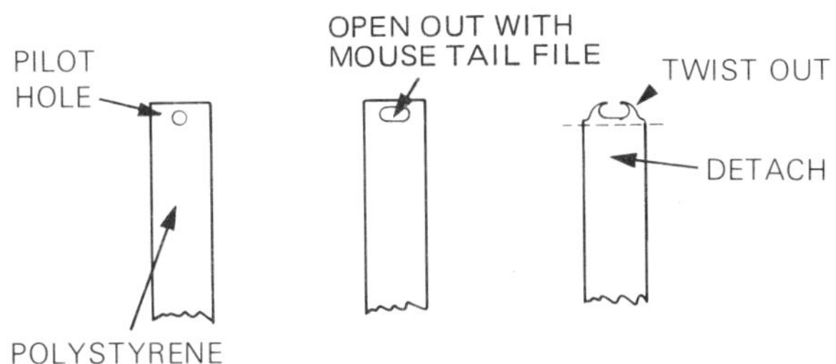

MAKING FAIRLEADS

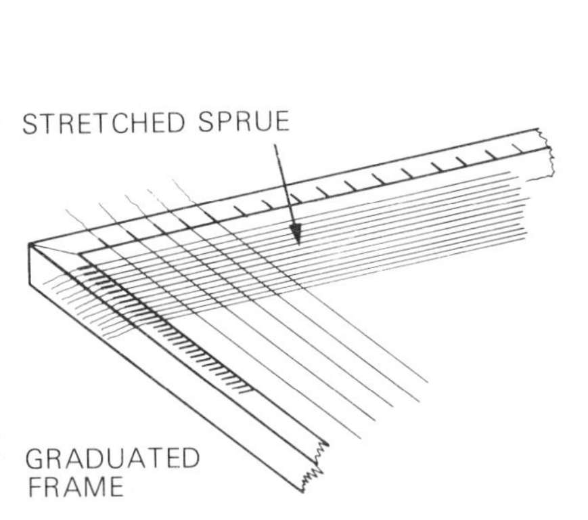

GUARD RAILS – GRID SYSTEM

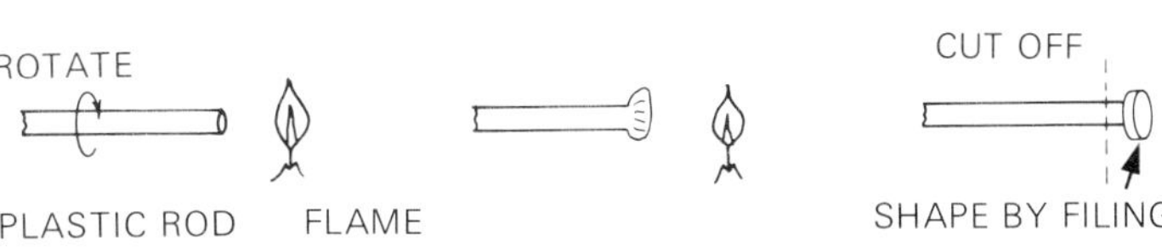

MUSHROOM TOP VENTILATORS

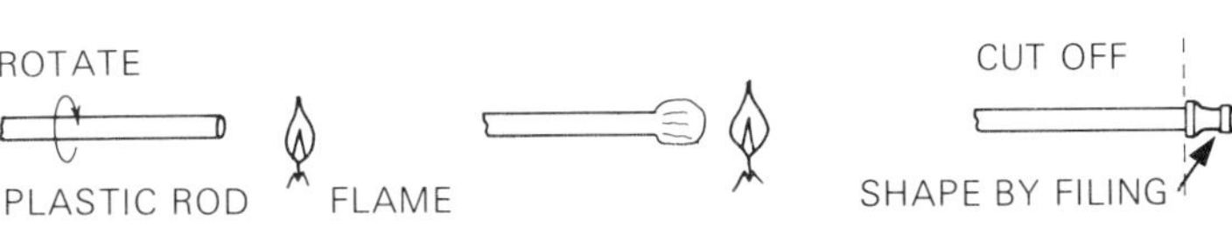

CAPSTAN

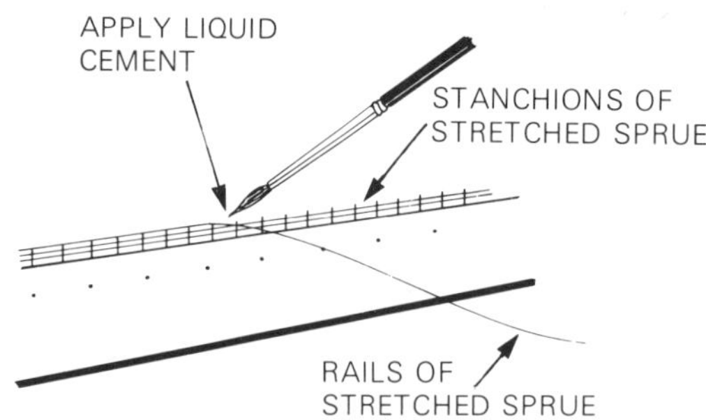

GUARD RAILS 'IN PLACE' METHOD

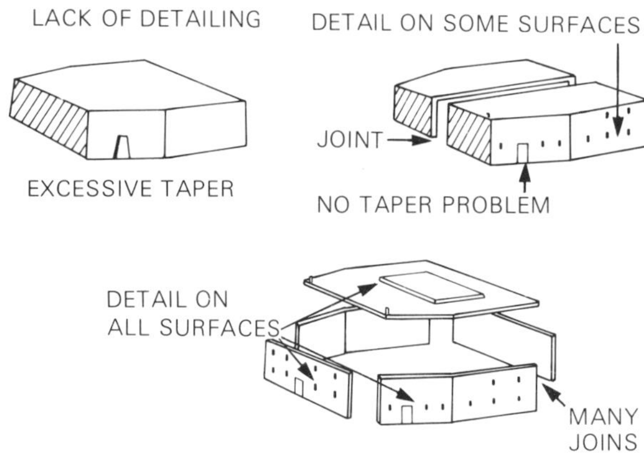

TYPES OF SUPERSTRUCTURE DESIGN IN PLASTIC KITS

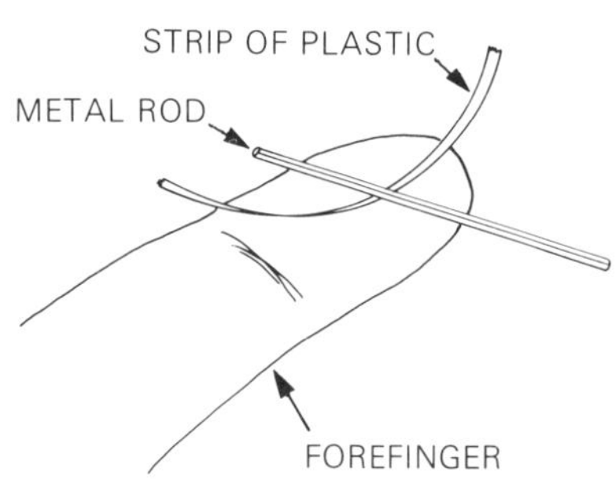

CURVING PLATING

KIT TURRET FRONT PLATES

be positioned in drilled holes, and the rail itself added when the stanchions are set. The usefulness of liquid cement is hardly more evident than in delicate operations such as these.

If one has a great deal of rail to fit, it is well worth while producing a large amount of stretched sprue, cutting it into lengths of, say, 12in, and grading it for future use. The one drawback of representing rail in this way is that it is difficult to reproduce any natural slackness, but in scales such as 1:600 or 1:700 this would hardly be a noticeable feature.

Superstructure assembly varies with each kit, but there are three basic ways in which the design may be approached by the manufacturer. Firstly, the individual structures may be supplied as complete units, with or without integral platforms or decks, which frequently means undue taper and always means no vertical detailing unless a four-way tool has been used. Secondly, they may be supplied as port and starboard halves, which cures the problem of taper but results in a lack of detailing fore and aft and a joint which has to be disguised. Thirdly, they may come as completely separate horizontal and vertical components, which enables detailing to be shown on all surfaces but requires some judicious cleaning up at the joints, especially if the parts fit poorly. The massive flights of steps that are supposed to represent access ladders should in all cases be removed.

Taper can usually be dealt with by filing, but any moulded detail will be destroyed in the process and will need to be replaced by using plastic strip, rod, etc. The opportunity can also be taken to improve and correct this where necessary. Scuttles, etc, will frequently need to be added, as will port lights, the latter usually being represented, if at all, by means of shallow recesses. In smaller scales, lights may be shown by carefully painting them on, but it may be preferable to replace the appropriate screens with sections of transparent plastic sheet which may then be painted, leaving the lights clear.

Moulding limitations are responsible for the grossly thick protective plating that is evident in all small-scale warship kits. The offending plastic should be carefully sliced away, and new strips prepared from thin polystyrene sheet. Curved sections can be produced by rolling the strip over the forefinger with a thin metal rod or piece of dowel.

Small fittings may be modified as required, or added where they are missing, by using thin plastic card, rod, or stretched sprue as appropriate, the only limitations being the individual modeller's skill . . . or patience!

The portrayal of a warship's armament has often been one of the weaker points of a plastic kit, though as with every other aspect of its anatomy, big improvements have been made in recent years. One of the most noticeable shortcomings has been the treatment of the front plates of turrets where, in order to simplify ejection, gun ports take the form of rectangular holes carried right down to barbette level. Some careful work with scrap plastic and filler is required in these instances, and sometimes it may be necessary to cut away the entire face and replace it

Top: Another view of HMS *Nelson,* showing the detail on the gun turrets — the 8-barrel pompom on 'B' and the 20mm single oerlikons on 'B' and 'C'. Note the lack of blast covers.

Bottom: The USS *South Dakota;* compare the gun turret detail on this 1/700 scale kit by Hasegawa with that on HMS *Nelson.* Blast covers have been included here.

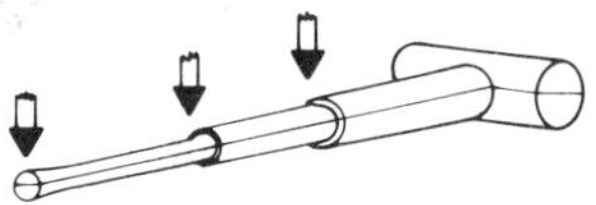

EXAGGERATED FEATURES FOUND ON SOME KIT GUN BARRELS

BLAST COVERS

Opposite top: The cruiser HMS *Exeter,* from the 1/700 (British) Matchbox kit. Note the simplified davits, which have been slimmed down, the open 4in mounting, ladder moulded on the funnel. The ¾in wingspan aircraft has hand painted insignia.

Opposite below: The USS *Saratoga,* which was assembled without alteration from the 1/700 Fujimi kit. The rigging has been simplified in this kit, and there is quite a lot of moulded-in detail.

with a more realistic product made from plastic card. Where blast covers are needed, the openings can merely be plugged and the turret faces sanded flush. The opportunity may also be taken here to sharpen up the edges with abrasive paper since these are commonly 'rounded off', again to facilitate ejection.

Blast covers, in fact, are supplied in only a tiny percentage of plastic kits, presumably to preserve the manufacturers' other prize gimmick, elevating guns. Before discussing how these particular features may be represented, it should be mentioned that a careful check should be made on the way the actual guns are mounted. The requirement that they should elevate often results in their appearing too high, too low, or too close together in relation to the turret front plate, and modifications may be called for. The barrels are frequently caricatured, with a very pronounced belling out at the muzzles and, more commonly, exaggerated 'steps' along their length, and if so should be altered accordingly.

Blast covers may be fabricated in a number of ways, but the following method is straightforward and produces a neat result. First, the guns should be separated into individual barrels if necessary, and a number of pieces of plastic card (0.01in) the same shape as the gun ports should be made. The barrels are then fixed on to these pieces of card, checking that the angles are correct by periodically 'dry-fitting' the assemblies to the turret. When the barrels are set, filling compound such as household Polyfilla is moulded on to them against the 'butt' ends. Any excess can be filed off in the normal way. The card backing ensures that a strong joint can be made with liquid cement. Barrels can be drilled out if required by first marking the drilling point with a needle.

Open mountings are always oversimplified, and some time spent with fragments of sprue and plastic card can work wonders. Open gunhouses are often moulded 'solid' and may have to be rebuilt entirely from styrene card. Torpedo tubes, and more frequently ships' aircraft, also lack detail and will benefit from some careful attention with stretched sprue, etc.

Boats and davits are also impossible to mould realistically, and compromises include such things as 'solid' interiors for motor boats, etc, 'solid' thwarts, overscale hull thickness and an absence of steering equipment. Some of these features are difficult, if not impossible, to correct, and it is often easier to scrap the kit offering and build anew from scratch. Methods of doing this will be considered in a moment. Covers are often moulded on to the boats and are always completely smooth and flat. Building up the height with a thin, slightly irregular layer of filler will bring a bit more character to these parts. Davits are almost always too thick and their operating gear completely absent. Stretched sprue will again come to the rescue, and the same material serves well for replacing overscale or moulded-on booms and derricks and for producing lattice work for cranes, etc. Boat crutches are sometimes ill-defined or missing altogether and should be attended to with card.

Masts, yards and radar aerials are other features which are often poorly represented, though this is not always the fault of the manufacturer. Careful work with plastic rod and sprue filament will improve the appearance of a model no end. Rigging is always something of a problem, and with very small scales it may be desirable to omit it altogether. Fine stretched sprue has yet another use if rigging is required, although certain adhesives such as Uhu can be drawn out into fine threads and used instead. One other snag concerning rigging is that if masts and yards are made from plastic, the strain imposed on them by the rigging can often bend them out of true, and more rigid material such as metal may be needed.

It will be apparent by now that a great deal of

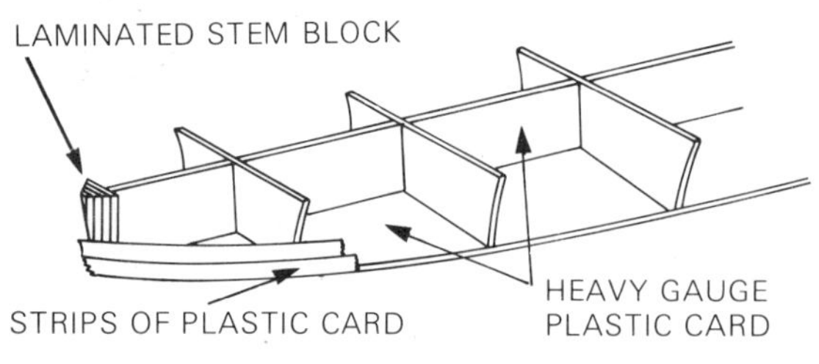

SCRATCH-BUILT HULLS:1

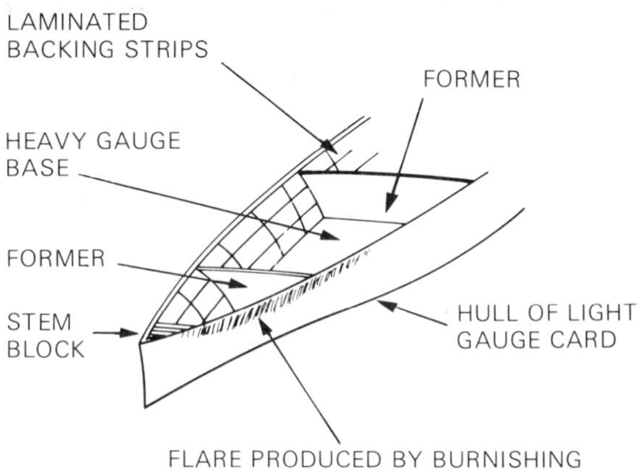

SCRATCH-BUILT HULLS:2

intricate work with tiny particles of material is required to turn the basic plastic kit into something approaching a good quality model. A stand-mounted lens is a useful investment and will considerably ease eyestrain. For attaching tiny parts, a fine pair of tweezers and a very fine, long-haired brush are essential, and some sort of rest for the wrist may be helpful.

CONVERTING AND SCRATCHBUILDING

Although the procedures outlined in the foregoing paragraphs refer to methods of improving kit models, it will not have gone unnoticed that we are already well into the realms of converting and scratchbuilding. However, one or two special techniques have not been covered, and these will be considered now.

Most of the methods used in the construction of large wooden ship models can, in a modified form, be applied to the building of small-scale plastic ship models. Hulls may be produced by building up a framework of plastic card on a keel or on a waterline base. The gauge of card used should be fairly heavy (0.04in or more), and laminated blocks may be required for areas of compound curves, for example at the stem and at the stern. Hull plating can be added using thin strips of plastic card, filled and sanded flush when set, although flat areas can be covered with larger pieces. The 'bread and butter' method familiar to all ship modellers can be used for superstructure blocks since plastic card lends itself admirably to lamination, but for large components such as complete hulls this method is rather wasteful.

Reference was made earlier, however, to the fact that polystyrene sheet can be shaped into compound curves, and this property is especially relevant when it comes to producing hull forms. There are three basic ways in which this shaping may be achieved.

The first method is useful for more gentle curves and simply involves burnishing the plastic sheet with a smooth, rounded object such as the back of a small spoon. Polystyrene will 'stretch' to a certain extent in normal room temperature and waterline hulls of, for example, early dreadnoughts, where the flare of the bows may be comparatively gentle and the hull itself fairly slab-sided, may adequately be produced in this way, although stem and stern blocks are required for strength. The plastic sheet used for this process should be of fairly light gauge (0.015 or 0.020in) and will need stiffening within the hull by means of backing strips laminated on to the sides and formers across the beam.

The second method can be used for curves that are too sharp to be produced merely by burnishing. A simple wooden jig is needed, and the card sheet should be taped or otherwise temporarily secured in its final configuration on to it. The whole thing is then immersed for a few seconds in very hot water (around 180°F), and the plastic sheet will then retain permanently the shape taken up. This procedure is helpful for producing such items as hull sections, life belts, Carley floats, and the like.

With more complex shapes, such as the hulls of ships' boats, moulded gunhouses, radar domes, etc, components may be produced by heating up a piece of polystyrene card and pressing the required shape, which may be carved from wood or plastic, into it. The commercial extension of this principle is the vacuum-former, which although used for producing kits of aircraft and body shells of vehicles, has not yet been applied to warships. In theory, there is no reason why complete hulls for fairly large ship models should not be produced in this way, and the choice of a plastic surface rather than a wooden one has its advantages where bonding and painting are concerned.

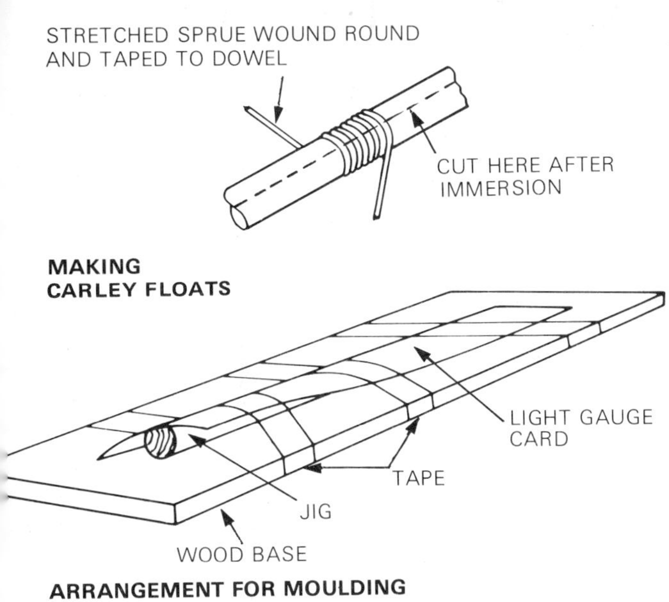

MAKING CARLEY FLOATS

ARRANGEMENT FOR MOULDING PLASTIC SHEET IN HOT WATER

Above: This is a scratch built hull for the battlecruiser HMS *Invincible.* Because the hull has gentle contours, it has been possible to produce these in the plasticard by burnishing rather than heat treatment; note internal stiffening. 1/600 scale.

Below: HMS *Sheffield,* a completely scratch built model at 1/600 scale by J L Geary, using plasticard and some stretched sprue. This model incorporates some fine detail, particularly the mattress for the Type 965 search radar forward of the foremast.

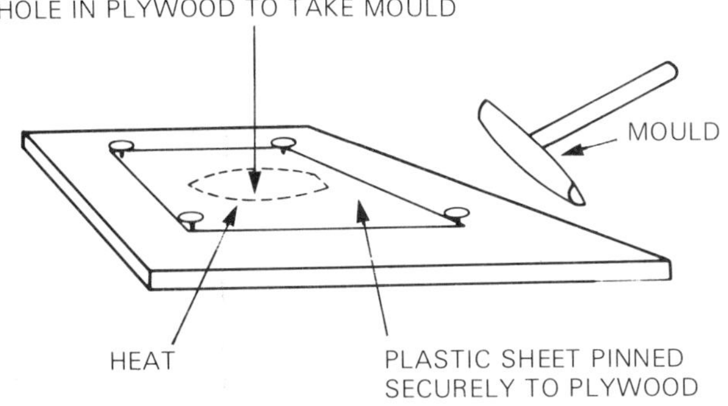

HEAT MOULDING PLASTIC COMPONENTS

PAINTING AND FINISHING

Perhaps the most helpful development in the world of model making over the last decade or so has been the quite prodigious range of specially-produced paints that has come on to the market. Companies like Humbrol, Pactra and Airfix now offer the modeller a variety of shades that a few years ago would have been unbelievable. However, it is not so much the choice of available colours as the quality of the paint itself that has had a really beneficial impact. Provided the paint is stirred well and carefully applied, an even density of finish is guaranteed, drying time is a matter of minutes, and brush marks are a thing of the past. The paint as supplied in the tin or jar is always too thick and needs to be mixed with enamel thinners or white spirit before it is used. Drying time is thereby prolonged also, a helpful factor when painting awkward spots.

The decision as to which particular shade of paint should be applied to a particular model is still a problem for the modeller to solve, for 'naval' shades do not appear in any great numbers and, even if they did, the variations apparent in different tins of the same colour would mean that a check would need to be carried out and modifications perhaps made before the paint is applied. A home-made colour chart, displaying chips from each tin in the modeller's personal stock, is therefore of considerable assistance when it comes to deciding which paint is to be used.

Scale effect is a topic about which there is much argument, but the writer's view is that, certainly with small-scale models, the tone of each matched colour should be scaled down by lightening it with white, and that extremes such as pure black and pure white should be avoided. Very much depends upon the distance from which the finished model is to be viewed, but it is worth remembering that a 1:600 scale model viewed from a point 8.8ft away represents a scale distance of one mile — and that's a lot of water to break up the light.

The plastic model requires very little preparation before it is painted. It should be as free from dust as possible, of course, a particularly important consideration for small scales, and any bare filler should be either sealed with a coat of liquid cement or primed with matt paint. Areas to be painted to represent scrubbed wood should be given an undercoat of matt white, particular if the plastic is a dark colour to begin with, but otherwise the finishing coat can be applied straightaway.

The model should, generally speaking, be painted as each sub-assembly is completed, starting with horizontal surfaces and then proceeding to the vertical surfaces, the latter being brushed with vertical strokes. Camouflaged finishes call for much patience in order to align the colour regions correctly. Each patch or band may be marked out with a thin line of colour with the sub-assembly held temporarily in place; the latter can then be removed to ease the task of infilling.

Should a pristine finish be required, there is no doubt that the airbrush offers advantages to those whose hand brushing is a little suspect, and although a good deal of time has to be spent in preparing the paint before use and cleaning the equipment afterwards, with practice it enables the job of painting a model to be accomplished very quickly. However, for miniatures, it is hardly worth the expense, and if subtle 'wear and tear' are to be shown on a model, it is quite unnecessary.

Paint erosion is perhaps not in keeping with full hull display models, but for a waterline model representing a ship in service it can be a very effective feature, and a technique known as dry-brushing is a useful skill that can be developed. The brush is dipped into the paint in the normal way, but before application it is wiped out on to a clean rag, thus removing virtually all the paint. However, enough will remain to leave tiny deposits as the brush is dusted over the surface of the model. By continuous application in this way on one particular spot, the paint will build up to give a 'splotch' or mottle effect and the same technique can be used to produce feathered edges on camouflage bands, etc.

Straight lines, such as the demarcation of boot topping or camouflage separation, may be facilitated by the use of thin strips of adhesive tape. Much has been written concerning the dire consequences of using sellotape as it is reputed to pull off paint that has been applied beneath it, but the writer has never experienced any problems with it. Previously painted surfaces should be thoroughly dried out and the tape should have a perfectly clean edge, precautions which need hardly be mentioned.

Many kits include paper flags and glossy decals for hull numbers, etc, but it goes without saying that these look quite preposterous on a model warship and should be discarded. Dry-print lettering is available for those with shaky hands, and if flags are required, home-made items can be produced quite easily.

Finally, a brief word about model presentation. The writer must confess to a marked partiality towards models displayed in their natural environments, and a sea base or diorama can add a

Opposite top: The battleship HMS *Prince of Wales,* built from the standard Tamiya 1/700 kit, but corrected in minor detail; note the camouflage paint scheme.

Centre: The importance of pre-painting sub assemblies is to be seen in this partly assembled model of the Italian heavy cruiser *Gorizia,* a 1/400 Italian Modelcraft kit. Masking tape had to be used for the camouflage, and the moulded-in detail makes straight lines somewhat difficult.

Bottom: Though based on the USS *Growler,* a 1/178 scale Revell kit, this model does not represent a particular submarine, but was used to show the official US colour scheme 32/3SS-B. The rust streaks were added by the dry brush method. Rails and aerials of stretched sprue.

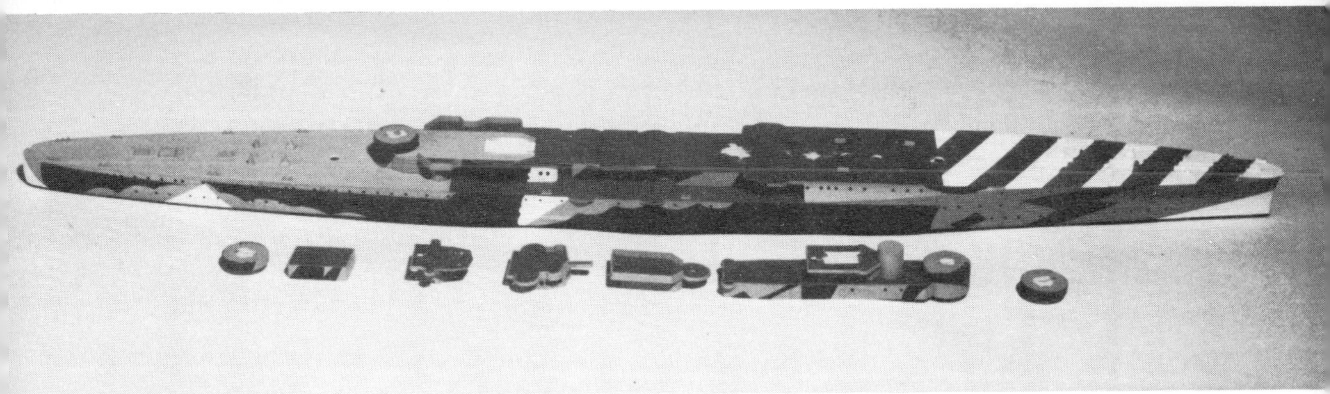

Above: A good example of a diorama of an historical incident, HMS *Campbeltown* ramming the lock at St Nazaire. The hull is from a 1/600 Airfix kit, modified and the detail built up with plastic card, etc. The base (sea) is polyfilla. This is one of those rare instances where damage to the ship can be shown. (Photos: Author's collection and by J L Bowen)

Opposite: This 1/200 model of the Japanese destroyer *Hatsutsuki* was built by Don Smith. It is basically a Nichimo kit (an expensive series) but with many additions by the builder, including much work on the radar equipment. (Photographs by Don Smith)

good deal of interest to the basic miniature warship.

A simple but effective base may be produced by making a tray from chipboard edged with beading, mounting the model within it and working Polyfilla around the hull. Waves can be produced by moulding the Polyfilla before it has set, a mixture of fairly stiff consistency lending itself to more dramatic effects. Other methods of representing water include the use of resin, painted foil, and cellophane pressed into thick, wet paint, but Polyfilla has considerable versatility and can be made to look very realistic. Ordinary gloss enamel paints may be applied to its surface, with disturbed water shown by using matt white applied either directly or by the dry-brushing method described above.

Diorama situations are perhaps limited when compared with other model subjects such as aircraft or military vehicles, as space may be a problem, but refuelling at sea, launching ceremonies, ships fitting out, vessels under refit, damaged or sinking ships (anathema to some, admittedly) and historical incidents can be modelled very effectively in plastic.

SUMMARY

One of the purposes of ship modelling is to produce a miniature version of a real vessel that is as accurate and as authentic as it can be. One hundred per cent success with regard to these ideals is impossible, for every model contains flaws, however small and insignificant they may be. By working from a plastic kit, the time taken to produce such a model can be (though is not necessarily) reduced and, after all, if one's primary consideration is authenticity, the choice of materials is relatively unimportant. The modeller who uses plastic as his medium will derive a great deal of enjoyment from his hobby. It is moreover possible for him to produce a model that is as pleasing to behold as any other.

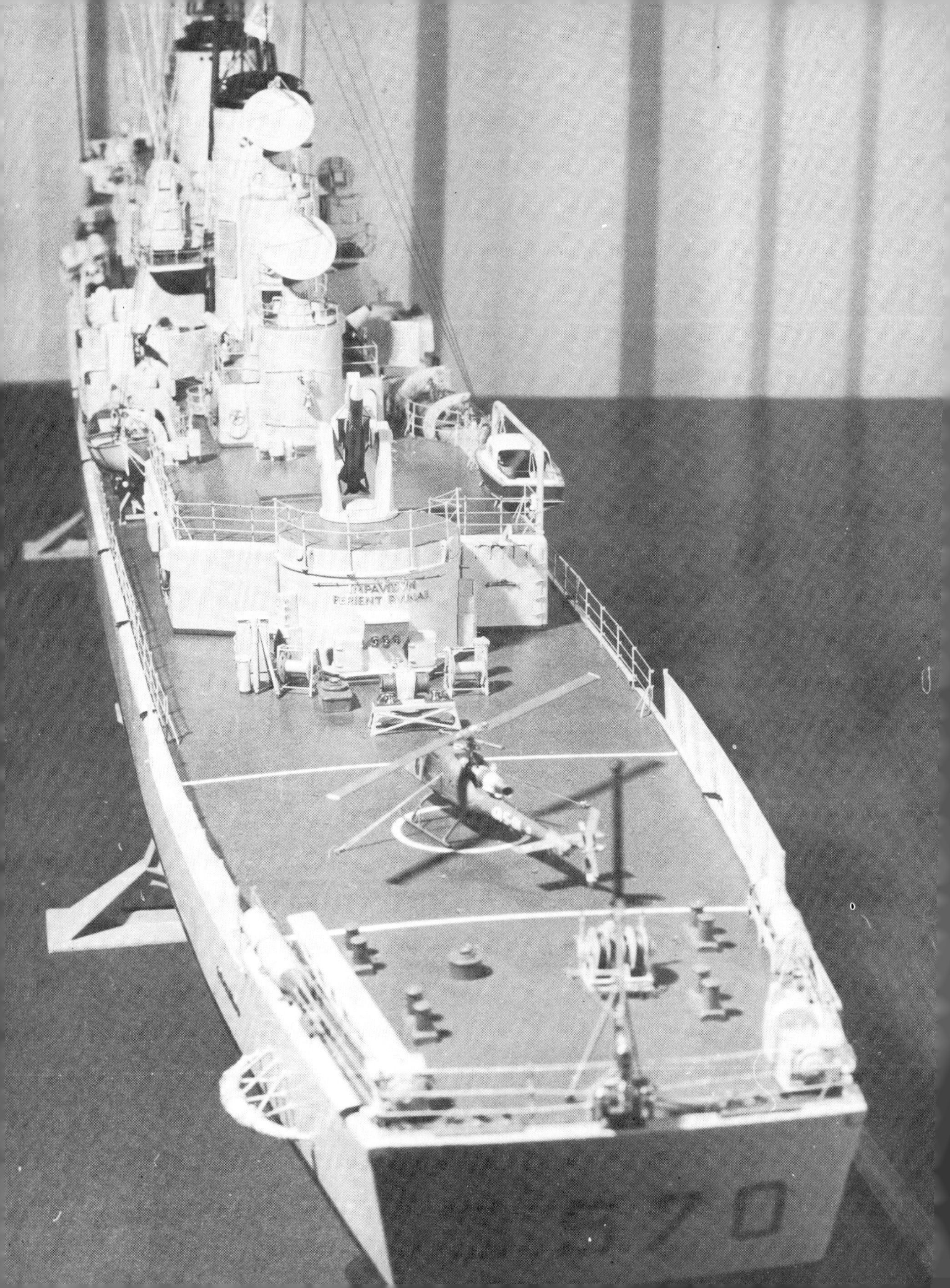
570

Bibliography

Compiled by ROBERT GARDINER

Model Shipwright. The only journal in English devoted to scale ship modelling of the highest standards. Articles specifically on warships occur frequently, but most of the value of the journal is in the general techniques covered and the high proportion of illustrations.

Warship. From the same 'stable' as *Model Shipwright*, and in the same format, this journal is also quarterly. It is principally concerned with the history of warships but a series on 'Classic Warship Models' has appeared. Both from Conway Maritime Press Ltd, 2 Nelson Road, London SE10 9JB.

Warship International, the quarterly journal of the International Naval Research Organisation, Toledo, Ohio, USA. An amateur publication whose material varies from highly abstruse 'PhD theses' to reworkings of popular subjects based on secondary sources. However, much of the journal is given over to readers' queries and answers, some of which is very valuable, although there is little of specific relevance to modelmakers.

Model Boats. (MAP Ltd, Hemel Hempstead, UK) A monthly modelling magazine; very rarely covers detailed scale models of warships.

Scale Models. (MAP Ltd) Also monthly; devoted to plastic models and occasionally has in-depth reviews of new ship kits.

Airfix Magazine. (Gresham Books Ltd, UK) A monthly magazine, largely based on Airfix plastic products.

Scale Modeler. (Challenge Publications, Canoga Park, California, USA) Another monthly devoted to plastic models, predominantly aircraft.

Sea Classics. (Challenge Publications) A popular monthly covering most aspects of maritime affairs; very little embodies original research, although modellers may find the photographs useful.

Ships of the World. (Tokyo, Japan) One of the best general maritime magazines; the text, of course, is in Japanese, but there are numerous photos and drawings, many of which are devoted to warships.

De Modelbouwer. (NVM, Leidschendam, Netherlands) A Dutch language general modelling magazine, with a regular section devoted to ships.

Modell-Werft. (Scholz-Verlag, Wolfsburg, West Germany) A monthly ship modelling magazine covering — mostly — top quality models; many photos and plans.

Modell Magazin. (Alba Publikation, Düsseldorf, West Germany) A German language plastic modelling monthly; very rarely covers warships.

Modell-Fan. (Schünemann, Bremen, West Germany) Another German plastic modelling magazine, with good news coverage; occasionally deals with warships.

BOOKS ON MODELLING

Scale Model Warships by Kozo Izumi
Although written in Japanese the author is also an artist and a modeller, and understanding the problems that modellers face has adapted a method of visual presentation that makes a knowledge of Japanese unnecessary. The book is based on literally hundreds of perspective line drawings — relating to an *Akitsuki* class destroyer — and covers in full detail every aspect of construction and fitting.

Building Warship Models by P C Coker. (Coker Craft, Charleston, 1974) A somewhat misleading title since the book is weak on description of constructional techniques. However, it does contain reprints of sketches from Izumi's book (see above) and a magnificent collection of photographs of superb warship models.

Shipbuilding in Miniature by Donald McNarry. Long out of print, and not specifically devoted to warship modelling, nevertheless this book by one of the world's greatest miniaturists is a must for anyone building small scale warships.

Radio Control Model Boats by Smeed and Connolly (MAP Ltd, Hemel Hempstead, numerous editions). Useful for the general techniques of fitting and operating radio control in models, but very little is applicable specifically to scale vessels, and modern developments in electronics have rendered much of the book old-fashioned if not actually out of date. Two other MAP publications may be of use to those making live steam models, K N Harris' *Model Stationary and Marine Steam Engines* and *Model Boilers and Boilermaking.*

Apart from these titles there is very little on warship modelling that is readily available, although readers may find the following useful if obtainable: Ed Schnepf's *Scale Model Warships and How to Build Them* (USA, 1968) and a Japanese series called *Picture Warship Models*, each booklet containing complete pictorial coverage of four detailed models of Japanese ships, with up to 50 photos devoted to each model. A complementary source for Japanese WWII warships is *Plans of Ships of the Imperial Japanese Navy*. Although very expensive and almost impossible to obtain in the West, it does contain over 100 official plans in large fold-out form, so that even the aircraft carrier *Shinano* is reproduced to a reasonable scale.

FULL SIZE PRACTICE

In view of the shortage of good books on warship modelling many modelmakers turn to technical manuals on warship construction. Textbooks on naval architectural theory are not particularly helpful (although a book like William White's *Manual of Naval Architecture* of 1877 is full of fascinating background information): the most useful are books on shipyard practice and the techniques of construction. Many of these are readily available secondhand in editions dating from the turn of the century, the best-known being E L Attwood's *Warships* (first edition 1904) and R C Newton's *Practical Construction of Warships* (first published 1941). Both contain a number of relevant drawings of construction and fittings. Attwood also wrote a book on *Laying Off*, and there are earlier works by McDermaid (*Shipyard Practice as Applied to Warship Construction*, 1910 — largely superceded by Newton) and J J Welch (*Text Book of Naval Architecture*, 1901). One relatively recent book, T C Gilmer's *Modern Ship Design* (1970) covers contemporary warships in some depth.

The *Transactions* of the Royal Institution of Naval Architects (annually from 1860) in the UK and of the Society of Naval Architects and Marine Engineers (annually from 1893) in the USA, occasionally include articles of interest to warship modellers.

One final source of value are the official Manuals of Seamanship and maintenance manuals for guns, etc, produced for the Royal Navy and for the USN from about the turn of the century. These are particularly useful for drawings of weapons, deck-fittings, boats and so on.

The literature of warships is enormous, very variable, and usually of marginal interest to modelmakers. Therefore what follows is highly selective, including only major reference works, and the most readily available of popular books. Foreign language books are only quoted where there is nothing available in English.

YEARBOOKS

The three best-known annual reference books are *Jane's Fighting Ships* (UK, from 1898), *Flottes de Combat* (France, from 1897) and Weyer's *Flottentaschenbuch* (Germany): *Flottes de Combat* is now available in English as *Combat Fleets*, published jointly in the USA and UK by the US Naval Institute Press and Arms & Armour. Although the reading public tends to treat these works as gospel truth, they often contain errors and misinformation. Sometimes this is simply a question of accepting false data from navies with something to hide (the misleading Italian trials figures between the wars are an example); or else it may be that their 'semi-official' status leads them to toe the official line. *Jane's*, for example, has long been the unofficial mouthpiece of British defence thinking (as an instance, until recently it was never allowed to quote RN sonar designations). Other year books include Fahey's *Ships and Aircraft of the US Fleet* (from 1939, but now ceased publication, although some of the wartime volumes have been reprinted), Brassey's *Naval Annual* (UK, from 1886 to 1949, when it became the more general *Armed Forces Yearbook*) and *The Naval Review* (US, from 1963).

MONOGRAPH SERIES

A notable feature of warship publishing in recent years has been the proliferation of uniform series of books. These have adopted the monograph approach, each being devoted to a particular navy, a ship type, a class, or even a single famous ship. Since these are widely available and much-used by modellers, a few general remarks about the salient features of each series would be appropriate.

Ian Allan 'Navies' series. (Available in the USA from various publishers). A large range of pocket books, each on a major navy of the First or Second World Wars. By a variety of authors, the standard is naturally variable, but each contains basic data on all major ships and a selection of small portrait photos: some contain appearance sketches, but generally speaking they are not clear enough to be used as visual reference by modellers.

Macdonald WWII pocket books. (Also available in the USA). A somewhat different approach from Ian Allan's, being devoted to the ship types of a particular navy (eg *British Cruisers*) but in a similar small format. Recently they have gone over to 'Fact Files', larger format softbacks, but treating the information in much the same way. Some of the first series, such as Meister's *Soviet Navy* and Lenton's *German Navy* have been edited and expanded from the smaller volumes.

Conway Warship Monographs. There were only two in this series, covering the WWI period: these were the *Queen Elizabeth* class and the *Invincible* class. This series introduced the approach-by-class which was later adopted by 'Ensigns'. Conway have now taken a broader view for the new 'Warship Specials' series, the first three titles being *Battlecruisers*, *Super Destroyers* and *Destroyer Weapons of WWII*.

Ensign. One of the few series produced with the specific needs of the modelmaker in mind. The text is usually short, but the large format is used to reproduce detail photos as large as possible, and there is a centrefold full colour camouflage scheme. The series only covered British ships of WWII and has now ceased publication, but the tradition is being carried on by the forthcoming 'Man o' War' series to be published in the USA.

Ship's Data. (Leeward Publications, USA). A series mostly devoted to single ships — and for sales reasons usually preserved vessels — each paperback volume contains a history of the ship, photos, line drawings and a full-colour spread.

US Navy Camouflage. A new series by Larry Sowinski and (published by the 'Floating Drydock' company) devoted to the WWII era. Because of the vagaries of colour printing, the author prefers to use clear black-and-white photos, although colour chips are available. So far there is one general volume and one on carriers with more in preparation.

Almark. A short-lived venture that published a number of pocket-books on WWII ship types. They were neither particularly well-conceived nor well-produced and probably only Peter Hodges' contributions added anything new. The company's output is now confined to military and aviation subjects.

Warship Profiles. A very well-known series, each devoted to a particular ship, with a potted history, some plans, photos and a full-colour centre-spread appearance drawing. The series ceased some years ago after producing over 40 titles. The quality of information and artwork varied enormously, but unfortunately the series seemed to be getting better and more adventurous just before it closed down.

Orrizonte Mare. For those that read Italian there is a range of profiles of Italian ship types of the WWII era. They have rather more text than most monographs, but also include appearance drawings and some colour camouflage patterns.

J F Lehmanns Verlag. This well-known German firm, now part of Bernard & Graefe, publish a number of pocket books on German warships, the most notable of which is the only book on German warship camouflage (*Die Anstriche und Tarnanstriche der deutschen Kriegsmarine*).

BACKGROUND READING

Pre-Dreadnought. There is no single modern reference work for the ironclad era although the publication in 1979 of *Conway's All The World's Fighting Ships 1860-1905* will remedy this. A good technical account is Hovgaard's *Modern History of Warships* (1921, reprinted 1971 and 1977 by Conway Maritime) and for America a contemporary volume is Bennett's *Steam Navy of the US* (also reprinted recently in the USA) although readers should beware of his engineering officer's prejudices.

Battleships. The classic work for the RN is Dr Oscar Parkes' *British Battleships*, (Seeley Service) which covers the period from the *Warrior* (1860) to *Vanguard* (scrapped in 1960). He is generally reliable up to the First World War, where he could work from official sources, but for the later period he has been largely superseded by Alan Raven and John Roberts'

British Battleships of WWII. (Arms & Armour Press). There is no equivalent work on US ships, although the recently published *Battleships* (Naval Institute Press) by Dulin and Garske, in many ways an unsatisfactory book, covers from the *North Carolinas* to the *Montanas*. Of the more general books, the most quoted is Breyer's *Battleships and Battlecruisers* (Macdonald & Janes). The vast documentation and elaborate line drawings give this book the air of a first class authority: unfortunately most of the research is based on secondary, published, sources, and outside the German Navy the author can be faulted on points of detail, interpretation and balance. Therefore a modeller must use the appearance drawings carefully — for example there is a drawing of *Vittorio Veneto* captioned 'as completed', but obviously based on a trials photo (the Italians ran trials before much of the fire control equipment had been fitted).

Aircraft Carriers. Probably the most useful for modellers, since it is illustrated with over 500 photos is Norman Polmar's *Aircraft Carriers* (1969).

Cruisers. For some reason this type seems to be the Cinderella among warship subjects — both for books and models. There is no definitive study of any country's cruisers, although Raven and Roberts are working on a study of British cruisers to complement their battleship book.

Destroyers. By contrast there are numerous books on destroyers, although few could be described as definitive. Edgar March's *British Destroyers* is often considered the ultimate authority — probably because it is produced as a uniform volume with Parkes' book on battleships — but it must be used with great care. Although based on official sources, it contains a number of serious errors — there is at least one case of a plan showing a destroyer leader which is a few feet too short, because it was based on March's figures! There is no work as detailed for US destroyers, but probably the best account of the design rationale is Norman Friedman's half of the forthcoming *Destroyer Weapons of WWII* (Conway Maritime).

Submarines. Although not particularly popular modelling subjects, the general interest in submarines is immense, and reflected in the number of books available. A recent all-inclusive book is Bagnasco's *Submarines of WWII*, which is much better in its English translation (Arms & Armour Press in the UK, Naval Institute Press in the US) than the original Italian, thanks to rigorous editing and picture choice. Undoubtedly the best book on U-boats is Eberhard Rössler's *Geschichte des deutschen U-bootbaus* (Lehmanns Verlag) which is full of plans and diagrams. This work is currently being translated into English for publication in the UK and USA.

Smaller vessels. These are not well documented. There is *Allied Escort Vessels of WWII* by Peter Elliott (Macdonalds, UK; Naval Institute Press, USA) which gives some of the background, if little of the detail of the ships themselves. One type that is well represented is fast patrol boats: Fock's *Schnellboote* has been translated and is available as *Fast Fighting Boats 1870-1945* (Nautical, UK; Naval Institute Press, USA) but for some reason it goes no further than the end of the war. However, although it is weak on non-German vessels, the plans are numerous and, mostly, excellent, and the information can be supplemented with Phelan and Brice's *Fast Attack Craft* (Macdonalds). There is no technical book on landing craft.

Major Navies. A number of books cover the ships of one navy rather than one type. For the present US Navy, Norman Polmar carries on in the Fahey tradition with *The Ships and Aircraft of the US Fleet* (Naval Institute Press). The Soviet Navy is the object of much interest and there is a reasonable *Guide to the Soviet Navy* (Naval Institute Press; PSL in the UK) for present ships and Jurg Meister's *Soviet Warships of WWII* (Macdonalds) for earlier vessels, while Rene Greger's *The Russian Fleet 1914-1917* (Ian Allan) contains many photographs of both ships and naval actions for that period.

For the Royal Navy there is no single book on WWI or II ships, except the pocketbook series already mentioned, but for present ships there is the frequently up-dated *Ships of the British and Commonwealth Navies* by Trevor Lenton (Ian Allan). The Japanese Navy is better served, with two studies *The Imperial Japanese Navy 1865-1945* by Watts and Gordon (Macdonalds) and Jentschura, Jung and Mickel's *Warships of the Imperial Japanese Navy 1869-1945* (Arms & Armour, UK; Naval Institute Press, USA). Of the two, Watts and Gordon is probably the more reliable, since they at least used Naval Intelligence reports, although the other is better illustrated. For the present 'Maritime Self-Defence Force', the new *Guide to Far Eastern Navies* (Naval Institute Press) is the best available.

The standard work on German warships is Gröner's two-volume *Die deutschen Kriegschiffe 1815-1945* (Lehmanns Verlag) but for some reason it has never been translated into English. Similarly, there is no authoritative work in English on French warships, although Editions d'Outre Mer produce a series in French.

PICTORIALLY USEFUL

A modelmaker is principally concerned with the appearance of a particular ship at a particular time, and as such tends to collect pictorial reference. The following are books which he would find useful for their illustrations, although it does not mean that the text should be dismissed. They are all in print or easily available.

American Steel Navy, Alden (Naval Institute Press)
Covers the period 1883-1909 — a magnificent collection of photographs.

Battleships of World War I, Antony Preston (Arms & Armour Press)

British Naval Aircraft since 1912, Thetford (Putnam)

Camera at Sea 1939-1945, edited by the staff of 'Warship' (Conway Maritime Press, UK; Naval Institute Press, USA)
A fine collection in a large format covering most aspects of the war at sea.

Carrier Operations in WWII 2 volumes, David Brown (Ian Allan, UK; Naval Institute Press, USA)

Carrier Air Groups, David Brown (Hylton Lacey)
A series on British Fleet Air Arm squadrons.

Dreadnought, Richard Hough (PSL)

Escort Carriers, Poolman (Ian Allan)

The German Navy 1939-45, Bekker (Hamlyn)

Guns at Sea, Padfield (Evelyn)

The Japanese Navy at the end of WWII, Shizuo Fukui
Line drawings of the ships that survived the war.

A Pictorial History of the Fleet Air Arm, Rawlings (Ian Allan)

A Pictorial History of the Royal Navy 1916-1914, 2 volumes, Watts (Ian Allan)

The Royal Navy in Old Photographs, Trotter (Dent)

Sailor: A Pictorial History, McGowan (Macdonalds)

Tirpitz: The Floating Fortress, Brown (Arms & Armour Press)

US Navy: An Illustrated History, Miller (Naval Institute Press)

US Navy Aircraft since 1911, Swanborough & Bowers (Putnam)

US Navy: Vietnam, photos by Moeser (Naval Institute Press)

Warships, Lyon (Salamander)

The World's Warships in Review, 1860-1906, Leather (Macdonalds)
Photographs by Beken of Cowes.